SCIENCE AND CULTURE TEXTS
JOSEPH HUSSLEIN, S.J., Ph.D., GENERAL EDITOR

THE GOSPEL OF SAINT MARK

MARK THE EVANGELIST

Miniature of the *Codex Aureus* in the British Museum, London

The GOSPEL
of SAINT MARK

Presented
in Greek Thought-Units and Sense-Lines
With a Commentary

By
JAMES A. KLEIST, S.J., Ph.D.
Professor of Classical Languages
at St. Louis University

(Μᾶρκος) ἀκούσας τὸν λόγον
λαλούμενον λέγει. (Mk. 5, 36)

THE BRUCE PUBLISHING COMPANY
New York   MILWAUKEE   Chicago

Imprimi potest:

   S. H. HORINE, S.J.
     Praepositus Provinciae Missourianae

Nihil obstat:

   H. B. RIES,
     Censor Librorum

Imprimatur:

   ✠ SAMUEL ALPHONSUS STRITCH
     Archiepiscopus Milwaukiensis

June, 1935

This Volume

is

respectfully dedicated

to

Young Readers of St. Mark

and to

All who begin Advanced Work in New Testament Greek

Ἀσπάζεται ὑμᾶς Μᾶρκος, ὁ ἀνεψιὸς Βαρνάβα,
περὶ οὗ ἐλάβετε ἐντολάς,—ἐὰν ἔλθῃ πρὸς ὑμᾶς,
δέξασθε αὐτόν.

Colossians 4, 10

Primitive man did not speak with the care required by the Art of Oratory nor in accordance with the rules that it lays down.

—*Quintilian.*

Our canonical writers and doctors possessed Eloquence as well as Wisdom, a kind of Eloquence becoming in men of their character.

—*St. Augustine.*

To read; to understand; to love—and to facilitate reading, understanding, and loving on the part of others—these are the first and second commandments of the critic.

—*Sainte-Beuve.*

PREFACE BY THE GENERAL EDITOR

The departments of classical languages in our colleges and universities are once more indebted to the Rev. James A. Kleist, S.J., for a valuable service rendered to teachers and students of Greek. The present sense-line edition of St. Mark's Gospel in the original Greek, enhanced by scholarly introductory chapters, scientific notes, and vocabulary, is the result of many years of research as well as of classroom experience.

The author's choice of this document for the preparation of a suitable text for students of college Greek or beginners in graduate work, is easily justified.

The Marcan Gospel, in the first place, is finely characteristic of all New Testament Greek. It uses the language spoken by the people in the days of the Apostles, the *Koine* or common tongue in vogue throughout the Greco-Roman world ever since the eventful conquests of Alexander in the fourth century before Christ. The language of this Gospel, as the author shows, is a pure, idiomatic Greek which, like the *Koine* generally, had developed naturally out of the speech of an earlier period. Rooted in the past, it is racy of the soil that nourished it. The various idioms pointed out by the author, particularly in the notes on general features of style, illustrate much that the student will later meet with in the study of New Testament writings and of classical masterpieces as well.

But there are still other and even more pertinent reasons for turning to St. Mark among all the New Testament writers. The first of these is the singular shortness of the Marcan account, which renders possible the thorough study of an entire Gospel within the student's limited time. To this fact must be added certain stylistic qualities of Marcan Greek which should not be overlooked. While St. Mark, it may justly be said, is a stranger to the art of the rhetorician, he excels in brevity and compactness of diction, in action and onward movement, in graphic detail and vigorous phrase.

Without exaggeration, therefore, we may claim that the study of the Marcan text, as here made possible, though apparently narrowing the student's vision to a single section of the New Testament, nevertheless supplies him with a sound and practical introduction for later ventures in the Greek of an earlier age no less than that of the Christian era.

JOSEPH HUSSLEIN, S.J., PH.D.
General Editor, Science and Culture Texts

ST. LOUIS UNIVERSITY
June 18, 1935

AUTHOR'S FOREWORD

THE GOSPEL OF ST. MARK is designed as a textbook for beginners in New Testament Greek who wish to read the Ἀρχὴ τοῦ Εὐαγγελίου. It contains first of all a presentation of the original in thought-units and sense-lines. In the Commentary that follows, Part I deals with Colometry and certain qualities of ancient artistic prose in so far as they affect the second Gospel; Part II contains Annotations, partly on general features of style, and partly on difficult passages in the text.

St. Mark was not a stylist in the modern sense, yet it would be an egregious error to suppose that he was indifferent as to how he spoke. All sentence structure, even when imperfect, adds point to the thought to be expressed. Like the other Evangelists St. Mark had his individual manner, and if there is a way of revealing it to us, it must be by some such presentation of the text as I have here attempted. Thought-units and sense-lines are a passport to any ancient writer's mind. They help us to look a little more deeply into his sentence building and to realize a little more vividly his development of thought. Above all, they supply the modern reader with preliminary aids to intelligent appreciation, with an indispensable background, we may say, with which the first readers were familiar from the very atmosphere wherein they breathed and from their greater nearness to antiquity, both in time and sympathy.

It may be well to state at the very outset, however, that, in presenting the Marcan text in thought-units and sense-lines, I do not profess to reconstruct with exactness the old colometric style of writing. No colometric autographs of any portion of the New Testament have survived, so that we do not know whether the sacred writers, or at least St. Mark, made any use of colon-writing at all. St. Jerome, who rendered the Bible *per cola et commata,* followed the practice of contemporary teachers of

Greek and Latin literature, but this fact alone does not prove that the original autographs were *written* colometrically.

Moreover, the so-called colometric copies which are extant present difficulties and problems of their own. Since St. Jerome used a *novum scribendi genus* for his *interpretatio nova*, and since this "new method of writing" consisted in his adoption of the colometric form in imitation of the secular teachers, we are led to believe that the *copies* of the New Testament which he had before him were not done in the colometric style. Furthermore, *habent sua fata libelli*, and the history of profane literature should be a warning to the student of New Testament colometry. Lindsay tells us that "the original colometry of the 'Palatine' recension [of Plautus] has been to a great extent obscured in the extant representatives of the 'Palatine' family, *owing to the scribe* of their immediate original having combined two or more short lines into one long line, and in various ways *having departed from the colometry* for the sake of saving space" (*The Captivi of Plautus*, 62). Against the possibility of similar liberties having been taken with the form of the New Testament writings, it will hardly do to argue that a Christian copyist would feel less free in handling the arrangement of a colometrized copy or even of a colometrized autograph than an ancient copyist would with texts of a profane character. St. Jerome, at all events, takes occasion somewhere to refer to "the malice or deficiency of the copyists" (*The Life of St. Jerome*, by Fray José de Siguenza, London: 1907, p. 324).

In view of this general uncertainty regarding the nature, the extent, and even the existence of New Testament colometry, a use of the term "colometry" on the title-page of this volume would be misleading. The question whether my arrangement of the Greek in thought-units and sense-lines tallies with what might be called a colometrization in the technical sense of that term is of no material importance to my purpose here. I have attempted to analyze St. Mark's sentences and paragraphs with attention both to his syntax, which is of the simplest kind, and to the ancient theory of sentence building. The final result is but a tentative reconstruction, yet one, I trust, that allows us to see the working of St. Mark's mind—a mind, we may safely say, that mirrors the mind of his voucher, St. Peter, and, in places, the mind of Christ Himself. The Papias-fragment is authority for the belief that St. Mark, who was St. Peter's "interpreter," wrote down carefully (ἀκριβῶς) whatever he had heard St. Peter tell the early Christians about "the words and works of the Lord," and that "he took forethought of one thing—not to omit anything he had heard nor to falsify in recording anything."

In the course of the Introduction occasion will be taken here and there to point out what advantages may be considered to be inherent in this use of thought-units and sense-lines. If, on account of the many handicaps encumbering a modern inquiry into ancient colometry, we cannot expect complete success, we may at least be reasonably sure that an arrangement of the Greek like the accompanying will contain many individual sense-lines and even whole sentences that could not be different in a duly colometrized original. And so we have a tolerable certainty that we are able, at least partially, to enter into the spirit of that great 'Αρχή which is being more and more admired as a masterpiece.

For an historical introduction to the second Gospel the student may be referred to several brief sketches in my *Memoirs* which deal, respectively, with "The Gospel and Its Author," "The Memoirs Called Gospels," "John the Ancient and St. Mark," "Features of the New Translation," and "Glimpses of Marcan Art."

For many New Testament scholars of the present day the study of structural form—*die Formgeschichte*—is of absorbing interest. But, since the present work looks to the needs of the beginner, it must be pardoned for not taking cognizance of matters that belong more properly to an advanced stage of investigation.

Modern scholarship very laudably tries to find a place for our Gospels in the literature of the time; after all, the evangelists were children of their age. One may be tempted to see in them "biography" (βίος; vita) or "history" (ἱστορία; historia) or mere "memorandum" (ὑπόμνημα; commentarius); but, to omit other considerations, such attempts to fit the Gospels into the ancient mold must fail because they lack one quality which enters into the very fiber of all ancient types: artistic form or rhetorical composition. Also writings of lesser pretensions have been mentioned as possible prototypes, such as the diatribe (διατριβή; sermo), of which the most noted example is Epictetus's *dissertationes* compiled by Arrian, or Sulla's memoirs (τὰς αὐτοῦ πράξεις, which Lucullus was expected to "work up into history": Plutarch, *Luc.* I, 3). The nearest ancient parallel to suggest itself to St. Justin the Martyr, in his endeavor to acquaint a pagan audience with our Gospels, was the type known as *memorabilia* (ἀπομνημονεύματα, sc. τῶν ἀποστόλων; see *Memoirs*, Ch. II). It seems best to take the Gospels for what they profess to be. Thus St. Luke, in the opening verse of his *actus apostolorum* or πράξεις ἀποστόλων, refers to his own Gospel as a λόγος or record of all ὧν ἤρξατο ὁ Ἰησοῦς ποιεῖν τε καὶ διδάσκειν. Similarly the Papias-fragment describes the Gospel of St. Mark as a careful transcript (ἀκριβῶς ἔγραψεν) of "what the Lord has said or done" (τὰ ὑπὸ τοῦ Κυρίου ἢ πραχθέντα ἢ λεχθέντα). And here we seem to be at the end of our search: there has been nothing just like the Gospels, either before or after—a result, no doubt, of our Lord's own καινὴ διδαχή.

The Greek here colometrized is that adopted for my *Memoirs* from the *Novum Testamentum Graece et Latine* by Dr. Henry Vogels, D.D., Professor of New Testament exegesis at the University of Bonn, Germany, published by L. Schwann, Düsseldorf, Germany (2d ed. 1922). To author and publisher I wish again to offer my warmest thanks for their kind permission to use their text.

I gladly take this opportunity to express my gratification at the welcome given to my *Memoirs of St. Peter* both here and abroad, in spite of its shortcomings. There was reason to expect criticism. Our current versions of the Bible have pervaded the whole texture of our very thought and style, and poured a wealth of meaning and association into phrases familiar to every child. Even the appearance of wishing to tamper with this heritage must have seemed to many readers little short of sacrilege. It might indeed be supposed that, unless a mountain of distrust and skepticism is first removed, a quiet estimate of the kind of work attempted in the *Memoirs* must be impossible. It was a pleasure, under the circumstances, to find that the reviewers of the *Memoirs*, far from setting up some existing version of the Bible as a final standard of excellence, were willing to judge the new translation in the light of the aims I had in writing it, namely, first, to re-read St. Mark with all the help which American and European scholarship has put at our disposal in the last three or four decades; secondly, to find in our everyday English (to quote a reviewer) "wholesome, effective, and virile locutions" as a medium for expressing St. Mark's everyday Greek. Since the original stands outside the stream of literary Greek, it seems inconceivable that a modern rendering should not be allowed to speak to the plain man in his own everyday English. The Gospels do not, like the Book of Job, "march with majestic harmonies"; why, then, cannot a modern rendering be content "to reflect the lowliest forms of human life" in a language, reverent, by all means, but comprehensible and attractive to the common man? The Gospel was preached to the poor, and Christ bent down to the level of humble folk to give them the Message of Salvation. It was a delight, therefore, to hear a professional student of Holy Scripture say that the *Memoirs* contain "innumerable lines in which the author has given us a version of incomparable excellence," and another, an English veteran of Biblical criticism, that it succeeds "over and over again in catching the precise meaning of a passage." Above all, there was hope held out in the statement of still another critic that "this first volume will facilitate and give a decided impetus to the study of the second Evangelist."

The present volume is not "just another book" among many others. It consists of material that has been actually used with classes of beginners. Though dealing exclusively with the Gospel of St. Mark, it wishes to reach two distinct types of student: first, the college freshman who has spent two or three years on ancient Greek and is content with a rapid reading (helped, perhaps, by a glance at the *Memoirs*) of St. Mark's Gospel in the original Greek; secondly, the student who intends to enter upon advanced work in New Testament Greek. In other words, the GOSPEL professes to offer enough matter for two distinct courses in Greek, the one elementary, the other somewhat advanced. The copious Notes with their references to standard works, while needless for the elementary reader, will, I trust, provide the advanced student with interesting starting-points in his quest of τὰ χαρίσματα which are τὰ μείζονα in all language study and literature.

This twofold appeal of my GOSPEL, I confess, has been a matter of some concern to me. I am sure I could have lightened my labor in preparing this volume, had I chosen my model from among the existing types of textbook and adhered rigorously to the conventional method of treatment. But then *vita brevis est*, and, therefore, since the economic crisis through which we are passing lays a heavy hand on Greek books, in this "Greekless age," it may seem doubtful whether the promise made in the Preface to my *Memoirs*, of devoting a separate treatise to Marcan philology, can ever be redeemed. In consequence a compromise was made, and the problem in writing the GOSPEL was, on the one hand, not to include too much that a college freshman would find altogether beyond his level, and, on the other, not to include too much that a beginner in graduate study should deem superfluous from his point of view. The final result may perhaps, in Horace's felicitous coinage, be a *concordia discors;* but the confident hope is entertained that a sympathetic teacher will find it no unpleasant task to minimize any disharmony that might arise.

And now that the linguistic foundation has been laid, both in the *Memoirs* and in this GOSPEL, it will be a delightful task to turn from the letter to the spirit and show the influence which the Marcan Good News has had on the religious thought and life of the world, beginning with the *Didache*, on through the Patristic age, down to our own times.

> Ὁμοία ἐστὶν ἡ βασιλεία τῶν οὐρανῶν ζύμῃ
> ἣν λαβοῦσα γυνὴ ἔκρυψεν εἰς ἀλεύρου σάτα τρία
> ἕως οὗ ἐζυμώθη ὅλον.

I wish to offer my sincere thanks to several publishing companies for their kind permission to quote some brief but pithy lines from their publications: namely, to the Oxford University Press (see the Foreword, p. xii; also pp. 203 and 112); to the Macmillan Company (see p. 98, footnote 12); to the Catholic University of America Press (see p. 98, footnote 14); to the University of California Press (see p. 99, footnote 15); to Ginn and Company (see pp. 153 and 197; selections from Genung's *Working Principles of Rhetoric*); to the North American Review (see p. 149; a quotation from H. Henderson).

J. A. K.

Pentecost, 1935
St. Louis University
St. Louis, Mo.

TABLE OF CONTENTS

II. Annotations

PART ONE

THE GOSPEL OF SAINT MARK PRESENTED
IN THOUGHT-UNITS

[ΚΑΤΑ ΜΑΡΚΟΝ]

1 1 <u>Ἀρχὴ</u> τοῦ εὐαγγελίου Ἰησοῦ Χριστοῦ, υἱοῦ τοῦ Θεοῦ.

2 <u>Καθὼς</u> γέγραπται ἐν τῷ Ἡσαΐα τῷ προφήτῃ·

ἰδοὺ ἐγὼ ἀποστέλλω τὸν ἄγγελόν μου
πρὸ προσώπου σου,
ὃς κατασκευάσει τὴν ὁδόν σου.

3 φωνὴ βοῶντος ἐν τῇ ἐρήμῳ·
ἑτοιμάσατε τὴν ὁδὸν Κυρίου,
εὐθείας ποιεῖτε τὰς τρίβους αὐτοῦ,

4 ἐγένετο Ἰωάννης
ὁ βαπτίζων ἐν τῇ ἐρήμῳ
καὶ κηρύσσων βάπτισμα μετανοίας
εἰς ἄφεσιν ἁμαρτιῶν.

5 καὶ ἐξεπορεύετο πρὸς αὐτόν
πᾶσα ἡ Ἰουδαία χώρα καὶ οἱ Ἱεροσολυμῖται πάντες,
καὶ ἐβαπτίζοντο ὑπ᾽ αὐτοῦ ἐν τῷ Ἰορδάνῃ ποταμῷ
ἐξομολογούμενοι τὰς ἁμαρτίας αὐτῶν.

6 καὶ ἦν ὁ Ἰωάννης ἐνδεδυμένος
τρίχας καμήλου καὶ ζώνην δερματίνην περὶ τὴν ὀσφὺν αὐτοῦ,
καὶ ἔσθων
ἀκρίδας καὶ μέλι ἄγριον.

7 καὶ ἐκήρυσσεν λέγων·

ἔρχεται ὁ ἰσχυρότερός μου ὀπίσω μου,
οὗ οὐκ εἰμὶ ἱκανὸς κύψας λῦσαι
τὸν ἱμάντα τῶν ὑποδημάτων αὐτοῦ·

3

1

8 ἐγὼ ἐβάπτισα ὑμᾶς ὕδατι,
αὐτὸς δὲ βαπτίσει ὑμᾶς ἐν πνεύματι ἁγίῳ.

9 Καὶ ἐγένετο ἐν ἐκείναις ταῖς ἡμέραις
ἦλθεν Ἰησοῦς ἀπὸ Ναζαρὲτ τῆς Γαλιλαίας
καὶ ἐβαπτίσθη εἰς τὸν Ἰορδάνην ὑπὸ Ἰωάννου.

10 καὶ εὐθὺς ἀναβαίνων ἐκ τοῦ ὕδατος,
εἶδεν σχιζομένους τοὺς οὐρανούς
καὶ τὸ πνεῦμα ὡς περιστερὰν καταβαῖνον εἰς αὐτόν·

11 καὶ φωνὴ ἐγένετο ἐκ τῶν οὐρανῶν·
σὺ εἶ ὁ υἱός μου ὁ ἀγαπητός,
ἐν σοὶ εὐδόκησα.

12 Καὶ εὐθὺς τὸ πνεῦμα αὐτὸν ἐκβάλλει εἰς τὴν ἔρημον.

13 καὶ ἦν ἐν τῇ ἐρήμῳ τεσσεράκοντα ἡμέρας
πειραζόμενος ὑπὸ τοῦ σατανᾶ·
καὶ ἦν μετὰ τῶν θηρίων,
καὶ οἱ ἄγγελοι διηκόνουν αὐτῷ.

14 Μετὰ δὲ τὸ παραδοθῆναι τὸν Ἰωάννην
ἦλθεν ὁ Ἰησοῦς εἰς τὴν Γαλιλαίαν
κηρύσσων τὸ εὐαγγέλιον τοῦ θεοῦ

15 καὶ λέγων

ὅτι πεπλήρωται ὁ καιρός
καὶ ἤγγικεν ἡ βασιλεία τοῦ θεοῦ·

μετανοεῖτε
καὶ πιστεύετε ἐν τῷ εὐαγγελίῳ.

16 Καὶ παράγων παρὰ τὴν θάλασσαν τῆς Γαλιλαίας
εἶδεν Σίμωνα καὶ Ἀνδρέαν τὸν ἀδελφὸν Σίμωνος
ἀμφιβάλλοντας ἐν τῇ θαλάσσῃ·
ἦσαν γὰρ ἁλεεῖς.

1

17 καὶ εἶπεν αὐτοῖς ὁ Ἰησοῦς·
   δεῦτε ὀπίσω μου,
   καὶ ποιήσω ὑμᾶς γενέσθαι ἁλεεῖς ἀνθρώπων.

18 καὶ εὐθὺς ἀφέντες τὰ δίκτυα
   ἠκολούθησαν αὐτῷ.

19 Καὶ προβὰς ὀλίγον
   εἶδεν Ἰάκωβον τὸν τοῦ Ζεβεδαίου
   καὶ Ἰωάννην τὸν ἀδελφὸν αὐτοῦ,
   καὶ αὐτοὺς ἐν τῷ πλοίῳ
   καταρτίζοντας τὰ δίκτυα.

20 καὶ εὐθὺς ἐκάλεσεν αὐτούς·
   καὶ ἀφέντες τὸν πατέρα αὐτῶν Ζεβεδαῖον
   ἐν τῷ πλοίῳ μετὰ τῶν μισθωτῶν
   ἀπῆλθον ὀπίσω αὐτοῦ.

21 Καὶ εἰσπορεύονται εἰς Καφαρναούμ·
   καὶ εὐθὺς τοῖς σάββασιν
   εἰσελθὼν εἰς τὴν συναγωγὴν ἐδίδασκεν.

or: καὶ εὐθὺς τοῖς σάββασιν εἰσελθών
    εἰς τὴν συναγωγὴν ἐδίδασκεν.

22 καὶ ἐξεπλήσσοντο ἐπὶ τῇ διδαχῇ αὐτοῦ·
   ἦν γὰρ διδάσκων αὐτούς
   ὡς ἐξουσίαν ἔχων,
   καὶ οὐχ ὡς οἱ γραμματεῖς.

23 Καὶ εὐθὺς ἦν ἐν τῇ συναγωγῇ αὐτῶν
   ἄνθρωπος ἐν πνεύματι ἀκαθάρτῳ·

24 καὶ ἀνέκραξεν ²⁴λέγων·
   ἔα, τί ἡμῖν καὶ σοί, Ἰησοῦ Ναζαρηνέ;
   ἦλθες ἀπολέσαι ἡμᾶς.
   οἶδά σε τίς εἶ, ὁ ἅγιος τοῦ θεοῦ.

1 25 καὶ ἐπετίμησεν αὐτῷ ὁ Ἰησοῦς λέγων·
φιμώθητι
καὶ ἔξελθε ἐξ αὐτοῦ.

26 καὶ σπαράξαν αὐτὸν τὸ πνεῦμα τὸ ἀκάθαρτον
καὶ φωνῆσαν φωνῇ μεγάλῃ
ἐξῆλθεν ἐξ αὐτοῦ.

27 καὶ ἐθαμβήθησαν ἅπαντες,
ὥστε συνζητεῖν πρὸς ἑαυτοὺς λέγοντας·

τί ἐστιν τοῦτο;
διδαχὴ καινὴ κατ᾽ ἐξουσίαν·

καί,
τοῖς πνεύμασι τοῖς ἀκαθάρτοις ἐπιτάσσει,
καὶ ὑπακούουσιν αὐτῷ.

28 καὶ ἐξῆλθεν ἡ ἀκοὴ αὐτοῦ
εὐθὺς πανταχοῦ
εἰς ὅλην τὴν περίχωρον τῆς Γαλιλαίας.

29 Καὶ εὐθὺς ἐκ τῆς συναγωγῆς ἐξελθόντες
ἦλθον εἰς τὴν οἰκίαν Σίμωνος καὶ Ἀνδρέου
μετὰ Ἰακώβου καὶ Ἰωάννου.

30 ἡ δὲ πενθερὰ Σίμωνος κατέκειτο πυρέσσουσα,
καὶ εὐθὺς λέγουσιν αὐτῷ περὶ αὐτῆς.

31 καὶ προσελθὼν ἤγειρεν αὐτήν
κρατήσας τῆς χειρός·
καὶ ἀφῆκεν αὐτὴν ὁ πυρετὸς εὐθύς,
καὶ διηκόνει αὐτοῖς.

32 Ὀψίας δὲ γενομένης, ὅτε ἔδυ ὁ ἥλιος,
ἔφερον πρὸς αὐτόν
πάντας τοὺς κακῶς ἔχοντας
καὶ τοὺς δαιμονιζομένους·
33 καὶ ἦν ὅλη ἡ πόλις ἐπισυνηγμένη πρὸς τὴν θύραν.

1

34 καὶ ἐθεράπευσεν πολλοὺς
κακῶς ἔχοντας ποικίλαις νόσοις,
καὶ δαιμόνια πολλὰ ἐξέβαλεν,
καὶ οὐκ ἤφιεν λαλεῖν τὰ δαιμόνια,
ὅτι ᾔδεισαν αὐτόν.

35 Καὶ πρωῒ ἔννυχα λίαν ἀναστὰς ἐξῆλθεν
καὶ ἀπῆλθεν εἰς ἔρημον τόπον,
κἀκεῖ προσηύχετο.

36 καὶ κατεδίωξεν αὐτὸν Σίμων καὶ οἱ μετ᾽ αὐτοῦ,
37 καὶ εὑρόντες αὐτὸν λέγουσιν αὐτῷ
ὅτι πάντες ζητοῦσίν σε.

38 καὶ λέγει αὐτοῖς·
ἄγωμεν ἀλλαχοῦ εἰς τὰς ἐχομένας κωμοπόλεις,
ἵνα καὶ ἐκεῖ κηρύξω·
εἰς τοῦτο γὰρ ἐξῆλθον.

39 καὶ ἦλθεν
κηρύσσων εἰς τὰς συναγωγὰς αὐτῶν
εἰς ὅλην τὴν Γαλιλαίαν
καὶ τὰ δαιμόνια ἐκβάλλων.

40 Καὶ ἔρχεται πρὸς αὐτὸν λεπρός

παρακαλῶν αὐτόν
καὶ γονυπετῶν αὐτόν

καὶ λέγων αὐτῷ
ὅτι ἐὰν θέλῃς δύνασαί με καθαρίσαι.

41 ὁ δὲ Ἰησοῦς,
σπλαγχνισθεὶς ἐκτείνας τὴν χεῖρα αὐτοῦ,
ἥψατο καὶ λέγει αὐτῷ·
θέλω, καθαρίσθητι.

42 καὶ εἰπόντος αὐτοῦ
εὐθὺς ἀπῆλθεν ἀπ᾽ αὐτοῦ ἡ λέπρα,
καὶ ἐκαθερίσθη.

43 | καὶ ἐμβριμησάμενος αὐτῷ
     εὐθὺς ἐξέβαλεν αὐτόν,
44 | καὶ λέγει αὐτῷ·

     ὅρα μηδενὶ μηδὲν εἴπῃς,
     ἀλλὰ ὕπαγε σεαυτὸν δεῖξον τῷ ἱερεῖ
     καὶ προσένεγκε περὶ τοῦ καθαρισμοῦ σου
     ἃ προσέταξεν Μωϋσῆς
     εἰς μαρτύριον αὐτοῖς.

45 | ὁ δὲ ἐξελθών
     ἤρξατο κηρύσσειν πολλὰ καὶ διαφημίζειν τὸν λόγον,
     ὥστε μηκέτι αὐτὸν δύνασθαι
     φανερῶς εἰς πόλιν εἰσελθεῖν,
     ἀλλ' ἔξω ἐπ' ἐρήμοις τόποις ἦν·

     καὶ ἤρχοντο πρὸς αὐτὸν πάντοθεν.

2 1 | Καὶ εἰσελθὼν πάλιν εἰς Καφαρναούμ
     δι' ἡμερῶν ἠκούσθη ὅτι εἰς οἶκόν ἐστιν.

2 | καὶ εὐθέως συνήχθησαν πολλοί,
     ὥστε μηκέτι χωρεῖν μηδὲ τὰ πρὸς τὴν θύραν.

     καὶ ἐλάλει αὐτοῖς τὸν λόγον,
3 | καὶ ἔρχονται φέροντες πρὸς αὐτὸν παραλυτικόν
     αἰρόμενον ὑπὸ τεσσάρων.

or: 2 | καὶ εὐθέως συνήχθησαν πολλοί,
     ὥστε μηκέτι χωρεῖν μηδὲ τὰ πρὸς τὴν θύραν,
     καὶ ἐλάλει αὐτοῖς τὸν λόγον.

3 | καὶ ἔρχονται φέροντες πρὸς αὐτὸν παραλυτικόν.

2

4 | καὶ μὴ δυνάμενοι προσενέγκαι αὐτῷ διὰ τὸν ὄχλον
ἀπεστέγασαν τὴν στέγην ὅπου ἦν,
καὶ ἐξορύξαντες
χαλῶσι τὸν κράβαττον ὅπου ὁ παραλυτικὸς κατέκειτο.

5 | καὶ ἰδὼν ὁ Ἰησοῦς τὴν πίστιν αὐτῶν
λέγει τῷ παραλυτικῷ·
τέκνον, ἀφίενταί σου αἱ ἁμαρτίαι.

6 | ἦσαν δέ τινες τῶν γραμματέων ἐκεῖ καθήμενοι
καὶ διαλογιζόμενοι ἐν ταῖς καρδίαις αὐτῶν·

7 | τί οὗτος οὕτως λαλεῖ ;
βλασφημεῖ·

τίς δύναται ἀφιέναι ἁμαρτίας
εἰ μὴ εἷς ὁ θεός ;

8 | καὶ εὐθὺς ἐπιγνοὺς ὁ Ἰησοῦς τῷ πνεύματι αὐτοῦ
ὅτι οὕτως διαλογίζονται αὐτοὶ ἐν ἑαυτοῖς,
λέγει αὐτοῖς·

τί ταῦτα διαλογίζεσθε ἐν ταῖς καρδίαις ὑμῶν ;
9 | τί ἐστιν εὐκοπώτερον,
εἰπεῖν τῷ παραλυτικῷ·
ἀφίενταί σου αἱ ἁμαρτίαι,

ἢ εἰπεῖν·
ἔγειρε καὶ ἆρον τὸν κράβαττόν σου
καὶ περιπάτει ;

10 | ἵνα δὲ εἰδῆτε
ὅτι ἐξουσίαν ἔχει ὁ υἱὸς τοῦ ἀνθρώπου
ἀφιέναι ἁμαρτίας ἐπὶ τῆς γῆς.

11 | λέγει τῷ παραλυτικῷ·
σοὶ λέγω,
ἔγειρε ἆρον τὸν κράβαττόν σου
καὶ ὕπαγε εἰς τὸν οἶκόν σου.

2 12 | καὶ ἠγέρθη
καὶ εὐθὺς ἄρας τὸν κράβαττον
ἐξῆλθεν ἐναντίον πάντων·

ὥστε ἐξίστασθαι πάντας
καὶ δοξάζειν τὸν θεὸν λέγοντας
ὅτι οὐδέποτε οὕτως εἴδομεν.

13 | Καὶ ἐξῆλθεν πάλιν παρὰ τὴν θάλασσαν·
καὶ πᾶς ὁ ὄχλος ἤρχετο πρὸς αὐτόν,
καὶ ἐδίδασκεν αὐτούς.

14 | Καὶ παράγων εἶδεν Λευὶν τὸν τοῦ Ἀλφαίου
καθήμενον ἐπὶ τὸ τελώνιον,
καὶ λέγει αὐτῷ·
ἀκολούθει μοι.

| καὶ ἀναστὰς ἠκολούθησεν αὐτῷ.

15 | Καὶ γίνεται κατακεῖσθαι αὐτὸν ἐν τῇ οἰκίᾳ αὐτοῦ,
καὶ πολλοὶ τελῶναι καὶ ἁμαρτωλοὶ
συνανέκειντο τῷ Ἰησοῦ καὶ τοῖς μαθηταῖς αὐτοῦ·
ἦσαν γὰρ πολλοὶ καὶ ἠκολούθουν αὐτῷ.

16 | καὶ οἱ γραμματεῖς, τῶν Φαρισαίων,
ἰδόντες αὐτὸν ἐσθίοντα μετὰ τῶν ἁμαρτωλῶν καὶ τελωνῶν
ἔλεγον τοῖς μαθηταῖς αὐτοῦ·
τί ὅτι μετὰ τῶν τελωνῶν καὶ ἁμαρτωλῶν ἐσθίει καὶ πίνει ;

17 | καὶ ἀκούσας ὁ Ἰησοῦς λέγει αὐτοῖς·

οὐ χρείαν ἔχουσιν οἱ ἰσχύοντες ἰατροῦ
ἀλλ᾽   οἱ κακῶς ἔχοντες·

οὐκ ἦλθον καλέσαι δικαίους
ἀλλὰ   ἁμαρτωλούς.

18 | Καὶ ἦσαν οἱ μαθηταὶ Ἰωάννου
καὶ   οἱ Φαρισαῖοι   νηστεύοντες.

2

καὶ ἔρχονται καὶ λέγουσιν αὐτῷ·
δὶα τί οἱ μαθηταὶ Ἰωάννου
καὶ οἱ μαθηταὶ τῶν Φαρισαίων   νηστεύουσιν,
οἱ δὲ σοὶ μαθηταὶ   οὐ νηστεύουσιν ;

19   καὶ εἶπεν αὐτοῖς ὁ Ἰησοῦς·

  μὴ δύνανται οἱ υἱοὶ τοῦ νυμφῶνος
   ἐν ᾧ ὁ νυμφίος μετ' αὐτῶν ἐστιν   νηστεύειν ;
  ὅσον χρόνον ἔχουσιν τὸν νυμφίον μετ' αὐτῶν,
   οὐ δύνανται   νηστεύειν·

20   ἐλεύσονται δὲ ἡμέραι
  ὅταν ἀπαρθῇ ἀπ' αὐτῶν ὁ νυμφίος,
  καὶ τότε   νηστεύσουσιν,
  ἐν ἐκείνῃ τῇ ἡμέρᾳ.

21   Οὐδεὶς ἐπίβλημα ῥάκους ἀγνάφου
  ἐπιρράπτει ἐπὶ ἱμάτιον παλαιόν·
  εἰ δὲ μή,
   αἴρει τὸ πλήρωμα ἀπ' αὐτοῦ τὸ καινὸν τοῦ παλαιοῦ,
   καὶ χεῖρον σχίσμα γίνεται.

22   καὶ οὐδεὶς βάλλει οἶνον νέον εἰς ἀσκοὺς παλαιούς·
  εἰ δὲ μή,
   ῥήξει ὁ οἶνος τοὺς ἀσκούς,
   καὶ ὁ οἶνος ἀπόλλυται καὶ οἱ ἀσκοί.

  ἀλλὰ οἶνον νέον εἰς ἀσκοὺς καινοὺς βλητέον.

23   Καὶ ἐγένετο αὐτὸν ἐν τοῖς σάββασιν
  παραπορεύεσθαι διὰ τῶν σπορίμων,
  καὶ οἱ μαθηταὶ αὐτοῦ ἤρξαντο ὁδὸν ποιεῖν
  τίλλοντες τοὺς στάχυας.

24   καὶ οἱ Φαρισαῖοι ἔλεγεν αὐτῷ·
  ἴδε τί ποιοῦσιν τοῖς σάββασιν ὃ οὐκ ἔξεστιν ;

25   καὶ αὐτὸς λέγει αὐτοῖς·
  οὐδέποτε ἀνέγνωτε

τί ἐποίησεν Δαυίδ,
ὅτε χρείαν ἔσχεν καὶ ἐπείνασεν
αὐτὸς καὶ οἱ μετ᾽ αὐτοῦ ;

26   πῶς εἰσῆλθεν εἰς τὸν οἶκον τοῦ θεοῦ
ἐπὶ ᾽Αβιάθαρ ἀρχιερέως
καὶ τοὺς ἄρτους τῆς προθέσεως ἔφαγεν,
οὓς οὐκ ἔξεστιν φαγεῖν
εἰ μὴ τοῖς ἱερεῦσιν,
καὶ ἔδωκεν καὶ τοῖς σὺν αὐτῷ οὖσιν ;

27 καὶ ἔλεγεν αὐτοῖς·

τὸ σάββατον διὰ τὸν ἄνθρωπον ἐγένετο,
καὶ οὐχ ὁ ἄνθρωπος διὰ τὸν σάββατον·

28 ὥστε κύριός ἐστιν ὁ υἱὸς τοῦ ἀνθρώπου
καὶ τοῦ σαββάτου.

3 1 Καὶ εἰσῆλθεν πάλιν εἰς συναγωγήν.

καὶ ἦν ἐκεῖ ἄνθρωπος ἐξηραμμένην ἔχων τὴν χεῖρα·
2 καὶ παρετήρουν αὐτόν
εἰ τοῖς σάββασιν θεραπεύσει αὐτόν,
ἵνα κατηγορήσωσιν αὐτοῦ.

3 καὶ λέγει τῷ ἀνθρώπῳ τῷ τὴν ξηρὰν χεῖρα ἔχοντι·
ἔγειρε εἰς τὸ μέσον.

4 καὶ λέγει αὐτοῖς·
ἔξεστιν τοῖς σάββασιν
ἀγαθοποιῆσαι ἢ κακοποιῆσαι,
ψυχὴν σῶσαι ἢ ἀποκτεῖναι ;

5 οἱ δὲ ἐσιώπων.

καὶ περιβλεψάμενος αὐτοὺς μετ᾽ ὀργῆς,
συνλυπούμενος ἐπὶ τῇ πωρώσει τῆς καρδίας αὐτῶν.

3

λέγει τῷ ἀνθρώπῳ·
  ἔκτεινον τὴν χεῖρα.

καὶ ἐξέτεινεν,
καὶ ἀπεκατεστάθη ἡ χεὶρ αὐτοῦ.

6 καὶ ἐξελθόντες οἱ Φαρισαῖοι
   εὐθὺς μετὰ τῶν Ἡρῳδιανῶν συμβούλιον ἐδίδουν
     κατ' αὐτοῦ,
   ὅπως αὐτὸν ἀπολέσωσιν.

7 Καὶ ὁ Ἰησοῦς μετὰ τῶν μαθητῶν αὐτοῦ
   ἀνεχώρησεν πρὸς τὴν θάλασσαν.

καὶ πολὺ πλῆθος ἀπὸ τῆς Γαλιλαίας ἠκολούθησεν·

     καὶ ἀπὸ τῆς Ἰουδαίας
8   καὶ ἀπὸ Ἱεροσολύμων

     καὶ ἀπὸ τῆς Ἰδουμαίας
     καὶ πέραν τοῦ Ἰορδάνου

     καὶ περὶ Τύρον καὶ Σιδῶνα,
       πλῆθος πολύ,

ἀκούοντες ὅσα ἐποίει, ἦλθον πρὸς αὐτόν.

9 καὶ εἶπεν τοῖς μαθηταῖς αὐτοῦ,
   ἵνα πλοιάριον προσκαρτερῇ αὐτῷ
     διὰ τὸν ὄχλον,
   ἵνα μὴ θλίβωσιν αὐτόν·

10 πολλοὺς γὰρ ἐθεράπευσεν,
   ὥστε ἐπιπίπτειν αὐτῷ,
   ἵνα αὐτοῦ ἅψωνται ὅσοι εἶχον μάστιγας.

11 καὶ τὰ πνεύματα τὰ ἀκάθαρτα, ὅταν αὐτὸν ἐθεώρει,
     προσέπιπτεν αὐτῷ
     καὶ ἔκραζεν λέγοντα
       ὅτι σὺ εἶ ὁ υἱὸς τοῦ θεοῦ.

3 12 | καὶ πολλὰ ἐπετίμα αὐτοῖς,
ἵνα μὴ αὐτὸν φανερὸν ποιήσωσιν.

13 | Καὶ ἀναβαίνει εἰς τὸ ὄρος,
καὶ προσκαλεῖται οὓς ἤθελεν αὐτός,
καὶ ἀπῆλθον πρὸς αὐτόν.

14 | καὶ ἐποίησεν δώδεκα
ἵνα ὦσιν μετ' αὐτοῦ,
καὶ ἵνα ἀποστέλλῃ αὐτούς
κηρύσσειν
15 | καὶ ἔχειν ἐξουσίαν ἐκβάλλειν τὰ δαιμόνια.

16 | καὶ ἐποίησεν τοὺς δώδεκα,
καὶ ἐπέθηκεν ὄνομα τῷ Σίμωνι Πέτρον·

17 | καὶ Ἰάκωβον τὸν τοῦ Ζεβεδαίου
καὶ Ἰωάννην τὸν ἀδελφὸν τοῦ Ἰακώβου,
καὶ ἐπέθηκεν αὐτοῖς ὀνόματα Βοανηργές,
ὅ ἐστιν υἱοὶ βροντῆς·

18 | καὶ Ἀνδρέαν καὶ Φίλιππον
καὶ Βαρθολομαῖον καὶ Ματθαῖον

καὶ Θωμᾶν καὶ Ἰάκωβον τὸν τοῦ Ἀλφαίου
καὶ Θαδδαῖον καὶ Σίμωνα τὸν Καναναῖον

19 | καὶ Ἰούδαν Ἰσκαριώθ,
ὃς καὶ παρέδωκεν αὐτόν.

20 | Καὶ ἔρχονται εἰς οἶκον·
καὶ συνέρχεται πάλιν ὁ ὄχλος,
ὥστε μὴ δύνασθαι αὐτοὺς μηδὲ ἄρτον φαγεῖν.

21 | καὶ ἀκούσαντες οἱ παρ' αὐτοῦ ἐξῆλθον κρατῆσαι αὐτόν·
ἔλεγον γὰρ ὅτι ἐξέστη.

22 | καὶ οἱ γραμματεῖς οἱ ἀπὸ Ἱεροσολύμων καταβάντες
ἔλεγον

3

ὅτι Βεελζεβοὺλ ἔχει,
καί,
ὅτι ἐν τῷ ἄρχοντι τῶν δαιμονίων ἐκβάλλει τὰ δαιμόνια.

23 καὶ προσκαλεσάμενος αὐτοὺς
ἐν παραβολαῖς ἔλεγεν αὐτοῖς·

πῶς δύναται σατανᾶς σατανᾶν ἐκβάλλειν ;

24 καὶ ἐὰν βασιλεία ἐφ' ἑαυτὴν μερισθῇ,
οὐ δύναται σταθῆναι ἡ βασιλεία ἐκείνη·
25 καὶ ἐὰν οἰκία ἐφ' ἑαυτὴν μερισθῇ,
οὐ δυνήσεται ἡ οἰκία ἐκείνη στῆναι.

26 καὶ εἰ ὁ σατανᾶς ἀνέστη ἐφ' ἑαυτὸν καὶ μεμέρισται,
οὐ δύναται στῆναι, ἀλλὰ τέλος ἔχει.

27 ἀλλ' οὐ δύναται οὐδεὶς
εἰς τὴν οἰκίαν τοῦ ἰσχυροῦ εἰσελθὼν
τὰ σκεύη αὐτοῦ διαρπάσαι,
ἐὰν μὴ πρῶτον τὸν ἰσχυρὸν δήσῃ,
καὶ τότε τὴν οἰκίαν αὐτοῦ διαρπάσει.

28 ἀμὴν λέγω ὑμῖν

ὅτι πάντα ἀφεθήσεται τοῖς υἱοῖς τῶν ἀνθρώπων
τὰ ἁμαρτήματα καὶ αἱ βλασφημίαι,
ὅσας ἐὰν βλασφημήσωσιν·

29 ὃς δ' ἂν βλασφημήσῃ εἰς τὸ πνεῦμα τὸ ἅγιον,
οὐκ ἔχει ἄφεσιν εἰς τὸν αἰῶνα,
ἀλλὰ ἔνοχός ἐστιν αἰωνίου ἁμαρτήματος.

30 ὅτι ἔλεγον·
πνεῦμα ἀκάθαρτον ἔχει.

31 Καὶ ἔρχονται ἡ μήτηρ αὐτοῦ καὶ οἱ ἀδελφοὶ αὐτοῦ,
καὶ ἔξω ἑστῶτες
ἀπέστειλαν πρὸς αὐτὸν καλοῦντες αὐτόν.

32 | καὶ ἐκάθητο περὶ αὐτὸν ὄχλος,
καὶ λέγουσιν αὐτῷ·
   ἰδοὺ ἡ μήτηρ σου
   καὶ οἱ ἀδελφοί σου
   [καὶ αἱ ἀδελφαί σου]
   ἔξω ζητοῦσίν σε.

33 | καὶ ἀποκριθεὶς αὐτοῖς λέγει·
   τίς ἐστιν ἡ μήτηρ μου καὶ οἱ ἀδελφοί μου ;

34 | καὶ περιβλεψάμενος τοὺς περὶ αὐτὸν κύκλῳ καθημένους
λέγει·

   ἴδε ἡ μήτηρ μου
   καὶ οἱ ἀδελφοί μου.

35 | ὃς γὰρ ἂν ποιήσῃ τὸ θέλημα τοῦ θεοῦ,
   οὗτος ἀδελφός μου
   καὶ ἀδελφή
   καὶ μήτηρ ἐστίν.

4 1 | Καὶ πάλιν ἤρξατο διδάσκειν παρὰ τὴν θάλασσαν.

   καὶ συνάγεται πρὸς αὐτὸν ὄχλος πλεῖστος,
   ὥστε αὐτὸν εἰς [τὸ] πλοῖον ἐμβάντα καθῆσθαι
      ἐν τῇ θαλάσσῃ,
   καὶ πᾶς ὁ ὄχλος πρὸς τὴν θάλασσαν
      ἐπὶ τῆς γῆς ἦσαν.

2 | καὶ ἐδίδασκεν αὐτοὺς ἐν παραβολαῖς πολλά,
   καὶ ἔλεγεν αὐτοῖς ἐν τῇ διδαχῇ αὐτοῦ·

3 | ἀκούετε.

   ἰδοὺ ἐξῆλθεν ὁ σπείρων τοῦ σπεῖραι.

4 | καὶ ἐγένετο ἐν τῷ σπείρειν
      ὃ μὲν ἔπεσεν παρὰ τὴν ὁδόν,
      καὶ ἦλθεν τὰ πετεινὰ καὶ κατέφαγεν αὐτό.

4 5   καὶ ἄλλο ἔπεσεν ἐπὶ τὸ πετρῶδες,
      ὅπου οὐκ εἶχεν γῆν πολλήν,
      καὶ εὐθὺς ἐξανέτειλεν
         διὰ τὸ μὴ ἔχειν βάθος γῆς·
6   καὶ ὅτε ἀνέτειλεν ὁ ἥλιος ἐκαυματίσθη,
      καὶ διὰ τὸ μὴ ἔχειν ῥίζαν ἐξηράνθη.

7   καὶ ἄλλο ἔπεσεν εἰς τὰς ἀκάνθας,
      καὶ ἀνέβησαν αἱ ἄκανθαι
      καὶ συνέπνιξαν αὐτό,
      καὶ καρπὸν οὐκ ἔδωκεν.

8   καὶ ἄλλα ἔπεσεν εἰς τὴν γῆν τὴν καλήν,
      καὶ ἐδίδου καρπὸν ἀναβαίνοντα καὶ αὐξανόμενον,
      καὶ ἔφερεν εἰς τριάκοντα
      καὶ   ἐν ἑξήκοντα
      καὶ   ἐν ἑκατόν.

9 καὶ ἔλεγεν·
   ὃς ἔχει ὦτα ἀκούειν ἀκουέτω.

10 Καὶ ὅτε ἐγένετο κατὰ μόνας, ἠρώτων αὐτόν
   οἱ περὶ αὐτὸν σὺν τοῖς δώδεκα τὰς παραβολάς.

11 καὶ ἔλεγεν αὐτοῖς·

   ὑμῖν τὸ μυστήριον δέδοται τῆς βασιλείας τοῦ θεοῦ·
   ἐκείνοις δὲ τοῖς ἔξω ἐν παραβολαῖς τὰ πάντα γίνεται,
12   ἵνα βλέποντες βλέπωσιν καὶ μὴ ἴδωσιν,
     καὶ ἀκούοντες ἀκούωσιν καὶ μὴ συνιῶσιν,
      μήποτε ἐπιστρέψωσιν καὶ ἀφεθῇ αὐτοῖς.

13 καὶ λέγει αὐτοῖς·

   οὐκ οἴδατε τὴν παραβολὴν ταύτην,
   καὶ πῶς πάσας τὰς παραβολὰς γνώσεσθε;

14 ὁ σπείρων τὸν λόγον σπείρει.

4 15 οὗτοι δέ εἰσιν οἱ παρὰ τὴν ὁδόν
ὅπου σπείρεται ὁ λόγος,
καὶ ὅταν ἀκούσωσιν,
  εὐθὺς ἔρχεται ὁ σατανᾶς
  καὶ αἴρει τὸν λόγον τὸν ἐσπαρμένον ἐν αὐτοῖς.

16 καὶ οὗτοί εἰσιν ὁμοίως οἱ ἐπὶ τὰ πετρώδη σπειρόμενοι,
οἳ ὅταν ἀκούσωσιν τὸν λόγον,
  εὐθὺς μετὰ χαρᾶς λαμβάνουσιν αὐτόν,
17 καὶ οὐκ ἔχουσιν ῥίζαν ἐν ἑαυτοῖς,
  ἀλλὰ πρόσκαιροί εἰσιν,
εἶτα γενομένης θλίψεως ἢ διωγμοῦ διὰ τὸν λόγον
  εὐθὺς σκανδαλίζονται.

18 καὶ ἄλλοι εἰσὶν οἱ εἰς τὰς ἀκάνθας σπειρόμενοι·
οὗτοί εἰσιν οἱ τὸν λόγον ἀκούσαντες,
19 καὶ αἱ μέριμναι τοῦ αἰῶνος
  καὶ ἡ ἀπάτη τοῦ πλούτου
  καὶ αἱ περὶ τὰ λοιπὰ ἐπιθυμίαι
εἰσπορευόμεναι συνπνίγουσιν τὸν λόγον,
καὶ ἄκαρπος γίνεται.

20 καὶ ἐκεῖνοί εἰσιν οἱ ἐπὶ τὴν γῆν τὴν καλὴν σπαρέντες,
οἵτινες ἀκούουσιν τὸν λόγον καὶ παραδέχονται,
  καὶ καρποφοροῦσιν ἐν τριάκοντα
  καὶ   ἐν ἑξήκοντα
  καὶ   ἐν ἑκατόν.

21 | Καὶ ἔλεγεν αὐτοῖς·

μήτι ἔρχεται ὁ λύχνος,
  ἵνα ὑπὸ τὸν μόδιον τεθῇ ἢ ὑπὸ τὴν κλίνην ;
οὐχ ἵνα ἐπὶ τὴν λυχνίαν τεθῇ ;

22 οὐ γάρ ἐστίν τι κρυπτόν,
  ἐὰν μὴ ἵνα φανερωθῇ·
οὐδὲ ἐγένετο ἀπόκρυφον,
  ἀλλ' ἵνα ἔλθῃ εἰς φανερόν.

4   23 | εἴ τις ἔχει ὦτα ἀκούειν, ἀκουέτω.

24 | Καὶ ἔλεγεν αὐτοῖς·

βλέπετε τί ἀκούετε.

ἐν ᾧ μέτρῳ μετρεῖτε μετρηθήσεται ὑμῖν,
καὶ προστεθήσεται ὑμῖν τοῖς ἀκούουσιν.

25 | ὃς γὰρ ἔχει,
 δοθήσεται αὐτῷ·
καὶ ὃς οὐκ ἔχει,
 καὶ ὃ ἔχει ἀρθήσεται ἀπ' αὐτοῦ.

26 | Καὶ ἔλεγεν·

οὕτως ἐστὶν ἡ βασιλεία τοῦ θεοῦ,
ὡς [ἐὰν] ἄνθρωπος βάλῃ τὸν σπόρον ἐπὶ τῆς γῆς,

27 | καὶ καθεύδῃ καὶ ἐγείρηται
 νύκτα καὶ ἡμέραν,
καὶ ὁ σπόρος βλαστᾷ καὶ μηκύνηται,
 ὡς οὐκ οἶδεν αὐτός.

28 | αὐτομάτη ἡ γῆ καρποφορεῖ,
 πρῶτον χόρτον,
 εἶτα στάχυν,
 εἶτα πλήρη σῖτον ἐν τῷ στάχυϊ.

29 | ὅταν δὲ παραδῷ ὁ καρπός,
εὐθὺς ἀποστέλλει τὸ δρέπανον,
ὅτι παρέστηκεν ὁ θερισμός.

30 | Καὶ ἔλεγεν·

πῶς ὁμοιώσωμεν τὴν βασιλείαν τοῦ θεοῦ,
ἢ ἐν τίνι αὐτὴν παραβολῇ θῶμεν ;

31 | ὡς κόκκον σινάπεως·

4

ὃς ὅταν σπαρῇ ἐπὶ τῆς γῆς,
μικρότερον ὂν πάντων τῶν σπερμάτων τῶν ἐπὶ τῆς γῆς

32   καὶ ὅταν σπαρῇ,
        ἀναβαίνει,
        καὶ γίνεται μεῖζον πάντων τῶν λαχάνων,
        καὶ ποιεῖ κλάδους μεγάλους,

        ὥστε δύνασθαι ὑπὸ τὴν σκιὰν αὐτοῦ
        τὰ πετεινὰ τοῦ οὐρανοῦ κατασκηνοῦν.

33   Καὶ τοιαύταις παραβολαῖς πολλαῖς
       ἐλάλει αὐτοῖς τὸν λόγον,
       καθὼς ἠδύναντο ἀκούειν·

34   χωρὶς δὲ παραβολῆς οὐκ ἐλάλει αὐτοῖς,
       κατ' ἰδίαν δὲ τοῖς ἰδίοις μαθηταῖς ἐπέλυεν πάντα.

35   Καὶ λέγει αὐτοῖς
       ἐν ἐκείνῃ τῇ ἡμέρᾳ ὀψίας γενομένης·
       διέλθωμεν εἰς τὸ πέραν.

36   καὶ ἀφέντες τὸν ὄχλον
       παραλαμβάνουσιν αὐτὸν ὡς ἦν ἐν τῷ πλοίῳ·

       καὶ ἄλλα δὲ πλοῖα ἦν μετ' αὐτοῦ.

37   καὶ γίνεται λαῖλαψ μεγάλη ἀνέμου,

       καὶ τὰ κύματα ἐπέβαλλεν εἰς τὸ πλοῖον,
       ὥστε ἤδη γεμίζεσθαι τὸ πλοῖον.

38   καὶ ἦν αὐτὸς ἐν τῇ πρύμνῃ
       ἐπὶ τὸ προσκεφάλαιον καθεύδων·

       καὶ διεγείρουσιν αὐτὸν καὶ λέγουσιν αὐτῷ·
       διδάσκαλε, οὐ μέλει σοι ὅτι ἀπολλύμεθα ;

39   καὶ διεγερθεὶς ἐπετίμησεν τῷ ἀνέμῳ
  καὶ   εἶπεν   τῇ θαλάσσῃ·

σιώπα,
πεφίμωσο.

καὶ ἐκόπασεν ὁ ἄνεμος,
καὶ ἐγένετο γαλήνη μεγάλη.

40 καὶ εἶπεν αὐτοῖς·
τί δειλοί ἐστε οὕτως ;
πῶς οὐκ ἔχετε πίστιν ;

41 καὶ ἐφοβήθησαν φόβον μέγαν,
καὶ ἔλεγον πρὸς ἀλλήλους·
τίς ἄρα οὗτός ἐστιν,
ὅτι καὶ ὁ ἄνεμος καὶ ἡ θάλασσα ὑπακούει αὐτῷ ;

5 1 Καὶ ἦλθον εἰς τὸ πέραν τῆς θαλάσσης
εἰς τὴν χώραν τῶν Γαδαρηνῶν.

2 καὶ ἐξελθόντος αὐτοῦ ἐκ τοῦ πλοίου,
εὐθὺς ὑπήντησεν αὐτῷ ἐκ τῶν μνημείων
ἄνθρωπος ἐν πνεύματι ἀκαθάρτῳ,
3 ὃς τὴν κατοίκησιν εἶχεν ἐν τοῖς μνήμασιν,

καὶ οὐδὲ ἁλύσει οὐκέτι οὐδεὶς ἐδύνατο αὐτὸν δῆσαι,
4 διὰ τὸ αὐτὸν πολλάκις πέδαις καὶ ἁλύσεσιν δεδέσθαι,
καὶ διεσπάσθαι ὑπ᾿ αὐτοῦ τὰς ἁλύσεις
καὶ τὰς πέδας συντετρῖφθαι,
καὶ οὐδεὶς ἴσχυεν αὐτὸν δαμάσαι·

5 καὶ διαπαντὸς νυκτὸς καὶ ἡμέρας
ἐν τοῖς μνήμασιν καὶ ἐν τοῖς ὄρεσιν ἦν
κράζων καὶ κατακόπτων ἑαυτὸν λίθοις.

6 καὶ ἰδὼν τὸν Ἰησοῦν ἀπὸ μακρόθεν
ἔδραμεν
καὶ προσεκύνησεν αὐτῷ,

5   7   καὶ κράξας φωνῇ μεγάλῃ λέγει·

τί ἐμοὶ καὶ σοί,
   Ἰησοῦ υἱὲ τοῦ θεοῦ τοῦ ὑψίστου ;
ὁρκίζω σε τὸν θεόν,
   μή με βασανίσῃς.

8 ἔλεγεν γὰρ αὐτῷ·
   ἔξελθε τὸ πνεῦμα τὸ ἀκάθαρτον ἐκ τοῦ ἀνθρώπου.

9 καὶ ἐπηρώτα αὐτόν·
   τί ὄνομά σοι ;

   καὶ λέγει αὐτῷ·
   λεγεὼν ὄνομά μοι, ὅτι πολλοί ἐσμεν.

10 καὶ παρεκάλει αὐτὸν πολλά,
   ἵνα μὴ αὐτοὺς ἀποστείλῃ ἔξω τῆς χώρας.

11 ἦν δὲ ἐκεῖ πρὸς τῷ ὄρει
   ἀγέλη χοίρων μεγάλη βοσκομένη·

12 καὶ παρεκάλεσαν αὐτὸν λέγοντες·
   πέμψον ἡμᾶς εἰς τοὺς χοίρους,
   ἵνα εἰς αὐτοὺς εἰσέλθωμεν.

13 καὶ ἐπέτρεψεν αὐτοῖς.

   καὶ ἐξελθόντα τὰ πνεύματα τὰ ἀκάθαρτα
   εἰσῆλθον εἰς τοὺς χοίρους,
      καὶ ὥρμησεν ἡ ἀγέλη κατὰ τοῦ κρημνοῦ
      εἰς τὴν θάλασσαν,
      ὡς δισχίλιοι,
   καὶ ἐπνίγοντο ἐν τῇ θαλάσσῃ.

14 καὶ οἱ βοσκόμενοι αὐτοὺς ἔφυγον
   καὶ ἀπήγγειλαν εἰς τὴν πόλιν καὶ εἰς τοὺς ἀγρούς·
   καὶ ἦλθον ἰδεῖν τί ἐστιν τὸ γεγονός.

5

15 | καὶ ἔρχονται πρὸς τὸν Ἰησοῦν,
καὶ θεωροῦσιν τὸν δαιμονιζόμενον
καθήμενον ἱματισμένον καὶ σωφρονοῦντα,
τὸν ἐσχηκότα τὸν λεγεῶνα,
καὶ ἐφοβήθησαν.

16 | καὶ διηγήσαντο αὐτοῖς οἱ ἰδόντες,
πῶς ἐγένετο τῷ δαιμονιζομένῳ
καὶ περὶ τῶν χοίρων.

17 | καὶ ἤρξαντο παρακαλεῖν αὐτόν
ἀπελθεῖν ἀπὸ τῶν ὁρίων αὐτῶν.

18 | καὶ ἐμβαίνοντος αὐτοῦ εἰς τὸ πλοῖον
παρεκάλει αὐτὸν ὁ δαιμονισθείς,
ἵνα μετ’ αὐτοῦ ᾖ.

19 | καὶ οὐκ ἀφῆκεν αὐτόν,
ἀλλὰ λέγει αὐτῷ·
ὕπαγε εἰς τὸν οἶκόν σου πρὸς τοὺς σούς,
καὶ ἀπάγγειλον αὐτοῖς,
ὅσα σοι ὁ κύριος πεποίηκεν
καὶ ἠλέησέν σε.

20 | καὶ ἀπῆλθεν
καὶ ἤρξατο κηρύσσειν ἐν τῇ Δεκαπόλει
ὅσα ἐποίησεν αὐτῷ ὁ Ἰησοῦς·

καὶ πάντες ἐθαύμαζον.

21 | Καὶ διαπεράσαντος τοῦ Ἰησοῦ ἐν τῷ πλοίῳ
πάλιν εἰς τὸ πέραν συνήχθη ὄχλος πολὺς ἐπ’ αὐτόν,
καὶ ἦν παρὰ τὴν θάλασσαν.

22 | Καὶ ἔρχεται εἷς τῶν ἀρχισυναγώγων, ὀνόματι Ἰάειρος,
καὶ ἰδὼν αὐτόν
πίπτει πρὸς τοὺς πόδας αὐτοῦ,
23 | καὶ παρακαλεῖ αὐτὸν πολλὰ λέγων

5

ὅτι τὸ θυγάτριόν μου ἐσχάτως ἔχει·
ἵνα ἐλθὼν ἐπιθῇς τὰς χεῖρας αὐτῇ,
ἵνα σωθῇ καὶ ζήσῃ.

24 καὶ ἀπῆλθεν μετ᾽ αὐτοῦ·
καὶ ἠκολούθει αὐτῷ ὄχλος πολύς,
καὶ συνέθλιβον αὐτόν.

25 Καὶ γυνή τις
οὖσα ἐν ῥύσει αἵματος δώδεκα ἔτη,

26 καὶ πολλὰ παθοῦσα ὑπὸ πολλῶν ἰατρῶν
καὶ δαπανήσασα τὰ παρ᾽ αὐτῆς πάντα,

καὶ μηδὲν ὠφεληθεῖσα
ἀλλὰ μᾶλλον εἰς τὸ χεῖρον ἐλθοῦσα,

27 ἀκούσασα περὶ τοῦ Ἰησοῦ,
ἐλθοῦσα ἐν τῷ ὄχλῳ ὄπισθεν,

ἥψατο τοῦ ἱματίου αὐτοῦ·
28 ἔλεγεν γάρ
ὅτι ἐὰν ἅψωμαι κἂν τῶν ἱματίων αὐτοῦ
σωθήσομαι.

29 καὶ εὐθὺς ἐξηράνθη ἡ πηγὴ τοῦ αἵματος αὐτῆς,
καὶ ἔγνω τῷ σώματι
ὅτι ἴαται ἀπὸ τῆς μάστιγος.

30 καὶ εὐθὺς ὁ Ἰησοῦς
ἐπιγνοὺς ἐν ἑαυτῷ τὴν ἐξ αὐτοῦ δύναμιν ἐξελθοῦσαν,
ἐπιστραφεὶς ἐν τῷ ὄχλῳ,
ἔλεγεν·
τίς μου ἥψατο τῶν ἱματίων ;

31 καὶ ἔλεγον αὐτῷ οἱ μαθηταὶ αὐτοῦ·
βλέπεις τὸν ὄχλον συνθλίβοντά σε,
καὶ λέγεις· τίς μου ἥψατο ;

5   32 | καὶ περιεβλέπετο ἰδεῖν τὴν τοῦτο ποιήσασαν.

33 | ἡ δὲ γυνή

φοβηθεῖσα καὶ τρέμουσα,
εἰδυῖα ὃ γέγονεν [ἐπ'] αὐτῇ,

ἦλθεν
καὶ προσέπεσεν αὐτῷ
καὶ εἶπεν αὐτῷ πᾶσαν τὴν ἀλήθειαν.

34 | ὁ δὲ εἶπεν αὐτῇ·

θύγατερ, ἡ πίστις σου σέσωκέν σε·

ὕπαγε εἰς εἰρήνην,
καὶ ἴσθι ὑγιὴς ἀπὸ τοῦ μάστιγός σου.

35 | Ἔτι αὐτοῦ λαλοῦντος
ἔρχονται ἀπὸ τοῦ ἀρχισυναγώγου λέγοντες
ὅτι ἡ θυγάτηρ σου ἀπέθανεν·
τί ἔτι σκύλλεις τὸν διδάσκαλον ;

36 | ὁ δὲ Ἰησοῦς εὐθέως παρακούσας τὸν λόγον λαλούμενον
λέγει τῷ ἀρχισυναγώγῳ·
μὴ φοβοῦ,
μόνον πίστευε.

37 | καὶ οὐκ ἀφῆκεν οὐδένα μετ' αὐτοῦ συνακολουθῆσαι
εἰ μὴ τὸν Πέτρον καὶ Ἰάκωβον
καὶ Ἰωάννην τὸν ἀδελφὸν Ἰακώβου.

38 | καὶ ἔρχονται εἰς τὸν οἶκον τοῦ ἀρχισυναγώγου,
καὶ θεωρεῖ θόρυβον, καὶ κλαίοντας καὶ ἀλαλάζοντας πολλά·

39 | καὶ εἰσελθὼν λέγει αὐτοῖς·
τί θορυβεῖσθε καὶ κλαίετε ;
τὸ παιδίον οὐκ ἀπέθανεν ἀλλὰ καθεύδει.

40 | καὶ κατεγέλων αὐτοῦ.

ὁ δὲ ἐκβαλὼν πάντας
παραλαμβάνει τὸν πατέρα τοῦ παιδίου
  καὶ τὴν μητέρα
  καὶ τοὺς μετ᾽ αὐτοῦ,
  καὶ εἰσπορεύεται ὅπου ἦν τὸ παιδίον ἀνακείμενον.

41   καὶ κρατήσας τῆς χειρὸς τοῦ παιδίου
λέγει αὐτῇ·

   ταλιθὰ κούμ,
   (ὅ ἐστιν μεθερμηνευόμενον)·
   τὸ κοράσιον, σοὶ λέγω, ἔγειρε.

42   καὶ εὐθὺς ἀνέστη τὸ κοράσιον
καὶ περιεπάτει·
  ἦν γὰρ ἐτῶν δώδεκα.

  καὶ ἐξέστησαν εὐθὺς ἐκστάσει μεγάλῃ.

43   καὶ διεστείλατο αὐτοῖς πολλά,
   ἵνα μηδεὶς γνῷ τοῦτο,
  καὶ εἶπεν δοθῆναι αὐτῇ φαγεῖν.

6 1 Καὶ ἐξῆλθεν ἐκεῖθεν,
καὶ ἔρχεται εἰς τὴν πατρίδα αὐτοῦ,
  καὶ ἀκολουθοῦσιν αὐτῷ οἱ μαθηταὶ αὐτοῦ.

2 καὶ γενομένου σαββάτου
  ἤρξατο ἐν τῇ συναγωγῇ διδάσκειν.

  καὶ πολλοὶ ἀκούοντες ἐξεπλήσσοντο λέγοντες·

   πόθεν τούτῳ ταῦτα,
  καί,
   τίς ἡ σοφία ἡ δοθεῖσα τούτῳ;
  καί,
   αἱ δυνάμεις τοιαῦται διὰ τῶν χειρῶν αὐτοῦ γινόμεναι;

6

3 | οὐχ οὗτός ἐστιν ὁ τέκτων,
ὁ υἱὸς τῆς Μαρίας
καὶ ἀδελφὸς Ἰακώβου καὶ Ἰωσῆτος
καὶ   Ἰούδα   καὶ Σίμωνος ;
καί,
οὐκ εἰσὶν αἱ ἀδελφαὶ αὐτοῦ ὧδε πρὸς ἡμᾶς ;

| καὶ ἐσκανδαλίζοντο ἐν αὐτῷ.

4 | καὶ ἔλεγεν αὐτοῖς ὁ Ἰησοῦς

ὅτι οὐκ ἔστιν προφήτης ἄτιμος
εἰ μὴ ἐν τῇ πατρίδι αὐτοῦ
καὶ ἐν τοῖς συγγενεῦσιν αὐτοῦ
καὶ ἐν τῇ οἰκίᾳ αὐτοῦ.

5 | καὶ οὐκ ἐδύνατο ἐκεῖ ποιῆσαι οὐδεμίαν δύναμιν,
εἰ μὴ ὀλίγοις ἀρρώστοις ἐπιθεὶς τὰς χεῖρας ἐθεράπευσεν.

6 | καὶ ἐθαύμαζεν διὰ τὴν ἀπιστίαν αὐτῶν.

| Καὶ περιῆγεν τὰς κώμας κύκλῳ διδάσκων.

7 | Καὶ προσκαλεῖται τοὺς δώδεκα,
καὶ ἤρξατο αὐτοὺς ἀποστέλλειν δύο δύο,
καὶ ἐδίδου αὐτοῖς ἐξουσίαν
τῶν πνευμάτων τῶν ἀκαθάρτων·

8 | καὶ παρήγγειλεν αὐτοῖς,

ἵνα μηδὲν αἴρωσιν εἰς ὁδὸν εἰ μὴ ῥάβδον μόνον,
μὴ ἄρτον,
μὴ πήραν,
μὴ εἰς τὴν ζώνην χαλκόν,

9 | ἀλλὰ ὑποδεδεμένους σανδάλια,
καί,
μὴ ἐνδύσησθε δύο χιτῶνας.

6 10 καὶ ἔλεγεν αὐτοῖς·

ὅπου ἐὰν εἰσέλθητε εἰς οἰκίαν,
ἐκεῖ μένετε ἕως ἂν ἐξέλθητε ἐκεῖθεν.

11 καὶ ὃς ἂν τόπος μὴ δέξηται ὑμᾶς
μηδὲ ἀκούσωσιν ὑμῶν,
ἐκπορευόμενοι ἐκεῖθεν
ἐκτινάξατε τὸν χοῦν τὸν ὑποκάτω τῶν ποδῶν ὑμῶν
εἰς μαρτύριον αὐτοῖς.

12 Καὶ ἐξελθόντες ἐκήρυξαν ἵνα μετανοῶσιν,
13 καὶ δαιμόνια πολλὰ ἐξέβαλλον
καὶ ἤλειφον ἐλαίῳ πολλοὺς ἀρρώστους
καὶ ἐθεράπευον.

14 Καὶ ἤκουσεν ὁ βασιλεὺς Ἡρῴδης,
φανερὸν γὰρ ἐγένετο τὸ ὄνομα αὐτοῦ,
καὶ ἔλεγεν
ὅτι Ἰωάννης ὁ βαπτίζων ἐγήγερται ἐκ νεκρῶν,
καὶ διὰ τοῦτο ἐνεργοῦσιν αἱ δυνάμεις ἐν αὐτῷ.

15 ἄλλοι δὲ ἔλεγον
ὅτι Ἡλίας ἐστίν.

ἄλλοι δὲ ἔλεγον
ὅτι προφήτης ὡς εἷς τῶν προφητῶν.

16 ἀκούσας δὲ ὁ Ἡρῴδης ἔλεγεν·
ὃν ἐγὼ ἀπεκεφάλισα Ἰωάννην,
οὗτος ἠγέρθη.

17 Αὐτὸς γὰρ ὁ Ἡρῴδης ἀποστείλας
ἐκράτησεν τὸν Ἰωάννην
καὶ ἔδησεν αὐτὸν ἐν φυλακῇ

διὰ Ἡρῳδιάδα τὴν γυναῖκα Φιλίππου τοῦ ἀδελφοῦ αὐτοῦ,
ὅτι αὐτὴν ἐγάμησεν·

6 18 ἔλεγεν γὰρ ὁ Ἰωάννης τῷ Ἡρῴδῃ
ὅτι οὐκ ἔξεστίν σοι
ἔχειν τὴν γυναῖκα τοῦ ἀδελφοῦ σου.

19 ἡ δὲ Ἡρῳδιὰς ἐνεῖχεν αὐτῷ
καὶ ἤθελεν αὐτὸν ἀποκτεῖναι,
καὶ οὐκ ἐδύνατο·

20 ὁ γὰρ Ἡρῴδης ἐφοβεῖτο τὸν Ἰωάννην,
εἰδὼς αὐτὸν ἄνδρα δίκαιον καὶ ἅγιον,
καὶ συνετήρει αὐτόν,
καὶ ἀκούσας αὐτοῦ πολλὰ ἠπόρει,
καὶ ἡδέως αὐτοῦ ἤκουεν.

21 καὶ γενομένης ἡμέρας εὐκαίρου,
ὅτε Ἡρῴδης τοῖς γενεσίοις αὐτοῦ δεῖπνον ἐποίησεν
τοῖς μεγιστᾶσιν αὐτοῦ
καὶ τοῖς χιλιάρχοις
καὶ τοῖς πρώτοις τῆς Γαλιλαίας,

22 καὶ εἰσελθούσης τῆς θυγατρὸς αὐτῆς τῆς Ἡρῳδιάδος
καὶ ὀρχησαμένης
καὶ ἀρεσάσης τῷ Ἡρῴδῃ καὶ τοῖς συνανακειμένοις,

εἶπεν ὁ βασιλεὺς τῷ κορασίῳ·
αἴτησόν με ὃ ἐὰν θέλῃς,
καὶ δώσω σοι·

23 καὶ ὤμοσεν αὐτῇ
ὅτι ὃ ἐάν με αἰτήσῃς δώσω σοι
ἕως ἡμίσους τῆς βασιλείας μου.

24 καὶ ἐξελθοῦσα εἶπεν τῇ μητρὶ αὐτῆς·
τί αἰτήσωμαι ;

ἡ δὲ εἶπεν·
τὴν κεφαλὴν Ἰωάννου τοῦ βαπτίζοντος.

6 25 | καὶ εἰσελθοῦσα εὐθὺς μετὰ σπουδῆς πρὸς τὸν βασιλέα
ᾐτήσατο λέγουσα·
θέλω ἵνα ἐξαυτῆς δῷς μοι ἐπὶ πίνακι
τὴν κεφαλὴν Ἰωάννου τοῦ βαπτιστοῦ.

26 | καὶ περίλυπος γενόμενος ὁ βασιλεύς
διὰ τοὺς ὅρκους καὶ τοὺς συνανακειμένους
οὐκ ἠθέλησεν ἀθετῆσαι αὐτήν.

27 | καὶ εὐθὺς ἀποστείλας ὁ βασιλεὺς σπεκουλάτορα
ἐπέταξεν ἐνέγκαι τὴν κεφαλὴν αὐτοῦ.

28 | ὁ δὲ ἀπελθὼν ἀπεκεφάλισεν αὐτὸν ἐν τῇ φυλακῇ,
καὶ ἤνεγκεν τὴν κεφαλὴν αὐτοῦ ἐπὶ πίνακι
καὶ ἔδωκεν αὐτὴν τῷ κορασίῳ,
καὶ τὸ κοράσιον ἔδωκεν αὐτὴν τῇ μητρὶ αὐτῆς.

29 | καὶ ἀκούσαντες οἱ μαθηταὶ αὐτοῦ
ἦλθον καὶ ἦραν τὸ πτῶμα αὐτοῦ
καὶ ἔθηκαν αὐτὸ ἐν μνημείῳ.

30 | Καὶ συνάγονται οἱ ἀπόστολοι πρὸς τὸν Ἰησοῦν,
καὶ ἀπήγγειλαν αὐτῷ
πάντα ὅσα ἐποίησαν
καὶ ὅσα ἐδίδαξαν.

31 | καὶ λέγει αὐτοῖς·
δεῦτε ὑμεῖς αὐτοὶ κατ' ἰδίαν εἰς ἔρημον τόπον
καὶ ἀναπαύσασθε ὀλίγον.

ἦσαν γὰρ οἱ ἐρχόμενοι καὶ οἱ ὑπάγοντες πολλοί,
καὶ οὐδὲ φαγεῖν εὐκαίρουν.

32 | καὶ ἀπῆλθον ἐν τῷ πλοίῳ εἰς ἔρημον τόπον κατ' ἰδίαν.

33 | καὶ εἶδον αὐτοὺς ὑπάγοντας
καὶ ἐπέγνωσαν πολλοί,
καὶ πεζῇ ἀπὸ πασῶν τῶν πόλεων συνέδραμον ἐκεῖ
καὶ προῆλθον αὐτούς.

6 34 | Καὶ ἐξελθὼν εἶδεν πολὺν ὄχλον,
καὶ ἐσπλαγχνίσθη ἐπ᾽ αὐτούς,
ὅτι ἦσαν ὡς πρόβατα μὴ ἔχοντα ποιμένα,
καὶ ἤρξατο διδάσκειν αὐτοὺς πολλά.

35 | Καὶ ἤδη ὥρας πολλῆς γενομένης
προσελθόντες αὐτῷ οἱ μαθηταὶ αὐτοῦ ἔλεγον

ὅτι ἔρημός ἐστιν ὁ τόπος,
καὶ ἤδη ὥρα πολλή·

36 | ἀπόλυσον αὐτούς,
ἵνα ἀπελθόντες εἰς τοὺς κύκλῳ ἀγροὺς καὶ κώμας
ἀγοράσωσιν ἑαυτοῖς τί φάγωσιν.

37 | ὁ δὲ ἀποκριθεὶς εἶπεν αὐτοῖς·
δότε αὐτοῖς ὑμεῖς φαγεῖν.

καὶ λέγουσιν αὐτῷ·
ἀπελθόντες ἀγοράσωμεν δηναρίων διακοσίων ἄρτους,
καὶ δώσομεν αὐτοῖς φαγεῖν ;

38 | ὁ δὲ λέγει αὐτοῖς·
πόσους ἄρτους ἔχετε ;
ὑπάγετε ἴδετε.

καὶ γνόντες λέγουσιν·
πέντε, καὶ δύο ἰχθύας.

39 | καὶ ἐπέταξεν αὐτοῖς ἀνακλῖναι πάντας
συμπόσια συμπόσια
ἐπὶ τῷ χλωρῷ χόρτῳ.

40 | καὶ ἀνέπεσαν πρασιαὶ πρασιαί
ἀνὰ ἑκατὸν καὶ ἀνὰ πεντήκοντα.

41 | καὶ λαβὼν τοὺς πέντε ἄρτους καὶ τοὺς δύο ἰχθύας
ἀναβλέψας εἰς τὸν οὐρανόν

6

εὐλόγησεν
καὶ κατέκλασεν τοὺς ἄρτους
καὶ ἐδίδου τοῖς μαθηταῖς,
ἵνα παρατιθῶσιν αὐτοῖς·

καὶ τοὺς δύο ἰχθύας ἐμέρισεν πᾶσιν.

42 | καὶ ἔφαγον πάντες καὶ ἐχορτάσθησαν·
43 | καὶ ἦραν κλάσματα δώδεκα κοφίνων πληρώματα
| καὶ ἀπὸ τῶν ἰχθύων.

44 | καὶ ἦσαν οἱ φαγόντες τοὺς ἄρτους πεντακισχίλιοι ἄνδρες.

45 | Καὶ εὐθὺς ἠνάγκασεν τοὺς μαθητὰς αὐτοῦ
ἐμβῆναι εἰς τὸ πλοῖον
καὶ προάγειν εἰς τὸ πέραν πρὸς Βηθσαϊδάν,
ἕως αὐτὸς ἀπολύει τὸν ὄχλον.

46 | καὶ ἀποταξάμενος αὐτοῖς
ἀπῆλθεν εἰς τὸ ὄρος προσεύξασθαι.

47 | καὶ ὀψίας γενομένης
ἦν τὸ πλοῖον ἐν μέσῳ τῆς θαλάσσης,
καὶ αὐτὸς μόνος ἐπὶ τῆς γῆς.

48 | καὶ ἰδὼν αὐτοὺς βασανιζομένους ἐν τῷ ἐλαύνειν,
ἦν γὰρ ὁ ἄνεμος ἐναντίος αὐτοῖς,
περὶ τετάρτην φυλακὴν τῆς νυκτός
ἔρχεται πρὸς αὐτοὺς περιπατῶν ἐπὶ τῆς θαλάσσης·

καὶ ἤθελεν παρελθεῖν αὐτούς.

49 | οἱ δὲ ἰδόντες αὐτὸν ἐπὶ τῆς θαλάσσης περιπατοῦντα
ἔδοξαν φάντασμα εἶναι, καὶ ἀνέκραξαν·
50 | πάντες γὰρ αὐτὸν εἶδον καὶ ἐταράχθησαν.

ὁ δὲ εὐθὺς ἐλάλησεν μετ' αὐτῶν,
καὶ λέγει αὐτοῖς·

θαρσεῖτε, ἐγώ εἰμι,
μὴ φοβεῖσθε.

51 | καὶ ἀνέβη πρὸς αὐτοὺς εἰς τὸ πλοῖον,
καὶ ἐκόπασεν ὁ ἄνεμος.

52 | καὶ λίαν ἐκ περισσοῦ ἐν ἑαυτοῖς ἐξίσταντο·
οὐ γὰρ συνῆκαν ἐπὶ τοῖς ἄρτοις,
ἀλλ' ἦν αὐτῶν ἡ καρδία πεπωρωμένη.

53 | καὶ διαπεράσαντες
ἐπὶ τὴν γῆν ἦλθον εἰς Γεννησαρέτ
καὶ προσωρμίσθησαν.

or: | καὶ διαπεράσαντες ἐπὶ τὴν γῆν
ἦλθον εἰς Γεννησαρέτ
καὶ προσωρμίσθησαν.

54 | καὶ ἐξελθόντων αὐτῶν ἐκ τοῦ πλοίου
εὐθὺς ἐπιγνόντες αὐτόν
55 | περιέδραμον ὅλην τὴν χώραν ἐκείνην·

καὶ ἤρξαντο ἐπὶ τοῖς κραβάττοις τοὺς κακῶς ἔχοντας περιφέρειν,
ὅπου ἤκουον ὅτι ἐστίν.

56 | καὶ ὅπου ἂν εἰσεπορεύετο
εἰς κώμας ἢ εἰς πόλεις ἢ εἰς ἀγρούς,
ἐν ταῖς ἀγοραῖς ἐτίθεσαν τοὺς ἀσθενοῦντας,
καὶ παρεκάλουν αὐτόν,
ἵνα κἂν τοῦ κρασπέδου τοῦ ἱματίου αὐτοῦ ἅψωνται.

καὶ ὅσοι ἂν ἥψαντο αὐτοῦ
ἐσῴζοντο.

7 | 1 | Καὶ συνάγονται πρὸς αὐτόν
οἱ Φαρισαῖοι καί τινες τῶν γραμματέων
ἐλθόντες ἀπὸ Ἱεροσολύμων.

7   2 | καὶ ἰδόντες τινὰς τῶν μαθητῶν αὐτοῦ
ὅτι κοιναῖς χερσίν, τοῦτ' ἔστιν ἀνίπτοις,
ἐσθίουσιν τοὺς ἄρτους,—

3   οἱ γὰρ Φαρισαῖοι καὶ πάντες οἱ Ἰουδαῖοι,
ἐὰν μὴ πυγμῇ νίψωνται τὰς χεῖρας,
οὐκ ἐσθίουσιν,
κρατοῦντες τὴν παράδοσιν τῶν πρεσβυτέρων·

4   καὶ ἀπ' ἀγορᾶς ἐὰν μὴ ῥαντίσωνται
οὐκ ἐσθίουσιν·

καὶ ἄλλα πολλά ἐστιν ἃ παρέλαβον κρατεῖν,
βαπτισμοὺς ποτηρίων καὶ ξεστῶν
καὶ   χαλκίων καὶ κλινῶν,—

5 | ἔπειτα ἐπερωτῶσιν αὐτὸν οἱ Φαρισαῖοι καὶ οἱ γραμματεῖς·
διὰ τί οὐ περιπατοῦσιν οἱ μαθηταί σου
κατὰ τὴν παράδοσιν τῶν πρεσβυτέρων,
ἀλλὰ κοιναῖς χερσὶν ἐσθίουσιν τὸν ἄρτον ;

6 | ὁ δὲ εἶπεν αὐτοῖς·

καλῶς ἐπροφήτευσεν Ἡσαΐας περὶ ὑμῶν τῶν ὑποκριτῶν,
ὡς γέγραπται

ὅτι οὗτος ὁ λαὸς τοῖς χείλεσίν με τιμᾷ,
ἡ δὲ καρδία αὐτῶν πόρρω ἀπέχει ἀπ' ἐμοῦ·
7   μάτην δὲ σέβονταί με,
διδάσκοντες διδασκαλίας ἐντάλματα ἀνθρώπων.

8   ἀφέντες γὰρ τὴν ἐντολὴν τοῦ θεοῦ
κρατεῖτε τὴν παράδοσιν τῶν ἀνθρώπων
βαπτισμοὺς ξεστῶν καὶ ποτηρίων
καὶ ἄλλα παρόμοια τοιαῦτα πολλὰ ποιεῖτε.

9 | καὶ ἔλεγεν αὐτοῖς·

καλῶς ἀθετεῖτε τὴν ἐντολὴν τοῦ θεοῦ,
ἵνα τὴν παράδοσιν ὑμῶν τηρήσητε.

7 10 | Μωϋσῆς γὰρ εἶπεν·

τίμα τὸν πατέρα σου καὶ τὴν μητέρα σου,
καί·
ὁ κακολογῶν πατέρα ἢ μητέρα θανάτῳ τελευτάτω.

11 | ὑμεῖς δὲ λέγετε·
ἐὰν εἴπῃ ἄνθρωπος τῷ πατρὶ ἢ τῇ μητρί·
κορβᾶν, ὅ ἐστιν δῶρον, ὃ ἐὰν ἐξ ἐμοῦ ὠφεληθῇς,
12 | οὐκέτι ἀφίετε αὐτὸν οὐδὲν ποιῆσαι τῷ πατρὶ ἢ τῇ μητρί,
13 | ἀκυροῦντες τὸν λόγον τοῦ θεοῦ
τῇ παραδόσει ὑμῶν ᾗ παρεδώκατε·

καὶ παρόμοια πολλὰ τοιαῦτα ποιεῖτε.

14 | Καὶ προσκαλεσάμενος πάλιν τὸν ὄχλον
ἔλεγεν αὐτοῖς·

ἀκούσατέ μου πάντες καὶ σύνετε.

15 | οὐδέν ἐστιν ἔξωθεν τοῦ ἀνθρώπου εἰσπορευόμενον εἰς αὐτόν
ὃ δύναται κοινῶσαι αὐτόν·
ἀλλὰ τὰ ἐκ τοῦ ἀνθρώπου ἐκπορευόμενα
ἐστὶν τὰ κοινοῦντα τὸν ἄνθρωπον.

16 | εἴ τις ἔχει ὦτα ἀκούειν, ἀκουέτω.

17 | Καὶ ὅτε εἰσῆλθεν εἰς οἶκον ἀπὸ τοῦ ὄχλου,
ἐπηρώτων αὐτὸν οἱ μαθηταὶ αὐτοῦ τὴν παραβολήν.

18 | καὶ λέγει αὐτοῖς·

οὕτως καὶ ὑμεῖς ἀσύνετοί ἐστε;

οὐ νοεῖτε
ὅτι πᾶν τὸ ἔξωθεν εἰσπορευόμενον εἰς τὸν ἄνθρωπον
οὐ δύναται αὐτὸν κοινῶσαι,

19 | ὅτι οὐκ εἰσπορεύεται αὐτοῦ εἰς τὴν καρδίαν,
ἀλλ᾽   εἰς τὴν κοιλίαν,

7

καὶ εἰς τὸν ἀφεδρῶνα ἐκπορεύεται ;

καθαρίζων πάντα τὰ βρώματα.

20 ἔλεγεν δέ

ὅτι τὸ ἐκ τοῦ ἀνθρώπου ἐκπορευόμενον,
ἐκεῖνο κοινοῖ τὸν ἄνθρωπον.

21 ἔσωθεν γὰρ ἐκ τῆς καρδίας τῶν ἀνθρώπων
οἱ διαλογισμοὶ οἱ κακοὶ ἐκπορεύονται,

πορνεῖαι, κλοπαί, φόνοι,
22 μοιχεῖαι, πλεονεξίαι, πονηρίαι,
δόλος, ἀσέλγεια, ὀφθαλμὸς πονηρός,
βλασφημία, ὑπερηφανία, ἀφροσύνη·

23 πάντα ταῦτα τὰ πονηρὰ ἔσωθεν ἐκπορεύεται
καὶ   κοινοῖ τὸν ἄνθρωπον.

24 Ἐκεῖθεν δὲ ἀναστάς
ἀπῆλθεν εἰς τὰ μεθόρια Τύρου καὶ Σιδῶνος.

Καὶ εἰσελθὼν εἰς οἰκίαν
οὐδένα ἤθελεν γνῶναι,
καὶ οὐκ ἠδυνήθη λαθεῖν.

25 ἀλλ’ εὐθὺς ἀκούσασα γυνὴ περὶ αὐτοῦ,
ἧς εἶχεν τὸ θυγάτριον αὐτῆς πνεῦμα ἀκάθαρτον,
ἐλθοῦσα προσέπεσεν πρὸς τοὺς πόδας αὐτοῦ·

26 —ἡ δὲ γυνὴ ἦν Ἑλληνίς, Συροφοινίκισσα τῷ γένει—·

καὶ ἠρώτα αὐτόν,
ἵνα τὸ δαιμόνιον ἐκβάλῃ ἐκ τῆς θυγατρὸς αὐτῆς.

27 καὶ ἔλεγεν αὐτῇ·
ἄφες πρῶτον χορτασθῆναι τὰ τέκνα·
οὐ γάρ ἐστιν καλόν
λαβεῖν τὸν ἄρτον τῶν τέκνων
καὶ τοῖς κυναρίοις βαλεῖν.

7

28 | ἡ δὲ ἀπεκρίθη καὶ λέγει αὐτῷ·
ναί, Κύριε·
καὶ τὰ κυνάρια ὑποκάτω τῆς τραπέζης
ἐσθίουσιν ἀπὸ τῶν ψιχίων τῶν παιδίων.

29 | καὶ εἶπεν αὐτῇ·
διὰ τοῦτον τὸν λόγον ὕπαγε,
ἐξελήλυθεν ἐκ τῆς θυγατρός σου τὸ δαιμόνιον.

30 | καὶ ἀπελθοῦσα εἰς τὸν οἶκον αὐτῆς
εὗρεν τὸ παιδίον βεβλημένον ἐπὶ τὴν κλίνην
καὶ τὸ δαιμόνιον ἐξεληλυθός.

31 | Καὶ πάλιν ἐξελθὼν ἐκ τῶν ὁρίων Τύρου
ἦλθεν διὰ Σιδῶνος εἰς τὴν θάλασσαν τῆς Γαλιλαίας
ἀνὰ μέσον τῶν ὁρίων Δεκαπόλεως.

32 | Καὶ φέρουσιν αὐτῷ κωφὸν μογιλάλον,
καὶ παρακαλοῦσιν αὐτόν
ἵνα ἐπιθῇ αὐτῷ τὴν χεῖρα.

33 | καὶ ἀπολαβόμενος αὐτὸν ἀπὸ τοῦ ὄχλου κατ' ἰδίαν
ἔβαλεν τοὺς δακτύλους αὐτοῦ εἰς τὰ ὦτα αὐτοῦ
καὶ πτύσας ἥψατο τῆς γλώσσης αὐτοῦ·

34 | καὶ ἀναβλέψας εἰς τὸν οὐρανὸν ἐστέναξεν,
καὶ λέγει αὐτῷ·
ἐφφαθά, ὅ ἐστιν διανοίχθητι.

35 | καὶ εὐθέως ἠνοίγησαν αὐτοῦ αἱ ἀκοαί,
καὶ ἐλύθη ὁ δεσμὸς τῆς γλώσσης αὐτοῦ,
καὶ ἐλάλει ὀρθῶς.

36 | καὶ διεστείλατο αὐτοῖς ἵνα μηδενὶ λέγωσιν·
ὅσον δὲ αὐτοῖς διεστέλλετο,
αὐτοὶ μᾶλλον περισσότερον ἐκήρυσσον.

37 | καὶ ὑπερπερισσῶς ἐξεπλήσσοντο λέγοντες·
καλῶς πάντα πεποίηκεν,

καὶ τοὺς κωφοὺς ποιεῖ ἀκούειν
καὶ ἀλάλους λαλεῖν.

8 1 Ἐν ἐκείναις ταῖς ἡμέραις
πάλιν πολλοῦ ὄχλου ὄντος
καὶ μὴ ἐχόντων τί φάγωσιν,
προσκαλεσάμενος τοὺς μαθητὰς αὐτοῦ
λέγει αὐτοῖς·

2 σπλαγχνίζομαι ἐπὶ τὸν ὄχλον,
ὅτι ἤδη ἡμέραι τρεῖς προσμένουσίν μοι
καὶ οὐκ ἔχουσιν τί φάγωσιν·

3 καὶ ἐὰν ἀπολύσω αὐτοὺς νήστεις εἰς οἶκον αὐτῶν,
ἐκλυθήσονται ἐν τῇ ὁδῷ·
καί τινες αὐτῶν ἀπὸ μακρόθεν ἥκουσιν.

4 καὶ ἀπεκρίθησαν αὐτῷ οἱ μαθηταὶ αὐτοῦ
ὅτι πόθεν τούτους δυνήσεταί τις
ὧδε χορτάσαι ἄρτων ἐπ᾽ ἐρημίας ;

5 καὶ ἠρώτα αὐτούς·
πόσους ἔχετε ἄρτους ;

οἱ δὲ εἶπον·
ἑπτά.

6 καὶ παραγγέλλει τῷ ὄχλῳ ἀναπεσεῖν ἐπὶ τῆς γῆς.

καὶ λαβὼν τοὺς ἑπτὰ ἄρτους
εὐχαριστήσας ἔκλασεν
καὶ ἐδίδου τοῖς μαθηταῖς αὐτοῦ,
ἵνα παρατιθῶσιν·

καὶ παρέθηκαν τῷ ὄχλῳ.

8

7 | καὶ εἶχον ἰχθύδια ὀλίγα·
καὶ εὐλογήσας αὐτά
εἶπεν καὶ ταῦτα παρατιθέναι.

8 | καὶ ἔφαγον καὶ ἐχορτάσθησαν·
καὶ ἦραν περισσεύματα κλασμάτων ἑπτὰ σπυρίδας.

9 | ἦσαν δὲ ὡς τετρακισχίλιοι.

| καὶ ἀπέλυσεν αὐτούς.

10 | Καὶ εὐθὺς ἐμβὰς εἰς τὸ πλοῖον μετὰ τῶν μαθητῶν αὐτοῦ
ἦλθεν εἰς τὰ μέρη Δαλμανουθά.

11 | Καὶ ἐξῆλθον οἱ Φαρισαῖοι
καὶ ἤρξαντο συνζητεῖν αὐτῷ,
ζητοῦντες παρ' αὐτοῦ σημεῖον ἀπὸ τοῦ οὐρανοῦ,
πειράζοντες αὐτόν.

12 | καὶ ἀναστενάξας τῷ πνεύματι αὐτοῦ
λέγει·
τί ἡ γενεὰ αὕτη ζητεῖ σημεῖον ;
ἀμὴν λέγω ὑμῖν,
εἰ δοθήσεται τῇ γενεᾷ ταύτῃ σημεῖον.

13 | καὶ ἀφεὶς αὐτούς
πάλιν ἐμβὰς ἀπῆλθεν εἰς τὸ πέραν.

14 | Καὶ ἐπελάθοντο λαβεῖν ἄρτους,
καὶ εἰ μὴ ἕνα ἄρτον
οὐκ εἶχον μεθ' ἑαυτῶν ἐν τῷ πλοίῳ.

15 | καὶ διεστέλλετο αὐτοῖς λέγων·
ὁρᾶτε, βλέπετε ἀπὸ τῆς ζύμης τῶν Φαρισαίων
καὶ   τῆς ζύμης Ἡρῴδου.

16 | καὶ διελογίζοντο πρὸς ἀλλήλους λέγοντες
ὅτι ἄρτους οὐκ ἔχομεν.

8

17　καὶ γνοὺς ὁ Ἰησοῦς λέγει αὐτοῖς·

τί διαλογίζεσθε ὅτι ἄρτους οὐκ ἔχετε;

οὔπω νοεῖτε καὶ συνίετε;
πεπωρωμένην ἔχετε τὴν καρδίαν ὑμῶν;

18　ὀφθαλμοὺς ἔχοντες οὐ βλέπετε,
καὶ ὦτα ἔχοντες οὐκ ἀκούετε;

καὶ οὐ μνημονεύετε,
19　　ὅτε τοὺς πέντε ἄρτους ἔκλασα εἰς τοὺς πεντακισχιλίους,
πόσους κοφίνους κλασμάτων πλήρεις ἤρατε;

λέγουσιν αὐτῷ·
δώδεκα.

20　ὅτε δὲ τοὺς ἑπτὰ εἰς τοὺς τετρακισχιλίους,
πόσων σπυρίδων πληρώματα κλασμάτων ἤρατε;

καὶ λέγουσιν·
ἑπτά.

21　καὶ ἔλεγεν αὐτοῖς·
οὔπω συνίετε;

22　Καὶ ἔρχονται εἰς Βηθσαϊδάν.

Καὶ φέρουσιν αὐτῷ τυφλόν,
καὶ παρακαλοῦσιν αὐτόν, ἵνα αὐτοῦ ἅψηται.

23　καὶ ἐπιλαβόμενος τῆς χειρὸς τοῦ τυφλοῦ
ἐξήνεγκεν αὐτὸν ἔξω τῆς κώμης·

καὶ πτύσας εἰς τὰ ὄμματα αὐτοῦ,
ἐπιθεὶς τὰς χεῖρας αὐτῷ,
ἐπηρώτα αὐτόν, εἴ τι βλέπει.

24　καὶ ἀναβλέψας ἔλεγεν·
βλέπω τοὺς ἀνθρώπους,
ὅτι ὡς δένδρα ὁρῶ περιπατοῦντας.

8 25 | εἶτα πάλιν ἐπέθηκεν τὰς χεῖρας ἐπὶ τοὺς ὀφθαλμοὺς αὐτοῦ·
καὶ διέβλεψεν
καὶ ἀπεκατέστη,
καὶ ἐνέβλεπεν τηλαυγῶς ἅπαντα.

26 | καὶ ἀπέστειλεν αὐτὸν εἰς οἶκον αὐτοῦ λέγων·
μηδὲ εἰς τὴν κώμην εἰσέλθῃς.

27 | Καὶ ἐξῆλθεν ὁ Ἰησοῦς καὶ οἱ μαθηταὶ αὐτοῦ
εἰς τὰς κώμας Καισαρίας τῆς Φιλίππου.

καὶ ἐν τῇ ὁδῷ ἐπηρώτα τοὺς μαθητὰς αὐτοῦ
λέγων αὐτοῖς·
τίνα με λέγουσιν οἱ ἄνθρωποι εἶναι ;

28 | οἱ δὲ εἶπον αὐτῷ λέγοντες

ὅτι Ἰωάννην τὸν βαπτιστήν,
καί·
ἄλλοι Ἠλίαν,
ἄλλοι δὲ ὅτι εἷς τῶν προφητῶν.

29 | καὶ αὐτὸς ἐπηρώτα αὐτούς·
ὑμεῖς δὲ τίνα με λέγετε εἶναι ;

ἀποκριθεὶς δὲ ὁ Πέτρος λέγει αὐτῷ·
σὺ εἶ ὁ Χριστός.

30 | καὶ ἐπετίμησεν αὐτοῖς,
ἵνα μηδενὶ λέγωσιν περὶ αὐτοῦ.

31 | Καὶ ἤρξατο διδάσκειν αὐτοὺς
ὅτι δεῖ τὸν υἱὸν τοῦ ἀνθρώπου πολλὰ παθεῖν,

καὶ ἀποδοκιμασθῆναι
ὑπὸ τῶν πρεσβυτέρων
καὶ τῶν ἀρχιερέων
καὶ τῶν γραμματέων

8

καὶ ἀποκτανθῆναι
καὶ μετὰ τρεῖς ἡμέρας ἀναστῆναι.

32 | καὶ παρρησίᾳ τὸν λόγον ἐλάλει.

καὶ προσλαβόμενος ὁ Πέτρος αὐτόν
ἤρξατο ἐπιτιμᾶν αὐτῷ.

33 | ὁ δὲ ἐπιστραφεὶς
καὶ ἰδὼν τοὺς μαθητὰς αὐτοῦ
ἐπετίμησεν Πέτρῳ καὶ λέγει·

ὕπαγε·
ὀπίσω μου, σατανᾶ·

ὅτι οὐ φρονεῖς τὰ τοῦ θεοῦ
ἀλλὰ   τὰ τῶν ἀνθρώπων.

34 | Καὶ προσκαλεσάμενος τὸν ὄχλον σὺν τοῖς μαθηταῖς αὐτοῦ
εἶπεν αὐτοῖς·

εἴ τις θέλει ὀπίσω μου ἐλθεῖν,
ἀπαρνησάσθω ἑαυτόν
καὶ ἀράτω τὸν σταυρὸν αὐτοῦ,
καὶ ἀκολουθείτω μοι.

35 | ὃς γὰρ ἐὰν θέλῃ τὴν ψυχὴν αὐτοῦ σῶσαι,
ἀπολέσει αὐτήν·
ὃς δ' ἂν ἀπολέσει τὴν ψυχὴν αὐτοῦ
ἕνεκεν ἐμοῦ καὶ τοῦ εὐαγγελίου,
σώσει αὐτήν.

36 | τί γὰρ ὠφελήσει ἄνθρωπον
κερδῆσαι τὸν κόσμον ὅλον
καὶ ζημιωθῆναι τὴν ψυχὴν αὐτοῦ ;

37 | τί γὰρ δῷ ἄνθρωπος ἀντάλλαγμα τῆς ψυχῆς αὐτοῦ ;

38 | ὃς γὰρ ἐὰν ἐπαισχυνθῇ με καὶ τοὺς ἐμοὺς λόγους
    ἐν τῇ γενεᾷ ταύτῃ τῇ μοιχαλίδι καὶ ἁμαρτωλῷ,
    καὶ ὁ υἱὸς τοῦ ἀνθρώπου ἐπαισχυνθήσεται αὐτόν,
    ὅταν ἔλθῃ ἐν τῇ δόξῃ τοῦ πατρὸς αὐτοῦ
    μετὰ τῶν ἀγγέλων τῶν ἁγίων.

9   1 | καὶ ἔλεγεν αὐτοῖς·

    ἀμὴν λέγω ὑμῖν

      ὅτι εἰσίν τινες τῶν ὧδε ἑστηκότων
      οἵτινες οὐ μὴ γεύσωνται θανάτου,
        ἕως ἂν ἴδωσιν τὴν βασιλείαν τοῦ Θεοῦ
      ἐληλυθυῖαν ἐν δυνάμει.

2 | Καὶ μετὰ ἡμέρας ἓξ

    παραλαμβάνει ὁ Ἰησοῦς
      τὸν Πέτρον καὶ τὸν Ἰάκωβον καὶ τὸν Ἰωάννην,
    καὶ ἀναφέρει αὐτοὺς εἰς ὄρος ὑψηλόν
    κατ' ἰδίαν μόνους.

3 | καὶ μετεμορφώθη ἔμπροσθεν αὐτῶν,
    καὶ τὰ ἱμάτια αὐτοῦ ἐγένετο στίλβοντα λευκὰ λίαν,
    οἷα γναφεὺς ἐπὶ τῆς γῆς οὐ δύναται οὕτως λευκᾶναι.

4 | καὶ ὤφθη αὐτοῖς Ἡλίας σὺν Μωϋσεῖ,
    καὶ ἦσαν συνλαλοῦντες τῷ Ἰησοῦ.

5 | καὶ ἀποκριθεὶς Πέτρος λέγει τῷ Ἰησοῦ·

    ῥαββί, καλόν ἐστιν ἡμᾶς ὧδε εἶναι,
    καὶ ποιήσωμεν τρεῖς σκηνάς,
      σοὶ μίαν
      καὶ Μωϋσεῖ μίαν
      καὶ Ἡλίᾳ μίαν.

9

6 | οὐ γὰρ ᾔδει τί ἀποκριθῇ·
ἔκφοβοι γὰρ ἐγένοντο.

7 | καὶ ἐγένετο νεφέλη ἐπισκιάζουσα αὐτοῖς,
καὶ ἐγένετο φωνὴ ἐκ τῆς νεφέλης·

οὗτός ἐστιν ὁ υἱός μου ὁ ἀγαπητός,
ἀκούετε αὐτοῦ.

8 | καὶ ἐξάπινα περιβλεψάμενοι
οὐκέτι οὐδένα εἶδον
ἀλλὰ τὸν Ἰησοῦν μόνον μεθ᾽ ἑαυτῶν.

9 | Καὶ καταβαινόντων αὐτῶν ἀπὸ τοῦ ὄρους
διεστείλατο αὐτοῖς,
ἵνα μηδενὶ ἃ εἶδον διηγήσωνται,
εἰ μὴ ὅταν ὁ υἱὸς τοῦ ἀνθρώπου ἐκ νεκρῶν ἀναστῇ.

10 | καὶ τὸν λόγον ἐκράτησαν,
πρὸς ἑαυτοὺς συνζητοῦντες
τί ἐστιν τὸ ἐκ νεκρῶν ἀναστῆναι.

11 | καὶ ἐπηρώτων αὐτὸν λέγοντες·
ὅτι λέγουσιν οἱ γραμματεῖς
ὅτι Ἡλίαν δεῖ ἐλθεῖν πρῶτον ;

12 | ὁ δὲ ἔφη αὐτοῖς·

Ἡλίας μὲν ἐλθὼν πρῶτον ἀποκαθιστάνει πάντα·
καὶ πῶς γέγραπται ἐπὶ τὸν υἱὸν τοῦ ἀνθρώπου,
ἵνα πολλὰ πάθῃ καὶ ἐξουδενηθῇ ;

13 | ἀλλὰ λέγω ὑμῖν
ὅτι καὶ Ἡλίας ἐλήλυθεν·
καὶ ἐποίησαν αὐτῷ ὅσα ἤθελον,
καθὼς γέγραπται ἐπ᾽ αὐτόν.

9

14 | Καὶ ἐλθὼν πρὸς τοὺς μαθητάς
εἶδεν ὄχλον πολὺν περὶ αὐτοὺς καὶ γραμματεῖς
συνζητοῦντας πρὸς αὐτούς.

15 | καὶ εὐθὺς πᾶς ὁ ὄχλος
ἰδόντες αὐτὸν ἐξεθαμβήθησαν,
καὶ προστρέχοντες ἠσπάζοντο αὐτόν.

16 | καὶ ἐπηρώτησεν αὐτούς·
τί συνζητεῖτε πρὸς αὐτούς ;

17 | καὶ ἀπεκρίθη αὐτῷ εἷς ἐκ τοῦ ὄχλου·

διδάσκαλε, ἤνεγκα τὸν υἱόν μου πρὸς σέ,
ἔχοντα πνεῦμα ἄλαλον·

18 | καὶ ὅπου ἐὰν αὐτὸν καταλάβῃ,
ῥήσσει αὐτόν,
καὶ ἀφρίζει
καὶ τρίζει τοὺς ὀδόντας
καὶ ξηραίνεται.

καὶ εἶπα τοῖς μαθηταῖς σου ἵνα αὐτὸ ἐκβάλωσιν,
καὶ οὐκ ἴσχυσαν.

19 | ὁ δὲ ἀποκριθεὶς αὐτοῖς λέγει·

ὦ γενεὰ ἄπιστος,
ἕως πότε πρὸς ὑμᾶς ἔσομαι ;
ἕως πότε ἀνέξομαι ὑμῶν ;

φέρετε αὐτὸν πρός με.

20 | καὶ ἤνεγκαν αὐτὸν πρὸς αὐτόν.

καὶ ἰδὼν αὐτὸν τὸ πνεῦμα εὐθὺς συνεσπάραξεν αὐτόν,
καὶ πεσὼν ἐπὶ τῆς γῆς ἐκυλίετο ἀφρίζων.

21 | καὶ ἐπηρώτησεν τὸν πατέρα αὐτοῦ·
πόσος χρόνος ἐστὶν ὡς τοῦτο γέγονεν αὐτῷ ;

9

ὁ δὲ εἶπεν·

ἐκ παιδιόθεν·

22 καὶ πολλάκις καὶ εἰς πῦρ αὐτὸν ἔβαλεν καὶ εἰς ὕδατα,
ἵνα ἀπολέσῃ αὐτόν.

ἀλλ' εἴ τι δύνῃ,
βοήθησον ἡμῖν σπλαγχνισθεὶς ἐφ' ἡμᾶς.

23 ὁ δὲ Ἰησοῦς εἶπεν αὐτῷ·
τὸ εἰ δύνῃ, πάντα δυνατὰ τῷ πιστεύοντι.

24 εὐθὺς κράξας ὁ πατὴρ τοῦ παιδίου
μετὰ δακρύων ἔλεγεν·
πιστεύω·
βοήθει μου τῇ ἀπιστίᾳ.

25 ἰδὼν δὲ ὁ Ἰησοῦς ὅτι ἐπισυντρέχει ὄχλος,
ἐπετίμησεν τῷ πνεύματι τῷ ἀκαθάρτῳ λέγων αὐτῷ·

τὸ ἄλαλον καὶ κωφὸν πνεῦμα,
ἐγὼ ἐπιτάσσω σοι,
ἔξελθε ἐξ αὐτοῦ
καὶ μηκέτι εἰσέλθῃς εἰς αὐτόν.

26 καὶ κράξας καὶ πολλὰ σπαράξας
ἐξῆλθεν·

καὶ ἐγένετο ὡσεὶ νεκρός,
ὥστε τοὺς πολλοὺς λέγειν ὅτι ἀπέθανεν.

27 ὁ δὲ Ἰησοῦς κρατήσας τῆς χειρὸς αὐτοῦ
ἤγειρεν αὐτόν,
καὶ ἀνέστη.

28 καὶ εἰσελθόντος αὐτοῦ εἰς οἶκον
οἱ μαθηταὶ αὐτοῦ κατ' ἰδίαν ἐπηρώτων αὐτόν·
ὅτι ἡμεῖς οὐκ ἠδυνήθημεν ἐκβαλεῖν αὐτό;

9   29 | καὶ εἶπεν αὐτοῖς·
τοῦτο τὸ γένος ἐν οὐδενὶ δύναται ἐξελθεῖν
εἰ μὴ ἐν προσευχῇ καὶ νηστείᾳ.

30 | Κἀκεῖθεν ἐξελθόντες
παρεπορεύοντο διὰ τῆς Γαλιλαίας,
καὶ οὐκ ἤθελεν, ἵνα τις γνῷ·

31 | ἐδίδασκεν γὰρ τοὺς μαθητὰς αὐτοῦ,
καὶ ἔλεγεν αὐτοῖς

ὅτι ὁ υἱὸς τοῦ ἀνθρώπου
παραδίδοται εἰς χεῖρας ἀνθρώπων,
καὶ ἀποκτενοῦσιν αὐτόν,
καὶ ἀποκτανθεὶς μετὰ τρεῖς ἡμέρας ἀναστήσεται.

32 | οἱ δὲ ἠγνόουν τὸ ῥῆμα,
καὶ ἐφοβοῦντο αὐτὸν ἐπερωτῆσαι.

33 | Καὶ ἦλθον εἰς Καφαρναούμ.

Καὶ ἐν τῇ οἰκίᾳ γενόμενος ἐπηρώτα αὐτούς·
τί ἐν τῇ ὁδῷ διελογίζεσθε ;

34 | οἱ δὲ ἐσιώπων·
πρὸς ἀλλήλους γὰρ διελέχθησαν ἐν τῇ ὁδῷ
τίς μείζων.

35 | καὶ καθίσας ἐφώνησεν τοὺς δώδεκα
καὶ λέγει αὐτοῖς·

εἴ τις θέλει πρῶτος εἶναι,
ἔσται πάντων ἔσχατος
καὶ πάντων διάκονος.

36 | καὶ λαβὼν παιδίον
ἔστησεν αὐτὸ ἐν μέσῳ αὐτῶν,
καὶ ἐναγκαλισάμενος αὐτὸ εἶπεν αὐτοῖς·

9 37   ὃς ἂν ἓν τῶν τοιούτων παιδίων δέξηται
   ἐπὶ τῷ ὀνόματί μου,
  ἐμὲ δέχεται·

  καὶ ὃς ἂν ἐμὲ δέχηται,
  οὐκ ἐμὲ δέχεται
   ἀλλὰ τὸν ἀποστείλαντά με.

38   Ἔφη αὐτῷ ὁ Ἰωάννης·

  διδάσκαλε, εἴδομέν τινα
  ἐν τῷ ὀνόματί σου ἐκβάλλοντα δαιμόνια·

  καὶ ἐκωλύομεν αὐτόν,
  ὅτι οὐκ ἠκολούθει ἡμῖν.

39   ὁ δὲ Ἰησοῦς εἶπεν·

  μὴ κωλύετε αὐτόν·
  οὐδεὶς γάρ ἐστιν
   ὃς ποιήσει δύναμιν ἐπὶ τῷ ὀνόματί μου
   καὶ δυνήσεται ταχὺ κακολογῆσαί με·

40   ὃς γὰρ οὐκ ἔστιν καθ' ἡμῶν,
  ὑπὲρ ἡμῶν ἐστιν.

41   Ὃς γὰρ ἂν ποτίσῃ ὑμᾶς ποτήριον ὕδατος
   ἐν ὀνόματι, ὅτι Χριστοῦ ἐστε,
  ἀμὴν λέγω ὑμῖν ὅτι οὐ μὴ ἀπολέσῃ τὸν μισθὸν αὐτοῦ.

42   Καὶ ὃς ἂν σκανδαλίσῃ ἕνα τῶν μικρῶν τούτων
   τῶν πιστευόντων εἰς ἐμέ,
  καλόν ἐστιν αὐτῷ μᾶλλον
   εἰ περίκειται μύλος ὀνικὸς περὶ τὸν τράχηλον αὐτοῦ
   καὶ βέβληται εἰς τὴν θάλασσαν.

43 Καὶ ἐὰν σκανδαλίζῃ σε ἡ χείρ σου,
  ἀπόκοψον αὐτήν·
   καλόν ἐστιν
   σὲ κυλλὸν εἰσελθεῖν εἰς τὴν ζωήν,
   ἢ τὰς δύο χεῖρας ἔχοντα ἀπελθεῖν εἰς τὴν γέενναν,
   εἰς τὸ πῦρ τὸ ἄσβεστον.

45 καὶ ἐὰν ὁ πούς σου σκανδαλίζῃ σε,
  ἀπόκοψον αὐτόν·
   καλόν ἐστιν
   σὲ εἰσελθεῖν εἰς τὴν ζωὴν χωλόν,
   ἢ τοὺς δύο πόδας ἔχοντα βληθῆναι εἰς τὴν γέενναν.

47 καὶ ἐὰν ὁ ὀφθαλμός σου σκανδαλίζῃ σε,
  ἔκβαλε αὐτόν·
   καλόν σέ ἐστιν
   μονόφθαλμον εἰσελθεῖν εἰς τὴν βασιλείαν τοῦ θεοῦ,
   ἢ δύο ὀφθαλμοὺς ἔχοντα βληθῆναι εἰς τὴν γέενναν
48   ὅπου ὁ σκώληξ αὐτῶν οὐ τελευτᾷ
   καὶ τὸ πῦρ   οὐ σβέννυται.

49 πᾶς γὰρ   πυρὶ ἁλισθήσεται
  καὶ πᾶσα θυσία ἁλὶ ἁλισθήσεται.

50 καλὸν τὸ ἅλας·
  ἐὰν δὲ τὸ ἅλας ἄναλον γένηται,
  ἐν τίνι αὐτὸ ἀρτύσετε ;

  ἔχετε ἐν ἑαυτοῖς ἅλα
  καὶ εἰρηνεύετε ἐν ἀλλήλοις.

10 1 Καὶ ἐκεῖθεν ἀναστὰς ἔρχεται
  εἰς τὰ ὅρια τῆς Ἰουδαίας
  καὶ πέραν τοῦ Ἰορδάνου,

 καὶ συμπορεύονται πάλιν ὄχλοι πρὸς αὐτόν,
 καὶ ὡς εἰώθει πάλιν ἐδίδασκεν αὐτούς.

10

2 | Καὶ προσελθόντες Φαρισαῖοι ἐπηρώτων αὐτόν,
　εἰ ἔξεστιν ἀνδρὶ γυναῖκα ἀπολῦσαι,
πειράζοντες αὐτόν.

3 | ὁ δὲ ἀποκριθεὶς εἶπεν αὐτοῖς·
　τί ὑμῖν ἐνετείλατο Μωϋσῆς ;

4 | οἱ δὲ εἶπον·
　ἐπέτρεψεν Μωϋσῆς
　　βιβλίον ἀποστασίου γράψαι
　　καὶ ἀπολῦσαι.

5 | ὁ δὲ Ἰησοῦς εἶπεν αὐτοῖς·

　πρὸς τὴν σκληροκαρδίαν ὑμῶν
　ἔγραψεν ὑμῖν τὴν ἐντολὴν ταύτην.

6 | ἀπὸ δὲ ἀρχῆς κτίσεως
　ἄρσεν καὶ θῆλυ ἐποίησεν αὐτοὺς ὁ θεός.

7 | ἕνεκεν τούτου
　καταλείψει ἄνθρωπος τὸν πατέρα αὐτοῦ καὶ τὴν μητέρα,
　καὶ προσκολληθήσεται πρὸς τὴν γυναῖκα αὐτοῦ·

8 | καὶ ἔσονται οἱ δύο εἰς σάρκα μίαν,
　ὥστε οὐκέτι εἰσὶν δύο ἀλλὰ μία σάρξ.

9 | ὁ οὖν ὁ θεὸς συνέζευξεν,
　ἄνθρωπος μὴ χωριζέτω.

10 | καὶ εἰς τὴν οἰκίαν
πάλιν οἱ μαθηταὶ περὶ τούτου ἐπηρώτων αὐτόν.

11 | καὶ λέγει αὐτοῖς·

　ὃς ἂν ἀπολύσῃ τὴν γυναῖκα αὐτοῦ
　καὶ γαμήσῃ ἄλλην,
　　μοιχᾶται ἐπ' αὐτήν·

10 12│ καὶ ἐὰν αὐτὴ ἀπολύσασα τὸν ἄνδρα αὐτῆς
  γαμήσῃ ἄλλον,
  μοιχᾶται.

13 │Καὶ προσέφερον αὐτῷ παιδία, ἵνα αὐτῶν ἅψηται·
  │οἱ δὲ μαθηταὶ ἐπετίμων τοῖς προσφέρουσιν.

14 │ἰδὼν δὲ ὁ Ἰησοῦς ἠγανάκτησεν
  │καὶ εἶπεν αὐτοῖς·

  ἄφετε τὰ παιδία ἔρχεσθαι πρός με,
  μὴ κωλύετε αὐτά·
  τῶν γὰρ τοιούτων ἐστὶν ἡ βασιλεία τοῦ θεοῦ.

15 │ ἀμὴν λέγω ὑμῖν,
  ὃς ἂν μὴ δέξηται τὴν βασιλείαν τοῦ θεοῦ ὡς παιδίον,
  οὐ μὴ εἰσέλθῃ εἰς αὐτήν.

16 │καὶ ἐναγκαλισάμενος αὐτὰ κατευλόγει
  │τιθεὶς τὰς χεῖρας ἐπ᾽ αὐτά.

17 │Καὶ ἐκπορευομένου αὐτοῦ εἰς ὁδόν
  προσδραμὼν εἷς καὶ γονυπετήσας αὐτόν
  ἐπηρώτα αὐτόν·

  διδάσκαλε ἀγαθέ,
  τί ποιήσω, ἵνα ζωὴν αἰώνιον κληρονομήσω;

18 │ὁ δὲ Ἰησοῦς εἶπεν αὐτῷ·

  τί με λέγεις ἀγαθόν;
  οὐδεὶς ἀγαθὸς εἰ μὴ εἷς ὁ θεός.

19 │ τὰς ἐντολὰς οἶδας·

  μὴ φονεύσῃς,
  μὴ μοιχεύσῃς,
  μὴ κλέψῃς,
  μὴ ψευδομαρτυρήσῃς,

10

μὴ ἀποστερήσῃς,
τίμα τὸν πατέρα σου καὶ τὴν μητέρα.

20 ὁ δὲ ἀποκριθεὶς εἶπεν αὐτῷ·
διδάσκαλε, ταῦτα πάντα ἐφυλαξάμην ἐκ νεότητός μου.

21 ὁ δὲ Ἰησοῦς ἐμβλέψας αὐτῷ
ἠγάπησεν αὐτόν
καὶ εἶπεν αὐτῷ·

ἕν σε ὑστερεῖ·
ὕπαγε, ὅσα ἔχεις πώλησον καὶ δὸς πτωχοῖς,
——καὶ ἕξεις θησαυρὸν ἐν οὐρανῷ,——
καὶ δεῦρο ἀκολούθει μοι ἄρας τὸν σταυρόν.

22 ὁ δὲ στυγνάσας ἐπὶ τῷ λόγῳ ἀπῆλθεν λυπούμενος,
ἦν γὰρ ἔχων κτήματα πολλά.

23 Καὶ περιβλεψάμενος ὁ Ἰησοῦς
λέγει τοῖς μαθηταῖς αὐτοῦ·
πῶς δυσκόλως οἱ τὰ χρήματα ἔχοντες
εἰς τὴν βασιλείαν τοῦ θεοῦ εἰσελεύσονται.

24 οἱ δὲ μαθηταὶ ἐθαμβοῦντο ἐπὶ τοῖς λόγοις αὐτοῦ.

ὁ δὲ Ἰησοῦς πάλιν ἀποκριθεὶς λέγει αὐτοῖς·

τέκνα,
πῶς δύσκολόν ἐστιν τοὺς πεποιθότας ἐπὶ χρήμασιν
εἰς τὴν βασιλείαν τοῦ θεοῦ εἰσελθεῖν.

25 εὐκοπώτερόν ἐστιν
κάμηλον διὰ τῆς τρυμαλιᾶς τῆς ῥαφίδος διελθεῖν
ἢ πλούσιον εἰς τὴν βασιλείαν τοῦ θεοῦ εἰσελθεῖν.

26 οἱ δὲ περισσῶς ἐξεπλήσσοντο λέγοντες πρὸς ἑαυτούς·
καὶ τίς δύναται σωθῆναι ;

27 ἐμβλέψας αὐτοῖς ὁ Ἰησοῦς λέγει·
παρὰ ἀνθρώποις ἀδύνατον, ἀλλ’ οὐ παρὰ Θεῷ·
πάντα γὰρ δυνατὰ   παρὰ τῷ Θεῷ.

10

28 | Ἤρξατο λέγειν ὁ Πέτρος αὐτῷ·
idoὺ ἡμεῖς ἀφήκαμεν πάντα
καὶ ἠκολουθήσαμέν σοι.

29 | ἀποκριθεὶς ὁ Ἰησοῦς εἶπεν·

ἀμὴν λέγω ὑμῖν,

οὐδείς ἐστιν ὃς ἀφῆκεν οἰκίαν
ἢ ἀδελφοὺς ἢ αδελφάς
ἢ μητέρα   ἢ πατέρα
ἢ τέκνα   ἢ ἀγρούς
ἕνεκεν ἐμοῦ καὶ ἕνεκεν τοῦ εὐαγγελίου,
30 | ἐὰν μὴ λάβῃ ἑκατονταπλασίονα,

νῦν ἐν τῷ καιρῷ τούτῳ
οἰκίας καὶ ἀδελφούς
καὶ ἀδελφὰς καὶ μητέρας
καὶ τέκνα καὶ ἀγρούς
μετὰ διωγμῶν,

καὶ ἐν τῷ αἰῶνι τῷ ἐρχομένῳ
ζωὴν αἰώνιον.

31 | πολλοὶ δὲ ἔσονται πρῶτοι ἔσχατοι
καὶ   οἱ ἔσχατοι πρῶτοι.

32 | Ἦσαν δὲ ἐν τῇ ὁδῷ
ἀναβαίνοντες εἰς Ἱεροσόλυμα,
καὶ ἦν προάγων αὐτοὺς ὁ Ἰησοῦς,

καὶ ἐθαμβοῦντο,
οἱ δὲ ἀκολουθοῦντες ἐφοβοῦντο.

καὶ παραλαβὼν πάλιν τοὺς δώδεκα
ἤρξατο αὐτοῖς λέγειν τὰ μέλλοντα αὐτῷ συμβαίνειν,

33 | ὅτι ἰδοὺ ἀναβαίνομεν εἰς Ἱεροσόλυμα,
καὶ ὁ υἱὸς τοῦ ἀνθρώπου
παραδοθήσεται τοῖς ἀρχιερεῦσιν καὶ τοῖς γραμματεῦσιν,

10

καὶ κατακρινοῦσιν αὐτὸν θανάτῳ
καὶ παραδώσουσιν αὐτὸν τοῖς ἔθνεσιν

34   καὶ ἐμπαίξουσιν αὐτῷ
καὶ ἐμπτύσουσιν αὐτῷ
καὶ μαστιγώσουσιν αὐτόν
καὶ ἀποκτενοῦσιν,

καὶ μετὰ τρεῖς ἡμέρας ἀναστήσεται.

35 | Καὶ προσπορεύονται αὐτῷ
Ἰάκωβος καὶ Ἰωάννης οἱ υἱοὶ Ζεβεδαίου
λέγοντες αὐτῷ·

διδάσκαλε, θέλομεν ἵνα ὃ ἐὰν αἰτήσωμέν σε
ποιήσῃς ἡμῖν.

36 | ὁ δὲ εἶπεν αὐτοῖς·
τί θέλετε ποιῆσαί με ὑμῖν ;

37 | οἱ δὲ εἶπον αὐτῷ·

δὸς ἡμῖν,
ἵνα εἷς σου ἐκ δεξιῶν
καὶ εἷς σου ἐξ ἀριστερῶν
καθίσωμεν ἐν τῇ δόξῃ σου.

38 | ὁ δὲ Ἰησοῦς εἶπεν αὐτοῖς·

οὐκ οἴδατε τί αἰτεῖσθε.

δύνασθε πιεῖν τὸ ποτήριον ὃ ἐγὼ πίνω,
ἢ τὸ βάπτισμα ὃ ἐγὼ βαπτίζομαι βαπτισθῆναι ;

39 | οἱ δὲ εἶπον αὐτῷ·
δυνάμεθα.

ὁ δὲ Ἰησοῦς εἶπεν αὐτοῖς·

τὸ ποτήριον ὃ ἐγὼ πίνω πίεσθε,
καὶ τὸ βάπτισμα ὃ ἐγὼ βαπτίζομαι βαπτισθήσεσθε·

10

40 | τὸ δὲ καθίσαι ἐκ δεξιῶν μου ἢ ἐξ εὐωνύμων
οὐκ ἔστιν ἐμὸν δοῦναι ἀλλ' οἷς ἡτοίμασται.

41 | Καὶ ἀκούσαντες οἱ δέκα
ἤρξαντο ἀγανακτεῖν περὶ Ἰακώβου καὶ Ἰωάννου.

42 | καὶ προσκαλεσάμενος αὐτοὺς ὁ Ἰησοῦς
λέγει αὐτοῖς·

οἴδατε ὅτι οἱ δοκοῦντες ἄρχειν τῶν ἐθνῶν
κατακυριεύουσιν αὐτῶν
καὶ οἱ μεγάλοι αὐτῶν
κατεξουσιάζουσιν αὐτῶν.

43 | οὐχ οὕτως δέ ἐστιν ἐν ὑμῖν·

ἀλλ' ὃς ἂν θέλῃ μέγας γενέσθαι ἐν ὑμῖν,
ἔσται ὑμῶν διάκονος,
44 | καὶ ὃς ἂν θέλῃ ἐν ὑμῖν εἶναι πρῶτος,
ἔσται πάντων δοῦλος·

45 | καὶ γὰρ ὁ υἱὸς τοῦ ἀνθρώπου οὐκ ἦλθεν διακονηθῆναι
ἀλλὰ   διακονῆσαι
καὶ δοῦναι τὴν ψυχὴν αὐτοῦ λύτρον ἀντὶ πολλῶν.

46 | Καὶ ἔρχονται εἰς Ἱεριχώ.

καὶ ἐκπορευομένου αὐτοῦ, ἀπὸ Ἱεριχώ,
καὶ τῶν μαθητῶν αὐτοῦ καὶ ὄχλου ἱκανοῦ,

ὁ υἱὸς Τιμαίου Βαρτιμαῖος, τυφλὸς προσαίτης,
ἐκάθητο παρὰ τὴν ὁδόν.

47 | καὶ ἀκούσας ὅτι Ἰησοῦς ὁ Ναζαρηνός ἐστιν
ἤρξατο κράζειν καὶ λέγειν·
υἱὲ Δαυὶδ Ἰησοῦ, ἐλέησόν με.

48 | καὶ ἐπετίμων αὐτῷ πολλοὶ ἵνα σιωπήσῃ·
ὁ δὲ πολλῷ μᾶλλον ἔκραζεν·
υἱὲ Δαυίδ, ἐλέησόν με.

49 | καὶ στὰς ὁ Ἰησοῦς εἶπεν·
      φωνήσατε αὐτόν.

| καὶ φωνοῦσιν τὸν τυφλὸν λέγοντες αὐτῷ·
   θάρσει, ἔγειρε,
   φωνεῖ σε.

50 | ὁ δὲ ἀποβαλὼν τὸ ἱμάτιον αὐτοῦ
      ἀναπηδήσας ἦλθεν πρὸς τὸν Ἰησοῦν.

51 | καὶ ἀποκριθεὶς αὐτῷ ὁ Ἰησοῦς εἶπεν·
      τί σοι θέλεις ποιήσω ;

| ὁ δὲ τυφλὸς εἶπεν αὐτῷ·
   ῥαββουνί, ἵνα ἀναβλέψω.

52 | καὶ ὁ Ἰησοῦς εἶπεν αὐτῷ·
      ὕπαγε, ἡ πίστις σου σέσωκέν σε.

| καὶ εὐθὺς ἀνέβλεψεν,
  καὶ ἠκολούθει αὐτῷ ἐν τῇ ὁδῷ.

11   1 | Καὶ ὅτε ἐγγίζουσιν εἰς Ἱεροσόλυμα
      εἰς Βηθφαγὴ καὶ Βηθανίαν
      πρὸς τὸ ὄρος τῶν ἐλαιῶν,
      ἀποστέλλει δύο τῶν μαθητῶν αὐτοῦ
   2 | καὶ λέγει αὐτοῖς·

      ὑπάγετε εἰς τὴν κώμην τὴν κατέναντι ὑμῶν,
      καὶ εὐθὺς εἰσπορευόμενοι εἰς αὐτήν
        εὑρήσετε πῶλον δεδεμένον,
          ἐφ᾽ ὃν οὐδεὶς οὔπω ἀνθρώπων ἐκάθισεν·
      λύσατε αὐτὸν καὶ φέρετε.

11

3 | καὶ ἐάν τις ὑμῖν εἴπῃ·
τί ποιεῖτε τοῦτο ;
εἴπατε·
ὁ κύριος αὐτοῦ χρείαν ἔχει,
καὶ εὐθὺς αὐτὸν ἀποστέλλει πάλιν ὧδε.

4 | καὶ ἀπῆλθον καὶ εὗρον πῶλον δεδεμένον
πρὸς τὴν θύραν ἔξω ἐπὶ τοῦ ἀμφόδου,
καὶ λύουσιν αὐτόν.

5 | καί τινες τῶν ἐκεῖ ἑστηκότων ἔλεγον αὐτοῖς·
τί ποιεῖτε λύοντες τὸν πῶλον ;

6 | οἱ δὲ εἶπον αὐτοῖς καθὼς εἶπεν ὁ Ἰησοῦς·
καὶ ἀφῆκαν αὐτούς.

7 | καὶ φέρουσιν τὸν πῶλον πρὸς τὸν Ἰησοῦν,
καὶ ἐπιβάλλουσιν αὐτῷ τὰ ἱμάτια αὐτῶν·
καὶ ἐκάθισεν ἐπ' αὐτόν.

8 | καὶ πολλοὶ τὰ ἱμάτια αὐτῶν ἔστρωσαν εἰς τὴν ὁδόν,
ἄλλοι δὲ στιβάδας, κόψαντες ἐκ τῶν ἀγρῶν.

9 | καὶ οἱ προάγοντες
καὶ οἱ ἀκολουθοῦντες ἔκραζον·

ὡσαννά·
εὐλογημένος ὁ ἐρχόμενος ἐν ὀνόματι Κυρίου·
10 | εὐλογημένη ἡ ἐρχομένη βασιλεία τοῦ πατρὸς ἡμῶν Δαυίδ·
ὡσαννὰ ἐν τοῖς ὑψίστοις.

11 | Καὶ εἰσῆλθεν εἰς Ἱεροσόλυμα εἰς τὸ ἱερόν·

καὶ περιβλεψάμενος πάντα,
ὀψίας ἤδη οὔσης τῆς ὥρας,
ἐξῆλθεν εἰς Βηθανίαν μετὰ τῶν δώδεκα.

12 | Καὶ τῇ ἐπαύριον
ἐξελθόντων αὐτῶν ἀπὸ Βηθανίας ἐπείνασεν.

11

13 | καὶ ἰδὼν συκῆν ἀπὸ μακρόθεν ἔχουσαν φύλλα
ἦλθεν, εἰ ἄρα τι εὑρήσει ἐν αὐτῇ·

καὶ ἐλθὼν ἐπ᾽ αὐτὴν
οὐδὲν εὗρεν εἰ μὴ φύλλα·
ὁ γὰρ καιρὸς οὐκ ἦν σύκων.

14 | καὶ ἀποκριθεὶς εἶπεν αὐτῇ·
μηκέτι εἰς τὸν αἰῶνα ἐκ σοῦ μηδεὶς καρπὸν φάγοι.

| καὶ ἤκουον οἱ μαθηταὶ αὐτοῦ.

15 | Καὶ ἔρχονται εἰς Ἱεροσόλυμα.

Καὶ εἰσελθὼν εἰς τὸ ἱερόν

ἤρξατο ἐκβάλλειν τοὺς πωλοῦντας
καὶ τοὺς ἀγοράζοντας ἐν τῷ ἱερῷ,

καὶ τὰς τραπέζας τῶν κολλυβιστῶν
καὶ τὰς καθέδρας τῶν πωλούντων τὰς περιστερὰς κατέστρε-
ψεν,

16 | καὶ οὐκ ἤφιεν
ἵνα τις διενέγκῃ σκεῦος διὰ τοῦ ἱεροῦ·

17 | καὶ ἐδίδασκεν καὶ ἔλεγεν αὐτοῖς·

οὐ γέγραπται
ὅτι ὁ οἶκός μου οἶκος προσευχῆς
κληθήσεται πᾶσιν τοῖς ἔθνεσιν ;
ὑμεῖς δὲ πεποιήκατε αὐτὸν σπήλαιον λῃστῶν.

18 | καὶ ἤκουσαν οἱ ἀρχιερεῖς καὶ οἱ γραμματεῖς,
καὶ ἐζήτουν πῶς αὐτὸν ἀπολέσωσιν·
ἐφοβοῦντο γὰρ αὐτόν,
πᾶς γὰρ ὁ ὄχλος ἐξεπλήσσετο ἐπὶ τῇ διδαχῇ αὐτοῦ.

19 | Καὶ ὅταν ὀψὲ ἐγένετο,
ἐξεπορεύετο ἔξω τῆς πόλεως.

11

20 | Καὶ παραπορευόμενοι πρωῒ
εἶδον τὴν συκῆν ἐξηραμμένην ἐκ ῥιζῶν.

21 | καὶ ἀναμνησθεὶς ὁ Πέτρος λέγει αὐτῷ·
ῥαββί, ἴδε ἡ συκῆ ἣν κατηράσω ἐξήρανται.

22 | καὶ ἀποκριθεὶς ὁ Ἰησοῦς λέγει αὐτοῖς·

ἔχετε πίστιν θεοῦ.

23 | ἀμὴν λέγω ὑμῖν
ὅτι ὃς ἂν εἴπῃ τῷ ὄρει τούτῳ·
ἄρθητι καὶ βλήθητι εἰς τὴν θάλασσαν,
καὶ μὴ διακριθῇ ἐν τῇ καρδίᾳ αὐτοῦ,
ἀλλὰ πιστεύῃ ὅτι ὃ λαλεῖ γίνεται,
ἔσται αὐτῷ.

24 | διὰ τοῦτο λέγω ὑμῖν,
πάντα ὅσα προσεύχεσθε καὶ αἰτεῖσθε,
πιστεύετε ὅτι ἐλάβετε,
καὶ ἔσται ὑμῖν.

25 | καὶ ὅταν στήκετε προσευχόμενοι,
ἀφίετε εἴ τι ἔχετε κατά τινος,
ἵνα καὶ ὁ πατὴρ ὑμῶν ὁ ἐν τοῖς οὐρανοῖς
ἀφῇ ὑμῖν τὰ παραπτώματα ὑμῶν.

26 | εἰ δὲ ὑμεῖς οὐκ ἀφίετε,
οὐδὲ ὁ πατὴρ ὑμῶν ὁ ἐν τοῖς οὐρανοῖς
ἀφήσει τὰ παραπτώματα ὑμῶν.

27 | Καὶ ἔρχονται πάλιν εἰς Ἱεροσόλυμα.

καὶ ἐν τῷ ἱερῷ περιπατοῦντος αὐτοῦ
ἔρχονται πρὸς αὐτόν
οἱ ἀρχιερεῖς καὶ οἱ γραμματεῖς καὶ οἱ πρεσβύτεροι,

28 | καὶ ἔλεγον αὐτῷ·
ἐν ποίᾳ ἐξουσίᾳ ταῦτα ποιεῖς ;
ἢ τίς σοι ἔδωκεν τὴν ἐξουσίαν ταύτην,
ἵνα ταῦτα ποιῇς ;

29 | ὁ δὲ ᾽Ιησοῦς εἶπεν αὐτοῖς·

ἐπερωτήσω ὑμᾶς ἕνα λόγον,
καὶ ἀποκρίθητέ μοι,
καὶ ἐρῶ ὑμῖν ἐν ποίᾳ ἐξουσίᾳ ταῦτα ποιῶ.

30 | τὸ βάπτισμα τὸ ᾽Ιωάννου,
ἐξ οὐρανοῦ ἦν
ἢ ἐξ ἀνθρώπων ;
ἀποκρίθητέ μοι.

31 | καὶ διελογίζοντο πρὸς ἑαυτοὺς λέγοντες·
ἐὰν εἴπωμεν· ἐξ οὐρανοῦ,
ἐρεῖ· διὰ τί οὖν οὐκ ἐπιστεύσατε αὐτῷ ;
32 | ἀλλὰ εἴπωμεν· ἐξ ἀνθρώπων ;

ἐφοβοῦντο τὸν ὄχλον·
ἅπαντες γὰρ εἶχον τὸν ᾽Ιωάννην
ὄντως ὅτι προφήτης ἦν.

33 | καὶ ἀποκριθέντες τῷ ᾽Ιησοῦ λέγουσιν·
οὐκ οἴδαμεν.

καὶ ἀποκριθεὶς ὁ ᾽Ιησοῦς λέγει αὐτοῖς·
οὐδὲ ἐγὼ λέγω ὑμῖν,
ἐν ποίᾳ ἐξουσίᾳ ταῦτα ποιῶ.

12 1 | Καὶ ἤρξατο αὐτοῖς ἐν παραβολαῖς λαλεῖν·

ἀμπελῶνα ἄνθρωπος ἐφύτευσεν,

καὶ περιέθηκεν φραγμόν
καὶ ὤρυξεν ὑπολήνιον
καὶ ᾠκοδόμησεν πύργον,

2

καὶ ἐξέδοτο αὐτὸν γεωργοῖς,
καὶ ἀπεδήμησεν.

2   καὶ ἀπέστειλεν πρὸς τοὺς γεωργοὺς τῷ καιρῷ δοῦλον,
ἵνα παρὰ τῶν γεωργῶν
λάβῃ ἀπὸ τῶν καρπῶν τοῦ ἀμπελῶνος.

3   καὶ λαβόντες αὐτὸν ἔδειραν
καὶ ἀπέστειλαν κενόν.

4   καὶ πάλιν ἀπέστειλεν πρὸς αὐτοὺς ἄλλον δοῦλον·
κἀκεῖνον ἐκεφαλαίωσαν καὶ ἠτίμασαν.

5   καὶ ἄλλον ἀπέστειλεν,
κἀκεῖνον ἀπέκτειναν,
καὶ πολλοὺς ἄλλους,
οὓς μὲν δέροντες,
οὓς δὲ ἀποκτέννοντες.

6   ἔτι ἕνα εἶχεν, υἱὸν ἀγαπητόν·
ἀπέστειλεν αὐτὸν ἔσχατον πρὸς αὐτοὺς λέγων
ὅτι ἐντραπήσονται τὸν υἱόν μου.

7   ἐκεῖνοι δὲ οἱ γεωργοὶ πρὸς ἑαυτοὺς εἶπον
ὅτι οὗτός ἐστιν ὁ κληρονόμος·
δεῦτε ἀποκτείνωμεν αὐτόν,
καὶ ἡμῶν ἔσται ἡ κληρονομία.

8   καὶ λαβόντες ἀπέκτειναν αὐτόν,
καὶ ἐξέβαλον αὐτὸν ἔξω τοῦ ἀμπελῶνος.

9   τί οὖν ποιήσει ὁ κύριος τοῦ ἀμπελῶνος ;

ἐλεύσεται καὶ ἀπολέσει τοὺς γεωργούς,
καὶ δώσει τὸν ἀμπελῶνα ἄλλοις.

10 οὐδὲ τὴν γραφὴν ταύτην ἀνέγνωτε·   Isaia 5/2

λίθον ὃν ἀπεδοκίμασαν οἱ οἰκοδομοῦντες,   Ps.117/22

12

11
    οὗτος ἐγενήθη εἰς κεφαλὴν γωνίας·
    παρὰ κυρίου ἐγένετο αὕτη,
    καὶ ἔστιν θαυμαστὴ ἐν ὀφθαλμοῖς ἡμῶν ;

12 καὶ ἐζήτουν αὐτὸν κρατῆσαι,
    καὶ ἐφοβήθησαν τὸν ὄχλον·
    ἔγνωσαν γὰρ ὅτι πρὸς αὐτοὺς τὴν παραβολὴν εἶπεν

καὶ ἀφέντες αὐτὸν ἀπῆλθον.

13 Καὶ ἀποστέλλουσιν πρὸς αὐτόν
τινὰς τῶν Φαρισαίων καὶ τῶν Ἡρῳδιανῶν,
    ἵνα αὐτὸν ἀγρεύσωσιν λόγῳ.

14 οἱ δὲ ἐλθόντες λέγουσιν αὐτῷ·

    διδάσκαλε, οἴδαμεν ὅτι ἀληθὴς εἶ
    καὶ οὐ μέλει σοι περὶ οὐδενός·
    οὐ γὰρ βλέπεις εἰς πρόσωπον ἀνθρώπων,
    ἀλλ' ἐπ' ἀληθείας τὴν ὁδὸν τοῦ θεοῦ διδάσκεις.

    ἔξεστιν κῆνσον Καίσαρι δοῦναι ἢ οὔ ;
    δῶμεν ἢ μὴ δῶμεν ;

15 ὁ δὲ εἰδὼς αὐτῶν τὴν ὑπόκρισιν
εἶπεν αὐτοῖς·
    τί με πειράζετε ;
    φέρετέ μοι δηνάριον·   ἵνα ἴδω.

16 οἱ δὲ ἤνεγκαν.

καὶ λέγει αὐτοῖς·
    τίνος ἡ εἰκὼν αὕτη καὶ ἡ ἐπιγραφή ;

οἱ δὲ εἶπον αὐτῷ·
    Καίσαρος.

17 καὶ ἀποκριθεὶς ὁ Ἰησοῦς εἶπεν αὐτοῖς·
    τὰ Καίσαρος ἀπόδοτε Καίσαρι,
    καὶ τὰ τοῦ Θεοῦ τῷ Θεῷ.

12

καὶ ἐξεθαύμαζον ἐπ' αὐτῷ.

18 | Καὶ ἔρχονται Σαδδουκαῖοι πρὸς αὐτόν,
οἵτινες λέγουσιν ἀνάστασιν μὴ εἶναι.

καὶ ἐπηρώτων αὐτὸν λέγοντες·

19 | διδάσκαλε, Μωϋσῆς ἔγραψεν ἡμῖν
ὅτι ἐάν τινος ἀδελφὸς ἀποθάνῃ
καὶ καταλίπῃ γυναῖκα
καὶ τέκνον μὴ ἀφῇ,
ἵνα λάβῃ ὁ ἀδελφὸς αὐτοῦ τὴν γυναῖκα
καὶ ἐξαναστήσῃ σπέρμα τῷ ἀδελφῷ αὐτοῦ.

20 | ἑπτὰ ἀδελφοὶ ἦσαν·

καὶ ὁ πρῶτος ἔλαβεν γυναῖκα,
καὶ ἀποθνῄσκων οὐκ ἀφῆκεν σπέρμα·

21 | καὶ ὁ δεύτερος ἔλαβεν αὐτήν,
καὶ ἀπέθανεν μὴ καταλιπὼν σπέρμα·

καὶ ὁ τρίτος ὡσαύτως·
22 | καὶ οἱ ἑπτὰ οὐκ ἀφῆκαν σπέρμα.

ἔσχατον πάντων καὶ ἡ γυνὴ ἀπέθανεν.

23 | ἐν τῇ ἀναστάσει, ὅταν ἀναστῶσιν,
τίνος αὐτῶν ἔσται γυνή;
οἱ γὰρ ἑπτὰ ἔσχον αὐτὴν γυναῖκα.

24 | ἔφη αὐτοῖς ὁ Ἰησοῦς·

οὐ διὰ τοῦτο πλανᾶσθε
μὴ εἰδότες τὰς γραφάς
μηδὲ τὴν δύναμιν τοῦ θεοῦ;

25 | ὅταν γὰρ ἐκ νεκρῶν ἀναστῶσιν,
οὔτε γαμοῦσιν οὔτε γαμίζονται,
ἀλλ' εἰσὶν ὡς ἄγγελοι ἐν τοῖς οὐρανοῖς.

12   **26**   περὶ δὲ τῶν νεκρῶν ὅτι ἐγείρονται,
            οὐκ ἀνέγνωτε ἐν τῇ βίβλῳ Μωϋσέως,   Εχ 3/6
               ἐπὶ τοῦ βάτου,
            πῶς εἶπεν αὐτῷ ὁ θεὸς λέγων·

               ἐγὼ ὁ θεὸς Ἀβραάμ
                 καὶ θεὸς Ἰσαάκ
                 καὶ θεὸς Ἰακώβ ;

     27   οὐκ ἔστιν θεὸς νεκρῶν ἀλλὰ (θεὸς) ζώντων.

            ὑμεῖς οὖν πολὺ πλανᾶσθε.

     28   Καὶ προσελθὼν εἷς τῶν γραμματέων,
               ἀκούσας αὐτῶν συνζητούντων,
               εἰδὼς ὅτι καλῶς ἀπεκρίθη αὐτοῖς,
            ἐπηρώτησεν αὐτόν·
               ποία ἐστὶν ἐντολὴ πρώτη πάντων ;

     29   ἀπεκρίθη ὁ Ἰησοῦς

               ὅτι πρώτη ἐστίν·

                 ἄκουε, Ἰσραήλ·
                 Κύριος ὁ θεὸς ἡμῶν Κύριος εἷς ἐστιν,
     30   καὶ ἀγαπήσεις Κύριον τὸν θεόν σου
                   ἐξ ὅλης τῆς καρδίας σου
                   καὶ ἐξ ὅλης τῆς ψυχῆς σου
                   καὶ ἐξ ὅλης τῆς διανοίας σου
                   καὶ ἐξ ὅλης τῆς ἰσχύος σου.

     31   δευτέρα αὕτη·
               ἀγαπήσεις τὸν πλησίον σου ὡς σεαυτόν.

            μείζων τούτων ἄλλη ἐντολὴ οὐκ ἔστιν.

     32   καὶ εἶπεν αὐτῷ ὁ γραμματεύς·

               καλῶς, διδάσκαλε, ἐπ' ἀληθείας εἶπας
               ὅτι εἷς ἐστιν καὶ οὐκ ἔστιν ἄλλος πλὴν αὐτοῦ·

12

33   καὶ τὸ ἀγαπᾶν αὐτόν
    ἐξ ὅλης τῆς καρδίας
    καὶ ἐξ ὅλης τῆς συνέσεως
    καὶ ἐξ ὅλης τῆς ἰσχύος,
    καὶ τὸ ἀγαπᾶν τὸν πλησίον ὡς ἑαυτόν
    περισσότερόν ἐστιν πάντων τῶν ὁλοκαυτωμάτων καὶ θυσιῶν.

34   καὶ ὁ Ἰησοῦς, ἰδὼν αὐτὸν ὅτι νουνεχῶς ἀπεκρίθη,
    εἶπεν αὐτῷ·
    οὐ μακρὰν εἶ ἀπὸ τῆς βασιλείας τοῦ θεοῦ.

    καὶ οὐδεὶς οὐκέτι ἐτόλμα αὐτὸν ἐπερωτῆσαι.

35   Καὶ ἀποκριθεὶς ὁ Ἰησοῦς ἔλεγεν
    διδάσκων ἐν τῷ ἱερῷ·

    πῶς λέγουσιν οἱ γραμματεῖς
    ὅτι ὁ Χριστὸς υἱὸς Δαυὶδ ἐστιν ;

36   αὐτὸς Δαυὶδ εἶπεν ἐν τῷ πνεύματι τῷ ἁγίῳ·
    εἶπεν ὁ Κύριος τῷ Κυρίῳ μου·   Ps. 109
    κάθου ἐκ δεξιῶν μου,
    ἕως ἂν θῶ τοὺς ἐχθρούς σου
    ὑποπόδιον τῶν ποδῶν σου.

37   αὐτὸς Δαυὶδ λέγει αὐτὸν Κύριον,
    καὶ πόθεν αὐτοῦ ἐστιν υἱός ;

    Καὶ ὁ πολὺς ὄχλος ἤκουεν αὐτοῦ ἡδέως.

38   Καὶ ἐν τῇ διδαχῇ αὐτοῦ ἔλεγεν·

    βλέπετε ἀπὸ τῶν γραμματέων
    τῶν θελόντων ἐν στολαῖς περιπατεῖν
    καὶ ἀσπασμοὺς ἐν ταῖς ἀγοραῖς

39   καὶ πρωτοκαθεδρίας ἐν ταῖς συναγωγαῖς
      καὶ πρωτοκλισίας ἐν τοῖς δείπνοις,

40   οἱ κατεσθίοντες τὰς οἰκίας τῶν χηρῶν
      καὶ προφάσει μακρὰ προσευχόμενοι,
      οὗτοι λήψονται περισσότερον κρίμα.

41   Καὶ καθίσας κατέναντι τοῦ γαζοφυλακίου
      ἐθεώρει πῶς ὁ ὄχλος βάλλει χαλκὸν εἰς τὸ γαζοφυλάκιον·
      καὶ πολλοὶ πλούσιοι ἔβαλλον πολλά.

42   καὶ ἐλθοῦσα μία χήρα πτωχή
      ἔβαλεν λεπτὰ δύο, ὅ ἐστιν κοδράντης.

43   καὶ προσκαλεσάμενος τοὺς μαθητὰς αὐτοῦ
      εἶπεν αὐτοῖς·

      ἀμὴν λέγω ὑμῖν
        ὅτι ἡ χήρα αὕτη ἡ πτωχὴ πλεῖον πάντων βέβληκεν
        τῶν βαλλόντων εἰς τὸ γαζοφυλάκιον·

44   πάντες γὰρ ἐκ τοῦ περισσεύοντος αὐτοῖς ἔβαλον,
      αὕτη δὲ ἐκ τῆς ὑστερήσεως αὐτῆς
        πάντα ὅσα εἶχεν ἔβαλεν,
        —ὅλον τὸν βίον αὐτῆς—.

13   1   Καὶ ἐκπορευομένου αὐτοῦ ἐκ τοῦ ἱεροῦ
             λέγει αὐτῷ εἷς τῶν μαθητῶν αὐτοῦ·
             διδάσκαλε, ἴδε ποταποὶ λίθοι
             καὶ ποταπαὶ οἰκοδομαί.

         2   καὶ ὁ Ἰησοῦς εἶπεν αὐτῷ·
             βλέπεις ταύτας τὰς μεγάλας οἰκοδομάς;
             οὐ μὴ ἀφεθῇ [ὧδε] λίθος ἐπὶ λίθον
               ὃς οὐ μὴ καταλυθῇ.

13

3 | Καὶ καθημένου αὐτοῦ εἰς τὸ ὄρος τῶν ἐλαιῶν
κατέναντι τοῦ ἱεροῦ,
ἐπηρώτα αὐτὸν κατ᾽ ἰδίαν
Πέτρος καὶ Ἰάκωβος καὶ Ἰωάννης καὶ Ἀνδρέας·

4 | εἰπὸν ἡμῖν, πότε ταῦτα ἔσται,
καὶ τί τὸ σημεῖον
ὅταν μέλλῃ ταῦτα συντελεῖσθαι πάντα ;

5 | ὁ δὲ Ἰησοῦς ἤρξατο λέγειν αὐτοῖς·

βλέπετε μή τις ὑμᾶς πλανήσῃ.
6 | πολλοὶ γὰρ ἐλεύσονται ἐπὶ τῷ ὀνόματί μου λέγοντες
ὅτι ἐγώ εἰμι,
καὶ πολλοὺς πλανήσουσιν.

7 | ὅταν δὲ ἀκούσητε πολέμους καὶ ἀκοὰς πολέμων,
μὴ θροεῖσθε·
δεῖ γὰρ γενέσθαι,
ἀλλ᾽ οὔπω τὸ τέλος.
8 | ἐγερθήσεται γὰρ ἔθνος ἐπ᾽ ἔθνος
καὶ βασιλεία ἐπὶ βασιλείαν.

ἔσονται σεισμοὶ κατὰ τόπους,
ἔσονται λιμοί.

ἀρχαὶ ὠδίνων ταῦτα.

9 | Βλέπετε δὲ ὑμεῖς ἑαυτούς·

παραδώσουσιν γὰρ ὑμᾶς εἰς συνέδρια,
καὶ εἰς συναγωγὰς δαρήσεσθε,
καὶ ἐπὶ ἡγεμόνων καὶ βασιλέων σταθήσεσθε
ἕνεκεν ἐμοῦ,
εἰς μαρτύριον αὐτοῖς.

10 | καὶ εἰς πάντα τὰ ἔθνη
πρῶτον δεῖ κηρυχθῆναι τὸ εὐαγγέλιον.

13 11 καὶ ὅταν ἄγωσιν ὑμᾶς παραδιδόντες,
μὴ προμεριμνᾶτε τί λαλήσητε,
ἀλλ' ὃ ἐὰν δοθῇ ὑμῖν ἐν ἐκείνῃ τῇ ὥρᾳ,
τοῦτο λαλεῖτε·

οὐ γάρ ἐστε ὑμεῖς οἱ λαλοῦντες
ἀλλὰ τὸ πνεῦμα τὸ ἅγιον.

12 καὶ παραδώσει ἀδελφὸς ἀδελφὸν εἰς θάνατον
καὶ πατὴρ τέκνον,
καὶ ἐπαναστήσονται τέκνα ἐπὶ γονεῖς
καὶ θανατώσουσιν αὐτούς.

13 καὶ ἔσεσθε μισούμενοι ὑπὸ πάντων
διὰ τὸ ὄνομά μου·
ὁ δὲ ὑπομείνας εἰς τέλος, οὗτος σωθήσεται.

14 Ὅταν δὲ ἴδητε τὸ βδέλυγμα τῆς ἐρημώσεως   *Daniel*
ἑστηκότα ὅπου οὐ δεῖ,
—ὁ ἀναγινώσκων νοείτω,—
τότε

οἱ ἐν τῇ Ἰουδαίᾳ φευγέτωσαν εἰς τὰ ὄρη·

15 ὁ δὲ ἐπὶ τοῦ δώματος
μὴ καταβάτω εἰς τὴν οἰκίαν
μηδὲ εἰσελθέτω τι ἆραι ἐκ τῆς οἰκίας αὐτοῦ·

16 καὶ ὁ εἰς τὸν ἀγρὸν
μὴ ἐπιστρεψάτω εἰς τὰ ὀπίσω
ἆραι τὸ ἱμάτιον αὐτοῦ.

17 οὐαὶ δὲ ταῖς ἐν γαστρὶ ἐχούσαις
καὶ ταῖς θηλαζούσαις
ἐν ἐκείναις ταῖς ἡμέραις.

18 προσεύχεσθε δὲ ἵνα μὴ γένηται χειμῶνος·
19 ἔσονται γὰρ αἱ ἡμέραι ἐκεῖναι θλίψις,

13

οἷα οὐ γέγονεν τοιαύτη
  ἀπ' ἀρχῆς κτίσεως, ἣν ἔκτισεν ὁ θεός,
  ἕως τοῦ νῦν,
  καὶ οὐ μὴ γένηται.

20 καὶ εἰ μὴ ἐκολόβωσεν Κύριος τὰς ἡμέρας,
  οὐκ ἂν ἐσώθη πᾶσα σάρξ·
  ἀλλὰ διὰ τοὺς ἐκλεκτοὺς οὓς ἐξελέξατο
  ἐκολόβωσεν τὰς ἡμέρας.

21 καὶ τότε ἐάν τις ὑμῖν εἴπῃ·
  ἴδε ὧδε ὁ Χριστός,
  ἴδε ἐκεῖ,
  μὴ πιστεύετε.

22 ἐγερθήσονται γὰρ ψευδόχριστοι καὶ ψευδοπροφῆται
  καὶ δώσουσιν σημεῖα καὶ τέρατα
    πρὸς τὸ ἀποπλανᾶν εἰ δυνατὸν τοὺς ἐκλεκτούς.

23 ὑμεῖς δὲ βλέπετε·
  ἰδοὺ προείρηκα ὑμῖν πάντα.

24 Ἀλλὰ ἐν ἐκείναις ταῖς ἡμέραις μετὰ τὴν θλίψιν ἐκείνην

  ὁ ἥλιος σκοτισθήσεται,
  καὶ ἡ σελήνη οὐ δώσει τὸ φέγγος αὐτῆς,

25 καὶ οἱ ἀστέρες ἔσονται ἐκ τοῦ οὐρανοῦ ἐκπίπτοντες,
  καὶ αἱ δυνάμεις αἱ ἐν τοῖς οὐρανοῖς σαλευθήσονται.

26 καὶ τότε ὄψονται τὸν υἱὸν τοῦ ἀνθρώπου
  ἐρχόμενον ἐν νεφέλαις
  μετὰ δυνάμεως πολλῆς καὶ δόξης.

27 καὶ τότε ἀποστελεῖ τοὺς ἀγγέλους αὐτοῦ,
  καὶ ἐπισυνάξει τοὺς ἐκλεκτοὺς αὐτοῦ,
  ἐκ τῶν τεσσάρων ἀνέμων ἀπ' ἄκρου γῆς,
  ἕως ἄκρου οὐρανοῦ.

13 28 Ἀπὸ δὲ τῆς συκῆς μάθετε τὴν παραβολήν·

ὅταν ἤδη αὐτῆς ὁ κλάδος ἁπαλὸς γένηται
καὶ ἐκφύῃ τὰ φύλλα,
γινώσκετε ὅτι ἐγγὺς τὸ θέρος ἐστίν.

29 οὕτως καὶ ὑμεῖς·
ὅταν ἴδητε ταῦτα γινόμενα,
γινώσκετε ὅτι ἐγγύς ἐστιν ἐπὶ θύραις.

30 ἀμὴν λέγω ὑμῖν
ὅτι οὐ μὴ παρέλθῃ ἡ γενεὰ αὕτη,
μέχρις οὗ ταῦτα πάντα γένηται.

31 ὁ οὐρανὸς καὶ ἡ γῆ παρελεύσονται,
οἱ δὲ λόγοι μου οὐ μὴ παρελεύσονται.

32 Περὶ δὲ τῆς ἡμέρας ἐκείνης ἢ τῆς ὥρας οὐδεὶς οἶδεν
οὐδὲ οἱ ἄγγελοι ἐν οὐρανῷ
οὐδὲ ὁ υἱός,
εἰ μὴ ὁ πατήρ.

33 Βλέπετε ἀγρυπνεῖτε καὶ προσεύχεσθε·
οὐκ οἴδατε γάρ, πότε ὁ καιρός ἐστιν.

34 ὡς ἄνθρωπος ἀπόδημος·
ἀφεὶς τὴν οἰκίαν αὐτοῦ
καὶ δοὺς τοῖς δούλοις αὐτοῦ τὴν ἐξουσίαν,
ἑκάστῳ τὸ ἔργον αὐτοῦ,
καὶ τῷ θυρωρῷ ἐνετείλατο, ἵνα γρηγορῇ.

35 γρηγορεῖτε οὖν·
οὐκ οἴδατε γὰρ πότε ὁ κύριος τῆς οἰκίας ἔρχεται,
ἢ ὀψὲ ἢ μεσονύκτιον
ἢ ἀλεκτοροφωνίας ἢ πρωΐ·

36 μὴ ἐλθὼν ἐξαίφνης εὕρῃ ὑμᾶς καθεύδοντας·

37 ὃ δὲ ὑμῖν λέγω, πᾶσιν λέγω,
γρηγορεῖτε.

14

1 | Ἦν δὲ τὸ πάσχα καὶ τὰ ἄζυμα μετὰ δύο ἡμέρας.

καὶ ἐζήτουν οἱ ἀρχιερεῖς καὶ οἱ γραμματεῖς,
πῶς αὐτὸν ἐν δόλῳ κρατήσαντες ἀποκτείνωσιν.

2 | ἔλεγον γάρ·
    μὴ ἐν τῇ ἑορτῇ,
    μήποτε ἔσται θόρυβος τοῦ λαοῦ.

3 | Καὶ ὄντος αὐτοῦ ἐν Βηθανίᾳ
    ἐν τῇ Σίμωνος τοῦ λεπροῦ,
κατακειμένου αὐτοῦ ἦλθεν γυνή
ἔχουσα ἀλάβαστρον μύρου νάρδου πιστικῆς πολυτελοῦς·

συντρίψασα τὴν ἀλάβαστρον
κατέχεεν αὐτοῦ τῆς κεφαλῆς.

4 | ἦσαν δέ τινες ἀγανακτοῦντες πρὸς ἑαυτούς·

    εἰς τί ἡ ἀπώλεια αὕτη τοῦ μύρου γέγονεν ;
5 | ἠδύνατο γὰρ τοῦτο τὸ μύρον
        πραθῆναι ἐπάνω δηναρίων τριακοσίων
        καὶ δοθῆναι τοῖς πτωχοῖς·

καὶ ἐνεβριμῶντο αὐτῇ.

6 | ὁ δὲ Ἰησοῦς εἶπεν·

    ἄφετε αὐτήν·
    τί αὐτῇ κόπους παρέχετε ;
    καλὸν ἔργον ἠργάσατο ἐν ἐμοί.

7 | πάντοτε γὰρ τοὺς πτωχοὺς ἔχετε μεθ' ἑαυτῶν,
    καὶ ὅταν θέλητε δύνασθε αὐτοῖς εὖ ποιῆσαι,
        ἐμὲ δὲ οὐ πάντοτε ἔχετε.

8 | ὃ ἔσχεν ἐποίησεν·
    προέλαβεν μυρίσαι μου τὸ σῶμα εἰς τὸν ἐνταφιασμόν.

14 9 ἀμὴν δὲ λέγω ὑμῖν,

ὅπου ἐὰν κηρυχθῇ τὸ εὐαγγέλιον τοῦτο
εἰς ὅλον τὸν κόσμον,
καὶ ὃ ἐποίησεν αὕτη λαληθήσεται
εἰς μνημόσυνον αὐτῆς.

10 Καὶ ᾽Ιούδας ὁ ᾽Ισκαριώθ, ὁ εἷς τῶν δώδεκα,
ἀπῆλθεν πρὸς τοὺς ἀρχιερεῖς,
ἵνα αὐτὸν παραδῷ αὐτοῖς.

11 οἱ δὲ ἀκούσαντες ἐχάρησαν,
καὶ ἐπηγγείλαντο αὐτῷ ἀργύριον δοῦναι·
καὶ ἐζήτει, πῶς αὐτὸν εὐκαίρως παραδῷ.

12 Καὶ τῇ πρώτῃ ἡμέρᾳ τῶν ἀζύμων,
ὅτε τὸ πάσχα ἔθυον,
λέγουσιν αὐτῷ οἱ μαθηταὶ αὐτοῦ·
ποῦ θέλεις ἀπελθόντες ἑτοιμάσωμεν,
ἵνα φάγῃς τὸ πάσχα ;

13 καὶ ἀποστέλλει δύο τῶν μαθητῶν αὐτοῦ
καὶ λέγει αὐτοῖς·

ὑπάγετε εἰς τὴν πόλιν,
καὶ ἀπαντήσει ὑμῖν ἄνθρωπος κεράμιον ὕδατος βαστάζων·

ἀκολουθήσατε αὐτῷ,
14 καὶ ὅπου ἐὰν εἰσέλθῃ εἴπατε τῷ οἰκοδεσπότῃ
ὅτι ὁ διδάσκαλος λέγει·
ποῦ ἐστιν τὸ κατάλυμά μου,
ὅπου τὸ πάσχα μετὰ τῶν μαθητῶν μου φάγω ;

15 καὶ αὐτὸς ὑμῖν δείξει ἀνάγαιον,
μέγα ἐστρωμένον ἕτοιμον·
καὶ ἐκεῖ ἑτοιμάσατε ἡμῖν.

14

16 | Καὶ ἐξῆλθον οἱ μαθηταὶ αὐτοῦ
καὶ ἦλθον εἰς τὴν πόλιν
καὶ εὗρον καθὼς εἶπεν αὐτοῖς,
καὶ ἡτοίμασαν τὸ πάσχα.

17 | Καὶ ὀψίας γενομένης ἔρχεται μετὰ τῶν δώδεκα.

18 | καὶ ἀνακειμένων αὐτῶν καὶ ἐσθιόντων
ὁ Ἰησοῦς εἶπεν·
ἀμὴν λέγω ὑμῖν
ὅτι εἷς ἐξ ὑμῶν παραδώσει με,
ὁ ἐσθίων μετ' ἐμοῦ.

19 | ἤρξαντο λυπεῖσθαι
καὶ λέγειν αὐτῷ εἷς κατὰ εἷς·
μήτι ἐγώ ;
καὶ ἄλλος·
μήτι ἐγώ ;

20 | ὁ δὲ εἶπεν αὐτοῖς·

εἷς τῶν δώδεκα,
ὁ ἐμβαπτόμενος μετ' ἐμοῦ εἰς τὸ τρύβλιον.

21 | ὅτι ὁ μὲν υἱὸς τοῦ ἀνθρώπου ὑπάγει,
καθὼς γέγραπται περὶ αὐτοῦ·
οὐαὶ δὲ τῷ ἀνθρώπῳ ἐκείνῳ,
δι' οὗ ὁ υἱὸς τοῦ ἀνθρώπου παραδίδοται·

καλὸν ἦν αὐτῷ,
εἰ οὐκ ἐγεννήθη ὁ ἄνθρωπος ἐκεῖνος.

22 | Καὶ ἐσθιόντων αὐτῶν λαβὼν ὁ Ἰησοῦς ἄρτον

εὐλογήσας ἔκλασεν
καὶ ἔδωκεν αὐτοῖς
καὶ εἶπεν·
λάβετε·
τοῦτό ἐστιν τὸ σῶμά μου.

14

23 | καὶ λαβὼν ποτήριον
    εὐχαριστήσας ἔδωκεν αὐτοῖς,
    καὶ ἔπιον ἐξ αὐτοῦ πάντες.

24 | καὶ εἶπεν αὐτοῖς·

    τοῦτό ἐστιν τὸ αἷμά μου τῆς διαθήκης
    τὸ ἐκχυννόμενον ὑπὲρ πολλῶν.

25 | ἀμὴν λέγω ὑμῖν
    ὅτι οὐκέτι οὐ μὴ πίω ἐκ τοῦ γενήματος τῆς ἀμπέλου,
    ἕως τῆς ἡμέρας ἐκείνης
    ὅταν αὐτὸ πίνω καινὸν ἐν τῇ βασιλείᾳ τοῦ θεοῦ.

26 | Καὶ ὑμνήσαντες ἐξῆλθον εἰς τὸ ὄρος τῶν ἐλαιῶν.

27 | Καὶ λέγει αὐτοῖς ὁ Ἰησοῦς

    ὅτι πάντες σκανδαλισθήσεσθε,
    ὅτι γέγραπται·
        πατάξω τὸν ποιμένα,
        καὶ τὰ πρόβατα διασκορπισθήσονται.

28 | ἀλλὰ μετὰ τὸ ἐγερθῆναί με
    προάξω ὑμᾶς εἰς τὴν Γαλιλαίαν.

29 | ὁ δὲ Πέτρος ἔφη αὐτῷ·
    εἰ καὶ πάντες σκανδαλισθήσονται,
    ἀλλ' οὐκ ἐγώ.

30 | καὶ λέγει αὐτῷ ὁ Ἰησοῦς·

    ἀμὴν λέγω σοι
        ὅτι σύ
        σήμερον
        ταύτῃ τῇ νυκτί
        πρὶν ἢ δὶς ἀλέκτορα φωνῆσαι
    τρίς με ἀπαρνήσῃ.

14   31 | ὁ δὲ ἐκπερισσῶς ἐλάλει·
          ἐάν με δέῃ συναποθανεῖν σοι,
          οὐ μή σε ἀπαρνήσομαι.

          ὡσαύτως δὲ καὶ πάντες ἔλεγον.

     32 | Καὶ ἔρχονται εἰς χωρίον
          οὗ τὸ ὄνομα Γεθσημανεί·

          καὶ λέγει τοῖς μαθηταῖς αὐτοῦ·
          καθίσατε ὧδε, ἕως προσεύξωμαι.

     33 | καὶ παραλαμβάνει
          τὸν Πέτρον καὶ Ἰάκωβον καὶ Ἰωάννην μετ' αὐτοῦ,
          καὶ ἤρξατο ἐκθαμβεῖσθαι καὶ ἀδημονεῖν·

     34 | καὶ λέγει αὐτοῖς·
          περίλυπός ἐστιν ἡ ψυχή μου ἕως θανάτου·
          μείνατε ὧδε καὶ γρηγορεῖτε.

     35 | καὶ προελθὼν μικρόν
          ἔπιπτεν ἐπὶ τῆς γῆς, καὶ προσηύχετο,
          ἵνα εἰ δυνατόν ἐστιν παρέλθῃ ἀπ' αὐτοῦ ἡ ὥρα,

     36 | καὶ ἔλεγεν·
          ἀββᾶ ὁ πατήρ,
          πάντα δυνατά σοι·
          παρένεγκε τὸ ποτήριον τοῦτο ἀπ' ἐμοῦ·
          ἀλλ' οὐ τί ἐγὼ θέλω, ἀλλὰ τί σύ.

     37 | καὶ ἔρχεται καὶ εὑρίσκει αὐτοὺς καθεύδοντας,
          καὶ λέγει τῷ Πέτρῳ·

          Σίμων, καθεύδεις ;
          οὐκ ἴσχυσας μίαν ὥραν γρηγορῆσαι ;

     38 | γρηγορεῖτε καὶ προσεύχεσθε,
          ἵνα μὴ εἰσέλθητε εἰς πειρασμόν·

14

τὸ μὲν πνεῦμα πρόθυμον,
ἡ δὲ σὰρξ ἀσθενής.

39 καὶ πάλιν ἀπελθὼν
προσηύξατο τὸν αὐτὸν λόγον εἰπών.

40 καὶ ὑποστρέψας
εὗρεν αὐτοὺς πάλιν καθεύδοντας,
ἦσαν γὰρ αὐτῶν οἱ ὀφθαλμοὶ καταβαρυνόμενοι·
καὶ οὐκ ᾔδεισαν τί ἀποκριθῶσιν αὐτῷ.

41 καὶ ἔρχεται τὸ τρίτον
καὶ λέγει αὐτοῖς·

καθεύδετε τὸ λοιπὸν καὶ ἀναπαύεσθε ;
ἀπέχει.

ἦλθεν ἡ ὥρα,
ἰδοὺ παραδίδοται ὁ υἱὸς τοῦ ἀνθρώπου
εἰς τὰς χεῖρας τῶν ἁμαρτωλῶν.

42 ἐγείρεσθε, ἄγωμεν·
ἰδοὺ ὁ παραδιδούς με ἤγγικεν.

43 Καὶ εὐθὺς ἔτι αὐτοῦ λαλοῦντος
παραγίνεται Ἰούδας, εἷς τῶν δώδεκα,
καὶ μετ' αὐτοῦ ὄχλος μετὰ μαχαιρῶν καὶ ξύλων
παρὰ τῶν ἀρχιερέων καὶ τῶν γραμματέων καὶ τῶν πρεσβυτέρων.

44 δεδώκει δὲ ὁ παραδιδοὺς αὐτὸν σύσσημον αὐτοῖς λέγων·
ὃν ἂν φιλήσω αὐτός ἐστιν·
κρατήσατε αὐτὸν καὶ ἀπάγετε ἀσφαλῶς.

45 καὶ ἐλθὼν εὐθὺς προσελθὼν αὐτῷ λέγει·
ῥαββί [ῥαββί],
καὶ κατεφίλησεν αὐτόν·

4

46 | οἱ δὲ ἐπέβαλον τὰς χεῖρας αὐτῷ
 | καὶ ἐκράτησαν αὐτόν.

47 | εἷς δέ τις τῶν παρεστηκότων σπασάμενος τὴν μάχαιραν
 | ἔπαισεν τὸν δοῦλον τοῦ ἀρχιερέως
 | καὶ ἀφεῖλεν αὐτοῦ τὸ ὠτίον.

48 | καὶ ἀποκριθεὶς ὁ Ἰησοῦς εἶπεν αὐτοῖς·

  ὡς ἐπὶ λῃστὴν ἐξήλθατε μετὰ μαχαιρῶν καὶ ξύλων
  συλλαβεῖν με·

49 | καθ᾽ ἡμέραν
  ἤμην πρὸς ὑμᾶς ἐν τῷ ἱερῷ διδάσκων,
  καὶ οὐκ ἐκρατήσατέ με.

 ἀλλ᾽ ἵνα πληρωθῶσιν αἱ γραφαί.

50 | καὶ ἀφέντες αὐτὸν ἔφυγον πάντες.

51 | Καὶ εἷς τις νεανίσκος συνηκολούθει αὐτῷ
 | περιβεβλημένος σινδόνα ἐπὶ γυμνοῦ,
 | καὶ κρατοῦσιν αὐτὸν οἱ νεανίσκοι·

52 | ὁ δὲ καταλιπὼν τὴν σινδόνα
 | γυμνὸς ἔφυγεν ἀπ᾽ αὐτῶν.

53 | Καὶ ἀπήγαγον τὸν Ἰησοῦν πρὸς τὸν ἀρχιερέα,
 | καὶ συνέρχονται αὐτῷ
  πάντες οἱ ἀρχιερεῖς
  καὶ οἱ πρεσβύτεροι
  καὶ οἱ γραμματεῖς.

54 | καὶ ὁ Πέτρος ἀπὸ μακρόθεν ἠκολούθησεν αὐτῷ
 | ἕως ἔσω εἰς τὴν αὐλὴν τοῦ ἀρχιερέως·

 | καὶ ἦν συνκαθήμενος μετὰ τῶν ὑπηρετῶν
 | καὶ θερμαινόμενος πρὸς τὸ φῶς.

14

55 | Οἱ δὲ ἀρχιερεῖς καὶ ὅλον τὸ συνέδριον
ἐζήτουν κατὰ τοῦ Ἰησοῦ μαρτυρίαν
εἰς τὸ θανατῶσαι αὐτόν,
καὶ οὐχ εὕρισκον·

56 | πολλοὶ γὰρ ἐψευδομαρτύρουν κατ' αὐτοῦ,
καὶ ἴσαι αἱ μαρτυρίαι οὐκ ἦσαν.

57 | καί τινες ἀναστάντες
ἐψευδομαρτύρουν κατ' αὐτοῦ λέγοντες

58 | ὅτι ἡμεῖς ἠκούσαμεν αὐτοῦ λέγοντος
ὅτι ἐγὼ καταλύσω τὸν ναὸν τοῦτον τὸν χειροποίητον,
καί·
διὰ τριῶν ἡμερῶν ἄλλον ἀχειροποίητον οἰκοδομήσω.

59 | καὶ οὐδὲ οὕτως ἴση ἦν ἡ μαρτυρία αὐτῶν.

60 | καὶ ἀναστὰς ὁ ἀρχιερεὺς εἰς μέσον
ἐπηρώτησεν τὸν Ἰησοῦν λέγων·
οὐκ ἀποκρίνῃ οὐδέν ;
τί οὗτοί σου καταμαρτυροῦσιν ;

61 | ὁ δὲ ἐσιώπα καὶ οὐκ ἀπεκρίνατο οὐδέν.

πάλιν ὁ ἀρχιερεὺς ἐπηρώτα αὐτόν
καὶ λέγει αὐτῷ·
σὺ εἶ ὁ Χριστὸς ὁ υἱὸς τοῦ εὐλογητοῦ ;

62 | ὁ δὲ Ἰησοῦς εἶπεν·

ἐγώ εἰμι·
καὶ ὄψεσθε τὸν υἱὸν τοῦ ἀνθρώπου
ἐκ δεξιῶν καθήμενον τῆς δυνάμεως
καὶ ἐρχόμενον μετὰ τῶν νεφελῶν τοῦ οὐρανοῦ.

63 | ὁ δὲ ἀρχιερεὺς διαρρήξας τοὺς χιτῶνας αὐτοῦ λέγει·
τί ἔτι χρείαν ἔχομεν μαρτύρων ;

4 64 | ἠκούσατε τῆς βλασφημίας·
τί ὑμῖν φαίνεται ;

| οἱ δὲ πάντες κατέκριναν αὐτὸν ἔνοχον εἶναι θανάτου.

65 | Καὶ ἤρξαντό τινες

ἐμπτύειν αὐτῷ
καὶ περικαλύπτειν αὐτοῦ τὸ πρόσωπον
καὶ κολαφίζειν αὐτόν
καὶ λέγειν αὐτῷ·
προφήτευσον.

| καὶ οἱ ὑπηρέται ῥαπίσμασιν αὐτὸν ἔλαβον.

66 | Καὶ ὄντος τοῦ Πέτρου κάτω ἐν τῇ αὐλῇ
ἔρχεται μία τῶν παιδισκῶν τοῦ ἀρχιερέως·

67 | καὶ ἰδοῦσα τὸν Πέτρον θερμαινόμενον
ἐμβλέψασα αὐτῷ λέγει·
καὶ σὺ μετὰ τοῦ Ναζαρηνοῦ ἦσθα τοῦ Ἰησοῦ.

68 | ὁ δὲ ἠρνήσατο λέγων·
οὔτε οἶδα οὔτε ἐπίσταμαι σὺ τί λέγεις.

| καὶ ἐξῆλθεν ἔξω εἰς τὸ προαύλιον,
καὶ ἀλέκτωρ ἐφώνησεν.

69 | καὶ ἡ παιδίσκη ἰδοῦσα αὐτόν
ἤρξατο πάλιν λέγειν τοῖς παρεστῶσιν
ὅτι οὗτος ἐξ αὐτῶν ἐστιν.

70 | ὁ δὲ πάλιν ἠρνεῖτο.

| καὶ μετὰ μικρὸν πάλιν οἱ παρεστῶτες ἔλεγον τῷ Πέτρῳ·
ἀληθῶς ἐξ αὐτῶν εἶ·
καὶ γὰρ Γαλιλαῖος εἶ.

71 | ὁ δὲ ἤρξατο ἀναθεματίζειν καὶ ὀμνύναι
ὅτι οὐκ οἶδα τὸν ἄνθρωπον τοῦτον ὃν λέγετε.

72 | καὶ εὐθὺς ἐκ δευτέρου ἀλέκτωρ ἐφώνησεν.

καὶ ἀνεμνήσθη ὁ Πέτρος τὸ ῥῆμα,
ὡς εἶπεν αὐτῷ ὁ Ἰησοῦς
ὅτι πρὶν ἀλέκτορα φωνῆσαι δὶς
τρίς με ἀπαρνήσῃ.

| καὶ ἐπιβαλὼν ἔκλαιεν.

15 1 | Καὶ εὐθὺς ἐπὶ τὸ πρωῒ συμβούλιον ποιήσαντες
οἱ ἀρχιερεῖς μετὰ τῶν πρεσβυτέρων καὶ γραμματέων,
καὶ ὅλον τὸ συνέδριον,
δήσαντες τὸν Ἰησοῦν ἀπήνεγκαν
καὶ παρέδωκαν Πιλάτῳ.

2 | καὶ ἐπηρώτησεν αὐτὸν ὁ Πιλᾶτος·
σὺ εἶ ὁ βασιλεὺς τῶν Ἰουδαίων ;

ὁ δὲ ἀποκριθεὶς αὐτῷ λέγει·
σὺ λέγεις.

3 | καὶ κατηγόρουν αὐτοῦ οἱ ἀρχιερεῖς πολλά.

4 | ὁ δὲ Πιλᾶτος πάλιν ἐπηρώτησεν αὐτὸν λέγων·
οὐκ ἀποκρίνῃ οὐδέν ;
ἴδε πόσα σου κατηγοροῦσιν.

5 | ὁ δὲ Ἰησοῦς οὐκέτι οὐδὲν ἀπεκρίθη,
ὥστε θαμάζειν τὸν Πιλᾶτον.

6 | Κατὰ δὲ ἑορτήν
ἀπέλυεν αὐτοῖς ἕνα δέσμιον ὅνπερ ᾐτοῦντο.

7 | ἦν δὲ ὁ λεγόμενος Βαραββᾶς
μετὰ τῶν συστασιωτῶν δεδεμένος,
οἵτινες ἐν τῇ στάσει φόνον πεποιήκεισαν.

15

8 | καὶ ἀναβοήσας ὁ ὄχλος ἤρξατο αἰτεῖσθαι
καθὼς ἀεὶ ἐποίει αὐτοῖς.

9 | ὁ δὲ Πιλᾶτος ἀπεκρίθη αὐτοῖς λέγων·
θέλετε ἀπολύσω ὑμῖν τὸν βασιλέα τῶν Ἰουδαίων ;
ἐγίνωσκεν γάρ
10 | ὅτι διὰ φθόνον παραδεδώκεισαν αὐτὸν οἱ ἀρχιερεῖς.

11 | οἱ δὲ ἀρχιερεῖς ἀνέσεισαν τὸν ὄχλον,
ἵνα μᾶλλον τὸν Βαραββᾶν ἀπολύσῃ αὐτοῖς.

12 | ὁ δὲ Πιλᾶτος πάλιν ἀποκριθεὶς ἔλεγεν αὐτοῖς·
τί οὖν ποιήσω
ὃν λέγετε τὸν βασιλέα τῶν Ἰουδαίων ;

13 | οἱ δὲ πάλιν ἔκραξαν·
σταύρωσον αὐτόν.

14 | ὁ δὲ Πιλᾶτος ἔλεγεν αὐτοῖς·
τί γὰρ ἐποίησεν κακόν ;

οἱ δὲ περισσῶς ἔκραξαν·
σταύρωσον αὐτόν.

15 | ὁ δὲ Πιλᾶτος βουλόμενος τῷ ὄχλῳ τὸ ἱκανὸν ποιῆσαι
ἀπέλυσεν αὐτοῖς τὸν Βαραββᾶν,
καὶ παρέδωκεν τὸν Ἰησοῦν φραγελλώσας, ἵνα σταυρωθῇ.

16 | Οἱ δὲ στρατιῶται ἀπήγαγον αὐτὸν ἔσω τῆς αὐλῆς,
ὅ ἐστιν πραιτώριον,
καὶ συνκαλοῦσιν ὅλην τὴν σπεῖραν.

17 | καὶ ἐνδιδύσκουσιν αὐτὸν πορφύραν
καὶ περιτιθέασιν αὐτῷ πλέξαντες ἀκάνθινον στέφανον.

18 | καὶ ἤρξαντο ἀσπάζεσθαι αὐτόν·
χαῖρε, βασιλεῦ τῶν Ἰουδαίων·

19 | καὶ ἔτυπτον αὐτοῦ τὴν κεφαλὴν καλάμῳ
καὶ ἐνέπτυον αὐτῷ,
καὶ τιθέντες τὰ γόνατα προσεκύνουν αὐτῷ.

15　20　καὶ ὅτε ἐνέπαιξαν αὐτῷ,
ἐξέδυσαν αὐτὸν τὴν πορφύραν
καὶ ἐνέδυσαν αὐτὸν τὰ ἱμάτια τὰ ἴδια.

Καὶ ἐξάγουσιν αὐτόν,
ἵνα σταυρώσωσιν αὐτόν.

21　καὶ ἀγγαρεύουσιν παράγοντά τινα Σίμωνα Κυρηναῖον
ἐρχόμενον ἀπ' ἀγροῦ,
τὸν πατέρα Ἀλεξάνδρου καὶ Ῥούφου,
ἵνα ἄρῃ τὸν σταυρὸν αὐτοῦ.

22　καὶ φέρουσιν αὐτὸν ἐπὶ τὸν Γολγοθᾶν τόπον,
ὅ ἐστιν μεθερμηνευόμενος κρανίου τόπος.

23　καὶ ἐδίδουν αὐτῷ ἐσμυρνισμένον οἶνον·
ὁ δὲ οὐκ ἔλαβεν.

24　καὶ σταυροῦσιν αὐτόν·
καὶ διαμερίζονται τὰ ἱμάτια αὐτοῦ,
βάλλοντες κλῆρον ἐπ' αὐτὰ τίς τί ἄρῃ.

25　ἦν δὲ ὥρα τρίτη καὶ ἐσταύρωσαν αὐτόν.

26　καὶ ἦν ἡ ἐπιγραφὴ τῆς αἰτίας αὐτοῦ ἐπιγεγραμμένη·
ὁ βασιλεὺς τῶν Ἰουδαίων.

27　Καὶ σὺν αὐτῷ σταυροῦσιν δύο λῃστάς,
ἕνα ἐκ δεξιῶν
καὶ ἕνα ἐξ εὐωνύμων αὐτοῦ.

28　[καὶ ἐπληρώθη ἡ γραφὴ ἡ λέγουσα·
καὶ μετὰ ἀνόμων ἐλογίσθη.]

29　Καὶ οἱ παραπορευόμενοι ἐβλασφήμουν αὐτόν
κινοῦντες τὰς κεφαλὰς αὐτῶν καὶ λέγοντες·
οὐὰ ὁ καταλύων τὸν ναόν
καὶ οἰκοδομῶν ἐν τρισὶν ἡμέραις,
30　　σῶσον σεαυτὸν καταβὰς ἀπὸ τοῦ σταυροῦ.

15

31 | ὁμοίως καὶ οἱ ἀρχιερεῖς
ἐμπαίζοντες πρὸς ἀλλήλους μετὰ τῶν γραμματέων
ἔλεγον·

ἄλλους ἔσωσεν,
ἑαυτὸν οὐ δύναται σῶσαι.

32 | ὁ Χριστὸς ὁ βασιλεὺς Ἰσραήλ
καταβάτω νῦν ἀπὸ τοῦ σταυροῦ,
ἵνα ἴδωμεν
καὶ πιστεύσωμεν.

καὶ οἱ συνεσταυρωμένοι σὺν αὐτῷ
ὠνείδιζον αὐτόν.

33 | Καὶ γενομένης ὥρας ἕκτης
σκότος ἐγένετο ἐφ᾽ ὅλην τὴν γῆν,   8/11 bega from sky
ἕως ὥρας ἐνάτης.

34 | καὶ τῇ ὥρᾳ τῇ ἐνάτῃ ἐβόησεν ὁ Ἰησοῦς φωνῇ μεγάλῃ·

ἐλωΐ, ἐλωΐ,
λιμὰ σαβαχθανεί;   Ps 21/2

ὅ ἐστιν μεθερμηνευόμενον·
ὁ θεός μου, ὁ θεός μου,
εἰς τί ἐγκατέλιπές με;

35 | καί τινες τῶν παρεστηκότων ἀκούσαντες ἔλεγον·
ἴδε Ἡλίαν φωνεῖ.

36 | δραμὼν δέ τις καὶ γεμίσας σπόγγον ὄξους
περιθεὶς καλάμῳ ἐπότιζεν αὐτόν, λέγων·
ἄφετε,
ἴδωμεν, εἰ ἔρχεται Ἡλίας καθελεῖν αὐτόν.

37 | ὁ δὲ Ἰησοῦς ἀφεὶς φωνὴν μεγάλην
ἐξέπνευσεν.

15

38 | Καὶ τὸ καταπέτασμα τοῦ ναοῦ ἐσχίσθη εἰς δύο
ἀπ' ἄνωθεν ἕως κάτω.

39 | Ἰδὼν δὲ ὁ κεντυρίων ὁ παρεστηκὼς ἐξ ἐναντίας αὐτοῦ
ὅτι οὕτως ἐξέπνευσεν,
εἶπεν·
ἀληθῶς οὗτος ὁ ἄνθρωπος υἱὸς θεοῦ ἦν.

40 | Ἦσαν δὲ καὶ γυναῖκες ἀπὸ μακρόθεν θεωροῦσαι,

ἐν αἷς καὶ Μαρία ἡ Μαγδαληνή
καὶ Μαρία ἡ Ἰακώβου τοῦ μικροῦ καὶ Ἰωσῆτος μήτηρ
καὶ Σαλώμη,

41 | αἳ ὅτε ἦν ἐν τῇ Γαλιλαίᾳ
ἠκολούθουν αὐτῷ καὶ διηκόνουν αὐτῷ,

καὶ ἄλλαι πολλαί
αἱ συναναβᾶσαι αὐτῷ εἰς Ἱεροσόλυμα.

42 | Καὶ ἤδη ὀψίας γενομένης,
ἐπεὶ ἦν παρασκευή, ὅ ἐστιν προσάββατον,
43 | ἐλθὼν Ἰωσήφ
ὁ ἀπὸ Ἀριμαθαίας, εὐσχήμων βουλευτής,
ὃς καὶ αὐτὸς ἦν προσδεχόμενος τὴν βασιλείαν τοῦ θεοῦ,
τολμήσας εἰσῆλθεν πρὸς τὸν Πιλᾶτον
καὶ ᾐτήσατο τὸ σῶμα τοῦ Ἰησοῦ.

44 | ὁ δὲ Πιλᾶτος ἐθαύμασεν, εἰ ἤδη τέθνηκεν·

καὶ προσκαλεσάμενος τὸν κεντυρίωνα
ἐπερώτησεν αὐτόν, εἰ πάλαι ἀπέθανεν·

45 | καὶ γνοὺς ἀπὸ τοῦ κεντυρίωνος
ἐδωρήσατο τὸ σῶμα τῷ Ἰωσήφ.

46 | καὶ ἀγοράσας σινδόνα
καθελὼν αὐτόν

ἐνείλησεν τῇ σινδόνι
καὶ κατέθηκεν αὐτὸν ἐν μνημείῳ
ὃ ἦν λελατομημένον ἐκ πέτρας,
καὶ προσεκύλισεν λίθον ἐπὶ τὴν θύραν τοῦ μνημείου.

47 | ἡ δὲ Μαρία ἡ Μαγδαληνὴ καὶ Μαρία ἡ Ἰωσῆτος
ἐθεώρουν ποῦ τέθειται.

16 1 | Καὶ διαγενομένου τοῦ σαββάτου
Μαρία ἡ Μαγδαληνὴ καὶ Μαρία ἡ τοῦ Ἰακώβου καὶ Σαλώμη
ἠγόρασαν ἀρώματα,
ἵνα ἐλθοῦσαι ἀλείψωσιν αὐτόν.

2 | καὶ λίαν πρωῒ τῇ μιᾷ τῶν σαββάτων
ἔρχονται ἐπὶ τὸ μνημεῖον,
ἀνατείλαντος τοῦ ἡλίου.

3 | καὶ ἔλεγον πρὸς ἑαυτάς·
τίς ἀποκυλίσει ἡμῖν τὸν λίθον
ἐκ τῆς θύρας τοῦ μνημείου ;

4 | καὶ ἀναβλέψασαι θεωροῦσιν
ὅτι ἀποκεκύλισται ὁ λίθος·
ἦν γὰρ μέγας σφόδρα.

5 | καὶ εἰσελθοῦσαι εἰς τὸ μνημεῖον
εἶδον νεανίσκον
καθήμενον ἐν τοῖς δεξιοῖς
περιβεβλημένον στολὴν λευκήν,
καὶ ἐξεθαμβήθησαν.

6 | ὁ δὲ λέγει αὐταῖς·

μὴ ἐκθαμβεῖσθε·
Ἰησοῦν ζητεῖτε,
τὸν Ναζαρηνόν,
τὸν ἐσταυρωμένον·

16

ἠγέρθη, οὐκ ἔστιν ὧδε·
ἴδε ὁ τόπος ὅπου ἔθηκαν αὐτόν.

7 ἀλλὰ ὑπάγετε,
εἴπατε τοῖς μαθηταῖς αὐτοῦ καὶ τῷ Πέτρῳ
ὅτι προάγει ὑμᾶς εἰς τὴν Γαλιλαίαν·
ἐκεῖ αὐτὸν ὄψεσθε, καθὼς εἶπεν ὑμῖν.

8 καὶ ἐξελθοῦσαι ἔφυγον ἀπὸ τοῦ μνημείου,
εἶχεν γὰρ αὐτὰς τρόμος καὶ ἔκστασις·

καὶ οὐδενὶ οὐδὲν εἶπον·
ἐφοβοῦντο γάρ.

9 Ἀναστὰς δὲ πρωῒ πρώτῃ σαββάτου
ἐφάνη πρῶτον Μαρίᾳ τῇ Μαγδαληνῇ,
παρ' ἧς ἐκβεβλήκει ἑπτὰ δαιμόνια.

10 ἐκείνη πορευθεῖσα ἀπήγγειλεν τοῖς μετ' αὐτοῦ γενομένοις
πενθοῦσι καὶ κλαίουσιν.

11 κἀκεῖνοι ἀκούσαντες ὅτι ζῇ καὶ ἐθεάθη ὑπ' αὐτῆς
ἠπίστησαν.

12 Μετὰ δὲ ταῦτα δυσὶν ἐξ αὐτῶν περιπατοῦσιν
ἐφανερώθη ἐν ἑτέρᾳ μορφῇ
πορευομένοις εἰς ἀγρόν.

13 κἀκεῖνοι ἀπελθόντες ἀπήγγειλαν τοῖς λοιποῖς·
οὐδὲ ἐκείνοις ἐπίστευσαν.

14 Ὕστερον ἀνακειμένοις αὐτοῖς τοῖς ἕνδεκα ἐφανερώθη,
καὶ ὠνείδισεν τὴν ἀπιστίαν αὐτῶν καὶ σκληροκαρδίαν,
ὅτι τοῖς θεασαμένοις αὐτὸν ἐγηγερμένον
οὐκ ἐπίστευσαν.

16

15 | καὶ εἶπεν αὐτοῖς

Πορευθέντες εἰς τὸν κόσμον ἅπαντα
κηρύξατε τὸ εὐαγγέλιον πάσῃ τῇ κτίσει.

16 | ὁ πιστεύσας καὶ βαπτισθεὶς σωθήσεται,
ὁ δὲ ἀπιστήσας κατακριθήσεται.

17 | σημεῖα δὲ τοῖς πιστεύσασιν ταῦτα παρακολουθήσει·
ἐν τῷ ὀνόματί μου

δαιμόνια ἐκβαλοῦσιν,
γλώσσαις λαλήλουσιν καιναῖς,

18 | ὄφεις ἀροῦσιν,
κἂν θανάσιμόν τι πίωσιν οὐ μὴ αὐτοὺς βλάψῃ,

ἐπὶ ἀρρώστους χεῖρας ἐπιθήσουσιν
καὶ καλῶς ἕξουσιν.

19 | Ὁ μὲν οὖν Κύριος Ἰησοῦς μετὰ τὸ λαλῆσαι αὐτοῖς
ἀνελήφθη εἰς τὸν οὐρανόν
καὶ ἐκάθισεν ἐκ δεξιῶν τοῦ θεοῦ.

20 | ἐκεῖνοι δὲ ἐξελθόντες ἐκήρυξαν πανταχοῦ,
τοῦ Κυρίου συνεργοῦντος
καὶ τὸν λόγον βεβαιοῦντος
διὰ τῶν ἐπακολουθούντων σημείων.

PART TWO

COLOMETRY AND ANNOTATIONS

I. COLOMETRY

A. Cola and Commata: Thought-Units and Sense-Lines
B. The Second Gospel in Thought-Units and Sense-Lines

When the reading of an author has begun, the teacher should allow no important point to pass unnoticed either as regards the resourcefulness or the style shown in the treatment of the subject.

—Quintilian

Le livre divin de l'Évangile offre une matière si riche qu'aucun travail humain ne saurait se flatter d'en embrasser tous les aspects.

—Paul Joüon

A. Cola and Commata: Thought-Units and Sense-Lines

> All the best scholars are convinced that the study of structure is of the utmost value, not merely for charming the ear, but for stirring the soul. For in the first place, nothing can penetrate to the emotions that stumbles at the portals of the ear, and secondly, man is naturally attracted by harmonious sounds.—Quintilian, IX, iv, 10. Tr. by H. E. Butler (Loeb L.)

1. *St. Jerome's Interpretatio Nova:*[1] When St. Jerome planned his Latin rendering of the Bible—the *Vulgate,* as we call it—and cast about for an appropriate medium of presentation, he chose colometry or colon-writing as the best means to that end. He tells us that his choice was determined by the fact that the teachers of Greek and Latin literature at his time were accustomed "to write Demosthenes and Tullius *per cola et commata.*" In adopting the practice of his day and colometrizing his rendering of the Bible, he wished to confer on his readers the same benefits which, he conceived, the teachers of profane literature were conferring on their pupils by the use of colometrized texts. St. Jerome was aware that colometry does not turn prose into poetry, but, since it invests prose with the semblance of verse, he felt that this very fact must be of great assistance in the public reading of the Word of God. It is easy to see how a duly colometrized text of the Bible enables even an otherwise not very skilful reader to express at least the sense of the sacred writer. It is of the nature of colometry that it presents a text, not *en bloc,* but broken up into short clauses (*membra* or *cola*) or even smaller divisions (*incisa* or *commata*), each

---

[1] For an account of "St. Jerome's Life and Work" and "The Vulgate in the Church," see Pope, *Aids,* I, 209–238; Dowd, *Gospel Guide,* 49 ff.; Merk, *Compendium, passim;* esp. 87 ff.; *The Catholic Encyclopedia,* XV, 515; VIII, 431; José de Siguenza, *The Life of St. Jerome,* London, 1907; Kaulen, *Bibl. Vulg.,* "Einleitung," 1 ff.; Pope, *Cath. Church and Bible,* Ch. IV, 46–50; Rönsch, *Itala und Vulgata;* Schaefer-Meinertz, *Einleitung,* pp. 53–63; Vaccari, *Alle origini della Volgata,* Rome, 1916.

91

of which contains no more matter than is enough to make sense.[2] In delivering a colometrized passage, all a reader has to do is to pronounce at one breath the words occurring in each colon or comma and make a slight pause at the end of each division. Thus words put together by the writer in order to make sense are kept together by the reader, and the writer's meaning is safely conveyed to the audience. St. Jerome chose colometry *utilitati legentium providentes*, or, in the blunt phrase of Cassiodorus, *propter simplicitatem fratrum*. In the preface to his edition of the prophet Isaias St. Jerome says:[3]

Nemo, cum prophetas versibus viderit esse descriptos, metro eos existimet apud Hebraeos ligari, et aliquid simile habere de Psalmis et operibus Salomonis: sed quod in Demosthene et Tullio *solet fieri*, ut per cola scribantur et commata, qui utique prosa et non versibus scripserunt, nos quoque utilitati legentium providentes, interpretationem novam *novo scribendi genere* distinximus.

In the centuries that gave birth to the New Testament, and long after, even ordinary audiences were alive to the charms of appropriate delivery, and insisted on harmony and finish both of composition and of presentation.[4] So extravagant was the cultivation of form that to this day the term *rhetoric* generally connotes affectation in the use of language. It is well to bear this fact in mind when we deal with the New Testament. The writers of the New Testament were far from

---

[2] *Colometry* (originally the measuring of a Ms. by the number of its cola or lines) and *colon-writing* or *colometrization* are often used interchangeably. Harris, *Stichometry*, 22; also *AJPh.*, IV, 151. For the use of colometry in the early centuries, see Merk, *l.c.*, 61; Schütz, *Bedeutung, passim;* Norden, *ATh.*, 364 ff.; Kleist, *Memoirs,* Ch. IV. The editors of the new Benedictine edition of St. Jerome's *Vulgate* accept Cassiodorus's statement that St. Jerome colometrized his entire version. *Biblia Sacra*, I, "Prolegomena," xliv; Zehetmeier, "Die Periodenlehre des Aristoteles" (*Philologus*, 85; pp. 192, 255, 414); Fraenkel, *Kolon und Satz;* Steinmayr, *Periode und Rhythmus der gr. und lat. Kunstsprache,* Halle, 1928; Schütz, *Parallele Bau,* Göttingen, 1920; Norden, *Antike Kunstprosa, passim;* Kaibel, *Stil und Text der* Πολιτεία 'Αθηναίων *des Aristoteles* (very practical), pp. 64 ff., 81 ff.; Wordsworth-White, *Novum Testamentum,* "De colis et commatibus codicis Amiatini," 733 ff.

[3] *Biblia Sacra*, I, "Prolegomena." *Distinguere* is t.t. for "punctuate." Quintilian XI, iii, 39: *virtus distinguendi*="correctness of punctuation." It is not quite clear, in what sense St. Jerome's *scribendi genus* was *novum*. Thompson, *Introduction,* 67 ff. For ancient methods of punctuation, see Harper's *Dict. of Class. Lit. and Ant.*, 1156; Whibley, *Companion*, 698; Merk, *Compendium*, 61, 2. Flock, *passim;* Kühner-Blass, I, 92, 93, "Lesezeichen." Wordsworth-White, *Novum Testamentum . . . sec. edit. Sancti Hieronymi* (see esp. *Praefatio* and *Epilogus*).

[4] Moore, *Orations*, xxi. Norden, *AK.*, "Einleitung." For Cicero's views on the validity of popular judgment in questions of style, see D'Alton, *Lit. Th.*, 234 ff., 385. For the effect of oratorical virtuosity on ordinary audiences, see Philostratus and Eunapius, *Lives of the Sophists, passim;* D'Alton, *l.c.*, 103.

consciously aiming at artistic effect or great rhetorical display; but it
is also evident that they were at pains, as indeed any intelligent person
would be, to facilitate, and even make agreeable, the public recita-
tion of their writings, and that in this effort they were supported by
the general view that *cola* and *commata*, in one form or another, were
indispensable elements of good writing. St. Jerome was convinced
that, in presenting his Latin rendering in that rhythmical arrangement
which we associate with the term *colometry*, he was doing no violence
to the Greek originals. Colometrization is not a thing foisted upon the
New Testament, but merely the outward symbol of an inner structure
that runs more or less through all ancient composition. We moderns
write ancient texts colometrically because the ancient authors composed them colometrically. It would seem that for St. Jerome this
use of "prose-verse" in the rendering of at least a portion of the Bible
was a novel experiment (*novo scribendi genere*). For us it is a return,
we are happy to think, to an old and well-tried tradition of the early
Church.

2. *Demetrius's Theory of Sentence Structure.* St. Jerome's expression
per cola et commata brings us face to face with the ancient theories of
style. We have an elaborate and authoritative exposition in Aristotle's
Rhetoric;[5] but for the modern beginner in New Testament colometry
it is a more practical procedure to acquaint himself, first of all, with
some later theory of style, such, for example, as that of *Demetrius*,
whose treatise *On Style* was not only more or less contemporaneous
with the New Testament, but also presents the essentials of good writing in a much less rigid form than does Aristotle.

According to Demetrius, artistic prose, by which he means a prose
not altogether content with the careless, meandering flow of unpre-
tentious speech, is differentiated from non-artistic by the use of *cola*
(κῶλα, pl. of κῶλον, "branch, limb, part"). The chief function of a colon,
in this theory, is to mark the conclusion of a thought *within* the sentence; for, although there are two kinds of colon, and a colon is occasionally the same as a *complete* sentence, yet generally a colon is only
an integral part of a sentence, much as an arm is a limb or integral
part of the human body. On the whole, the ancients loved to present
their thoughts not in the straightforward diction resulting from a mere

---

[5] Lane Cooper, *The Rhetoric of Aristotle;* Appleton, 1932. J. H. Freese, *Aristotle,
The "Art" of Rhetoric;* Loeb L. 1926. W. Rhys Roberts, *Demetrius On Style;* Cam-
bridge, 1902; see Sections 1–35. Zehetmeier, *l.c*; see footnote 2.

accumulation of words, but as it were piecemeal and by a sort of interlocking of clauses or phrases, in such a way that the complete thought to be expressed was held in suspense till the end of the whole sentence. At the beginning of Xenophon's *Anabasis*, Demetrius tells us, the words "Darius and Parysatis" down to "the younger Cyrus" are a fully completed sentence, consisting of two cola: yet each of these two parts conveys a meaning which is in a measure complete. The thought that sons were born to Darius and Parysatis has a certain completeness; so has the second colon: "The elder was Artaxerxes, the younger, Cyrus." Consequently, a colon, "as I maintain (ὥς φημι), comprises a thought that is either a complete sentence or forms an integral part of one."[6] Xenophon's sentence is not a mere conglomeration of words, but rather a (more or less compact) grouping of several integral phrases which by their arrangement give artistic expression to a completely rounded-out thought.

1. Δαρείου καὶ Παρυσάτιδος γίγνονται παῖδες δύο,
2. πρεσβύτερος μὲν Ἀρταξέρξης, νεώτερος δὲ Κῦρος.

Cola should not be too long; otherwise "the composition becomes unwieldy and hard to follow." Long cola are appropriate in elevated passages; short ones are in place when the subject is small. But even elevated passages may derive vigor and intensity from the use of short cola. Phrases of smaller compass are termed commata (κόμματα, pl. of κόμμα, "a piece cut off; chip"). A comma is defined as a phrase "less than a colon," as, for example, the saying "Know thyself." Later rhetoricians say that a comma is an expression of less than eight syllables, a colon, one of more than eight, but less than seventeen, which is the ordinary length of a hexameter.[7] A jerky, commatic style may suit persons under powerful emotion.[8]

A certain combination of two or more cola, with or without commata, *which suspends the thought till the end* of the complete sentence, is called a period. The period is a system (σύστημα) of cola (and commata) arranged so dexterously as to fit exactly the thought to be expressed. Ancient writers on the whole expressed themselves, preferably, in large masses of thought made up of smaller entities or logical elements, and this no doubt from a certain innate delight in artistic

---

[6] Quintilian IX, iv, 122: "in my opinion." Compare, for instance, the grouping of phrases or cola in Mk. 5, 25–28, or in 5, 30.

[7] L. Laurand, *Discours de Cicéron*, II, pp. 138 ff.

[8] See, for example, our Lord's utterances in Mk. 14, 30 and 14, 41.

structure.[9] It is therefore essential to a period to have a certain round-ing-out at the close (καμπήν τινα καὶ συστροφήν) in such a way that the thought (if not the syntax) is sustained till the end. The following is an example:

1. Chiefly because I thought the abrogation of the law was to the interest of the State,
2. but also for the sake of Chabrias's boy,
3. I have agreed to plead my client's case.

This is a period of three cola, says Demetrius. Aristotle's definition[10] of the period as "a form of expression that has a beginning and an end" is, according to Demetrius, appropriate, for the very word *period* (περί-οδος) implies that "there has been a beginning at one point and there will be an ending at another, and that we are hastening towards a definite goal as runners do after leaving the starting-place." The name *period* conveys the image of a path traversed in a circle. Destroy the circular form, and the period is gone, although the subject-matter remains the same:

I will support the complainants.
For Chabrias's boy is dear to me;
and much more so is the State, whose cause it is right for me to plead.

As to *style in general*, there are two kinds, the compacted, which consists of periods, as explained above, and the disconnected, so called because the cola are but loosely united. The following is an instance of the loose or running style: "Hecataeus thus relates. I write these things as they seem to me to be true. For the tales told by the Greeks are, as it appears to me, many and absurd." Here the cola (see below under 3, *a*) seem thrown upon one another in a heap without the union of propping, and without the mutual support which we find in periods. The cola in the periodic style may be compared to stones which support and hold together a vaulted roof. Every colon, however, which

---

[9] Quintilian IX, iv, 1–20. Yet Kaibel, *Stil und Text*, p. 64, rightly points out that the general demand for clear and strictly logical exposition had more to do with the tendency to periodic structure than mere fondness for artistic grouping: "Die Kunst der Periodisierung, gleichzeitig mit der Kunst zu denken und die Gedanken in Worte zu fassen ausgebildet, hat ihre eigentliche Quelle nicht sowol im Verlangen nach schöner Form wie im Bedürfnis nach Klarheit und Verständlichkeit."

[10] For a searching inquiry into Aristotle's theory, see Zehetmeier, "Die Perioden-lehre des Aristoteles," *Philologus*, 85, pp. 192, 255, 414. For Cicero's various ways of rendering the Greek term περίοδος, see *Festschrift Poland*, "Philol. Wochen-schrift," 25. Aug. 1932; (W. Stegemann).

possesses the requisite length and is rounded out at the end may, as also Aristotle admits, form a period of a single colon (μονόκωλον).

Compare the rambling style of Xenophon (*Anab.* 1, 3, 1) with the compact style of Thucydides (1, 26, 3):

Ἐνταῦθα ἔμεινεν ὁ Κῦρος καὶ ἡ στρατιὰ ἡμέρας εἴκοσιν·
οἱ γὰρ στρατιῶται οὐκ ἔφασαν ἰέναι τοῦ πρόσω·
ὑπώπτευον γὰρ ἤδη ἐπὶ βασιλέα ἰέναι·
μισθωθῆναι δὲ οὐκ ἐπὶ τούτῳ ἔφασαν.
πρῶτος δὲ Κλέαρχος τοὺς στρατιώτας ἐβιάζετο ἰέναι.

Πλεύσαντες εὐθὺς πέντε καὶ εἴκοσι ναυσί
καὶ ὕστερον ἑτέρῳ στόλῳ
τούς τε φεύγοντας ἐκέλευον δέχεσθαι αὐτούς,
τούς τε φρουροὺς οὓς Κορίνθιοι ἔπεμψαν
καὶ τοὺς οἰκήτορας ἀποπέμπειν.

The former passage leisurely adds item to item; in the second the thought is not complete until the last word is reached. Note the clamping of the clauses by the use of an initial participle and of such particles as τὲ and καί.

There are three varieties of period, the historical, the rhetorical, and the conversational. Readers of the second Gospel should be interested in Demetrius's description of the least ambitious of these, the conversational: the period of dialogue or conversation is one which remains loose or lax; it scarcely betrays the fact that it is a period (cf. Plato *Rep.* 1, 1):

Κατέβην χθὲς εἰς Πειραιᾶ μετὰ Γλαύκωνος τοῦ Ἀρίστωνος
προσευξόμενός τε τῇ θεῷ
καὶ ἅμα τὴν ἑορτὴν βουλόμενος θεάσασθαι
τίνα τρόπον ποιήσουσιν
ἅτε νῦν πρῶτον ἄγοντες.

St. Mark's sentences illustrate Demetrius's rule (*On Style* 19) that narrative periods should be "neither too carefully rounded (περιηγμένη), nor yet too relaxed, but between the two." An observation of Quintilian's is pat to our purpose: the historical style "requires continuity of motion," i.e., a fluent, forward movement which adds item to item without much attention to rhythmical combination. "All its cola are linked together and, because it glides on fluently (*lubrica est*), it flows this way and that—just like men who link hands to steady their movements, and lend each other support" (IX, iv, 129). A glance at the

Greek text above will help the reader to understand Quintilian's meta-phor: Marcan diction is *lubrica;* it follows no fixed rule; its cola are not strongly compacted; it glides on as the whim may suggest or the subject may require. Among the Evangelists St. Mark's diction is the λόγος διαλελυμένος *par excellence.*

3. *Ancient Cola and Commata: Modern Thought-Units and Sense-Lines.* Since the title-page of this volume promises a presentation of the Greek of the second Gospel, not *per cola et commata* or in a strictly colometrized form, but in thought-units and sense-lines, it may be asked what relation these elements of sentence structure bear to the ancient cola and commata. Thought-units and sense-lines as here understood are the lineal descendants of colon, comma, and period. A group of words which an ancient theorist would regard as a "sentence" is here called a thought-unit; a group which he would consider a colon or comma is here called sense-line. This terminology is true only in a large way; to justify it, we should keep two or three things in mind.

a) Whatever definition of colon or comma we adopt—for the ancient rhetoricians were by no means agreed in defining the terms—one characteristic stands out clearly: colon and comma are such parts of a sentence as, when taken by themselves, are able to make sense. A definition of colon frequently met with in ancient writers (as Aristides and Cornutus) is the following: στίχος διάνοιαν ἀπαρτίζουσα: "A stichos (or line) that expresses a (more or less) complete thought." In the passage quoted above, Demetrius tells us that each of the two cola in Xenophon's opening sentence conveys, within its own limits, a meaning which is in a measure complete. This description of colon (and the same applies to comma as a diminutive colon) runs through all the rhetorical literature of the Greeks. And if it is not perhaps directly deducible from Aristotle's description of a period, "The end of the period must coincide with the sense" (δεῖ τὴν περίοδον καὶ τῇ διανοίᾳ τετελειῶσθαι),[11] the *sense-making* quality of a colon (for he does not mention the comma) is made evident by the many examples which he gives in the same chapter.

I have said above that for the aims of the beginner in New Testament Greek Demetrius's definition of a period is more relevant and of more practical value than that of Aristotle. Demetrius was con-

---

[11] *Rhetoric*, III, ix, 4. See *Rhetores Graeci;* ed. by L. Spengel; 3 vols; Teubner 1853-1856; *passim.*

temporary with the writers of the New Testament, and by his time
the old Aristotelian insistence on *rhythm* (ῥυθμός, Aristotle; *numerus*,
Cicero) as the dominating characteristic of the period had largely
yielded to more practical considerations. Henceforth, while rhythm
was still tolerated, the element of *thought* became more conspicuous in
the framing of a period. Aristotle's period has been cleverly described
as "a sentence movement forecast and fulfilled by the speaker, divined
and held by the hearer, as a definite rhythmical and logical unit. Its
characteristic is that conclusiveness which satisfies at once ear and
mind. In sound and syntax it is the opposite of formless aggregation,
of the addition of clause to clause as by afterthoughts."[12] In this more
rigorous acceptation, the "beginning" and the "end" of a period correspond almost like prelude and main theme in a musical composition.
In other respects, however, even a Marcan sentence is a logical unit,
whether periodical or not, because it holds one complete *thought;* it
is a phonetic unit, because it is utterable at one breath. It is, occasionally, an emotional unit, because, as St. Augustine[13] intimates, emotion has power to determine of what kind or how many shall be the
cola or commata of a period. It may be added that Aristotle's "simple
period," consisting of but one lengthy and rounded-out colon, occurs
occasionally, in the form explained by Demetrius, in the second Gospel.

b) A presentation of a Greek or Latin text in *thought*-units and
sense-lines answers, therefore, the same purpose as the ancient colometric style of *writing:* it is the outward expression of a certain inner
structure which the ancients associated with colometry or the colometric form of *composition*. So far as we know, Aristotle was the first
to mention the colon as a part of a sentence built on artistic principles.
But, if we would understand New Testament "colometry," it is well
to bear in mind that in course of time the terms *colon* and *comma*[14]
came to be applied also to parts of non-periodic sentences, and it is in
this wider acceptation, supported by ancient rhetoricians, that we can
speak of *colon* and *comma* in analyzing the non-artistic diction of the
New Testament. Here the terms often mean no more than thought-
units and lines of *sense*.

---

[12] C. S. Baldwin, *Ancient Rhetoric and Poetic*, 29. (Macmillan, 1924.)

[13] *De Doctrina Christiana Liber IV*, vii, 11 ff. Kleist, *Classical Bulletin;* Jan. 1932.

[14] A satisfactory translation of *colon* and *comma* is wanting. "Since the distinction which they conveyed to the ancients is no longer regarded, they have no equivalent in modern English. The terms *clauses, phrases, commas, pauses, members, sections,* express in some part the proper meaning, but they also differ, each one, in
some fundamental point." Sr. Sullivan, *S. Aurelii Augustini De Doctrina Christiana
Liber Quartus*, p. 68; Cath. U. Patristic Studies.

c) St. Mark's style in particular is, on the whole, of the running or loose or disconnected type. To us moderns it is perhaps best brought home by saying that it abounds in paratactic structures, though not in the manner of Sir John Mandeville,[15]

And in that country is an old castle that stands upon a rock, the which is cleped the Castle of Sparrowhawk, that is beyond the city of Layas, beside the town of Pharsipee, that belongeth to the lordship of Cruk, that is a rich Lord, and a perch fair and right well made, and a fair lady of Fayrye that keepeth it.

nor like early Latin which was for the most part loose and running. An Ennian passage for example, "rattles to pieces like a mosaic set in clay. It is in the main a string of coördinate clauses hung on *que*, *atque, ibi, tum*, and without any appreciation of the differences which we attempt to convey by commas, semicolons, and full stops."[15]

Practically, then, it makes little difference whether we classify St. Mark's prose as disconnected diction, or as periodic diction of the conversational style, in the sense intended by Demetrius. His straggling composition resembles that *oratio* which Cicero describes in the words: *quae fluit et vagatur:*[16] like a river that overflows its banks, it runs on at large and without much inner need for limits. It is the direct antithesis to that periodic diction which "has *within itself* a beginning and an end" (λέξις ἔχουσα ἀρχὴν καὶ τελευτὴν αὐτὴ καθ' αὑτήν), a diction whose very thought and rhythm *require* structure and compactness.

However much St. Mark's Gospel may fail to conform to any ancient theory of artistic prose, which required the use of periods or larger structures diversified by a clever sprinkling of colon and comma strictly so-called, it yet bears the hall-marks of ancient composition in that it conveys its message by a simple, yet clearly visible, lattice of *thought*-units and *sense*-lines. The total impression of its sentence structure is ancient, and not modern. It is in the light, and by the aid, of these structural elements that we should try to read and understand the second Gospel.

B. *The Second Gospel in Thought-Units and Sense-Lines*

> He who has a taste for the unaffected, artless talk of a man of the people will read St. Mark with great delight.—H. J. Cladder.

---

[15] Tenney Frank, *Life and Literature in the Roman Republic;* U. of California. 133, 139. Ancient and modern periods are contrasted by Moore, *l.c.*, Introd.,xxii ff.
[16] *De Oratore*, III, 190.

1. The nature of colometry is one of the knottiest problems antiquity has bequeathed to modern classical scholarship. At the present stage of inquiry, for example, modern scholars are not able to decide whether a given colometrization of some larger portion of the New Testament, no matter how conscientiously it may have been made, would exactly correspond with a colometrized autograph. The explanations which the old rhetoricians give of colon, comma, and period, are at times "hazy and contradictory."[17] Some grammarians speak with undisguised hesitation, as when Quintilian[18] writes: "A comma, *in my opinion*, may be defined. . . ." Demetrius has told us above what *in his judgment* (ὥs φημι) should be properly styled a colon. The five great authorities on colometry are Aristotle, Cicero, Demetrius, Quintilian, and St. Augustine, and it is not surprising that within this span of seven or eight centuries the theory of style should have undergone changes. As a matter of fact, Demetrius differs from Aristotle in two or three essential points; Cicero, in turn, differs from Aristotle and Demetrius, and Quintilian assures us that he has reason to differ from his great predecessors.[19] Evidently there was no complete agreement among the theorists regarding certain minutiae of sentence structure. This is so true that it is a misnomer to speak of "*the* ancient theory of style" without further qualification.

In view of all this uncertainty, if we wish to read the second Gospel in *thought*-units and *sense*-lines, how are we going to determine what constitutes a thought, how many words are needed to make a thought-unit, how many are required to make "sense"? In particular, where does a *thought* begin and end?

Modern scholars have pointed out that any attempt at recognizing the so-called clausulae or rhythmical cadences *inside* a period must depend on subjective criteria and, consequently, on possible error, for the reason that "infallible criteria for recognizing cola and commata

---

[17] "Verschwommen und widerspruchsvoll"; Debrunner, *Theol. Blätter*, Sept., 1926. Zehetmeier, *l.c.*, p. 434: "Dass der Periodenbegriff Wandlungen unterworfen war, dafür finden sich . . . Anhaltspunkte." Der Asianismus "ist es, unter dessen Einfluss *schon das blosse Zusammenfassen von Gliedern* zu einem ohne Einhalten gesprochenen Ganzen zur 'Periode' wird, gegenüber dem in lauter kurze Einzelglieder zerfallenden Stil" (*Philologus*, 85 [39]). He warns that "Man kommt nicht weiter, wenn man an der Annahme festhält, die Unstimmigkeiten seien in der Unzulänglichkeit jener Autoren begründet" (p. 435).

[18] Quintilian IX, iv, 122.

[19] Zehetmeier, *l.c.*, pp. 192 ff.

have not yet been discovered."[20] E. Norden thinks he has found such
criteria in certain colometric manuscripts of the *Vulgate*, but prefers to
delay the publication of the results of his inquiry until more illustrative
material has been collected. R. Schütz, another pathfinder in this
field of study, is constrained to admit that, because colometry rests on
the psychology of spoken speech, there remains of necessity a measure
of arbitrariness in our dealing with ancient cola and commata. This
arbitrariness is apparent in the very witnesses to ancient writing to
which Norden appeals. Schütz for his own part lays down two criteria for disentangling cola and commata; first, a well-measured delivery (*wohlabgemessener Vortrag*); secondly, grammatical sentence
structure κατὰ σύνεσιν (*grammatische Satzgliederung κ. σ.*). The second
of these criteria, while necessary and helpful when nothing is at stake,
will leave us at a loss when we need it most, as in cases of textual criticism or in texts of dogmatic significance. The addition of the phrase
κατὰ σύνεσιν, moreover, necessarily opens the door to subjective interpretation; for the σύνεσις of each interpreter will influence his analysis
of the text. The first of the two criteria, too, is vague; for, it may be
asked, what is it that constitutes "well-measured and appropriate
delivery"? To mention but one source of doubt: no reading is appropriate unless it conveys feeling as well as thought; hence, St.
Augustine makes the mood of writer or reader a criterion for analyzing
longer sentences into their constituent cola and commata. He rightly
maintains that the Scriptures should not only be analyzed with care,
but also be read with a glow of feeling (*ardenter pronuntientur*).[21] Yet
surely, that evanescent thing called ἦθος is difficult to lay hold of,
and the modern reader is in constant danger of missing the ancient
point of view and dropping into false pathos.

In our quest of the principles on which to divide a period into cola
and commata, we are often left to shift for ourselves. Colon, comma,
and period differ in length, we know; but length is a mechanical criterion that must fail in disentangling intricate passages. A. Debrunner's conclusion is disheartening: "Therefore all colometrization is
subjective" (*Alle Kolometrie ist subjektiv*). He adds that all those who
have thus far done work in New Testament colometry have followed

---

[20] Norden, *AK.*, 952 with "Nachträge." For the so-called Euthalian MSS., see
Merk, *l.c.*, 10 c; Harris, *l.c.*, 34 ff.; Schaefer-Meinertz, 30, 176, 403; Von Dobschütz,
Einleitung, 35, 42, 90, 92; Von Soden, *Untersuchungen*, 637 ff.; Thompson, *l.c.*, 70.
[21] *De Doctrina Chr.*, IV, vii, 21.

but one norm, Syntax—a norm that has its disadvantages. He closes his essay with an outline of inquiry for anyone who would hereafter advance our knowledge of colometry. It is a formal course of investigation, mapped out in scientific style, which it would take a lifetime to carry out, and that without the cheering prospect of reaching absolutely final results.

Another New Testament scholar, H. J. Cladder, S.J., in a study of the structural form of the Epistle of St. James,[22] is convinced that several of the so-called colometric codices of the New Testament show conclusively that their authors "were no longer familiar with the structure of that Epistle as a whole," and that the stichic laws (*die stichischen Gesetze*) "had already dropped out of their consciousness." His own presentation of the Epistle in verses and cola is content with "mere *sense*-lines" (*Sinnzeilen*) and does not profess to offer more than that. He is aware that this system of sense-lines carries with it an element of subjectiveness, but, he adds, it is all that can be attempted under the limitations cramping the modern study of colometry. He reaches the same conclusions in his inquiry into the structure of the Epistle to the Hebrews.[23]

Difficulties, therefore, and inconveniences there undoubtedly are in our attempts to colometrize the New Testament, but it would be a mistake to exaggerate them. At all events the colometrizer of the New Testament is greatly helped in his task by the fact that both the old Greek writers and all Semitic authors (whether they composed in Hebrew or in Greek) were fond of expressing their minds by the figure called *Parallelism of Structure*, so that the principles of colometrization applicable to the Greek type of Parallelism can guide us also in our dealing with Parallelism of the Hebrew type. It should be added, however, that in other respects the two types are essentially different, the Greek type being a Parallelism of Form only, the other being a Parallelism of Thought (with, of course, a consequent parallel structure). Illustrations of the Greek παρίσωσις may be taken from Aristotle's Πολιτεία 'Αθηναίων (6, 1):

---

[22] *Zeitschrift für kath. Theol.*, "Der formale Aufbau des Jakobusbriefes"; 28, pp. 37 ff. and 295 ff.; also 29, 1 ff. and 500 ff. Cladder's inquiries are important, both in their positive and in their negative results.

[23] Thompson, *l.c.*, 70: "As might be expected, one arrangement of the text of the Bible in rhythmical sentences or lines of sense would not be consistently followed by all editors and scribes; and hence we find variations in the length of lines and sentences in the different extant Biblical MSS."

κύριος δὲ γενόμενος τῶν πραγμάτων ὁ Σόλων
a   τόν τε δῆμον ἠλευθέρωσε
b   καὶ ἐν τῷ παρόντι καὶ εἰς τὸ μέλλον,
c   κωλύσας δανείζειν ἐπὶ τοῖς σώμασιν,
a′ καὶ χρεῶν ἀποκοπὰς ἐποίησε
b′ καὶ τῶν ἰδίων καὶ τῶν δημοσίων
c′   ἃς συνάχθειαν καλοῦσι, ὡς ἀποσεισαμένων τὸ βάρος.

Or from 5, 3:

ἦν δὲ ὁ Σόλων
a   τῇ μὲν φύσει καὶ τῇ δόξῃ τῶν πρώτων,
a′ τῇ δ᾽ οὐσίᾳ καὶ τοῖς πράγμασι τῶν μέσων,
b   ὡς ἔκ τε τῶν ἄλλων ὁμολογεῖται
b′ καὶ αὐτὸς ἐν τοῖσδε τοῖς ποιήμασιν μαρτυρεῖ,
c   παραινῶν τοῖς πλουσίοις μὴ πλεονεκτεῖν.

                              (Kaibel, *Stil und Text*, 81-83)

With his eye on illustrations such as these, the colometrizer of the New Testament is sure that he cannot go wrong in colometrizing, for instance, the following passage in Mt. 7, 13-14, for the guiding principles are the same:

εἰσέλθετε διὰ τῆς στενῆς πύλης.
ὅτι πλατεῖα ἡ πύλη
καὶ εὐρύχωρος ἡ ὁδός
ἡ ἀπάγουσα εἰς τὴν ἀπώλειαν
καὶ πολλοί εἰσιν οἱ εἰσερχόμενοι δι᾽ αὐτῆς.
ὅτι στενὴ ἡ πύλη
καὶ τεθλιμμένη ἡ ὁδός
ἡ ἀπάγουσα εἰς τὴν ζωήν
καὶ ὀλίγοι εἰσὶν οἱ εὑρίσκοντες αὐτήν

                              (Norden, *AK.*, II, 818)

Akin in spirit, though not entirely in the form, is the following passage from the Codex Amiatinus, representing John 10, 7-9:

Amen amen dico vobis
quia *ego sum ostium ovium*
omnes quotquot venerunt
    fures sunt et latrones
sed non audierunt eos oves
ego sum ostium·
per me si quis introierit
    salvabitur.

                              (Wordsworth-White, p. 578)

Since, then, our information concerning the ancient colometric style is still deficient, I make no larger claims for my presentation of St. Mark's Gospel than are warranted by the facts. Whether this presentation is called a division into thought-units or sense-lines, or even a downright "colometrization," is immaterial and, with the proviso stated above, not misleading. I have analyzed St. Mark's sentences into shorter portions in the light of his simple syntax; structures deemed too cumbrous for convenient utterance in one breath I have broken up into smaller "phonetic units"; here and there I have allowed a voice to that unsteady element of personal emotion.[24] The result thus achieved is in all probability a very close approach to the old colometry. but it is well to remember that the terms *colon* and *comma* cannot, without qualification, be transferred from artistic rhetorical prose to so non-artistic and non-rhetorical a composition as the second Gospel. On the other hand, while such a wholesale transfer of terms would be hazardous, we need not hesitate to follow the example of some ancient grammarians and apply those terms in a wider sense. In strictness, cola, being in the Aristotelian theory rhythmical parts of a period, should not be looked for in the running style of St. Mark. But modern psychology assures us that all human thinking of whatever kind proceeds by means of small thought-units,[25] and these thought-units serve, after all, the same purpose as the ancient cola and commata. The question of the extent to which St. Mark's sentences conform to ancient periods is purely academic and has, therefore, no bearing on our present inquiry. The more immediate and practical aim of this study is to help the student to see *in what different ways St. Mark welds his words into sentences and molds his sentences into a progressive development of thought.* To see this with eye and mind is to look into the simple yet robust mind of a fellow creature, untaught, untutored, and unlettered, yet successful in producing a noteworthy Summary of the Message of Salvation. Art or no art,[26] the second Gospel is rightly admired for its bold strokes and graphic descriptions of a subject dear to us. Studying it, thought-unit by thought-unit, sense-line by sense-line, we study the

---

[24] See below, section 5, pp. 114 ff.

[25] Flagg, *A Writer of Attic*, 66: "The articulations which enable the speaker or writer to convey his thought with distinctness to another's mind are determined primarily for the most part by groups of words, not by words apprehended singly." Havers, *Handbuch der Syntax*, 13: "Der Satz besteht in der Regel nicht aus Wörtern, sondern aus Wortgruppen. Auch das Hören und Lesen der Rede erfolgt nach Wortgruppen, nicht nach einzelnen Wörtern." See *ib.*, "Das sukzessive Denken"; pp. 43–48.

[26] *Memoirs*, Ch. V, "Glimpses of Marcan Art"; see also below, sections 2–5.

mind of St. Peter and, in a limited sense, even the mind of Christ Himself. And furthermore, if the student is prompted by this inquiry, in spite of its limitations, to carry his researches deeper into the New Testament, and, particularly, into the more promising field of St. Paul's more vigorous and more elaborate Epistles, it is impossible to say beforehand what rewards may repay his labor.

2. By way of practical illustration of *the Marcan architecture of speech*—if the term be not too ambitious—we may examine the eight first verses of the first chapter of this Gospel, and see what becomes of them under "colometrization" in accordance with the principles explained above. We may see incidentally how the current division of the Gospel into chapter and verse is apt at times to miss the constructive relations, let alone, the finer affiliations, of thought to thought.

1 | Ἀρχὴ τοῦ εὐαγγελίου Ἰησοῦ Χριστοῦ υἱοῦ τοῦ Θεοῦ

2 | Καθὼς γέγραπται ἐν τῷ Ἡσαΐᾳ τῷ προφήτῃ
     ἰδοὺ ἐγὼ ἀποστέλλω τὸν ἄγγελόν μου πρὸ προσώπου σου
     ὃς κατασκευάσει τὴν ὁδόν σου

3 | φωνὴ βοῶντος ἐν τῇ ἐρήμῳ
         ἑτοιμάσατε τὴν ὁδὸν Κυρίου
         εὐθείας ποιεῖτε τὰς τρίβους αὐτοῦ

4 | ἐγένετο Ἰωάννης
     ὁ βαπτίζων ἐν τῇ ἐρήμῳ
     καὶ κηρύσσων βάπτισμα μετανοίας
         εἰς ἄφεσιν ἁμαρτιῶν

5 | καὶ ἐξεπορεύετο πρὸς αὐτόν
     πᾶσα ἡ Ἰουδαία χώρα καὶ οἱ Ἱεροσολυμῖται πάντες

    καὶ ἐβαπτίζοντο ὑπ' αὐτοῦ ἐν τῷ Ἰορδάνῃ ποταμῷ
     ἐξομολογούμενοι τὰς ἁμαρτίας αὐτῶν

6 | καὶ ἦν ὁ Ἰωάννης ἐνδεδυμένος
    τρίχας καμήλου καὶ ζώνην δερματίνην περὶ τὴν ὀσφ'ν αὐτοῦ

   καὶ ἔσθων
     ἀκρίδας καὶ μέλι ἄγριον

7   καὶ ἐκήρυσσεν λέγων·

     | ἔρχεται ὁ ἰσχυρότερός μου ὀπίσω μου
     | οὗ οὐκ εἰμὶ ἱκανὸς κύψας λῦσαι
     | τὸν ἱμάντα τῶν ὑποδημάτων αὐτοῦ

8 | ἐγὼ ἐβάπτισα ὑμᾶς ὕδατι
     | αὐτὸς δὲ βαπτίσει ὑμᾶς ἐν πνεύματι ἁγίῳ

The selection given above shows a number of devices intended to emphasize structure.

The opening line or *stichos* does perhaps not answer to an ancient "simple" period, for this should have length and final rounding. If either condition is absent, there is no period. The sentence is "loose." The vertical bar at the head of the *stichos* indicates that here *stichos* and thought-unit (or, logical unit) coincide.

The second unit is more ambitious, presenting its thought on an ampler scale than is usual with St. Mark. It embraces ten *stichoi* or sense-lines. There are several vertical lines at certain intervals. The line coinciding with the margin indicates the length of the logical unit. The fact that it touches two *stichoi* (one at καθώς and one at ἐγένετο) shows that they are "coördinate," if not in grammar, at least in St. Mark's mind: "It is written . . . and, therefore, John appeared." All other *stichoi* are thrown in to clothe the skeleton, and their indention marks them visually as subordinate to the two main sense-lines. At the first distance from the margin there are three vertical lines: the first (at ἰδού) sets off a quotation from Malachi; the second (at φωνή), one from Isaias; the third (at ὁ βαπτίζων), an apposition to the proper name Ἰωάννης. The quotation from Malachi consists of two parallel clauses and is therefore bracketed by one coördination line: "I will send" and "he will prepare." The quotation from Isaias pictures John as a φωνὴ βοῶντος, of which the two following asyndetic imperatives are explanatory; hence their indention. They touch the same coördination line, because they are of equal rank with each other.

In general it may be remarked that clauses of the same rank touch the same vertical coördination line; clauses of subordinate rank are marked by distance from the left. Note, however, that the terms "coördinate" and "subordinate" are taken in a broader sense. Thus, although the καθώς-clause is, in syntax, subordinate to the main clause (ἐγένετο), yet for the progress of the narrative as such the two clauses are coördinate: "It is written . . . and he appeared accordingly."

Since the καθώς-clause is subordinate in grammar to the main sentence, the whole thought-unit preserves the essence of an ancient period which reserves until the end its chief statement. The underlined words show the salient points of the narrative: it is *written* that God will send His *messenger* who shall be a *herald's voice* proclaiming that people should *prepare* the *way* of the Lord and make straight His *paths:* this herald was *John* who *baptized* in the desert and *preached* the need of a *baptism.* The phrase εἰς ἄφεσιν ἁμαρτιῶν is best taken as a comma stating the purpose both of the βαπτίζειν and of the κηρύσσειν. Its indention shows that it somehow belongs to both *stichoi.*

As the connection of the opening verses is disputed (see the Notes), their colometrization must depend on interpretation. As a rule, interpretation should follow colometrization.

The third logical unit coincides with verse 5 of the current division. It is a true thought-unit because it conveys one definite thought—the response of the people to John's invitation: *they streamed out* from their homes to *have themselves baptized* at his hands. As the two *stichoi* in this unit are too bulky for oral reading, they have been broken up each into two divisions. This unit is "loose" in structure and is in the typical, that is, paratactic, manner of St. Mark.

The fourth logical unit is of the same build as the third. There are two main coördinated *stichoi:* John was *clothed,* and John was *eating.* The style is loose. Here too the *stichoi* were broken up in keeping with that ancient preference for antithesis. Each main *stichos* ends with a participle, ἐνδεδυμένος and ἔσθων; each participle is followed by its object in the accusative plural, τρίχας and ἀκρίδας. The antithesis here is not in the thought, but in the words only. In ancient colometry, subject and object need not appear in the same *stichos.*

The fifth unit, which contains a specimen of John's manner of preaching, neatly rounds out the entire pericope describing his preparatory ministry. The stage is thus set for the appearance of our Lord. The selection from verses one to eight, then, falls into two grand divisions. The first gives the superscription of the entire Gospel. The second is not unlike a modern paragraph with ἐγένετο Ἰωάννης for its topic sentence. It has four units, each compact enough to stress one aspect of John's ministry. The first shows him as preëxistent in ancient prophecy and states the purpose of his mission; the second sketches his success as Christ's forerunner; the third lets us glimpse into his austere private life; the fourth tells the burden of his preaching.[27]

As each logical unit is held together by a coördination line along the

---

[27] *Memoirs,* pp. 45, 46.

margin, so each paragraph or pericope is marked as such by the capitalization of the opening word, ᾿Αρχή and Καθώs.

St. Mark's units are not physical measures depending on some ideal artistic standard. They are the spontaneous products of a simple mind bent on telling some of "the words and works of the Lord"; they are measures of untutored thought, and differ as much as thoughts will differ. Some require but one *stichos* containing all that the writer or speaker was able or willing to crowd into one syntactical unit. Others are more ambitious. Some have sharply balanced members when the thoughts are sharply contrasted. Others run along in meandering fashion, but never lose sight of the goal. All are photographs of St. Mark's or St. Peter's mind. Their "rhetoric" is of a kind which any plain man in similar circumstances would light upon.

In the colometrization of the Gospel several of the devices used above were dropped to avoid crowding the page.

3. Scanning the entire Gospel in colometric form, we notice great diversity of structure coupled with great simplicity. It is just what we should expect if we recall the origin of this ᾿Αρχή. There is no need of exaggerating St. Peter's lack of education, but he was certainly a plain, unlettered man. Suddenly he finds himself facing the world and telling what he has seen and heard as a disciple of Christ. Here we have *the clue to St. Mark's workmanship*.[28] The nature of the subject (partly human, partly divine), the circumstances of speaker and listener, the personal interest in many an incident close to the Apostle's heart—all contribute to this mosaic of word-pictures which we call the second Gospel. Here everything is simple, direct, graphic, and intensely interesting to the speaker. There is here no "labor," no unwholesome straining after cleverness. A poet or a master of prose may give illumination to a great concept or invest the statement of truth with glory. All that St. Peter or St. Mark is able to do is to tell directly what has happened,

[28] The phrases "Marcan Art" and "Marcan Workmanship," occasionally used in this volume, are meant to leave it undecided whether an expression singled out for comment is attributable to the writer St. Mark or to his voucher St. Peter or to any other person whose words are quoted in the Gospel. Cf. Merk, *l.c.*, 345 ff.; Lagrange, *L'Évangile*, Ch. VI, cviii ff.; Knabenbauer, "Prolegomena"; Schaefer-Meinertz, *l.c.*, 261 ff.; Huby, *The Church and the Gospels*, 77–85; Lagrange, *The Gospel according to St. Mark*, Introd.; Cladder, *Unsere Evangelien*, 105 ff.; *The Cath. Encyclop.*, Vol. IX, 672; VI, 658; on Codex Amiatinus, see IV, 81; on Codex Claromontanus, see IX, 631.

and this is the very thing that pleases us so much. There is here no "Art" but just common sense.

Let us see how St. Mark can relate a scene that culminates in some pithy or pointed sayings of our Lord's:

Καὶ γίνεται κατακεῖσθαι αὐτὸν ἐν τῇ οἰκίᾳ αὐτοῦ
καὶ πολλοὶ τελῶναι καὶ ἁμαρτωλοί
συνανέκειντο τῷ Ἰησοῦ καὶ τοῖς μαθηταῖς αὐτοῦ·
ἦσαν γὰρ πολλοὶ καὶ ἠκολούθουν αὐτῷ.

καὶ οἱ γραμματεῖς τῶν Φαρισαίων,
ἰδόντες αὐτὸν ἐσθίςντα μετὰ τῶν ἁμαρτωλῶν καὶ τελωνῶν,
ἔλεγον τοῖς μαθηταῖς αὐτοῦ·
τί ὅτι μετὰ τῶν τελωνῶν καὶ ἁμαρτωλῶν ἐσθίει καὶ πίνει;

καὶ ἀκούσας ὁ Ἰησοῦς λέγει αὐτοῖς·

οὐ χρείαν ἔχουσιν οἱ ἰσχύοντες ἰατροῦ
ἀλλ᾽   οἱ κακῶς ἔχοντες·

οὐκ ἦλθον καλέσαι δικαίους
ἀλλὰ   ἁμαρτωλούς.

A glance at this selection will convince us that St. Mark's way of writing is simple, yet effective. His aim is to preserve two of our Lord's memorable sayings. How does he go about it—he, I say, who was not trained in the schools? He builds up a pericope of three units. The first unit pictures the background: Jesus, surrounded by His disciples and a multitude of publicans, is Levi's guest at a banquet given in His honor. The second acquaints us with the immediate provocation of our Lord's dictum: the Scribes and Pharisees whisper their indignation at His free-and-easy intercourse with sinners and publicans. The third records the crowning answer with neat attention to that old cherished parallelism of form[29] which sinks into ear and heart alike. Accordingly, the first unit culminates in two words: κατακεῖσθαι and συνανέκειντο; the second in οἱ γραμματεῖς ἔλεγον; the third in ὁ Ἰησοῦς λέγει. Shall we not credit St. Mark or his voucher St. Peter with enough good sense to be able to construct so simple a frame as that? And be it remembered, the frame as a matter of fact

---

[29] Sr. Barry, *St. Augustine the Orator*, 194 ff.; Campbell, 92 ff.; Norden, *AK.*, 509 ff. and 817 ff.   See above, B, section 1, p. 102.

was furnished by the nexus of the events themselves. St. Peter merely had to look at what was going on and listen carefully to what was being said, and later to reproduce his simple, though vivid, impressions. Here, then, we have the secret of St. Mark's manner. If he has to tell a particular incident, he tells it in a simple, clear, and orderly way. He has to tell it effectively, of course; so, without any training in "art," relying merely on his good sense, he tells it in a single-minded, straightforward way. His narrative is simple, because it avoids bewildering detail; direct, because it makes straight for the goal and eschews what is irrelevant; graphic, because it abounds in descriptive particulars. The result, in the selection quoted above, is admirable: our Lord's dictum is placed before us in an unforgettable form.

Some critics are at pains to show that St. Mark did not write like a professional historian. A professional historian, so we are told, acquaints us fully with a character when first introducing it.[30] St. Mark, on the contrary, scatters his details, leaving us to gather the *disiecta membra*. Thus St. Luke states the age of Jairus's daughter when he mentions her father's coming to Jesus for help. In St. Mark, we are left to learn her age at the end of the story, as by an afterthought: she rises and walks *and she was twelve years of age*. This, no doubt, is clumsy composition, but it is not St. Mark's:

> And she rose at once and moved about again;
> *for* she was twelve years old.

St. Mark withholds the mention of the girl's age until the reader needs the information to account for her ability to walk about. She was alive, for she walked about; she could walk about, for she was twelve years old, and, St. Mark wishes to *imply*, fully capable of appreciating the great boon bestowed upon her. And what a joyous reunion of all the parties concerned! If this is not professional writing, it is certainly relishable writing. Again: A rich man presents himself before Jesus to ask what he must do to obtain eternal life. While St. Luke pictures him as a man of rank, St. Mark does not mention his social position until the moment when he became sad at our Lord's call, for he had great possessions. But, here again, there is no literary canon to compel the mention of that detail earlier in the story; and besides, coming after the Lord's call to complete renunciation, it comes as a great surprise; "it is striking in effect," as the same critic admits, "and more

---

[30] See J. Huby, *The Church and the Gospels*, 95 ff. Huby does, however, pay a just tribute to St. Mark as an excellent story-teller.

than one reader has received a healthy shock from it!'' *Ex uno* (vel
duobus) *disce omnes*. In getting acquainted with the real St. Mark, the
student must start, not by appealing to some mystical canon of writing,
but by supposing St. Mark to have been a very sensible man, and then
follow him through his narrative.

For our immediate purpose in this volume it is not necessary to try
to enter fully into the knotty question of the literary type to which
the second Gospel belongs. It is enough to recall that all our Gospels
are classified by St. Justin[31] in the second century as "Memoirs of the
Apostles," Ἀπομνημονεύματα τῶν Ἀποστόλων, and that the Papias-fragment describes the second Gospel as a careful transcript of St. Peter's
catechetical instructions. That explains why this Gospel contains a
collection of pieces of narrative, description, parable, allegory, exposition, discourse, and argument, all directed to its great object, to furnish a Summary of the Gospel of Jesus Christ, Son of God. Its form
is admirably suited to its function. Regarding the great structural
features of the composition as a whole, all that need be said here is
that it falls naturally into two parts which supplement each other.[32]
As to the minor units of form, the student must gain a knowledge of
them by direct acquaintance with the text.

Readers of the second Gospel are apt to be betrayed into thinking
that these memoirs are a mere jumble of events presented in a rugged,
dry, and unattractive fashion. Such an impression would be unfair to
St. Mark, for, although his Gospel is not a *Short Story* in the most
modern and technical sense of that term, yet it possesses in a greater or
less degree all those elements which give that type of literature its
distinctive tone and invest it with so much charm and interest. At all
events, the second Gospel has *plot*, for the series of acts, events, or
incidents narrated in it is a body of more or less related influences each
of which has a share in hastening the close, both tragic and glorious,
of the life of Christ. From the moment when "a voice rings in the
wilderness" (ɪ, 3), there is a constant onward rush of happenings,
first in Galilee (Chapters I to IX), then in the Jewish Capital (Chapters
X to XV), in fact, event follows event rapidly (εὐθύς!), until the con-
summation is reached in the Resurrection. The Gospel has *dramatic
plot*, for the Death of Christ is a result that grows out of the traits of
character of the chief persons involved in the drama: Christ and His
relentless enemies; a result, *logical* on the part of Christ, who, even

---

[31] See *Memoirs*, Chapters II and III.   See the Author's Foreword, p. xiv.
[32] *Memoirs*, 55, 56.

though He foresaw His tragic end from the outset (2, 20) could not act differently; and perversely logical or *inevitable* on the part of the Scribes, who, once they had hardened themselves against believing the Message of Salvation and committed the "unpardonable sin" (3, 29), were driven to the destruction of Jesus. Furthermore, if the Short Story requires *persons in action in a time of crisis*, it is easy to see how in a true (though perhaps not technical) sense each act and event in the life of Christ was really a "time of crisis." From the start (2, 6) He was constantly under the vigilant eyes of His sworn enemies (3, 2: παρετήρουν), and whatever He did or said was later set down to His account as a perverter of the people and a traitor to the Jewish cause. Again, if the typical Short Story aims at *singleness of effect*, such singleness is evidently a characteristic trait of this very Gospel, for, looking back from the heights of Golgotha (Ch. XV), and the consequent glorification of Jesus (Ch. XVI), we can see how everything narrated in the earlier portions of the book contributes to the total effect of this "Summary" of events connected with the "Message of Salvation," namely, the proof that *Jesus* is the *Son of God* (1, 1). Again, if we examine the nature of the *action* described in this Gospel, we find that, after a brief exposition (1, 1–13), the action begins to *rise*, and continues to do so until the grand *climax, height, or climactic moment* is reached when Jesus is condemned to death (15, 15); what follows after the decisive moment is merely the carrying out of the sentence, or, technically, the *falling action* of the story. From another angle of view, the *catastrophe* may be said to occur in the Crucifixion (15, 24) and the Death of Jesus upon the Cross (15, 37).[33]

The Gospel of St. Mark is in a sense the most profoundly stirring Short Story ever written by man. If upon scrutiny it is found to fall short of the technical requirements of this modern type of literature, it yet vastly outruns it in another direction: penned by man, it was designed by heaven. The Gospel of St. Mark, with all its literary deficiencies, peculiarities, or mannerisms, is, in its deepest source and inspiration, not human but divine.

When certain terms of Greek literary theory are used in elucidating the second Gospel, it is not implied that Marcan prose was literary,

---

[33] Shipherd, *Manual and Models*, 64 ff.; Genung, *Working Principles*, Ch. IX; Baldwin, *College Composition*, Ch. II, "The Technic of Plan and Paragraphs," 38 ff.; Greever and Bachelor, *The Century Book of Selections*, 3 ff. Robert Wilson Neal, *Short Stories in the Making* and *Today's Short Stories Analyzed;* Oxf. U. Press; 1914 and 1918. Here and on page 119 I have followed Mr. Neal's exposition.

but merely that literary types of composition have each its own coun-
terpart older than itself and rooted in the native forces of the human
mind. Art is but a grandiose Μίμησις of Nature.[34]

4. *The process of subdividing the Marcan sentences* may, obviously,
be carried to greater lengths than has been done here. Thus, for example, in 10, 28, we might wish to isolate the common and emphatic
subject (ἡμεῖς) of both verbs, as if to say: *Look*, there are two things
we did:

> Ἤρξατο λέγειν ὁ Πέτρος αὐτῷ·
>
> ἰδοὺ ἡμεῖς   ἀφήκαμεν πάντα
> καὶ ἠκολουθήσαμέν σοι.

Or, again, since colon-writing brings out what in artistic prose is called
rhythm of sentence structure (τάξις),[35] we might wish to present 10, 11
either as a specimen of dichotomy (division by pairs) or of trichotomy
(division into three parts), both of which are familiar to St. Mark.
Dichotomic arrangement:

> ὃς ἂν ἀπολύσῃ τὴν γυναῖκα αὐτοῦ καὶ γαμήσῃ ἄλλην μοιχᾶται ἐπ᾽ αὐτήν·
> καὶ ἐὰν αὐτὴ ἀπολύσασα τὸν ἄνδρα αὐτῆς γαμήσῃ ἄλλον μοιχᾶται.

Trichotomic combined with dichotomic arrangement:

1. ὃς ἂν ἀπολύσῃ τὴν γυναῖκα αὐτοῦ   :ἀπολῦσαι
2.   καὶ γαμήσῃ ἄλλην   :γαμῆσαι
3.   μοιχᾶται ἐπ᾽ αὐτήν   :μοιχᾶσθαι

1. καὶ ἐὰν αὐτὴ ἀπολύσασα τὸν ἄνδρα αὐτῆς   :ἀπολῦσαι
2.   γαμήσῃ ἄλλον   :γαμῆσαι
3.   μοιχᾶται   :μοιχᾶσθαι.

The first grouping shows the long, impressive sweep of the parallel
pronouncements on divorce: the parties to a marriage contract have

---

[34] Aristotle, *Poetics*, 1, 2. On the relation between artistic and natural expression,
see, for example, Brugmann (675) on Hyperbaton: "Auch die ungekünstelte Umgangssprache gebraucht solche Mittel"; or on Parenthesis: "Die Parenthese kann
natürlich ebenfalls als stilistisches Kunstmittel verwendet werden, wenngleich sie
in der Alltagssprache ihren Ausgangspunkt hat." Cf. Hofmann, *Lat. Umgangssprache, passim.* Quintilian (IX, iv, 5) explains how, since art is rooted in nature,
artistic devices are in a sense "natural"; in fact "that which is most natural is that
which nature permits to be done to the greatest perfection."

[35] Quintilian, IX, iv, 1 ff. See footnote 29.

equal rights. The second throws into relief the three salient elements in the matter of divorce, by giving prominence to each in a separate colon: divorce, remarriage, adultery. This latter presentation, when read aloud, points out the three steps in the procedure condemned by Christ. Note, incidentally, how this effect is heightened by indention.[36] At all events, just as reading aloud and proper pausing make a writer's mind as it were audible, so proper colometrization makes it visible and throws it as it were on a canvas.

The difficulties inherent in our attempts at colometrizing the Greek classics are met with in editing the Latin as well. Thus a passage in Sallust's *Bellum Catilinae* (53, 1) has been punctuated by Schmalz as follows:

Postquam Cato adsedit, consulares omnes itemque senatus magna pars sententiam eius laudant, virtutem animi ad caelum *ferunt;* alii alios increpantes timidos *vocant,* Cato clarus atque magnus habetur; senati decretum fit, sicuti ille censuerat.

Rolfe, on the contrary, puts a comma after *ferunt* and a full stop after *vocant*. Divergence of punctuation means divergence of interpretation. Correct punctuation and correct colometrization are fundamentally the same problem.[37]

Another source of uncertainty in editing the ancient classics is in our failure to understand the ancient point of view in distinguishing between what we call principal and subordinate clauses. The Latin particle *ut*, for example, like Greek, ἵνα or ὥστε, was often used to introduce a thought "felt" by the ancient writer as independent.[38]

·5. The term "logical unit" or "thought-unit" used above must not lead the student to assume that St. Mark's sentences may not also be emotional units. Speech conveys emotion as inevitably as it communicates thought.[39] "Even the simplest speech implies as much as

---

[36] J. H. Scott, *Rhythmic Prose*, in "U. of Iowa Humanistic Studies," III.

[37] Von Wilamowitz-Moellendorff, *Griechisches Lesebuch*, II, 2. Norden, *Aeneis* VI, 386.

[38] Pohlenz (on Cic. *Tusc.* I, 50): "*Ut* leitet wie ὥστε oft einen als selbständig empfundenen Gedanken ein." For independent ἵνα, see on Mk. 2, 10. Comparative grammar shows that, historically, subordination was gradually developed from juxtaposition and coördination. Gildersleeve, *AJPh.*, 23, 253 ff.; Smyth 2161; Brugmann 643, w. footnote.

[39] Algernon Tassin, *Oral Study of Literature, passim.* Havers, *Handbuch*, p. 29, has an interesting chapter on "Lautes und Stilles Lesen." See Hendrickson, *Classical Journal*, 25, on "Ancient Reading"; p. 182; J. Balogh, *Voces Paginarum*, "Philologus" 82 (1927), 84–109; 202–240.

it asserts." Of the four Gospels, the second is the last we feel tempted
to turn to for the priceless pearl of human emotion. May we not suspect that we have been too busy in the past gathering grammatical
statistics, instead of studying more sympathetically *the emotional side
of St. Mark's* 'Αρχή? We have had it dinned into our ears that St.
Mark is dry, and matter-of-fact, and rugged, and uncouth, and pleonastic; but before we raise such charges against a fellow man, we must
linger over his words to feel beneath them the pulse of the human heart.
Let us not be unjust: "Even the simplest speech implies as much as it
asserts." St. Mark wrote at a time when the world was filled with
novel sounds; when the Chosen People had come to a turning-point
in their history; when the preaching of the Εὐαγγέλιον, destined to
upheave the ancient world, was at its freshest and most inspiring.
Who could listen to St. Peter telling of the Redemption and his relations to the Son of God (Mt. 16, 16), without being stirred with emotion? And would not men's hearts burn within them as he wove into
his account many an utterance that had fallen fresh and warm from
the lips of the Saviour? To see in the second Gospel no more than material for grammatical statistics is to see in the preaching of the Gospel
an event in which the heart had no share. As to the charge of pleonastic expression, even such use may have a redeeming feature; for
what to a cold analyzer seems a waste of words may be no more than
normal in one whose mouth speaketh out of the abundance of the heart.

That emotion may play a part in colometrization is not a fanciful
assumption but a conviction based on a passage in St. Augustine's *De
doctrina Christiana*, IV, vii, 13. He says that the sentence (II Cor.
11, 16): *Alioquin velut insipientem suscipite me, ut et ego modicum quid
glorier* is a *circuitus trimembris*, a period consisting of three cola, but
fails to tell us how he contrived to find in it three cola where we should
expect but two. In all probability he wished the first word *alioquin*,
as being very emphatic ("However, if you MUST consider me a
fool"), to be taken by itself. We who are acquainted with the ways of
modern impressionistic poetry find no difficulty in accepting St.
Augustine's interpretation. In the following stanza, for instance,[40]

> Secret-wise
> I trespass on your guarded eyes
> And see—
> What shatters all my dreams for me,

---

[40] The first stanza of *Renunciation* by John Craig, published in *America*, May 30,
1931. For a brief note on St. Mark's *spoken* Gospel, see *Memoirs*, p. 168, on 12, 23.
For St. Augustine, see Kleist, *Classical Bulletin*, for January, 1932.

the principle governing this ultra-modern form of verse is none other than that which led St. Augustine to set apart *alioquin* from the rest of the sentence as an independent emotional *colon:*

> Alioquin
> velut insipientem suscipite me,
> ut et ego modicum quid glorier.

The principle was understood by the scribe of the Codex Claromontanus (of the sixth century) who wrote I Cor. 13, 7 as follows:

> Omnia suffert
> omnia credit
> omnia sperat
> omnia sustinet
> CARITAS
> nunquam excidit.

Caritas has a whole line to itself because it is stressed by emotion, as *alioquin* is above. Evidently St. Augustine, who in his theory of style harks back to Cicero over a gap of several centuries of rhetorical rioting, felt that he should interpret St. Paul as a man of flesh and blood, and not as an automaton. Can we interpret St. Mark in any other way? Is not his Gospel from beginning to end *spoken* Greek?

The plain prose of the Gospel of St. Mark is at times of so bare and rugged a sort that it becomes a challenge to an imaginative reader. The reader wants *atmosphere;* he wants it because he is human; he wants it even more because the Gospel is the story of the Saviour and should, therefore, re-echo the profound stir made in the world by the "new preaching." But where will he find this atmosphere? The answer can only be that, provided he is interested in the Marcan narrative, he will—with effort and ingenuity—succeed in capturing its spirit, as he goes from scene to scene; he will learn to feel its internal quality; he will taste *sensu interiore* that psychological, emotional, and tonal environment in which the characters and the actions depicted in the Gospel are seen to move. Clues to this atmosphere he will find if he looks for them, sometimes in an outright assertion, more often perhaps in certain assumptions with which St. Mark expects him to approach the narrative. In 6, 27 and 28, for instance, we read that

> The man went and beheaded him in prison
> and brought his head on a platter
> and gave it to the girl,
> and the girl gave it to her mother.

Here we have an account almost cruel in its jejuneness, and yet, if we fall back on elemental human nature, we should at least suspect, if we cannot comprehend, the agonies the Baptist went through when he realized that he, God's chosen vessel, was sacrificed to the whims of a lustful woman and her debauched daughter, and that, too, when the real Master of life and death was within easy reach. We can suspect the fiendish joy of mother and daughter in gloating over the blood-dripping head of the hated preacher of morality. All that is required of us, for this purpose, is that we understand a few basic facts of our nature. On other occasions St. Mark, even in spite of his brevity, furnishes a clue to the spirit of the scene, as when in 5, 33 he says:

> The woman, frightened and trembling,
> conscious of what had happened to her,
> came and threw herself down before Him,
> and told Him the whole truth.

We will, of course, carefully note those significant hints, those indexes, of the woman's emotion: φοβηθεῖσα and τρέμουσα and εἰδυῖα ὃ γέγονεν αὐτῇ. It is only too plain that, overpowered by the appearance of the great Teacher and Benefactor, she cast all reserve to the winds, as being out of place in the circumstances, and told, aloud and with a tremor in her voice, the whole story of her illness and her final cure; we can picture to ourselves how she nerved herself to a desperate action and, with full faith in Christ's power, touched His garment.

In 2, 12 we learn that the paralyzed man

> rose to his feet
> and, taking up his mat at once,
> walked away before the eyes of all.

We might conjecture, on general principles, that there followed an outburst of applause and admiration, even if St. Mark had not taken the trouble to tell us so: "*so that* all were beside themselves and praised God." Here, then, the emotional effect of the miracle on the masses is stated outright, while another effect, that on the Scribes, is passed over in silence: nettled as they must have been by all that Jesus said and did, they undoubtedly did not join in the popular demonstration; and this mental state of theirs we are justified in inferring, even in spite of St. Mark's seeming denial of it by the use of (ἐξίστασθαι) πάντας, which with aid from text and context we have no trouble in reading aright. In 7, 37, where the cure of the blind man is related, the situation is somewhat different; for, although there, too, the overwhelming emotional effect on the people rings out in clear and, indeed, pleonastic language,

> People were free beyond all bounds
> in expressing their delight,

St. Mark helps us to *relish* the popular outburst much more truly by indicating that it was a violation of our Lord's prohibition:

> The more strictly He charged them,
> the more freely, for their part, they published the fact.

Here, then, the "foil" motive, so effective in the Short Story, appears to good advantage: the people *relish* their outburst of applause all the more keenly because it flies in the face of what they considered to be undue modesty on the part of their Benefactor. The same undercurrent is at work in 1, 45, where the cured leper disregarded our Lord's prohibition and

> *set about* noising the fact abroad
> and publishing it so widely
> that Jesus could no longer go openly into town.

In 5, 20, too, the man cured of demoniacal possession

> *made a point* of telling publicly,
>   throughout the Decapolis,
> all that Jesus had done for him,

and we are all the better prepared to know how he felt if we know the connotations of St. Mark's favorite ἤρξατο with the present infinitive, which is of itself a hint of brisk activity. (See below, pp. 154 ff.)

The chapters dealing with the trial of Jesus are, as might be expected, steeped in emotion. Here almost every line has its ethos or pathos. Most dramatic perhaps is the solemn adjuration of Caiaphas, who challenges Jesus to tell the court outright whether He is the Son of God. So at last the vexed question as to Christ's identity is to be solved by a direct appeal to Himself: the atmosphere of the courtroom is charged with intense expectation. The words come slowly and solemnly from our Lord's lips. But—

> Then the high priest rent his garments
> and said:
>   What further need have we of witnesses?
>   You have heard the blasphemy!
>   What is your verdict?

There is not a word here to indicate St. Mark's (or St. Peter's) inward reaction to this brazen display of hypocrisy. We need no comment; we are better off without any; we are human and can read between the lines. We know who Christ is, and are, therefore, shocked at hearing

the charge of blasphemy hurled against the Son of God. Unfortunately
also Caiaphas's perverse reasoning and warped attitude toward Christ
is perfectly human and, therefore, perfectly intelligible to us; and,
surely, we should make an effort to understand these things, for St.
Mark's data are sufficient *sapienti*. It is with this same understanding
and appreciation that we should read the memorable four lines which
relate our Lord's sojourn in the desert (1, 13):

> And He was in the wilderness forty days
> and was put to the test by Satan.
> And He was among the wild beasts,
> and the angels waited on Him.

The outlines of the picture are clear: Christ, the Son of God, spends
of His own free choice forty days in the desert, is put to the test by
Satan, lives outside of all human intercourse, associates with the
wild beasts, but is nonetheless strengthened, as we must suppose, by
prayer to His heavenly Father, and refreshed by the sweet presence
and ministrations of the holy angels. Each line is a fresh glimpse into
our Lord's great Heart. St. Mark is brief, and yet he knew as much
about Christ as we do, and so did St. Peter, his voucher. They are not,
therefore, insensible to the deeper things in Christ's sojourn in the
desert; but there are facts and situations in human life "so great and
fundamental as to imply, without comment or addition, the quality
or mood inherent in them. They make their emotional appeal simply,
directly, and unaided." The bare assertion, "Jesus wept," often cited
as an illustration of the power and adequacy of the simple word to
excite emotion, is more than matched by St. Mark's statements of the
Crucifixion (15, 24) and the Death of Christ (15, 37):

> And they crucified Him.
> And Jesus uttered a loud cry and expired.

Writers of Short Stories know the secret of such appalling bareness, of
"the superb economy of speech" in dealing with self-interpreting facts
and situations. When a scene is intrinsically emotional, as all scenes
in which Christ takes a part must be, it needs no "verbal exploitation":
the brevity of the narrative is eked out by the primal, basic instincts
of the reader. This is especially true of the second Gospel, because
St. Mark wrote primarily, not for a pagan audience, that could not be
supposed to know the nature and work of the Saviour, but for Christian converts: his words are more like aids to memory for those Christians who had heard St. Peter's catechetical instructions at Rome.

In speaking to such an audience, St. Mark surely could afford to take much for granted.

And he does. There are scores of illustrations, in this Gospel, of the kind just analyzed, and the young reader is invited to interpret them for himself. Living interpretation is ultimately, not the commentator's business, but the reader's privilege. It should be *his* delight, after working his way through the (more or less necessary) undergrowth of notes and explanations, to penetrate to the bright clearing and there enjoy the *manna absconditum*. But the present writer cherishes the hope that, in presenting to the young reader the text of the second Gospel in sense-lines and thought-units, he has helped him very materially in his noble endeavor. One great advantage of the colometric system of writing is that it *invites meditation*.

6. The Greek and Latin literatures were intended to convey their message through the ear of the attentive hearer, rather than through the eye of the silent reader.[41] For an ancient student of rhetoric skilful reading was an indispensable accomplishment. Now, a necessary condition for skilful reading was, in the opinion of the rhetoricians, *appropriate pausing*. They ruled, in describing the plain style of composition, that cola and commata should be short, affording the reader a chance to pause frequently, even in a sentence of small compass. To illustrate this method of reading, Demetrius (204, 205) quotes the following clause from Plato (*Rep.* 327 a), Κατέβην χθὲς εἰς Πειραιᾶ μετὰ Γλαύκωνος: "I went down yesterday to the Peiraeus together with Glaucon," and adds that "here the rests and cadences are many." W. Rhys Roberts explains this to mean that the reader is expected to pause slightly after χθές, Πειραιᾶ, and Γλαύκωνος. Since colon and comma are *rhythmical* entities,[42] frequent pauses allow the various rhythms to make their separate impressions on the ear of an attentive hearer. In the sentence from Aeschines, Ἐκαθήμεθα μὲν ἐπὶ τῶν θάκων ἐν Λυκείῳ οὗ οἱ ἀθλοθέται τὸν ἀγῶνα διατιθέασιν, "We sat upon the

---

[41] Norden, *AK.*, "Einleitung." Hendrickson, *Classical Journal*, 25, pp. on "Ancient Reading."

[42] Quintilian IX, iv, 122; VIII, vi, 64: "The reason why those four words in which Plato in the noblest of his works states that he had gone down to the Peiraeus were found written in a number of different orders upon his wax tablets, was simply that he desired to make the rhythm as perfect as possible." Dionysius of Halicarnassus, *Ep.tome*, 133. Kleist, *Classical Bulletin*, January 1930.

benches in the Lyceum, where the stewards of the games order the contests," Demetrius requires a pause after "sat" and after "Lyceum."

But more important to us than the quantitative rhythm of a Greek sentence is that structural rhythm (or τάξις) by which a writer conveys a composite thought in all its ramifications; for he does convey it primarily "by groups of words, not by words apprehended singly."[43] These articulations by which he expresses his mind distinctly and intelligently should be "marked by a perceptible pause in reciting, sometimes merely by the inflection and intonation of the voice." At any rate, a sympathetic reader has an instinctive feeling for the right grouping of words. There can be little doubt that in training their students to read pausefully the ancients were assisted by the use of colometrized texts. St. Jerome tells us that the practice of colometrizing Demosthenes and Cicero was common in his day, and Cassiodorus (born 480) states that colon-writing was introduced to help persons unskilled in the art of reading aloud.

In the New Testament we are not on artistic ground, but are in a colometric atmosphere just the same. St. Jerome did not think he was doing violence to the original by rendering it *per cola et commata*. Now cola and commata call for pauses. A sure way, then, of unlocking the Biblical treasures, the *Manna absconditum*, as it were, is a kind of reading, now abrupt, now meditative, that marks the numerous pauses suggested by sense and structure. In Mk. 1, 24, for instance, abrupt pausing will emphasize the fright as well as the impotence of the demon in the presence of Christ:

> Ha! Let us alone—Jesus of Nazareth!
> You come to destroy us!
> I know Who You are—God's Holy One!

On the other hand, in reading the Angel's Easter message (16, 6) a few meditative pauses will help us to feel how sweetly Heaven's messenger removes the fright of the pious visitors to the tomb and how gently he breaks the glad tidings of the resurrection:

> Do not be frightened!
> It is Jesus you are looking for—
> > the Nazarene,
> > the Crucified.
> He is not here.
> He is risen.

---

[43] See footnote 25. For "structural rhythm," see Quintilian IX, iv, 1–19.

In what other than that pauseful, reflective utterance which is invited by colometry can we fancy our Lord driving home to the rich man, blow by blow, those unpleasant demands which in the end repelled the worldling:

> One thing is still wanting to you:
> go; sell all you have,
> and give the proceeds to the poor
> —for which you will have treasure in heaven—
> and, when you have thus taken up your cross,
> you may return and be one of My followers.

Undue haste in uttering this Call would have defeated its purpose: the young man had to be brought to realize each separate step in his becoming Christ's disciple. To us the New Testament is familiar from constant reading and pious meditation: to the original hearers or readers some of its truths were strange and many of its demands distasteful. Frequent pausing and repetition of unpleasant teachings were, we know, among the pedagogical methods constantly employed by our Lord. In this, as in other respects, He was the great Pattern of the teacher. Quintilian lets us glimpse into the secrets of ancient speakers and writers, by carefully distinguishing between "full stops," "slight pauses," and "mere checks in breathing,"[44] and gives us besides a *demonstratio ad oculos* applied to the opening lines of Virgil's *Aeneid*. The old schoolmaster sums up his long experience in this memorable dictum: "Correctness of punctuation may seem to be a trifling merit, but without it all the merits of oratory are worth nothing." We shall do well to apply this principle to our reading. In reading Lk. 23, 32, for instance, καὶ ἕτεροι κακοῦργοι δύο, only a pause after ἕτεροι can redeem the expression from downright blasphemy (Smyth 1272). See notes on 1, 19; 10, 46; 13, 34; 14, 30.

7. Perhaps a word should here be added about *St. Mark's ways of disposing the common element* in his composite sentences. By a common element we mean a word or phrase common to two (or more) parts of the same sentence. When Polybius says (1, 86, 1) that someone τὴν χώραν ἐπῄει καὶ τὰς πόλεις, the verb governs both nouns, but is placed only with the first. Evidently this common element might have been joined to the second object. There is room in this idiom, therefore, for great variety, especially when the common element con-

---

[44] Quintilian IX, iv, 67 ff.; XI, iii, 35 ff.

sists of two or more words. Thus Isocrates, wishing to say that a certain defense is "best and fairest," arranges the words as follows: (ἐγὼ) καλλίστην (ἡγοῦμαι) καὶ δικαιοτάτην (εἶναι τὴν τοιαύτην ἀπολογίαν). This interlocking is not due to chance, but was chosen for effect: it throws all emphasis on the two adjectives "best" and "fairest." Latin writers resort to the same device for the same purpose. In Horace's line, "aut prodesse (volunt) aut delectare (poetae)," both *volunt* and *poetae* belong with either alternative, and their clever disposal brings *prodesse* and *delectare* into sharp relief. The poet's *curiosa felicitas* has enabled him to indicate in the tersest way possible, and therefore in a classic way, the two polar purposes of poetry.

If the student of Latin would see to what lengths a writer can go in disposing the common elements of his sentences, he should go to the works, particularly the speeches, of Cicero. The Fourth Catilinarian contains the following comparatively simple passage:

> aspectus *Cethegi* et furor
> in vestra caede bacchantis.

Here the genitive *bacchantis* shows that the entire second colon is an apposition to *Cethegi*. The following, from the same source, is more complicated:

> qui nos omnis,
> qui populum Romanum *vita privare conati sunt,*
> qui delere imperium,
> qui populi Romani nomen exstinguere.

Of these four cola, the second contains all the common elements, although *vita privare* belongs to colon one and two, while *conati sunt,* the predicate of the entire sentence, is understood with colon two, three, and four. In delivering this oration Cicero had no fear of being misunderstood, for undoubtedly his *pronuntiatio* with its oral (and possibly facial) accessories made his meaning perfectly clear. Students of rhetoric will at once see why Cicero did not place *conati sunt* at the very end, for there the phrase would have prevented the double cretic ($- \smile -, - \smile -$: *nomen exstinguere*) from exerting its full force, and destroyed the phrasal symmetry or rythm of the passage.

Knowing what we do about St. Mark, we should not look for great artistry in his way of disposing the common element. However, in any given passage this element is where it is, not because it strayed there, but because St. Mark put it there. Acquaintance with his methods of marshaling the common element may be of use in elucidating some difficult passage. If we colometrize Mk. 9, 14 as follows:

Καὶ ἐλθὼν πρὸς τοὺς μαθητάς
(εἶδεν) ὄχλον πολὺν (περὶ αὐτοὺς) καὶ γραμματεῖς
(συνζητοῦντας πρὸς αὐτούς),

we see at a glance that εἶδεν governs both ὄχλον πολύν and γραμματεῖς ; also that the participle συνζητοῦντας belongs both with γραμματεῖς and with ὄχλον πολύν. Consequently, when commentators wonder why our Lord's question (τί συνζητεῖτε), addressed, it might seem, to the Scribes, was answered by the father of the epileptic boy, we know at once that they erred in connecting συνζητοῦντας with γραμματεῖς exclusively, instead of including the ὄχλος πολύς with which the father had come along. It is clear, also, that when our Lord appeared on the scene, πᾶς ὁ ὄχλος = the entire multitude, γραμματεῖς as well as ὄχλος πολύς, hastened to meet Him. Cf. the note on 1, 45 where πολλά and τὸν λόγον may be common elements.

There is a more important problem in Mk. 10, 46, where the solution of the *crux interpretum* may depend on our recognizing ἐκπορευομένου and ἀπὸ Ἰεριχώ, as common elements. Our Lord was traveling, and so of course were His disciples; He was ἀπὸ Ἰεριχώ, and so again were His disciples. Now, just when He and His disciples were "at a distance from Jericho," Bartimaeus sat beside the road begging. There is not the least difficulty in harmonizing this account with that of St. Luke who says that a blind man was cured just as Jesus approached the city. It is not denied that other ways out of the impasse may be more acceptable; all that is contended is that, once we clearly understand St. Mark's ways of disposing the so-called common elements of his sentences, the *crux* in 10, 46 vanishes into thin air. A writer's way of distributing his common elements is one way of speaking his mind to us. St. Mark makes use of more than half a dozen ways of distributing them.

Compare, for instance:

9, 22 : (πολλάκις) καὶ εἰς πῦρ (αὐτὸν ἔβαλεν) καὶ εἰς ὕδατα.

1, 45 : κηρύσσειν (πολλὰ) καὶ διαφημίζειν (τὸν λόγον).

13, 22 : (δώσουσιν) σημεῖα καὶ τέρατα (πρὸς τὸ ἀποπλᾶν).

1, 26 : σπαράξαν αὐτὸν (τὸ πνεῦμα) καὶ φωνῆσαν.

5, 19 : (ὅσα) σοι (ὁ κύριος) πεποίηκεν καὶ ἠλέησέν σε.

8. When Alexander the Great invaded the East, his engines of war were followed by more peaceful means of conquest—the treasures of Hellenic culture. Among these was *the charm and music of Hellenic*

speech. As the accents of Hellas fell on foreign ears, they were, no doubt, but imperfectly caught by the barbarian mind, and reëchoed but haltingly by the barbarian tongue; yet we should err were we to suppose that in the days of the Koine the old Greek sense of rhythm of language had vanished from the earth.[45] Three centuries after the heyday of Greek speech, we find Dionysius of Halicarnassus discoursing at Rome on the euphoniousness of Greek vowels, on nobility and charm in style, on the means by which these qualities may be attained, on melody, rhythm, and variety of speech, on susceptibility to harmonious sounds as "nature's universal gift to man." He is at one with Aristotle in laying down the rule that prose must be metrical, rhythmical, and melodious—though not meter, rhythm, and poem. It would be strange if genuine, though broken, strains of the music of Hellenic speech had not been floating in the air even in that late day, and had not "strayed" even into the Gospel of St. Mark. When St. Mark records our Lord's weary complaint in 9, 19, it is impossible to suppose that he was utterly insensible to its quantitative and structural rhythm:

| ἕως | πότε | πρὸς | ὑμᾶς | ἔσομαι |
| ἕως | πότε | ἀνέξομαι | | ὑμῶν. |

Or let us take the two parallel lines which open St. Mark's account of our Lord's parabolic teaching with this stately introductory measure, a sort of Anacrusis (Mk. 4, 2):

καὶ ἐδίδασκεν αὐτοὺς ἐν παραβολαῖς πολλά
καὶ ἔλεγεν αὐτοῖς ἐν τῇ διδαχῇ αὐτοῦ.

The very rhythm, even apart from the meaning of the words, puts the hearer in a solemn and attentive mood.

The last verses of the Gospel picture the glorious reign of the Risen Christ in Heaven and the triumphant march of the Gospel on earth. The theme is lofty, too lofty almost for human words; but St. Mark, with a sure instinct for values of sound, uses large expressions, and renders his *finale* melodious by sonorous "o" sounds and by syllables long by nature:

---

[45] Quintilian IX, iv, 10: "Nihil intrare potest in adfectus, quod in aure velut quodam vestibulo statim offendit." For Cicero's views on *numerus* = ῥυθμός, see Laurand, II, 118 ff. Moore, *Orations*, Introd. xxvi. Butcher, *Originality*, 169 ff. Havers stresses "Ton- und Satz-melodie" as clues to the sense of a phrase or passage.

’Εκεῖνοι δὲ ἐξελθόντες
ἐκήρυξαν πανταχοῦ
τοῦ Κυρίου συνεργοῦντος
καὶ τὸν λόγον βεβαιοῦντος
διὰ τῶν ἐπακολουθούντων σημείων.

It has been said, not untruly, that "in so entirely musical a language as Greek, and one in which the art of literary composition was so minutely and diligently taught, the absence of rhythm is perhaps as interesting a phenomenon as its presence" (Robson). If this be so, the general lack of music in the second Gospel is one of the most decisive arguments for the tradition which sees in it a more or less faithful reproduction of words originally *spoken* by untrained men. "Non-rhythmical Greek," says the same writer, "will be either a rough translation, or a piece of mere copy, to be worked up, perhaps, later, but at present artless and naïve." We are glad to think that the writer of the second Gospel, St. Mark, has left his original copy as artless and naïve—if these be the right epithets for his Message of Salvation—in the same state in which he had caught them from the artless lips of his voucher, St. Peter.[46]

But enough. In point of artistry, the second Gospel, viewed as a whole, falls considerably below the general ancient achievement; yet even St. Mark, we should think, was human enough to wish to impress his message on the ear of his hearers. Knowing that the Memoirs of St. Peter would be read aloud and in full assembly, even he must have

---

[46] In recent years the question of NT rhythm has attracted attention. E. S. Robson's inquiry into "Rhythm and Intonation in St. Mark 1–10" (*JThSt.* XVII, 270 ff.) proves that our knowledge of NT rhythm is extremely meager. The author finds that "every-day private letters" (including Theon's naughty letter to his father) "exhibit touches of rhythm." No wonder Blass felt obliged to warn against that "hunt for verse-rhythming in NT." Robson is more felicitous in calling attention to vowel tones playing a considerable part in literary Greek. "Rhythm includes consonant and vowel colorings which all go to swell the musical element of Greek." Robson gives a brief and rapid survey of some more striking instances in the first ten chapters of St. Mark of conscious or unconscious rhythm, but the results are "meagre enough." The beginner in NT Greek should leave questions of mere theory to more advanced study, but strenuously develop the habit of reading the NT with close attention to both quantitative and structural rhythm.

For the latest literature on NT rhythm, see Blass-Debrunner 487, with "Nachträge," p. 321. Grandmaison, *Jésus-Christ*, Note C. pp. 203 ff. Marcel Jousse's *Le Style Oral*, etc.; criticized by Chapman, *The Dublin Review*, July, 1929. Cornely-Merk, *Compendium*, 61, 2, b. *Zeitschr. f. k. Theol.;* see above, footnote 22. Cp Aristotle, *Rhet.*, III, ch. 8.

hoped that they would penetrate to the Christian heart "without stumbling at the portals of the ear." It is our plain duty, then, to read these Memoirs, these precious reminiscences about Christ, in a manner in which any ancient document requires to be read: with attention to accent and quantity (Quantitative Rhythm); with advertence to the distribution of cola and commata (Structural Rhythm); with frequent pauses dictated by sympathy (Pauses); with a feeling which echoes the ethos or pathos of each passage read (Emotion); and, above all, with reverence due to the Word of God (Summary of the Message of Salvation).[47]

The sun of Hellas sets in the New Testament; but that sun, even in its setting, is still the sun:[48]

$$\text{Δυόμενος γὰρ ὅμως ἥλιός ἐστιν ἔτι.}$$

---

[47] For the "music" of Greek and Latin speech, see Bennett, *The Latin Language*, 54. Sturtevant, *The Pronunciation of Greek and Latin*, 216 ff. Buck, *Comparative Grammar of Greek and Latin*, 217 ff. Butcher, *Originality*, 240. Leumann, on "Betonung" and "Silben-, Wort-, und Satz-akzent," p. 180. Dionysius of Halicarnassus, *De Compos. Verborum*, xi. For St. Augustine's estimate of St. Ambrose as a speaker, see Aug. *Confess.*, V, 13. Aug. *De Doctr. Chr.*, IV, xxvi, 56.

Plato (*Protag.*, 326) tells us that the παιδεία of a Greek boy consisted largely of the study of μουσική. "When the boy learns to play the harp, he is taught the works of the lyrical poets, those builders of song. And the masters insist on familiarizing the boy's soul with the rhythms and scales, that it may gain in gentleness, and that by advancing in rhythm and harmonic grace he may be *efficient in speech* and action, for the whole round of man's life requires the graces of rhythm and harmony." Dionysius holds that the feeling for melody is not the monopoly of a few chosen souls. "When a player on the harp or flute strikes a false note, the ἄμουσος ὄχλος (the unmusical, uneducated masses) at once raise a disturbance." From which he infers that "there is a touch of inborn affinity in all of us for beauty of melody and beauty of rhythm"; φυσική τίς ἐστιν ἁπάντων ἡμῶν οἰκειότης πρὸς εὐμέλειάν τε καὶ εὐρυθμίαν.

[48] Mr. Norden, in the excellent *Einleitung* to his *Antike Kunstprosa*, very aptly likens Greek prose in its final decay to the sun in its setting.

II. ANNOTATIONS

A. Notes on General Features of Style.
B. Brief Notes on Special Passages.

Cognoscere semper aliquid atque discere.

—Cicero

Διπλοῦν ὁρῶσιν οἱ μαθόντες γράμματα.

—Menander

Δεῖ ἀσκεῖν ἅμα τῇ μαθήσει τὴν εὕρεσιν.

—Plutarch

Expositio ita nescientibus fiat cognita ut tamen scientibus non sit onerosa.

—Saint Gregory the Great

There is so much taken for granted in philological and linguistic tradition, so many formulas afloat that need mooring or sinking, that even the novice can render acceptable service.

—Basil Lanneau Gildersleeve

Till four years ago, my own teaching work scarcely touched the Greek Testament, classics and comparative philology claiming the major part of my time. But I have not felt that this time was ill spent as a preparation for the teaching of the New Testament.

—James Hope Moulton

PREFATORY NOTE

The subjoined Notes are not concerned with Marcan Accidence, embracing Orthography, Declension, and Conjugation, but with Marcan idiom only. To find that *this idiom is essentially Greek*, is no surprise to anyone who considers that St. Mark's diction is but a typical cross-section of the spoken Koine, and that the spoken Koine in turn derives by a natural growth from the spoken speech of Hellas. Already in the sixth and fifth centuries B.C., the Greek vernacular had expanded its sphere of influence, timidly at first and sporadically, beyond the confines of Attica. After the downfall of Greek freedom, at the end of the fourth century, it entered, boldly and with the ardor of a conqueror, on its mission as a civilizer on a gigantic and cosmopolitan scale. Naturally its purity suffered somewhat in the conquest, and for four centuries prior to the rise of the New Testament, Greek idiom was in the crucible. For four centuries, it was put to the test in a subtle conflict with the varying vernaculars of the Eastern peoples; but even so, when it finally appeared in the New Testament, as a vehicle of ideas unheard of in the world before, it still rang true. This is the irresistible conviction that forces itself on all those who, after devoting years of study to ancient Greek, abruptly turn to the Greek of the New Testament. Traces of an inevitable wear and tear are of course recognizable here and there; but one is struck with the tenaciousness of a language that held its own through so many centuries. The New Testament, so far as the language is concerned, stands rooted in antiquity, and modern scholars do not hesitate to elucidate New Testament Greek by references to ancient Greek. The student whom these Notes are expected to benefit is, therefore, primarily one who has a fair knowledge of the ancient tongue and is now anxious to see how that knowledge will stand him in good stead in trying to appreciate the Gospel of St. Mark.

Marcan Greek is worth studying with loving care. It is worth studying for its own sake, because such study means a deeper understanding of a precious Christian document. We do not expect to find in St. Mark's Gospel the rounded periods of Isocrates or those devices of rhetoric that give life and grace to a Greek sentence. Our search is

131

for something better: in reading St. Mark we listen to the Prince of the Apostles explaining "the words and works of the Lord"; in a sense we listen to Christ Himself, for the Apostle, a first-class eye-witness, was no doubt anxious to save as much as possible of the actual words of Christ. Style—there is none in this Gospel; but there is idiom, and there is life, in it. Every word is vibrant with the high seriousness of those "eye-witnesses from the beginning," those "ministers of the word." It is to this precious content that the knowledge of ancient Greek idiom must furnish a clue.

Marcan Greek is also worth studying for the sake of the entire New Testament; for, strange as that may sound, the syntactical and linguistic problems met with in this Gospel are the same as those we meet in the rest of the New Testament. Paul, James, Matthew, John, were they not all men of the people who spoke the spoken Greek of their time? There are degrees observable in their social status, but their language is the same.

Scholars have given us a bird's-eye view of *the peculiarities of Marcan style*. St. Mark, it has been said, is fond of diminutives. True; but so is the Koine and, to an extent, older Greek, at least in certain types of a more popular kind. The participle with forms of $\epsilon\mathrm{\grave{\iota}}\mu\iota$ is common in St. Mark; but, again, the periphrastic tenses are common in the Koine generally (Mayser, 223 ff.) and are not wanting in the Greek of older days. St. Mark multiplies the pictorial participle. The truth is he merely overdoes a feature of genuine Greek. He loves the double negative; but negative combinations of the most varied kinds abound in every sort of Greek. The articular infinitive is frequent in the second Gospel, and frequent enough in better Greek to be known even to the novice. St. Mark is fond of pleonastic expression; but Demosthenes, for example, has more striking specimens of "redundancy," and that for no better purpose than the Evangelist; both wish to be vivid, the one because he is a literary artist, the other because he follows a natural instinct. Besides, are we consistent in praising St. Mark for his graphic descriptions and, in the same breath, censuring him for fullness of expression? In this, as in other respects, we should measure St. Mark by ancient standards, not by our own. Demetrius (*On Style*, 208–220) teaches that vividness arises from "repetition" and from "an exact narration overlooking no detail." In the following quotation let us substitute *Mark* for *Ctesias:* "The charge of garrulity often brought against Ctesias on the ground of his repetitions can perhaps in many cases be established, but in many instances it is his critics who fail to appreciate the writer's vividness." With this in mind, let us read, for example, Mk. 11, 13, where ἦλθεν is closely followed by ἐλθὼν ἐπ' αὐτήν; or 14, 16, where ἐξῆλθον is followed by ἦλθον εἰς τὴν πόλιν. St. Mark *sees* things, and describes them as he sees them. Again, he has anacolutha and parentheses; but so have good writers. In self-defense St. Mark can plead scrupulous adherence (ἀκριβῶς) to St. Peter's manner of instructing his converts. St. Mark uses εὐθύς 41 times. This "idiosyncrasy" may perhaps help us to understand in what light he looked at our Lord's brief but eventful ministry. He "confuses" his tenses. In reality his sixteen chapters do not contain a single tense that is out of order. His universal connective is καί; but the prevalence of καί in the Koine is well established. He abounds in parataxis; but, from Homer down, parataxis is of the very fiber of Greek. There is little artistry in his Gospel. But he is a first-rate story-teller, vivid, picturesque, full of life. His stories are brief and told with effect.

The upshot is simple: Marcan Greek is a particular kind of Greek, not because it is foreigner's Greek, but because it overworks genuine idioms, or accentuates tendencies seen in ancient Greek only sporadically. In this St. Mark is a child of his times. In what is his own he is far from contemptible. His limited vocabulary is made to do wonders. His Ἀρχή is a readable composition. His colloquial Greek arrests attention. What a distance between it and the best Papyrus! An eminent student of the New Testament has said: "He who has a taste for the unaffected, artless talk of a man of the people will read St. Mark with great delight" (H. J. Cladder). No doubt when we have finished reading him and abruptly turn to ancient prose, we are glad once more to bask in the pure light of classic finish. By the side of such transcendent beauty, the best in St. Mark is crude. But the keenest esthetic pleasure palls when long indulged in, and we are glad to return from Art to Nature, from the master of prose to the man of the people, whose lifelike, natural manner refreshes us. Approached in that sympathetic mood, St. Mark's mannerisms are like an antidote against the cult of flawless perfection. In the genial company of this plain man we breathe more freely, and feel the human pulse more directly, than we can in communion with the consummate masters. The very thought of a Gospel fixed in the faultless forms of classic prose is repellent. In the Gospel of St. Mark we are at home.

I can assure the beginner that I have tried to make the Notes in this volume readable, tangible, usable. Genuine Greek idiom is the point of attack for him if he would learn to do constructive work in

New Testament exegesis. Let him regard each Note, not as a thing that ends in itself, but as something to lead him on to independent research; and he will find that he cannot go far in the rest of the New Testament without stumbling on scores of illustrations of the very idioms here pointed out to him. It is in this (limited) sense that I am offering this GOSPEL OF ST. MARK as a sort of miniature introduction to New Testament Greek in general.

As to details regarding St. Mark's diction, the student will find much that is pertinent, in some well-known commentaries on the second Gospel, as those by Lagrange, Knabenbauer, and others; in several volumes of the *Journal of Theological Studies* and of the *Recherches de science religieuse;* and in New Testament Grammars. Illustrations of Marcan Greek from the Papyri are readily accessible in works like Moulton's *Prolegomena*, Deissmann's *Licht vom Osten*, Robertson's Historical *Grammar*, Moulton-Milligan's *Vocabulary*, Milligan's *Selections from the Greek Papyri*, Hunt's *Papyri* in the Loeb Library, Witkowski's *Epistulae Privatae Graecae*, Mayser's *Grammatik der griechischen Papyri*. Also the two standard dictionaries by Zorrell and Bauer abound in illustrations and references. Two very recent studies are Dom B. Botti's *Grammaire Grecque du Nouveau Testament* (Paris, 1933) and H. Pernot's *Etudes sur la langue des Evangiles* (Paris, 1927). See below, p. 160; and Brief Note on Mk. 14, 8.

> Τὰ ῥήματα τῆς θείας γραφῆς ἐξετάσωμεν,
> κατὰ τὸ δυνατὸν ἡμῖν
> ἀναπτύσσοντες αὐτῶν τὴν διάνοιαν.
>
> —*St. Basil the Great*

> Τὸ ἀφανὲς ἐκ τοῦ φανεροῦ ταχίστην ἔχει τὴν διάγνωσιν.
>
> *Isocrates, To Demonicus,* 34

ABBREVIATIONS

acc.—accusative.
adv.—adverb.
Aes.—Aeschylus.
  Eum.—Eumenides.
AJPh.—American Journal of Philology.
al.—*alii.*
Arist.—Aristophanes.
aor.—aorist.
cf.—*confer,* compare.
Cicero
  de or.—de oratore.
  or.—orator.
class.—classical.
Colometry, A 1, etc.—Refers to the essay on Ancient Colometry, above.
Cor.—Epistle to the Corinthians.
cpd. cpds.—compound(s).
dat.—dative.
Diog. Laert.—Diogenes Laertius.
Epict.—Epictetus.
equiv.—equivalent.
ex. exx.—example(s).
Eur.—Euripides.
  HF.—Hercules Furens.
  Iph. T.—Iphigenia Taurica.
  Or.—Orestes.
  Tro.—Troades.
f. ff. foll.—following.
fut. ft.—future.
gen.—genitive.
Gr.—Greek.
Herod.—Herodotus.
Hesiod—
  Theog.—*Theogonia.*
Hom. Hymn Dem.—*Homeric Hymn to Demeter.*
hist.—historical.
ib. ibid.—*ibidem.*
impf.—imperfect.
impv. imper.—imperative.
ind. indic.—indicative.
indecl.—indeclinable.

indef.—indefinite.
intr.—intransitive.
Introd.—Introduction.
Is.—Isocrates.
  Anti.—Antidosis.
  Demon.—To Demonicus.
  Pan.—Panegyricus.
Jn.—John.
L&S.—Liddle and Scott; new edition.
Lk.—St. Luke.
Mk.—St. Mark.
ms. mss.—manuscript(s).
Mt.—St. Matthew.
Note A, etc.—Refers to the Notes on General Features of Style.
NT.—New Testament.
obj.—objective.
opp.—opposed.
part. partic.—participle.
pass.—passive.
Pd. Pind.—Pindar.
  Ol.—Olympians.
  Nem.—Nemeans.
  Pyth.—Pythians.
pf.—perfect.
pl. plur.—plural.
Pl.—Plato.
  Apol.—Apologia.
  Ph. Phaed.—*Phaedo.*
  Phil.—Philebus.
  Protag.—Protagoras.
  Rep.—Republic.
  Theaet.—Theaetetus.
Plautus
  Poen.—Poenulus.
pred.—predicate.
pref.—preface.
prep.—preposition.
pres.—present.
pron.—pronoun.
ref.—reference.
refl.—reflexive.

rel.—relative.	Th. Thuc.—Thucydides.
sc.—scilicet.	Thess.—Epistle to the Thessalonians.
sg.—singular.	tr.—transitive.
So.—Sophocles.	v.—verse.
Ant.—Antigone.	vv.—verses.
OT.—Oedipus Rex.	Vergil *Aen.—Aeneid.*
Phil.—Philoctetus.	Xen.—Xenophon.
El.—Electra.	*Anab.—Anabasis.*
subj.—subjective.	*Cyr.—Cyropedia.*
subjv.—subjunctive.	*Hell.—Hellenica.*
s.v.—*sub verbo.*	*Memor.—Memorabilia.*

LARGER NOTES

A. Parataxis
B. Potential Phraseology
C. Apparent Tautology
D. Relativity of Terms
E. Modal Interpretation
F. Parallel Orientation
G. Stressing the Starting-Point
H. "Pliable and Good-natured Καί"
I. Marcan Ἤρξατο
K. Marcan Εὐθύς
L. Biblical Ἀποκρίνεσθαι
M. Marcan Ἐκπλήττεσθαι
N. Marcan Σκανδαλίζεσθαι
O. Varying the English Equivalent
P. Marcan Flexibility of Expression
Q. The Spoken Gospel
R. The Semitic Strain in the Second Gospel
S. St. Mark's Vocabulary
T. Points of Syntax:
    1. The Aoristic Present
    2. Coincident Action
U. Glimpses of Marcan Rhetoric

IMPORTANT NOTE: Throughout this work, all references to books or publications are made, *wherever possible*, to sections or marginal numbers, and not to pages. Reference to an author does not necessarily imply agreement with his view.

A. NOTES ON GENERAL FEATURES OF STYLE

A. Parataxis

If, on being invited to deliver a speech, we reply that "we shall try and do our best," we are using a mode of expression that has left a deep imprint on Greek and Latin Literature. Instead of subordinating our ideas and expressing them hypotactically ("We shall try to do our best"), we are coördinating them and expressing them paratactically. Cicero, *De oratore*, I, 187, says: "Experiar et dicam planius." In Plato's *Philebus*, 13 c, Socrates says: Πειρασόμεθα καὶ ἐροῦμεν.

In all languages parataxis is a natural way of speaking, and the languages of some Indians know no other way but this. Children, illiterate folk, and the plain man—all prefer to speak paratactically. They set words, phrases, or even clauses side by side (παρα- and τάσσω), sometimes joining them by some coördinating particle (Coördination), sometimes leaving them unconnected (Asyndeton; Juxtaposition). People who are averse to mental exertion find parataxis very convenient; they would rather save their energies than use them either to discover the finer relations of thought to thought or, if they know them, to formulate them by means of some device of language. The plain man's speech, moreover, is apt to be charged with feeling, but feeling is impatient of restraint, tends to burst its fetters, dispenses with tedious connectives, unloads itself in short and pithy phrases, and thus avoids the intricacies of hypotaxis. Besides allying itself with mental sloth and the inability of an excited mind to discharge its emotion through the more quiet channels of utterance, parataxis also takes the line of least resistance because the human mind does its thinking successively and piecemeal, rather than simultaneously and at a glance. Children tell a story bit by bit and feel uneasy in their attempts to subordinate. Sometimes parataxis is due to conditions extraneous to the mind. Perhaps foremost among these is the power to express the relation of thought to thought by other means than the spoken word. Gestures, tricks, and looks have expressional value, and may reveal one soul to another more intimately than bare words can do. To say that parataxis is the language of children and uneducated folk is to state a half-truth. In the closing chapter of the *Phaedo*, Plato yields consciously to the quiet charms of paratactic sentence structure in describing the last moments of Socrates. Rooted in the speech of everyday life, parataxis may be assumed by a writer or speaker for effect and thus made an artistic device. Hence the distinction between natural and artistic parataxis. One who uses parataxis for effect says apparently less than he means, yet gains in other respects; one who uses hypotaxis speaks more "logically," yet leaves less to the imagination or acumen of his hearer.

Greek parataxis has a long and noble ancestry. Homer is the great master of parataxis in poetry; Herodotus, in a less degree, in prose. When Greek became conscious of its powers, hypotaxis was widely cultivated, but parataxis remained a typical mode of structure. In the New Testament, parataxis is on the whole of the natural and primitive kind, a conclusion, however, that wants verification from case to case. No doubt the knowledge of the Hebrew *parallelismus membrorum* confirmed the New Testament writers in their tendency to paratactic presentation. Hence great caution is needed in estimating the effect of any given case of parataxis in the Gospels, especially where our Lord's parabolic teaching is reported.

As for St. Mark, we cannot suppose that he always uses parataxis with full advertence to its literary effect; but neither can we take for granted that he never noticed its possibilities. In 6, 42, for example, when he might have said, "All ate *until* they had their fill"—for he uses such subordination in 6, 10, "Stay there *until* you leave that district"—he did use coördination, "They all ate *and* everyone had his fill" (just as St. Luke writes in 9, 4, "Stay there *and* leave from there"). Shall we qualify St. Mark's wording as naïve or careless writing, or, may we not see design in it? Scholars have quoted the sentence as an example of St. Mark's supposed love for fullness of expression, merely on the ground that χορτασθῆναι already implies φαγεῖν! Surely St. Mark never thought of this subtle implication. As a faithful recorder, all he wished to do was to tell how St. Peter had told the incident and had stressed the miraculous character of the feeding: "*All ate* of the bread given them and, mind you, *everyone* of the five thousand persons had his *fill!*"

To recognize genuine parataxis is not always easy. Parataxis is genuine when one of the two notions, which are coördinated in grammar, is subordinated to the other in thought. In Mk. 2, 25, the distress (χρεία) is not, as one might hastily infer from καί, a fresh inconvenience extrinsic to the hunger (ἐπείνασεν). It rather specifies the hunger and tells in what it consisted; the phrase χρείαν ἔσχεν καὶ ἐπείνασεν is therefore paratactic: "he felt the pinch of hunger." Again, growth in age or stature is not simply coördinate with growth in grace or wisdom (Lk. 2, 52); hence, the use of καί in that passage is paratactic: "He grew in grace, *as* in age, and in wisdom." In Ephes. 4, 26, ὀργίζεσθε καὶ μὴ ἁμαρτάνετε, the first imperative is not a direct exhortation to anger, but the sense is: "*If* angry, beware of sinning" (Weymouth). But the imperative may be permissive: "Be angry; but do not sin" (Goodspeed)—a concise way of saying, "You may be angry, if necessary; only, *when* you are angry, do not sin." The phrase (Mk. 1, 17), δεῦτε ὀπίσω μου, καὶ ποιήσω ὑμᾶς . . . , is probably not paratactic, for here the imperative may have absolute value: "Come, and follow Me. I will make you fishers of men"; not "*If* you come. . . ." In Arist. *Wasps*, 300 ff., the chorus says: "I have to buy fuel, and bread, and sauce; *and* you want me to buy figs for you?" ἔχειν ἄλφιτα δεῖ, σὺ δὲ σῦκά μ᾽ αἰτεῖς; This is genuine parataxis, meant to show the incongruity of the request for figs under those circumstances. Just so St. Mark makes the disciples say: "You see the crowd push again st You *and* You ask, 'Who touched Me?' " (5, 31.)

A vivid realization of the ubiquity of parataxis in the New Testament will make the student cautious: instead of being content with the face value of καί or μέν–δέ, he will look beneath the surface and try to understand the relation of thought to thought. A μέν-clause usually pictures the background against which the corresponding δέ-clause needs to be viewed (Jebb). With regard to rendering St. Mark's paratactic passages, no general rule can be given. Frequently an obvious parataxis may be retained to good advantage especially as a concession to Marcan simplicity of diction.

The following conjunctions may express parataxis. Copulative: καί, δέ, οὐδέ, μήτε; adversative: ἀλλά, δέ, μέντοι, καίτοι; disjunctive: ἤ, ἤ–ἤ, εἴτε–εἴτε; inferential: ἄρα, οὖν, τοίνυν; causal: γάρ. Smith 2163. Gerth (516, 5) points out that, when γάρ or οὖν, etc., is used, there is grammatical parataxis, but the subordination of the thought is *revealed* instead of being concealed. For paratactic οὔτε—οὔτε, see Theognis, 107–108.

Study the foll. Marcan passages: 2, 15, ἦσαν καὶ ἠκολούθουν; 2, 18, τί νηστεύουσιν- οὐ νηστεύουσιν; 2, 25, χρείαν ἔσχεν καὶ ἐπείνασεν; 5, 4, δεδέσθαι καὶ διεσπάσθαι; 5, 19, πεποίηκεν καὶ ἠλέησεν; 6, 42, ἔφαγον καὶ ἐχορτάσθησαν; 9, 4, ὤφθη καὶ ἦσαν συνλαλοῦντες; 9, 39; ὃς ποιήσει καὶ δυνήσεται; 9, 42, περίκειται καὶ βέβληται; 10, 32, καὶ ἐθαμβοῦντο; 15, 25, ὥρα τρίτη καὶ ἐσταύρωσαν; 6, 50, εἶδον καὶ ἐταράχθησαν.

A typical illustration of Homeric Parataxis is *Il.* I, 453–455, where Chryses offers his second prayer to Apollo:

453: ἠμὲν δή ποτ' ἐμεῦ πάρος ἔκλυες εὐξαμένοιο
455: ἠδ' ἔτι καὶ νῦν μοι τόδ' ἐπικρήηνον ἐέλδωρ.

This coupling of the reference to the priest's first prayer (453) with the petition addressed to Apollo (455) is awkward in English: "You heard me in the past *and* now again fulfil my hope." The use of μὲν—δέ shows that we are to view each clause in the light of the other. Now, the reference to the prayer in the past rouses the petitioner to greater confidence and is meant to insure Apollo's good will a second time. Chryses means to say:

As you heard me once before, when I made prayer,
so now again fulfil this hope of mine.

But matters are complicated by the insertion of a second paratactic structure within the first:

454: τίμησας μὲν ἐμέ, μέγα δ' ἴψαο λαὸν Ἀχαιῶν.

This line records the double effect of the first prayer: honor bestowed on Chryses and trouble inflicted on the Greeks. It, too, is intended to strengthen the priest's claim to help: just as Apollo had heard his prayer when he cursed the Greeks, so the god ought fitly to hear his prayer now that he blesses them. Here, again, the μέν-clause contains the thought which we should subordinate:

As you heard me once before when I made prayer,
—indeed, *to* honor me
you mightily chastized the Grecian host—
so now in turn fulfil this hope of mine.

Literature on Parataxis. Smyth 2159–2172; 1839; Howard pp. 420 ff.; Donovan 395–404; Colwell 17–21; Moulton (*passim*); *Classical Journal*, Dec., 1925, on "Paratactic Καί"; Hofmann *Synt.* 227; id., *Umgangssprache* 100–108; Radermacher 218–222; Gildersleeve *AJPh.*, Vol. 23, 241 ff.; *Festschrift Poland* 119; Brugmann 643–646; Sommer 95 ff.; Gerth 515 ff.; Errandonea 288; Blass 438; 442 ff.; 458. Lagerkrantz in *Eranos* XIV, 171 ff.; Norden *AK.*, *passim;* id. *ATh.*, 355; id., *Aeneis* VI, 178 ff.; 307; 378 ff.; Robertson 426 ff.

Wackernagel I, 62, points out the connection between parataxis and hendiadys. Havers (*passim*) discusses parataxis as an emotional element of style. For parataxis in Homer, see Classen; for Sophocles, see Jebb's commentaries (Index). The psychology of asyndeton is discussed by Aristotle *Rhet.* III, xii, 4 ff.; Quintilian IX, iii, 50–54; *Demetrius On Style* 192–194; Barry 97; Campbell 44; Genung 318 footnote and 298; Wilamowitz, *Euripides, Herakles* (*passim*); see esp. on 101, 494, 509. For Plato's use of parataxis by way of parody, see Norden *ATh.* 368. For Asyndeton, see also Kroll, *Studien*, 367.

Herodotus is generally named as an example of the paratactic style because Aristotle (*Rhet.* 3, 9, 2) cites him among those παλαιοί who used the λέξις εἰρομένη: to be quite precise, however, the style of that historian betrays acquaintance with Sophistic theories and marks a transition from the "continuous" to the "periodic" (κατεστραμμένη) diction. See Norden *ATh.* 368.

B. *Potential Phraseology*

The writings of Aristotle and the discussions of Socrates in Plato are proof that Greek writers could express themselves with all the precision the subject matter might require. But hand in hand with this meticulous exactness went at times a tendency to brachylogical diction which, from our point of view, was a tendency to be obscure. "All human speech," says Havers (p. 64), "is essentially elliptical." Greek is no exception to the rule (see, for instance, Gerth 596 and 597. Smyth 3017; 3018). Now, one form of this brachylogy (or, shall we say, nonchalant carelessness?) is met with in our own language when, for instance, we say "I beg to remark," though strictly the thing begged for is not the actual remarking, but "leave or permission to remark" or "the right or privilege of remarking." Or, again, when a mother says to her naughty child, "You are the death of me," she means of course "the cause of my death." Or, "A family is a great responsibility," for "a charge that brings with it much responsibility." And so in a thousand ways.

In Greek, too, the object of a verb is, in numerous cases, not the *res in se*, but a *via ad rem;* not the thing in itself, but a way of coming by it, a means of approaching it, permission to do it, or that which brings something else with it. In Xen. *Hell.* 1, 6, 31, the ships were arranged in a certain way ἵνα μὴ διέκπλουν διδοῖεν, "so as not to give the enemy *a chance* of breaking through" (Brownson). Eur. *HF.* 732: Ἔχει ἡδονὰς θνῄσκων ἀνὴρ ἐχθρός, not "a dying enemy *feels* pleasure," but "is *a cause of* joy to others," ("Joy it is to see an enemy die"; Way). In John 11, 25, our Lord says: Ἐγώ εἰμι ἡ ἀνάστασις καὶ ἡ ζωή, "Ego sum resurrectionis et vitae Auctor" (A metonymy: Zorell). Aes. *Eum.* 588, οὗτις ἄρνησις πέλει, "I *cannot* well deny." So. *Phil.* 61, ἅλωσις, "*a means* of capture." Pl. *Theaet.* 146 b, ἔχει ἐπίδοσιν, "*admits* of improvement." Th. 3, 53, 2, λόγον ᾐτησάμεθα, "we asked for *permission* to speak." Th. 3, 39, 2, ἔχω συγγνώμην, "I *can* pardon it" (Lamberton). Th. 3, 60, λόγος ἐδόθη, "they were given *leave* to speak." (But see Herod. 3, 50.) Pindar *Pyth.* 2, 20, δρακεῖσα ἀσφαλές implies "the *right* to look confident" (Gild.). See Classen-Steup on Th. 6, 16, 5; Naegelsbach 58, w. footnote. Our English rendering, as indicated above, may sometimes copy the Greek, as in Hesiod *Eoiae* 16, τὴν ὑλακὴν ἀπώλεσαν, "they lost their bark"=their *power* of barking.

The oldest Greek example of what is here styled Potential Phraseology is *Iliad* I, 18: ὑμῖν μὲν θεοὶ δοῖεν ἐκπέρσαι Πριάμοιο πόλιν, "May the gods *enable* you to destroy (give you *the ability* to destroy) Priam's city." Mutzbauer (*Das Wesen des Griechischen Infinitivs*) accounts for this idiom by the substantive nature of the infinitive: "may the gods give you the city with a view to destroying it, or, for destruction." For this dative, see Smyth 1457. He explains *Iliad* VII, 203, by the additional use of Parataxis: "Give victory to Ajax," δὸς νίκην Αἴαντι "and appoint Ajax (δὸς Αἴαντα to be understood) for the winning of glory, εὖχος ἀρέσθαι." In course of time this original use of the infinitive was evidently lost sight of and replaced, in the Greek consciousness, by a sort of Ellipsis, as above supposed. See also Smyth 1969 and 2008.

Mark has several instances of this idiom. 3, 29, οὐκ ἔχει ἄφεσιν. 10, 40, δοῦναι τὸ καθίσαι. 10, 37, ἵνα καθίσωμεν. 3, 26, τέλος ἔχει, "is at an end," that is, at a point or in a state which inevitably *brings* his doom *with it*. 4, 11, δέδοται "the *right* to know the secret." 5, 18, ἵνα ᾖ. Cf. Luke 9, 1, ἔδωκεν αὐτοῖς θεραπεύειν "*power* to cure." Xen. *Cyr.* 7, 2, 12, διαπέπραγμαι παρὰ σοῦ μὴ ποιῆσαι ἁρπαγήν, "I have secured from you the *promise* not to plunder" (Miller). Epictetus 1, 29, 37, μονομαχῆσαι, "*leave* to enter the arena." So in Latin. *Res habet excusationem*, "the matter *may* be pardoned." *Habeo dicere*, "I am *able* to say." Vergil *Aeneid* vi, 313, *orantes transmittere cursum*, "begging for *leave* to ferry across." For the difficult passage in Lk. 17, 20, μετὰ παρατηρήσεως, see Note E, p. 148; and cf. Joüon. The coming of the Kingdom of God "does *not have to be* watched for." See Heinze on Horace, *Ars P.*, 243; "dynamisches Praesens."

That the Greek mind explained this idiom by an Ellipsis might be gathered from *Epist. ad Diognetum* 1, where the link between the two end terms is actually inserted, αἰτοῦμαι <u>δοθῆναί</u> μοι εἰπεῖν. But the explanation is questionable. In his notes on So. *El.* 527 and 913, Kaibel discusses the abstract quality of Greek nouns and verbs. A noun like ἅλωσις, which of itself means neither past nor present nor future capture, but just capture in the abstract, may under pressure from the context even mean the desire to capture. Similarly a verb like λαλεῖν denotes speaking in the abstract (*die abstrakte Verbal-handlung an sich.* See Brugmann 540 Anm. 1); but in a given context the general notion is narrowed down to actual or possible speaking. Hence *Acts* 4, 29, δὸς λαλεῖν = "give thy slaves *the power* to speak" (Goodspeed); "*enable* thy slaves to speak" (Weymouth). For the quotation from Kaibel, see below, Note E. For a definition of Context, see Morris, *Principles and Methods in Latin Syntax*, 79. Modern grammarians rightly warn against using Ellipsis indiscriminately to "explain" grammatical phenomena. See Löfstedt, *Syntactica*, II, p. 233 ff., where the most recent literature is noted. In these notes the term Ellipsis is used in a more popular sense.

Sometimes light falls on New Testament idiom from unexpected sources. Aristotle says that the continuous style οὐδὲν ἔχει τέλος καθ' αὑτήν; "it admits of no end"; "it *has* nothing in it *requiring* a stop." This sense of ἔχω is common Greek. See L&S, A I, 11. Applying this to Mk. 3, 26, we get the perfectly legitimate sense: if Satan rises up against himself, "there is that in him which requires an end, which brings destruction with it;=he is doomed"; his end is a mere matter of time. For ἔχω = "have to face," see L&S, A III, 1, b. Satan has to face destruction if he wars against himself. For another possible meaning of τ. ἔχει, see the note on Mk. 3, 26. Cf. Luke 12, 50: ἔχω βαπτισθῆναι "I have to be baptized." Cf. *habeo facere* = (1) "possum facere"; (2) "debeo facere"; Hofmann, *Lat. Gr.*, § 150 g.

C. Apparent Tautology

St. Mark has been charged with a love for fullness of expression or even downright tautology. One ground for this charge is the fact that in a number of passages he amplifies a noun by the addition of a (subordinate or coördinate) clause. Some think this amplification has a Semitic coloring; but "there is, of course, no violence to Greek idiom in it"; and "in view of Epictetus 1, 29, 49, τὴν κλῆσιν, ἣν κέκληκεν ὁ θεός, it seems needless to label this idiom Semitic" (Howard 420). In Mk. 7, 13, for instance, our Lord reproves the Pharisees for annulling God's commandment τῇ παραδόσει ὑμῶν, ᾗ παρεδώκατε. "By *your* tradition." The Pharisees might have rejoined that this was a tradition "of the Elders," not their own. To show *how* it was their own, the relative clause is added: "by your tradition—I mean, a tradition, started by others, but which you are handing down." The clause adds a touch not yet fully brought out in the preceding pronoun ὑμῶν. To describe this idiom as "pleonastic" or as a tautology is to overlook the important fact that St. Mark merely reports the exact manner in which our Lord was trying to impress the Pharisees with a sense of their share in the burdensome "tradition of the Elders." *Memoirs:* on 12, 23, p. 168, 169. See below, Note Q.

The best writers of ancient Greece have naturalized this more apparent than real tautology, this stranger coming in from the vernacular or the classroom or the lower strata of literature. *Iliad* 2, 286: ὑπόσχεσιν, ἥν περ ὑπέσταν. *Iliad* 9, 124: ἀθλοφόρους, οἳ ἀέθλια ποσσὶν ἄροντο. *Odyssey* 6, 326: ῥαιομένου, ὅτε μ' ἔρραιε. So. *Electra* 360: τὰ σὰ δῶρα, ἐφ' οἷσι νῦν χλιδᾷς, w. comment by Kaibel. St. Mark was not consciously copying the ways of the old masters; he learnt Greek from his environment; but the Greek of his environment had with marvelous tenacity retained the mode of speech here styled apparent tautology, and that all the more readily because it falls in conveniently with the mannerisms of the classroom or the ways of catechetical instructors. That St. Mark may have made some original contributions to the stock of examples already existing need not be denied. Proper colometrization, which requires pauseful reading, will often strip such peculiarities of their awkwardness. See Colometry, B6.

Cf. Mk. 1, 42, ἀπῆλθεν ἡ λέπρα, foll. by καὶ ἐκαθερίσθη. 3, 6, κατ' αὐτοῦ, explained by the ὅπως-clause. 3, 9, διὰ τὸν ὄχλον, made clear by the ἵνα-clause. 3, 28, αἱ βλασφημίαι, made more precise by the relative clause. 5, 15, τὸν ἐσχηκότα τὸν λεγεῶνα: an item not to be forgotten! 5, 36, λαλούμενον, a vivid touch after τὸν λόγον. 12, 44, ὅλον τὸν βίον, restricts the seemingly sweeping phrase πάντα ὅσα εἶχεν. 13, 20, "the ones whom He deigned to choose," after "the elect"; let the elect remember that their election is due to God's grace. 13, 34. 14, 72, τὸ ῥῆμα, ὡς εἶπεν.

In Mk. 13, 19, ἥν ἔκτισεν adds a personal touch to that impersonal date ἀπ' ἀρχῆς κτίσεως (note the absence of the art.). From impersonal creation we rise to the personal Creator, and are reminded of Genesis:

ἐν ἀρχῇ ἐποίησεν ὁ θεὸς τὸν οὐρανόν. Why this reminder here? Just as
God Almighty created the world for the benefit of mankind, so God
Almighty will disrupt the harmony of the universe, as He alone can
disrupt it, for the punishment of men; hence,

> Pray that it may not happen in winter;
> for those days will surely be a trying time
> such as never has existed
>> from the beginning of creation
>> —*from the day when God created*—
>> down to this hour,
> and never will exist again.

With regard to Mk. 1, 42, ἀπῆλθεν ἡ λέπρα, καὶ ἐκαθερίσθη, St. Mark
has been blamed for expressing "one fact in two ways." But such
criticism is not illuminating. When Jesus uttered the command,
θέλω, καθαρίσθητι, there must have been a moment's pause among the
multitude, watching what would happen. When the miracle occurred,
the people burst out exclaiming: "The leprosy has left the man!" "The
man is cleansed!" For editorial καί, see Note H.

In his note on So. *El.* 360, Kaibel criticizes Dio Chrysostom (XIII
9) for aping an idiom once used to better advantage by classical writers.
Men go to Delphi, says Dio, περὶ ἀπαιδίας, εἴ τωι μὴ γίγνοιντο παῖδες.
People go to Delphi to consult the god "concerning childlessness"—a
distressing condition, no doubt, "when year in year out no child is
born to the parent" (in spite of his yearning for an heir. Disappoint-
ment: Gild. 216). The question is not whether Dio was an "epigone,"
as all Koine writers must be, but whether his phraseology, judged by
older Greek, makes sense or not. Genung (307) says that tautology can
be obviated by making sure that each successive term *emphasizes a
new aspect* of the thought. The following quotation not only reflects its
author's quaint humor, but incidentally illustrates the idiom here discussed: "I say of extra-mural lectures that, in my opinion, the chief
fault with them is *their multitude—that there are too many of them*"
(Quiller-Couch, *Lecture on Lectures*). Smyth 3042, l. Gerth 601, 9.
Howard, pp. 419–420.

D. Relativity of Terms

Relative terms as here understood are terms not meant to be taken
absolutely. They are true, so long as we know that they are not absolutely true. Once people brought "all" their sick to Jesus (Mk. 1, 32),

but the word πάντας does not prove that St. Mark wished to speak with mathematical precision. His sweeping assertion may call for a tacit qualification, to be gathered from the context. When he tells us that "from that time on no one dared ask Him any more questions" (12, 34), we must not hastily charge him with error because he omitted to limit οὐκέτι and to define ἐπερωτῆσαι. (Lagrange: "No other attempt was made to *catch* Jesus by questions.") When it is said (2, 12) that "all" gave glory to God for the cure of the paralytic, we need not infer that even the Scribes who were present joined in the chorus of praise. The rest of the Gospel makes this clear.

In reading any Greek writer it is necessary to keep in mind this principle of interpretation. Much of what the ancients have written is *simplex rectumque*, plain, direct, straightforward, which leaves something to the intelligence of the reader. Quintilian (VIII, ii, 19) goes so far as to regard as "otiose" any word that a hearer is intelligent enough to assume as implied: "Ego otiosum sermonem dixerim, quem auditor suo ingenio intellegit." When a sweeping assertion is made, there may be something in the narrower or wider context to furnish a needful correction. This is especially true of fragments of religious truth scattered about in the New Testament, which need to be supplemented from the ensemble of Bible teaching in order to be seen in their proper light. To fail to see the whole is to fail to see the part. Our Evangelists, bent on narrating incidents in the life of Christ, did not set out to write dogmatic treatises or catechisms of Christian doctrine, but simply tell "what was said or done" on certain occasions. The fact of their inspiration does not interfere with their conventional manner of writing. In their way they tell the truth, nor will they mislead the modern reader who knows their way. We too allow ourselves to use at times large expressions, as when, to describe the enthusiastic reception of some actor or public speaker, we say that "the *whole* house rose to its feet and applauded."

The principle here discussed is known to exegetes. Commenting on Mk. 1, 5, Knabenbauer says: "πάντες, potius *in universum*, nullo pacto *ad unum omnes*." In a note on 4, 11, Lagrange accounts for τὰ πάντα by recourse to the Hebrew: "τὰ πάντα ne doit pas être pris d'une façon trop universelle; le style sémitique permettait ces généralisations qu'il ne faut point prendre en toute rigueur." In Mk. 11, 24, it would be absurd to take πάντα ὅσα as including even things entirely derogatory to God's honor. Whether this form of "exaggeration" is a general Oriental trait, or a Petrine peculiarity, or a Marcan idiosyncrasy, or, in fact, a perfectly human way of speaking, it will certainly not mislead the judicious reader of the New Testament.

E. Modal Interpretation of the Indicative

The Greek indicative is primarily used to denote fact or reality. Fact or reality is that special mode or manner in which a speaker or writer conceives of an assertion concerning the subject (Smyth 1759), or that tone which he gives to the predication (Gild. 183), when using the indicative mood. When the Greek language expresses possibility and power, obligation and necessity, and abstract notions generally, it may express them "as facts; whereas our translation often implies the failure to realize" (Gildersleeve 363). Kaibel, another great expounder of Greek syntax, in a note on So. *Electra* 914, takes an even wider sweep and explains that, since the Greek present indicative represents action in the abstract (*die abstrakte Verbalhandlung an sich, losgelöst von allem Zeitbegriff;* i.e., detached from the notion of time), it readily lends itself to all manner of specifications in the mind of the speaker or writer. He lays down this far-reaching principle that, in each passage, it is the personal manner or mood (*die persönliche Art oder Stimmung des Subjekts*) and the context (*und der Zusammenhang*) that give the necessary clue to correct interpretation (*geben die jedesmal nötige Auffassung an die Hand*). By way of illustration he says that a phrase like γίγνεται τοῦτο may be equivalent to δεῖ (or προσήκει, or εἰκός ἐστι) τοῦτο γίγνεσθαι, just as well as to δύναται τοῦτο γίγνεσθαι. For the timeless character of the Greek present indicative, see Wackernagel, I, 157 ff. For modality in the future indicative, see Gildersleeve 267; Smyth 1910 a; Wackernagel I, 206; Moulton 149 ff. For the tone of the imperative, see Moulton 172 ff. For the modal force of the imperfect, see the remarks by Robertson, 885 ff.; Gildersleeve 216; Smyth 1896; Peppler, *AJPh.*, 54, pp. 52 ff. ("Durative and Aoristic.") It is necessary to emphasize that in the NT the present indicative is widely used to express modality. Gild. 364, w. footnote.

A few illustrations may suffice. Pl. *Rep.* 8, 562, πῶς τὸ τοιοῦτον λέγομεν; "How *can* we say such a thing?" (Wackernagel I, 43; also 206: ἐρεῖς.—τινὸς ἐρούντος: "Wobei vielleicht einer sagen *könnte.*") *Iliad* 2, 24, οὐ χρὴ εὕδειν; either "It *is* unseemly for a councillor to sleep" (as a general principle applicable to all), or, with a thrust at Agamemnon, "A councillor *ought* not to sleep." So. *Oed. Tyr.* 68, ηὕρισκον, "they *could* find" (Jebb). So. *El.* 1037, δεῖ, "*Ought* I to make your rule of honor mine?" Krüger 54, 1, Anm. 3: πῶς οἶδα; "How *should* I know?" Lysias 12, 99, οὐχ ἑνὸς κατηγόρου ἔργον ἐστίν, "It *would* take, not one or two, but many accusers to do this." A special case is Lysias 12, 2 where πείσεσθαι does not denote actual necessity but a matter of propriety. The foll. rendering brings out "the failure to realize": "It seems to me we *ought* to reverse our usual practice; for, whereas in the past an accuser was expected to set forth the grounds for his enmity towards the defendant, in the present case inquiry *ought* really to be made of the defendants to find out what in the world possessed them to hate the city to the extent of committing such audacious offences against her. Of course I am not saying this as though I had no griev-ances of my own." Latin knows the same idiom. Hofmann 147; 149; 150; 155 (On "modale Verwendungsweisen"). Stegmann 44. Menge 330. *Quid ago?* "What shall I do?" Cic. *Tusc.* I, 116, *quos enume-rare magnum est*, "The bare mention of whom would be a feat."

In the NT, Joüon sees modality in John 13, 7, οὐκ οἶδας, "you *cannot* understand it now" (said "avec une nuance virtuelle 'pouvoir'; tu ne peux pas le comprendre maintenant"). Lk. 2, 29, νῦν ἀπολύεις: "Now you *may* let your servant depart." For this nuance, see Note B. Mt. 5, 43, μισήσεις, "tu pourras ne pas aimer." Mt. 7, 4; 12, 10; 26, 61. John 10, 18; 16, 22; 18, 28. We may add John 13, 8, οὐκ ἔχεις, "you *cannot* have a share." Possibly Lk. 2, 49, οὐκ ᾔδειτε, "You *could* not know" (Gild. 216). I Cor. 7, 6, θέλω, "I *would* all the world were like myself." Here θέλω = "I will" = "command," would be totally out of place.

Cf. Mk. 1, 31, διηκόνει. 3, 27, διαρπάσει. 3, 28, ἀφεθήσεται. 4, 13, γνώσεσθε. 5, 42, περιεπάτει. 7, 16, ἀκουέτω. 7, 35, ἐλάλει. 8, 17, οὔπω νοεῖτε. 8, 23, βλέπει. 8, 24, βλέπω. 8, 25, ἐνέβλεπεν. 8, 34, ἀκολουθείτω. 9, 42, καλόν ἐστιν. 10, 7, καταλείψει. 10, 35, θέλομεν. 10, 43, οὐχ οὕτως ἐστίν. 11, 14, ἤκουον.

The difficult passage in Lk. 17, 20 and 21, may perhaps be cleared up by modal interpretation:

> The Kingdom of God does not *have to* come
> and *have* to be watched for;
> nor will people *have* to say.
>   See there! or, See here!,
> for the Kingdom of God is already in your midst.

The necessity of modal interpretation is based on the fact that no writer in any language has either the power or the patience to express, down to the minutest detail, all his thoughts and sentiments, his fancies and feelings, and leave nothing to the imagination of the reader. "All human terms are vague, for they must be defined in terms of other terms. Our most precise language is only approximate. This is one of the many reasons why emotion transcends in validity the nicest academic phrase; why our swift intuition eternally outvalues the most labored statement. We can genuinely share another man's feeling, while at best we can only approximate his language" (H. Henderson, "The Aristocratic Spirit," *Contemporary Essays*, p. 182). Modal interpretation goes, therefore, beyond the letter and seeks for the spirit: where the ancient writer has stated a fact, it seeks to find a more congenial mode or mood. In Lk. 2, 29, old Simeon does not tell what God here and now is doing (νῦν ἀπολύεις), but merely hints at what God may do now that He has shown him the Christ: "Now Thou *mayest* dismiss Thy servant." In Mk. 10, 7, the future indicative καταλείψει expresses God's general designs regarding mankind, and announces a law of general validity: "Therefore a man *must* leave father and mother and cling to his wife." In 10, 43, οὐχ οὕτως ἐστίν, stating apparently a fact, is finely chosen to disguise an admonition: "It *ought* not to be so among you."

This tendency to look for special moods or modes in the indicative tenses of ancient writers is sound, because the ancient tongues were on the whole more objective, while the modern are more subjective; the ancient were more generic, the modern love to be more specific; the ancient mind was more concerned with facts, the modern revels in analysis of motives and in subjective colorings of thought. But most of all, the ancient writer or speaker made his principal appeal through oral delivery with all its adjuncts of gesture, tone, and facial expression, while the modern reader has nothing but the bare letter to guide him, unless he falls back upon modal interpretation to enliven and warm the printed page. Modal interpretation has its pitfalls because it seems to open the door to the caprice of the reader. But, although its application to individual cases may fail to carry conviction, its general validity as a principle of exposition cannot be questioned. To read a Greek or Latin text without regard to the author's state of mind is but to skim the page. Human speech, whether artistic or unsophisticated, implies as much as it asserts. Greek expressions, especially the vernacular Greek of the Gospels, have a way at times of being stiff and rude, so as to be almost offensive. An instance in point is the Divine Child's answer to His mother in the temple of Jerusalem: οὐκ ᾔδειτε, commonly rendered, "Did you not know that I had to be about My

Father's business?" Now, we cannot admit that Jesus spoke offensively to His parents. Here, then, modal interpretation must take the seeming rudeness and stiffness out of those Greek words. There is nothing in them to forbid our taking them as a gentle statement meant to excuse the parents. They had looked for the Child "sorrowing," but Jesus adds, "Really, you *could not* know that I had to be about My Father's business!" They *could not* know that on this occasion His Father would require Him to stay in Jerusalem without the consent of His parents. Cf. Joüon's explanation of John 13, 7.

F. Parallel Orientation

This somewhat fanciful name has here been given to a Greek idiom which requires that, when two (or more) expressions denoting relations of place occur in the same clause and depend on the same verb, both (or all) are "pointed" in the same direction. Just as the pyramids of old were carefully oriented and built with reference to the same point of the compass, so in a Greek sentence two (or more) adjoining expressions of place are so construed as to face the same direction: both express place where, or both place whither, or both place whence. Latin has the same idiom. Thus "he wrote to Caesar at Rome" is "Rom*am* ad Caesarem scripsit." The psychology of this idiom is simple. When we go *"to* a city situated *on* a mountain," we really go both *to* the city and *to* the mountain. And that is the Greek or Latin way of taking it. In other words, Parallel Orientation is but a variety of Parataxis (see Note A), the second designation of place being in apposition to the first. In such phrases the wider of the two terms usually comes first: our letter goes first to Rome; once being in Rome, it goes to the friend. The opposite process would be: "Rom*a ab* amico accepi epistulam."

For Marcan illustrations of this idiom, see Mk. 1, 28; 1, 38; 1, 39; 5, 1; 5, 19; 6, 45; 6, 51; 6, 56; 9, 43; 11, 1; 11, 11; 12, 2; 13, 27; 14, 3; 14, 9. A typical case occurs in 11, 1:

$$\text{Καὶ ὅτε ἐγγίζουσιν } \underline{\text{εἰς}} \text{ Ἱεροσόλυμα,}$$
$$\underline{\text{εἰς}} \text{ Βηθφαγὴ καὶ Βηθανίαν,}$$
$$\underline{\text{πρὸς}} \text{ τὸ ὄρος τῶν ἐλαιῶν,}$$
$$\text{ἀποστέλλει δύο τῶν μαθητῶν αὐτοῦ.}$$

The preposition πρός is sometimes found of *place where;* but coming directly after the double εἰς, both colon three and two seem to be an instance of Parallel Orientation:

And when they drew near to Bethphage and Bethany,
in the neighborhood of Jerusalem,
on the slope of the Mount of Olives,
He sent two of His disciples.

A clear knowledge of this idiom may be required for interpreting Mk. 13, 27, which has given much trouble to commentators. See the note. Perhaps the most elaborate illustration of Parallel Orientation occurs in Lk. 2, 4: "Joseph also went up *from* the city of Nazareth *in* Galilee *to* a city *in* Judea called Bethlehem":

> Ἀνέβη δὲ καὶ Ἰωσήφ
> ἀπὸ τῆς Γαλιλαίας ἐκ πόλεως Ναζαρέθ
> εἰς τὴν Ἰουδαίαν εἰς πόλιν Δαυίδ.

Compare the elegant use of parallel orientation in Menander, 562 K: ἐπὶ κλίμακα πρὸς τεῖχος ἀναβαίνων: "Scaling the wall on a ladder."

G. Stressing the Starting-Point

In describing local relations, the Greek is fond of stressing the starting-point of an action or the point of view of an observer (Smyth 1660). When Jesus rode to Jerusalem (Mk. 11, 8), the enthusiastic crowds scattered in His path branches which they had lopped "*in* the fields"; but the Greek has ἐκ τῶν ἀγρῶν. The Son of Man is seated "at the right side" of the Father; the Greek has ἐκ δεξιῶν. Latin, too, would say *a latere*. This use of ἐκ, called by Jebb "the surveying use" (So. *Ant.* 411), is natural because the reader is led by the use of ἐκ (or ἀπό) to see in spirit how the branches were brought *from* the fields, or, in general, to draw an imaginary line from one object to another. Scholars like Jebb, Kaibel, Havers, and others, have explained the psychology of this tendency to stress the starting-point, but it is needful to add that, in using this form of expression, the Greek mind was more concerned with the goal of the action than with the point of departure. Polybius, for instance, tells us (1, 53, 1) that after a certain naval victory Adherbal "*sent* the captured vessels *to* Carthage." He does not mean to tell us that, in order to reach their destination, they had to be "sent *away from*" the scene of the battle, yet he uses the double compound ἐξ-απ-έστειλεν. In some verbs, as in ἀφ-ικνέομαι, the thought of the goal has completely crowded out the notion of departure: "to come to; arrive at" (Moulton 247).

Familiarity with this typical Greek construction may be of value in interpretation. When *Diog. Laertius* (v 83) says: τοὺς φίλους ἐπὶ μὲν τὰ ἀγαθὰ παρακαλουμένους ἀπιέναι (δεῖ), ἐπὶ δὲ τὰς συμφορὰς αὐτομάτους, he means of course: "To enjoy your good things (ἐπί w. acc.), your friends should come to you by invitation only; to share in your misfortunes, they ought to come unasked." St. Mark has many examples of this idiom, and the student is advised to be on his guard whenever he meets the prepositions ἐκ or ἀπό, whether by themselves or in compounds. See the important note on Mk. 10, 46, ἐκ-πορευομένου.

For Aristotle's characteristic use of ἐκ, see L. Cooper's *Rhetoric of Aristotle*, xxiii; and cp. Mk. 6, 2; 8, 4; 12, 37, w. Notes on πόθεν.

H. *"Pliable and Good-natured* Καί*"*

From Homer down, Greek writers can do wonders with a simple καί, a particle so common in every type of composition that its very commonness has led somewhat to its neglect. Its homely form hides scores of fine nuances. It is like ore—crude, dull, and unattractive; but capable of receiving luster from sympathetic treatment. In the New Testament the evident preference for καί is matched by a similar preference in the Koine generally. Even the master of Greek prose could find no more appropriate vehicle for his melancholy reflections in the closing chapter of the *Phaedo* (116 d) than a string of sentences joined by καί. That its prevalence in St. Mark is due to other reasons than conscious imitation of the classics is clear, but this fact does not relieve the interpreter of his duty to inquire into the finer shades of καί even in the second Gospel. Some scholars are inclined to think that the use of "serial καί-clauses" in the New Testament has its origin, not in the λόγος ἰδιώτης of the Greeks, but in the λόγος κατεσκευασμένος of the Semites. Be this as it may, we have a right to presume that this use resembles other idioms which are Greek in origin, but owe their over-use to Aramaic influence. In other words, καί represents a thought more or less present to the writer's mind, but which that writer, following his Greek or Semitic instinct, did not care to specify more clearly.

In Mk. 15, 1, "The high priests with the Elders and Scribes, *that is to say*, the whole Sanhedrin, came to a decision." The καὶ ὅλον τὸ συνέδριον merely explains that these three groups made up the entire Sanhedrin. 4, 27, "Night *and* day *respectively*"; "night *and* day *by turns*." 13, 10: "*Yes*, all the nations must have the Gospel preached to them." Here καί introduces a parenthesis, just as in 10, 21, καὶ ἕξεις, almost like our colloquial: "*and, by the way*, for this you will have treasure in heaven." 15, 25, "It was the third hour *when* they crucified Him" (Temporal Parataxis: Jebb). 12, 30: "*Therefore* love the Lord." 14, 55, "*But* they could not find any." Here, "The context makes contrast" (Robertson); "The sense implies contrariety" (Abbott). 7, 3, "*As in fact* all the Jews"; "*Like* the Jews generally." 1, 5, "All Judea *and especially* (including even) Jerusalem." Thus καί sometimes adds the whole to a part, sometimes a part to the whole (augmentative or particularizing καί). In Mk. 4, 17, καί (*but*) is followed by ἀλλά (*and*) in the same sense as in Thuc. 7, 3, 3: καὶ ὁ Νικίας οὐκ ἐπῆγε, ἀλλ' ἡσύχαζε: "*But* Nicias did not lead the Athenians against him, *and* kept quiet." Cp. Mk. 15, 1, καί=*that is to say* w. Thuc. 5, 84, 1, ξυμμάχων καὶ νησιωτῶν : the allies were islanders.

Literature: Smyth 2868 ff.; Dana 221; *Classical Journal*, Dec., 1925, on "Paratactic Καί"; Joüon, *passim* (see his Index); Moulton-Milligan, *Vocabulary*, 314; Colwell, pp. 17–18; 86–89; Botte, 77; Gerth 521 (gives many illustrations); Blass, *passim* (see "Wortregister"); also Thayer, Bauer, Zorell, Robertson. For an "and-" sentence from John Mandeville, see above, Colometry, A 3. For an example of Herodotus's running style, see Dobson, p. 25. Genung (298) touches on the psychology of retaining "and" in certain forms of composition, and comments on "the ellipsis of such elements and relations as the reader may be trusted mentally to supply, and yet of things so important that some vigor of thought is connoted in supplying them." In the following passage *and* is used condensively for *and yet*:

> They know that the world is transitory
> *and* they act as if it were eternal;
> they know eternal life is a truth,
> *and* they act as if it were a dream.

For St. Mark's "editorial καί," stringing together separate utterances, see *Memoirs* on Mk. 14, 58, p. 173; it occurs in 1, 27; 3, 22; 6, 2 and 3; 7, 10; 8, 28; 14, 58. For the effect of "Introductory 'And' " in English composition, see Baldwin, *College Composition*, p. 68. In Xen. *Cyr.* 4, 1, 6, Cyrus addresses his troops much as a father would speak to his children: ὡς θεοφιλεῖς καὶ ἀγαθοὶ καὶ σώφρονες ἄνδρες δειπνοποιεῖσθε καὶ σπονδὰς τοῖς θεοῖς ποιεῖσθε καὶ παιᾶνα ἐξάρχεσθε καὶ ἅμα τὸ παραγγελλόμενον προνοεῖτε. Some exquisite comment on καί may be found in standard editions of the classics, as in Jebb's commentaries on Sophocles, Forman's notes on Plato, etc. For the use of καί in Parataxis, see Note A. For "serienartige Häufung von καί-Sätzen," see Norden *ATh.* 367 ff.

I. Marcan Ἤρξατο

The Marcan use of ἤρξατο with the present infinitive is a characteristic of style which almost all writers on New Testament Greek consider a pleonasm and a proof of slovenly diction. Out of a total of over sixty-five passages scattered through the Gospels, the idiom occurs twenty-six times in St. Mark alone. Blass believes that the New Testament use of ἄρχομαι with the infinitive conforms to classical usage, and that in none of the New Testament passages could the infinitive be replaced by the participle. Perhaps a thought or two may here be offered to show that in using this "peculiarity" St. Mark was only following his unerring Greek instinct. Here, as elsewhere, Marcan Greek is reliable Greek.

Whenever in the history of a language a word or phrase acquires a definite meaning, we reasonably suppose that this meaning continues more or less faithfully, until we can show its disappearance. Now, classical scholars tell us that the essence of the idiom here discussed is in the present tense and in the infinitive mood. The infinitive after ἄρχομαι, as after many other Greek verbs, is of the final-consecutive kind, showing that the action denoted by it is somehow the result of ἄρχομαι. Just what ἄρχεσθαι in this connection means, is of course difficult to describe; but, at all events, besides containing an inevitable reference to "beginning" (ἀρχή), it implies that the action to be begun is contemplated (by the writer or by the person acting) as *one to be continued*. The present tense means here what it means elsewhere: it conjures up the vision of a course of action. English writers may use the word "begin" in much the same sense, and there would be little quarrel about the Marcan idiom if this use of "begin" were always univocal and obvious, and if "begin" were as rich in content as the Greek ἄρχεσθαι. The phrase "He began to teach," instead of meaning, "He set Himself to instruct; He set about instructing; He proceeded to teach; He entered upon a course of instruction; He devoted or applied Himself to the task of teaching; He made a point of instructing the people"; etc., may obviously mean: "He was just beginning to teach (when this or that occurred); this was the first time that He taught; He began to teach, but did not continue, or someone else continued to teach"; etc. So when Plummer notes on Mk. 6, 7: "Note the ἤρξατο: the pairs were *not* sent out *all at one moment*," one is utterly at a loss to see how this sense could be gotten out of the simple Greek. St. Mark informs us, in that text, that Jesus *made a definite and conscious effort* to bring the good news before the people and for that purpose sent His disciples two by two into the villages. Jesus *made a point of sending* them out invested with His powers. Jesus *made preparations* for sending them out. If one were forced to choose one English word or phrase as expressing the essence of this idiom one might propose "proceed" in the sense of "adopt a course of action." Note *adopt*, as hinting at the idea of *beginning*, and a *course of action*, as bringing out vigorously the durative character of the present infinitive. One gets the same result by analyzing the Latin equivalent *in-cipere*, "take in hand," "undertake," "attempt." In fact ἄρχεσθαι in this sense is but a synonym of ἐπιχειρέω.

The gist of the matter is well stated by Smyth (2128): "ἄρχομαι *with the infinitive, begin to do something and continue with the same thing.*" This is correct, provided the word *continue* is given a little latitude: "either actually continue or at least intend to continue." It is *this intention to go through with the action once begun* that gives ἄρχομαι with the infinitive all its appositeness as an idiom. There are several instances in this Gospel where an action, prefaced with ἤρξατο, is, as appears from the context, soon interrupted. Zorell (181) goes so far as to hold this accidence of "interruption" as responsible for the use of ἄρχεσθαι: "actio, quae dum fit, ab aliis interrumpitur," a view in which it is difficult to concur.

A few examples of ἄρχομαι with the present infinitive may help to clarify the nuances of which this idiom is capable. Mk. 10, 47, ἤρξατο κράζειν: "he *began* to shout"; not in contrast to 10, 48, μᾶλλον ἔκραζεν, "he shouted all the louder"; but, seeing the distress he was in, and realizing vividly the unusual opportunity for a cure now offered him, "he *set to work* and shouted"; "he shouted *lustily.*" The French say: "Il *se mit* à crier" (not quite the same as: il commença à crier); the Germans: "Er machte sich ans Schreien." Colloquialisms always go to the heart of the matter. Thus Moulton renders ἐπιβαλὼν συνέχωσεν (Pap Tb P 50) "he *set to* and damned up" (p. 131), and rightly intimates that the writer might have said, without a change in meaning, ἤρξατο συγχοῦν; just as St. Mark's phrase in 14, 72, ἐπιβαλὼν ἔκλαιεν, might be changed to ἤρξατο κλαίειν, "he broke into sobs and tears." In *Memor.* 3, 5, 22, Xenophon writes: παλαίειν ἤρξω μανθάνειν: "You undertook, or, made it a business, to learn wrestling"; "You *went in for* wrestling." Notice how the idea of "beginning" is gently overshadowed in this idiom by the stronger notion of "undertaking; enterprise; attempt." Similarly Epictetus (2, 17, 1) says: "It is impossible for a man *seriously to apply himself* to learning" (ἄρξασθαι μανθάνειν) "that which he fancies he already masters." "Seriously to apply oneself": much like ἐπιχειρέω with the infinitive. In Mk. 5, 17, after the destruction of the swine, the inhabitants, fearing lest Jesus should inflict on them still greater harm, "asked Him in good earnest" (ἤρξαντο παρα-καλεῖν) or "set about seriously asking Him" to depart from them. One can feel that, when actions are prefaced with ἤρξα(ν)το, there is a certain solemnity or fuss or ado connected with them. Farrar, in a note on Lk. 7, 24, had, one is pleased to see, a glimpse of the truth when he said: "The word (ἤρξατο) introduces solemn and important remarks." Indeed, there is not an instance of ἄρχεσθαι with the present infinitive anywhere but shows that actions so characterized are never stumbled upon; one and all, they are undertaken of set purpose. This nuance, it is true, is more readily realized in certain contexts than in others. For instance, in Xen. *Hell.* 2, 3, 13, ἐπεὶ δὲ ἤρξαντο συμβουλεύεσθαι, the use of ἤρξαντο indicates a deliberate change of policy: "Once they changed their policy and cast about for ways and means. . . ." Yet hidden or obvious, the nuance is present everywhere. Bauer seems to hint at this when he describes the force of ἄρχεσθαι by saying: "Die Handlung setzt *neu* ein," for writers as a rule do not advert to actions as "neu einsetzend" unless they attach to them some importance and significance. One day our Lord sat on the Mount of Olives (Mk. 13). Before Him lies the Holy City and its magnificent Temple. He predicts that all this glory must crumble into dust. The disciples are eager for information. The moment has come when Jesus must, for their benefit as well as for that of future generations, make an important statement, a statement which in fact occupies the entire Chapter 13. We want a fitting prelude to this statement. St. Mark's way of preluding is humble, but significant:

> Then Jesus composed Himself, and began.
> Then Jesus launched forth into a set discourse.
> Then Jesus gave them a formal explanation.
> Ὁ δὲ Ἰησοῦς ἤρξατο λέγειν αὐτοῖς.

Note, now, that the subject of ἄρχομαι, as used in Greek literature, need not be a rational being. Even inanimate things can ἄρχεσθαι, and it is interesting to see what becomes of the "*intention* to continue" which seems to be of the essence of the idiom. Thuc. 3, 18, tells us that Mitylene had just been surrounded, καὶ ὁ χειμὼν ἤρχετο γίγνεσθαι: "when (and now) winter was making in earnest" ("Da war der Winter auch schon ernstlich im Anzuge"). Robert Louis Stevenson, whose idiom no one will question, gives us, without a thought of the corresponding Greek, a splendid illustration of its force. He says: "At last the path crossed the Chasseezac upon a bridge, and, forsaking this deep hollow, *set itself* to cross the mountain." Again: "It *began* to grow dark *in earnest*." Were we to render these sentences into Greek, we might meet idiom with idiom and say ἤρξατο διαβαίνειν, in the first passage, and ἤρξατο συσκοτάζειν, in the second. This reminds us of Lk. 9, 12: ἡ δὲ ἡμέρα ἤρξατο κλίνειν: "The evening or night was now well under way"; or: "The day was declining in earnest." In a ludicrous scene in Arist. *Frogs* 221, the pampered god Dionysus, not used to sitting on the hard rowing bench, exclaims: ἐγὼ δέ γ' ἀλγεῖν ἄρχομαι: "But I—I'm in for a siege of belly-ache!" In Lk. 14, 9, ἄρξῃ κατέχειν, the sense is not, "you will begin to take the lowest place"; for κατέχειν does not mean "to take"; and why should a guest's punishment consist in *beginning* (which is a momentary act) to take the lowest place? The puzzle disappears if we credit St. Luke with the knowledge of a common Greek idiom and find in ἄρξῃ (do not overlook the future), owing to its ever-present connotation of strenuous activity, a hint of the grin-and-bear attitude (for no guest takes the lowest place willingly and with a zest):

> And then you have to be content,
>   to your disgrace,
> to occupy the lowest place.

> And then you must resign yourself,
>   with shame,
> to occupying the lowest place.

A neat way of rendering the present infinitive with its durative force after ἄρχομαι will often be the use of a noun; as in *Diog. Laert.*: σχολαρχεῖν ἤρξατο: "So-and-So assumed the *headship* of the school" (Hicks). Hence: ἄρχεσθαι="beginnen die *Beschäftigung* mit etwas; anfangen mit einer *dauernden Tätigkeit*." Debrunner, p. 310.

Greek and Latin idioms are twin sisters; know the one, and you (often) know the other. Horace, Vergil, Cicero, and Plautus, for example, understand the subtle effect of an *incipio* (*occipio*) or *coepi* neatly thrown into a statement. Like ἄρχεσθαι, *incipere* implies effort, ado, fuss, attention to business. Thus Horace, to coax Torquatus to come and dine with him (*Epp.* 1, 5), says:

> Potare et spargere flores
> *incipiam* patiarque vel inconsultus haberi.

Who would wish to spoil this line by rendering, "I will *begin* to drink"? In inviting Torquatus to attend the banquet, Horace, naturally, holds out to him "a jolly good time"; he promises *to be serious* (note the twinkle in his eye) in the discharge of his *duties* as a host. It was the host's *business* to cheer his guests by drinking and scattering flowers: Do come, he says, and I (see below: p. 159)

> will do my share: I'll drink and scatter flowers
> and let the world imagine I'm a fool!

> With gusto will I drink and scatter scents:
> what care I if the world deems me a fool!

After enumerating the various topics he is to treat of in the *Georgics* (I, 5), Vergil says: *hinc canere incipiam*. What does he mean? Literally: *"These* are the things *I set myself* to sing about."* Hence Rhoades's rendering: "Such are my *themes.*" In Horace, *Ars Poetica,* 14–22, the current renderings of the noun *inceptis* and the verb *coepit* completely obscure the poet's meaning. Knapp, in the Index to his edition of Vergil, hints at the many-sidedness of *incipio* by rendering it: "lay hold of, take in hand; begin, commence; essay, undertake, attempt"; and of the noun *inceptum,* by rendering "beginning; attempt, undertaking, essay, purpose, resolve." For our English word "beginning," as used before and after 1500, see the new Oxf. Dictionary. Georges's *Ausführliches Wörterbuch,* too, gives significant renderings for *inceptum:* "Beginnen, Unternehmen, Vorhaben." Note, however, that Latin *incipio* and *coepi* seem to do duty both for ἄρχεσθαι with the infinitive (as here explained) and for ἄ. with the participle. By the way, Vergil's *canere incipiam* is a reminiscence of Hesiod *Theog.* 1, ἀρχώμεθ' ἀείδειν, and of *Hymn to Dem.* 1, ἄρχομ' ἀείδειν.

Marcan ἤρξατο may be studied in the following passages: 1, 45; 2, 23; 4, 1; 5, 17; 5, 20; 6, 2; 6, 7; 6, 34; 6, 55; 8, 11; 8, 31; 8, 32; 10, 28; 10, 32; 10, 41; 10, 47; 11, 15; 12, 1; 13, 5; 14, 19; 14, 33; 14, 65; 14, 69; 14, 71; 15, 8; 15, 18. Joh. Weiss is the only commentator, so far as I know, that has given the old classical idiom a little furbishing, and that only in five or six Marcan passages. In Mk. 14, 65, he renders ἤρξαντο ἐμπτύειν: "sie unterfingen sich"; "they made free to spit upon Him."

Two instances of ἄρχεσθαι, occurring in widely different contexts, have a special interest. Epictetus (1, 17, 16) says that, when he fails to understand the will of Nature, he goes for light to Chrysippus. But suppose, he says, ἄρχομαι μὴ νοεῖν τί λέγει? What then? Now,

Epictetus does not mean to tell us that, *as soon as* he fails to see Chrysippus's explanation, he *at once* rushes to another interpreter. That thought would require the participle νοῶν; and, besides, such conduct would be unbecoming in a philosopher. No; Epictetus *tries* to understand Nature. Failing in this, he goes to Chrysippus. But if, after repeated efforts to understand Chrysippus (note the present νοεῖν), he still fails to make headway, then he looks for τὸν ἐξηγούμενον. If ἄρχομαι ποιεῖν means "I commit myself to a course of action," then ἄρχομαι μὴ ποιεῖν must mean "I am doomed to a course of failure." Hence: "But suppose I am hopelessly stuck and do not understand Chrysippus? Well, in that case I look for τὸν ἐξηγούμενον."

Isocrates, *Antidosis* 82, has occasion to refer to the origin of mankind, a time ὅτε ἤρχετο τὸ γένος τὸ τῶν ἀνθρώπων γίγνεσθαι καὶ συνοικίζεσθαι κατὰ πόλεις. The reference is not to the precise moment when the human race sprang into being; for that thought would require the aorist γενέσθαι (often, by the way, used by Thucydides; also, e.g., by Aristotle *Rhet.* 3, 1, 8: ἤρξαντο κινῆσαι τὸ πρῶτον: "The poets were the first to give an *impulse* to style"); moreover, at the very beginning there could be no question of settling in cities (κατοικίζεσθαι κατὰ πόλεις). The present γίγνεσθαι pictures a gradual process, "to continue to come into being"; hence "to increase and multiply" (see Isocr. *Nicocles* 31). That Isocrates really refers to a time when the human race "was already in a fair way to multiply and to organize city life," seems clear from a passage in his *Panegyricus* (32): "If we carry our inquiry back to the beginning, we shall find that those who first appeared on the earth did *not at once* find the kind of life which we enjoy to-day, but that they procured it *little by little* through their own joint efforts" (Norlin).

As to *coepi* and *incipio* with the infinitive, modern grammarians see in them mere circumlocutions for the aorist-perfect and the future respectively, and pronounce the idiom in the main colloquial and late Latin. Hofmann is not far from the truth, however, when he claims for a phrase like *incipiet annuntiare* (Itala act. 26, 23) the sense of *annuntiaturus est* or μέλλει καταγγέλλειν (Hofmann, pp. 551, 557, 561); for even this slight admission will help us to appreciate Horace's *potare incipiam*: Come, he says, and dine with me; *I am ready* to do my duty; *I am resolved* to drink and scatter flowers: *poturus et sparsurus sum*, μέλλω πίνειν. This sense is clearly discernible in the very earliest instances of the idiom in Latin poetry, instances, therefore, that have helped to mold the taste of succeeding generations of Latin writers.

When Medea (Ennius fr. 232) says she is at a loss which way to turn (*quo nunc me vortam? quod iter incipiam ingredi?*), her *incipiam*, instead of focusing her vision on the starting-point, in reality ranges over two entire roads, each lying before her in full length: *quod iter?* the one leading *domum paternam*, or the one leading *ad Peliae filias?* The verb hints that a courageous decision is called for: which road shall I now nerve myself to take? Remember *in-cipio:* I take in hand, undertake, apply myself to. Nor is there any reference to bare beginning in Pacuvius (fr. 95, Ribbeck): *incipio, saxum temptans, scandere vorticem:* and, clutching at a rock, I with an effort mount the height; or in fr. 15: *increpare dictis saevis incipit:* and now he launches out into fierce invective. Plautus finds this idiom well suited to his horse-play. It would be uncritical to dilute it, for it was taken over from the Greek, where its sense was well established, by men *who were at home in Greek* no less than in Latin. As to the fate of *coepi* in late Latin, that is another question, but even here one might wish for a more thoroughgoing investigation. Latin idioms whose roots are Greek are more profitably pursued from their early beginnings forward than from their latest developments backward. Kroll (*Wiss. Synt.* 57), who shares Hofmann's view, rightly insists that *coepi* is often used with no hint of a beginning ("wo der Begriff des Anfangens nicht vorliegt"), an admission which might well be made the starting-point for further inquiry. Note that *in this idiom incipiam* for *incipio* is due to a kind of assimilation in tense (just as -*turus ero* for -*turus sum*. Hofmann, pp. 556 and 557), much like Mk. 3, 25 δυνήσεται for 3, 24 δύναται. For all New Testament instances of *incipio*=μέλλω, see Rönsch, *Itala und Vulgata*, 369. See also Löfstedt, Syntactica II, pp. 450-452.

H. Pernot's interesting inquiry into NT Greek from the side of its youngest modern descendant (*Études sur la langue des Évangiles*) does not, in the case of ἄρχομαι, advance beyond Hesseling (*Byzant. Zt.*, xx, 147). His statement that St. Matthew often "corrects Mk.'s familiar expression by suppressing ἄρχομαι," is not enlightening, because its validity depends on the solution of the Synoptic Problem. If St. Matthew uses the bare aorist or imperfect in those passages where St. Mark has ἤρξατο, he does not *correct* St. Mark, any more than St. Luke's ταῦτα ἐφύλαξα (18, 21) is a correction of St. Mark's ταῦτα ἐφυλαξάμην (10, 20): the former being excellent Greek for "I have observed these commandments," the latter no less excellent for "I have always guarded against these sins." One is almost wholly reconciled to Pernot's findings, however, when he says that *se mettre à* (the ordinary French rendering of ἄρχεσθαι) is a stronger expression (*le sens fort*) than *commencer à*, which renders the simple imperfect. Most welcome is his acceptance of a principle of interpretation that is only too frequently lost sight of by NT scholars, *sc.* that one evangelist in omitting ἄρχομαι does not stress the same point of view as another who uses it: *Mt. a souligné son point de vue, qui n'était peut-être pas celui de Mc.* Here we are at the very core of many linguistic differences observable between the two evangelists. It is always a risky thing to set two ancient writers by the ears without at least making a conscientious effort to understand each from his own point of view.

Literature. For the classical sense of ἄρχομαι with the infinitive, see Smyth 2128, with 1734 and 2098; Gerth 484, 27; Krüger, *Sprachlehre*, 56, 5, 1; Curtius-Hartel-Weigel, *Gr. Schulgrammatik*, 236, 2, b Zusatz; Kaegi 202, Note 5; Blass 414, 2 (Blass-Debrunner, p. 310); Hesseling, *Byz. Zeitschrift*, Vol. 20, 147 ff.; Hunkin's essay in *JThSt.*, xxv, 390 ff.; Plummer's notes on ἄρχεσθαι are not enlightening; nor is Allen's elaborate *Appendix;* see also Lagrange, Joüon, Zorell, etc. Moulton (p. 15) discusses St. Luke's "substitution" of μὴ ἄρξησθε λέγειν (3, 8) for St. Matthew's μὴ δόξητε λέγειν (which is good Greek for "do not presume to say"); but we need not suppose that Lk.'s ἄρξησθε was meant exactly to cover Mt.'s δόξητε; and besides, that "editorial" change does support the view here advanced; for to say "do not in good earnest plead that you are children of Abraham" is a mere variant for "do not dare or presume to say." See Weiss's rendering of Mk. 14, 65, quoted above. Brugmann, p. 603. On Lk. 4, 21, Lagrange cannot help remarking: "ἤρξατο a une certaine solennité!"

Much that has been written on New Testament ἄρχομαι with the present infinitive is utterly useless, because vitiated by false premises. In discussing Marcan Greek we cannot with impunity *begin by assuming* that it is a corrupt sort of Greek. Quite the contrary. Marcan Greek is good and honest Koine Greek which requires to be approached from the side of ancient Greek. (See below, p. 171, footnote 1.)

K. Marcan Εὐθύς

No single feature of Marcan diction is so familiar as the use of this constantly recurring adverb. St. Mark was not a litterateur (Eakin, *Expositor*, March, 1923), and "the frequent repetition of a word may have been an offence, but it was not so to him." But the Greeks had no such dread of repetition as we moderns have (Gildersleeve), and

the original readers of the second Gospel took the word, in all probability, at its face value. Its repetition (over 40 times) makes the life
of Christ seem to pass before us in a rush. "To explain this we must
take into account what Mark's conception of the public ministry of
Jesus was. As he saw it, things had happened rapidly." In fact, the
word εὐθύς may reflect our Lord's own attitude toward His ministry.
His public career was brief; and a multiplicity of work had to be crowded into it. There was, as it were, "no time to lose," and perhaps it was
this special aspect of the ministry that struck St. Mark so forcibly. If
so, the adverb εὐθύς ceases to be excessive. It is possible, however, to
take it in a weakened sense. Perhaps the essence of its meaning is
that "the event related is regarded as happening *in due sequence* to
what has gone before" (Burkitt). The Orientalist Joüon sees in εὐθύς
"une nuance affaiblie" and accounts for its frequence in the Gospel
"par un goût personnel." Sometimes one suspects that "at once"
is no more than "without losing time; without unnecessary delay."
For a special sense, see on Mk. 1, 29. Εὐθύς as used in the second Gospel may be one of St. Mark's "strong" words, or evidence of St. Peter's
"impetuosity," or a trait of Oriental exaggeration. *Memoirs* 56. Note
the wider sense of εὐθέως in 3 John 14: ἐλπίζω εὐθέως σε ἰδεῖν.

L. 'Biblical' Ἀποκρίνεσθαι

Commenting on Mt. 26, 25, Joüon takes ἀποκριθείς in a weakened
sense: "Ici, comme souvent, ἀποκρίνομαι est simplement 'prendre la
parole' au sens faible de 'parler, dire,' " as in Hebrew and Aramaic.
German writers render, "Er ergriff das Wort und sprach." Bauer de-
termines the sense of ἀποκρίνομαι more accurately: it is often used
without a previous question in contexts where the statement to be
made implies a contrast to what precedes ("in solchen Fällen bezieht
die Rede sich inhaltlich auf das Vorhergehende und führt einen Gegen-
satz dazu ein"). Zorell notes that "ex usu biblico ἀποκρίνεσθαι etiam is
dicitur qui, etiamsi eum alius allocutus non est, dicere incipit, quae
hominibus praesentibus rerumque adiunctis *congruant.*" Plummer, on
Mk. 9, 5 (where according to Howard, p. 453, this locution is strictly
redundant; so again in 11, 14 and 12, 35) says: "Peter's 'answer' was
not to words addressed to him but to facts which appealed to him";
and on 12, 35: "As in 9, 5; 11, 14; 15, 12, we have ἀποκριθείς of re-
sponding to circumstances which elicit utterance." (See below, p. 178.)

A statement prefaced by ἀποκριθείς is thereby characterized as answering a purpose, or appropriate to the occasion, or intended to meet some emergency, or elicited by some suggestion, or arising spontaneously out of a given situation, or, finally, as an *answer* to a question latent in the mind of the person addressed. See, for instance, 10, 51. *Memoirs*, p. 167.

Our English rendering should take note of this idiomatic sense of ἀποκρίνεσθαι and be suited to the context. In Mk. 6, 37, our Lord and the people are in the desert; there is no food at hand; the disciples thoughtlessly advise that the crowd be dismissed so that they may get provisions for themselves in some near-by villages. That is *their* way of meeting the emergency. But Jesus knows a more efficient way:

> To meet the difficulty He said to them.
> Upon their suggestion He said to them.
> And He took this up, replying to them.
> As a way out of the predicament, He said.

As Bengel aptly remarks: "*Respondet* non modo, qui . . . rogatus est, sed etiam, cui causa loquendi data est." The word means literally: "to decide for oneself back"; see Howard 115. Darby-Smith, in a note on Lk. 13, 2, admirably describe the force of ἀποκριθείς thus: "Hearing of the massacre of the Galileans, Jesus *took advantage of the opportunity* to warn the guilty nation." It were a pity if no effort were made to embody the force of ἀποκρίνεσθαι in the translation.[1]

The Greeks on the whole avoided using ἀποκρίνεσθαι in the sense here discussed. They used it as a legal term, "to defend oneself," "to answer charges." So in Latin *respondere*. Pliny *ep.* 3, 9: "Claudius mihi respondit"; "Claudius acted as counsel to the defence (in a suit in which I was the complainant)." There are instances of this 'biblical' use of ἀποκρίνομαι in Xenophon, *Anab*. 4, 1, 20: Xenophon had blamed Cheirisophus ὅτι οὐχ ὑπέμενεν; then, "*to clear himself* Cheirisophus said": ἀποκρίνεται Χειρίσοφος. Lit. "he answered to questions *implied* in Xenophon's censure." *Cyr*. 3, 3, 56: Cyaxares said Cyrus was making a serious mistake; then Cyrus ἀπεκρίνατο; "said by way of *protest*" or "to defend his conduct." Arrian stands in the midst of the later development of this idiom. *Anab*. 3, 10, 2, ὁ δὲ ἐκείνῳ ἀποκρίνεται, "Upon this proposal" or "At that suggestion" he remarked; etc. So again in 3, 23, 8: "He met their proposal with the statement . . ." (δεομένοις σπείσασθαι σφίσιν) ἀπεκρίνατο.

---

[1] To see the difference, compare, for instance, Lk. 6, 3, "Jésus leur dit en réponse" or Lk. 7, 40, "A ce propos, Jésus lui dit" (Soubigou) with the jejune "Jésus leur (lui) dit."

Homer and later writers often use (ἀπ-) ἀμείβομαι in the same sense. *Iliad* 1, 172, τὸν δ' ἠμείβετο. No *question* had been asked, yet Agamemnon "answered" to the charges made against him by Achilles: "Then Agamemnon said in his own defence." A close parallel is Mk. 14, 40, where the drowsy disciples, when found asleep, "had nothing to say in their own defence." So Pilate to our Lord in 15, 4: οὐκ ἀποκρίνῃ οὐδέν, "Have You nothing to say to defend Yourself?" Hermione in Eur. *Androm.* 154 replies "to the attitudes and looks of the Chorus who perhaps show their feelings in their faces" (Hyslop): "This is what I say to you to justify myself" or "in my own behalf," ἀνταμείβομαι.

Cf. the following Marcan passages: 7, 28; 8, 4; 9, 5; 9, 6; 10, 20; 10, 51; 11, 14; 14, 40; 14, 48; 15, 12. See *Memoirs* on 3, 33.

In St. John's Gospel οὖν often approaches to the sense of ἀποκριθείς. Thus 4, 8 and 4, 9: "Give Me to drink," Jesus said. "But the woman *met His request* by asking" (λέγει οὖν). Mark would perhaps have written: ἡ δὲ γυνὴ ἀποκριθεῖσα λέγει (However Johannine οὖν has its own history; see Bauer, Zorell; Dana 223; Blass 451, 1).

In classical writers λέγειν πρὸς ταῦτα serves the same purpose. Xen. *Anab.* 1, 3, 19: Clearchus advises the sending of a deputation to Cyrus which is to report ὅ, τι ἂν πρὸς ταῦτα λέγῃ (for which a NT writer might say: ὅ,τι ἐὰν ἀποκριθεὶς λέγῃ): "whatever he may have to say to our proposals." The use of πρός shows that the report is to represent *Cyrus's side* of the question; and that is exactly what ἀποκριθείς expresses in similar contexts. For πρός, see Bauer 1139 and 1140. Howard 126. Gerth 441. Compare Aeschines's celebrated reply: "You would not marvel thus if you had heard Demosthenes *in reply to* these arguments," εἰ Δημοσθένους λέγοντος πρὸς ταῦτα ἠκούσατε (Philostratus, *Lives of the Sophists*, 510).

Two other classical equivalents are πάλιν and ἑτέρωθεν. *Iliad* 13, 835, "The host shouted behind, and the Argives ἑτέρωθεν ἐπίαχον," shouted *in answer;* = ἀποκριθέντες ἐπίαχον. The adverb πάλιν has all the uses of Latin *rursus* (Souter). Menander 562 K: "So I explain in all seriousness, but they *for reply* turn up their noses" (Allinson): οἱ δὲ πάλιν ἐπεμυκτήρισαν; in effect: = ἀποκριθέντες ἐπεμυκτήρισαν or ἐπιμυκτηρίσαντες ἀπεκρίθησαν. This use of πάλιν throws light on Mk. 15, 13.

To sum up: ἀποκρίνεσθαι, as often used in NT, expresses, not an answer to an actual question, but a response or reaction to a stimulus received (whether by word, act, or circumstances) from without. It would be an exaggeration to say that in such passages our word "answer" is never an exact equivalent. Swete, in note on 7, 28, says that the woman's saying was "in the strictest sense an answer: she laid hold of Christ's word and based her plea upon it." Other passages are not so easily dismissed. On 9, 5, for instance, Swete notes that Peter felt that "some response was *called for*," yet modern translators shrink from using "answer" or "response" in that passage.

The fact that in parallel passages St. Matthew and St. Luke are content with εἶπεν αὐτοῖς is *no proof whatever* that the Marcan ἀποκρι-θεὶς εἶπεν is meaningless and redundant. St. Mark has suffered much by unfair comparison with the other evangelists. His idiom wants to be investigated in its own right. (See p. 160, last paragraph.)

M. Marcan Ἐκπλήττομαι

We are so accustomed to find the notion of fright or amazement expressed in the verb ἐκπλήττεσθαι throughout Greek literature that we have neglected somewhat its more pleasant sense. In Mk. 11, 18, we hear that πᾶς ὁ ὄχλος ἐξεπλήσσετο ἐπὶ τῇ διδαχῇ αὐτοῦ. Our Lord's teaching was novel, and not like that of the Scribes and Pharisees. He was the great Friend of the people; He spoke in His own name; He backed up His word of command with unlimited power; best of all, He used His power for the alleviation of suffering humanity. The people could not help being favorably impressed by His ministry, and it is this favorable impression made on them that finds voice in ἐκπλήττεσθαι: "The mass of the people was thrilled by His teaching." When Mary and Joseph, after a three days' sorrowful search for the Divine Child, found Him at last alive and radiant with joy, and even honored by the great doctors of the law, no wonder ἰδόντες αὐτὸν ἐξεπλάγησαν: they would not have been human had they not been "in a transport of joy at sight of Him" (Lk. 2, 48).

Meaning by etymology "to be struck out of one's senses," the word receives its color from the context. Usually a dative like φόβῳ or χαρᾷ removes all doubt. Where this is absent, the context alone must decide. In the vocabulary of ancient lovers, the word means simply "to fall in love." Medea was ἔρωτι θυμὸν ἐκπλαγεῖσ' Ἰάσονος, "with love for Jason thrilled through all her soul" (Eur. *Medea* 8). Aesch. *Cho.* 233, χαρᾷ δὲ μὴ 'κπλαγῇς φρένας, "Be not distraught for joy." Socrates confesses in a playful mood to a thrill of excitement in the presence of youth and beauty; ἀεί ποτε, it was his usual way, ὑπὸ τῶν νέων τε καὶ καλῶν ἐκπλήττομαι. The passage is interesting (Pl. *Erastae* 133 a) as enriching our vocabulary with two more significant terms, πάσχειν and ἀγωνιᾶν. In Plut. *Thes.* 19, 3, Ariadne was "smitten with the appearance of Theseus," πρὸς τὴν ὄψιν ἐξεπλάγη, "and admired," ἐθαύμασε (expressed admiration for; cf. Mk. 5, 20) "his athletic prowess." "Minos, too, was delighted," ἤσθη. Here ἐκπλαγῆναι is a synonym for ἡσθῆναι and θαυμάσαι. So. *Trach.* 629, "Indeed my heart's athrob (ἐξεπλάγη) with sheer delight." Cf. Aes. *Cho.* 233; Eur. *Hipp.* 38; Xen. *Cyr.* 1, 4, 25 and 27: "struck with admiration of Cyrus's beauty." Pl. *Phaedr.* 250 a; 234 d; 259 b. *Symp.* 216 d. Polybius 2, 56, 10, and 11: it is the tragedian's business "to thrill and charm": ἐκπλῆξαι καὶ ψυχαγωγῆσαι.

Mark has several instances of ἐκπλήττεσθαι. See *Memoirs* on 1, 22; 6, 2; 7, 37; 10, 26; 11, 18. See Zorell, 405, and L&S. Joined to περισσῶς or even ὑπερπερισσῶς (Mk. 7, 37), the word is one of Mark's "strong" expressions, and recalls Xenophon's ὑπερεκπλαγῆναι, *Cyr.* 1, 4, 25.

N. Marcan Σκανδαλίζομαι

The precise sense of this verb, as that of the noun σκάνδαλον, has been thoroughly examined in modern times. The student may consult Thayer's *Lexicon;* Bauer's *Wörterbuch;* Zorell's *Lexicon Graecum;* Stählin's *Skandalon;* Moulton-Milligan's *Vocabulary;* Lagrange's note on Mk. 4, 17, and Joüon's *L'Évangile.* The original meaning seems to be "I set a trap for," rather than "I put a stumbling block in the way of." The word occurs eight times in St. Mark: 4, 17; 6, 3; 9, 42; 9, 43; 9, 45; 9, 47; 14, 27; 14, 29. The Orientalist Joüon renders the passive of this verb everywhere by *trébucher,* the active by *faire trébucher,* except in 9, 42 where he has *scandaliser.* Whatever may be said of the trap-idea as representing the root meaning of the word, it seems impossible to make use of it in an English translation; nor is it possible to find one uniform rendering to match the various contexts in which the word occurs. Certain it is that, in one sense or another, the notion of "being the occasion of spiritual ruin to anyone" predominates wherever σκάνδαλον or σκανδαλίζω is used in the Gospels. In this sense our English word to "scandalize" is, according to the New Oxf. Engl. Dict., now *rare.* Good modern synonyms are "to shock" (Card. Newman) and "to horrify," sometimes "to surprise" (cf. the Concise Oxf. Dict.: "*I am surprised at you,* shocked, scandalized"). In chapter 9 the word seems to mean "to be a temptation to" or "an occasion of sin to anyone." *Memoirs,* pp. 155 and 156.

O. Varying the English Equivalent

In rendering the second Gospel I have not translated Greek words or phrases invariably by the same English equivalent in all contexts. The practice of the best modern writers is opposed to such rigid uniformity of expression. An exception has been made, however, at least to some extent, in the case of καί because it was felt that this point of style was too pronounced a peculiarity of St. Mark to justify its sacrifice. It is difficult in matters of this kind to strike the golden mean, for strict adherence either to absolute uniformity or to the principle of unlimited variety is out of place. All standards of translation are relative. For the place of "Translation" in Roman literary theory, see D'Alton, pp. 2, 20, 206, 429; 143 *n.*, 147, 206, 429–430. See the *Memoirs*, pp. 33 ff. Consult Shorey's Preface to Plato's *Republic* (Loeb L.).

Roberts (*Companion to the Revised Version;* 145 ff.) says: "If not practically very important, it is at least interesting and desirable that uniformity of rendering should be preserved in regard to expressions which are fitted to suggest the individuality of the sacred writers to an English reader. They have all a more or less marked style of their own." "It is obvious that such marked features in the first two Gospels" (as, for instance, the frequency of εὐθύς or St. Mark's "somewhat rude yet graphic character") "should be preserved, as they easily may be, in translation."

P. Marcan Flexibility of Expression

St. Mark's literary ability was mediocre. One need but read a page of his Gospel and then turn to a master of prose to see the difference. One of St. Mark's "deficiencies" of style is his lack of flexibility of expression: he generally uses the same word or phrase to denote the same thing. We need not minimize this "blemish" of style, a capital offense in the eyes of the modern critic, by saying that the Greeks did not feel the same dread of repetition as we do; for, even so, what is an artistic embellishment in a classic, may yet be a flaw in an inferior writer. Nor need we point out that in the second Gospel this peculiarity of style is mainly due to St. Mark's source of information. It is more important to note that repetition is at home in any kind of exposition, and was—as we know from the rest of the Gospels—habitually employed by the Pattern of all teachers. A further consideration is that our Lord's and

St. Peter's audiences were of a mentality to profit more by sameness of expression than by constant variation. At all events, we have no right to exaggerate this Marcan trait, for the simple reason that it was actually offset by a certain ability to vary. Contrast, for instance, the two descriptions of the man with the withered hand, both of which are couched in splendid Greek: 3, 1, ἐξηραμμένην ἔχων τὴν χεῖρα, and 3, 3, ὁ τὴν χεῖρα ἔχων ξηράν. Again, verses 15, 16, and 20 of chapter 4 refer to the same fact in three different participles, each used with perfect precision: ἐσπαρμένος, σπειρόμενος, and σπαρείς. See also 5, 15 and 5, 18: δαιμονιζόμενος, δαιμονισθείς, and ὁ ἐσχηκὼς τὸν λεγεῶνα.

Because St. Mark has a limited stock of words, we are doubly unfair to him if we accentuate his weakness by giving the same rendering in those passages in which he actually varies his expression. Joüon renders "qui avait la main desséchée" both in 3, 1 and in 3, 3. Huby and Lagrange offer "qui avait la main sèche" in 3, 3. The alteration is very slight, but even so a tribute to St. Mark. In English we may balance "a man who had a withered hand" or "a man whose hand was withered" against "the man with the withered hand." We may remember that among English writers "Matthew Arnold . . . is the great practitioner of this mode of iteration" in the interests of precision. Genung, *more suo*, gives the psychology of this device, under the headings: "Repetition of Grammatical Elements," "Iteration," "Repetition in Disguise," "Repetition of Construction" (pp. 302–310). The constant problem in the use of repetition is how to effect it with skill and grace. To know exactly what degree of flexibility St. Mark commands, we should compare all his phrases describing the same thing. The list of variants would be surprisingly extended. In a note on Mt. 15, 36, Joüon admits as "fort possible" that St. Matthew has εὐχαριστέω because "l'écrivain *grec* ait *voulu varier* son expression," a truly valuable admission from a declared Orientalist. See Note Q, and *Memoirs* on 7, 15, p. 160. There is a curious illustration of both Marcan weakness and strength in the change from οὐδεὶς ἐδύνατο αὐτὸν δῆσαι (5, 3) to οὐδεὶς ἴσχυεν αὐτὸν δαμάσαι (5, 4); there is a monotonous sameness in the general tone of the two phrases, but there is strength in the change from δῆσαι to δαμάσαι, and from ἐδύνατο to ἴσχυεν, just as Thuc. in 6, 18, 6, changes μηδὲν δύνασθαι to μάλιστ' ἂν ἰσχύειν. Illustrations like these show the ultimate soundness of St. Mark's idioms. In Mk. 1, 23, the phrase εὐθὺς ἦν is awkward, but a glance at Thuc. 3, 36, 4 is illuminating: καὶ τῇ ὑστεραίᾳ μετάνοιά τις εὐθὺς ἦν αὐτοῖς: "But on the very next day a feeling of repentance came over them" (Smith). Note ἦν: "came"; not "was." Gild. 212. So in Mk.: "And at once there came into the synagogue." (For ἐν=εἰς in the Koine, see Moulton 62 ff.)

Q. The Spoken Gospel

A clue to many of the peculiarities of the second Gospel is furnished by the fact that it is the Spoken Gospel *par excellence*. Not only are the speeches it contains actual speeches, but its descriptive and narrative portions are a transcript of oral discourse. Antiquity testifies that St. Mark was St. Peter's "interpreter" and as such transmitted to posterity instructions which he had heard the Apostle give to his converts. The Papias fragment insists on the extreme care St. Mark used in writing down what he had heard St. Peter *say*, and St. Peter in turn, we may suppose, would be careful to repeat exactly what he had *heard*.

With this clue to guide us, we can see why the diction of this Gospel differs in many respects from that of the others: the hand of the "editor" did not appreciably recast St. Peter's reminiscences about Christ.[1] Viewed in this light, St. Mark's blemishes of style are, in a sense, hall-marks of excellence because they make us realize more vividly the trustworthiness of this Ἀρχὴ τοῦ Εὐαγγελίου. Now, where there is actual speech—and that on the lips of uneducated folk—there must be repetition, there must be awkward constructions, there must be parentheses and anacolutha, there must be vernacular phrasing. Above all, the expression must mirror the speaker's emotion. All actual speech, flowing warm and direct from men under stress of emotion, is tinged with feeling. "It is wonderful what subtleties of tone, of feeling, of sentiment, of emotion, can be put into written words, and into very common little words at that. . . . Words hold just what you entrust to them, both the sense and the spirit, and keep it to show to any pair of eyes that comes looking for it, and have a discerning and sympathetic mind behind them" (Edward Sandford Martin, in "Writing"). The past has dealt hardly with St. Mark as a writer, and it is only in recent times that the psychology of spoken speech is being studied more systematically (Paul Frisk; Havers; Wundt). For illustrations of spoken speech and its peculiarities in St. Mark, see the brief notes in *Memoirs* on 12, 23; 14, 41; 2, 10; 3, 5; 6, 25; 8, 24; and consult Chapter V on Marcan Art, *passim*.

---

[1] Here as elsewhere in this volume, when the Petrine origin of the second Gospel is pointed out, it is not implied that St. Mark may not also have used other sources of information. See Merk, *l.c.*, 370 ff. Camerlynck, x ff.

Père Lagrange discusses this aspect of the second Gospel with wonted acuteness. "Le style de Mc. est surtout un style *populaire* et le plus *parlé* ... Il faut aussi tenir compte de la *précision* du conteur qui tient à garder aux choses leur contours et leurs couleurs car il les envisage en elles-mêmes." Referring to St. Mark's anacolutha, he says: "C'est encore une figure qui rappelle *le langage parlé* ..." Even anacolutha have their bright side: "Il est des cas où l'anacoluthe exprime admirablement le mouvement de la pensée." The so-called pleonasms in the second Gospel are due to the fact that the style "est un style *parlé*": it is artless, and has nothing to do with "l'art qui retranche les mots inutiles." Nor are they all genuine cases of pleonasm: "D'ailleurs on ne saurait ranger toutes les expressions plus pleines de Mc. dans la catégorie des simples pléonasmes." In telling a story, St. Mark brings us into direct contact with the *dramatis personae:* "Quand Marc raconte, on entre en contact avec les personnes tant il sait les animer." Lagrange charges some modern critics with a lack of good taste: "Les exégètes qui n'ont pas perdu tout sens esthétique reconnaissent à l'envie le charme des tableaux de Marc." *Évangile selon saint Marc*, Chapitre IV, lxvii ff.

St. Mark's Gospel is essentially the Spoken Gospel, the great λόγος λαλούμενος (to borrow a phrase from St. Mark: 5, 36). It was caught by him "as it was being spoken" by St. Peter. Many of the Evangelist's mannerisms must be traced to its character as λαλούμενος; and we may perhaps apply to St. Mark what Eupolis is reported to have said of Alcibiades: λαλεῖν ἄριστος, ἀδυνατώτατος λέγειν (Plut. *Alc.* 13). Speaking of the ancients in general, Kaibel takes occasion to warn us: "Wir sind meist viel zu sehr Leser der Texte, wo wir Hörer sein sollten" (So. *Electra* 1358, footnote).

R. The Semitic Strain in the Second Gospel

It is a burning question among New Testament scholars to what extent the Semitic languages, Hebrew and Aramaic (the tongue spoken in Palestine at the time of Christ), have affected the purity of New Testament Greek. As might be expected, considering the knottiness of the problem, opinions differ. There are those who scent Semitic influence in almost every expression of the New Testament; and there are others who stoutly refuse to admit such influence except where it can be established by the most rigorous proofs. When all has been said, the presumption should be, I think, that, since in the days of the Koine the knowledge of Greek was spreading in every direction, men who spoke Greek in their social intercourse with a non-Jewish population could not fail to acquire the genuine spoken Greek of their times. As this volume is destined for the young beginner, I may perhaps content myself with reiterating my point of view: Marcan Greek is a segment of Koine Greek; and Koine Greek is best understood from its contact with ancient Greek. Idioms once enshrined in a language continue to live, though not necessarily with the same freshness, as long as that language continues to be spoken by large masses of people. This is, to be sure, a broad formula which needs qualification, and is in this elastic form perhaps of little value to the student. But, at any rate, it reveals the point of view which has had an appreciable effect on this entire work, as well as on the *Memoirs of St. Peter*.

But to be more specific. The student need not be told that in the New Testament he breathes a Semitic air. He cannot help scenting the strange atmosphere, and he would like to lay hold of it in certain definite forms. What, then, may be suggested to him as a workable method of acquainting himself with this intruder and coming to terms with him? As there is question here of advising one presumably ignorant of the Oriental tongues, I should like to urge him to call in the aid of a faithful companion, I mean *L'Évangile de Notre-Seigneur Jésus-Christ*, by Père Paul Joüon, an Orientalist and author of several works on Hebrew and Arabic philology. There are two reasons for doing this: the work just named will take the student through the four Gospels in a *modern* (French) *translation* which attends to the differences between the Greek and Aramaic idioms, and will, moreover, point out to him, in very brief notes, to what extent it might be *possible* to find a *substrat araméen* for any Greek expression of the Evangelists. These notes are fairly numerous, so that it might appear that the learned author is designedly adding the weight of his authority to the already long list of scholars who see in the New Testament Aramaic documents. This is, however, far from being the case; for, while the notes register conscientiously almost every possibility of contact between Greek and Aramaic,[1] the *avant-propos* (xvii) sums up the results

---

[1] Occasionally Père Joüon creates a wrong impression, as when in Mk. 3, 29 he qualifies οὐκ ἔχει ἄφεσιν as "very un-Greek" on the authority of Turner (*JThSt.*, 28, p. 359), or when in Mk. 8, 31 he considers ἤρξατο as "justifié" because "c'est pour la première fois que Jésus parle de sa Passion." In reality, the phrase in 3, 29 is excellent Greek, and in 8, 31 ἤρξατο is justified for an entirely different reason.

of the author's inquiry in a statement free from bias: "The principal difference between Greek and Aramaic in the New Testament consists in this that, Greek being grammatically and stylistically more differentiated (*une langue plus nuancée*) than Aramaic, there are of necessity distinctions and finesses in our Greek text which *did not exist* in the Aramaic substratum. Now, there is no doubt that it is proper (*il convient*) to render into French, in the measure which our language permits, *all the finesses of the Greek* (*toutes les finesses*), while at the same time the possibility of an Aramaic substratum [as pointed out in the notes] underlying the Greek will allow the translator to avoid excessive anxiety in the matter (*l'attention donnée au substrat permettra au traducteur d'éviter une anxiété excessive*)."[2]

I am convinced we have here at last a formula which shows due appreciation of both the Greek and the Aramaic influences in the New Testament. It culminates in this advice: "As a translator of the New Testament, attend to all the finesses proper to the Greek; only do not be so meticulous in doing it as you would be if you had to render Plato or Thucydides." This, I submit, is an excellent working rule. It does justice to the facts as we know them, and is moreover intelligible to the student. It inspires confidence, while warning against an overdose of it. In idiom, the New Testament is essentially a Greek document. Its authors wrote Greek, and wished to be understood by Greek-speaking readers. Its message is addressed to the whole world—an echo, as it were, of that solemn catholic injunction:

Πορευθέντες εἰς τὸν κόσμον ἅπαντα
κηρύξατε τὸ εὐαγγέλιον πάσῃ τῇ κτίσει.

For a discussion of particulars, consult: Howard, "Semitisms in the New Testament," in Moulton's *Grammar of New Testament Greek*, Vol. II, part iii; Moulton, *Prolegomena, passim;* Moulton-Milligan, *Vocabulary of the Greek Testament;* Robertson, "The Semitic Influence," in *Grammar of the Greek New Testament in the Light of Historical Research;* Bauer, *Wörterbuch zum neuen Testament*, "Einleitung"; Zorell, *Lexicon Graecum Novi Testamenti;* Errandonea, *Epitome Grammaticae*

---

[2] Père Joüon has no patience with those who find in the Greek NT mistranslations from the Aramaic (xi): "Quelques aramaïstes, notamment Wellhausen, Burney, Torrey, ont cru relever dans nos évangiles quelques fausses traductions. Mais aucune de ces prétendues 'métraductions' n'est vraiment convaincante, aucune ne prouve qu'un de nos évangiles soit la traduction d'un texte araméen." He advances the interesting theory that St. Matthew was qualified to do his own Aramaic Gospel into Greek. For the theory of mistranslations, see Colwell, *passim*.

Graeco-Biblicae; Lagrange, *Évangile selon Saint Marc,* Introd. Ch. V; Abel, *Grammaire du Grec Biblique,* Introd.; Colwell, *The Greek of the Fourth Gospel;* Blass-Debrunner, 4.

S. *St. Mark's Vocabulary*

A scientific study of St. Mark's Vocabulary being outside the scope of the present volume, it may suffice here to indicate some of the problems involved in such an inquiry. Scholars like Hawkins, Lagrange, Joüon, Howard, and others have gone into the work thoroughly, but by no means exhaustively. Some interesting and valuable detail will be found in three somewhat older works: Thayer's *Greek-English Lexicon of the New Testament;* Vincent's *Word Studies,* and Trench's *Synonyms of the New Testament.* The most up-to-date dictionaries at the present moment are Zorell's *Lexicon Graecum Novi Testamenti* and Bauer's *Wörterbuch zum Neuen Testament.* For beginners, in particular, Souter's *Pocket Lexicon* (called by Dr. Milligan "a marvellous *multum in parvo"*) should be recommended. See also E. Pfeiffer, *Ev. nach Markus,* "Präparationen"; Teubner, 1932. (See above, p. 134.)

Taken as a whole, the Greek of the New Testament is not Jewish Greek.[1] It is not even a special brand of Hellenistic Greek. It is the Greek spoken at the time of Christ throughout the Graeco-Roman world. "We have now abundant proof," says Dr. Milligan, "that the so-called peculiarities of Biblical Greek are due simply to the fact that the writers of the New Testament for the most part made use of the ordinary colloquial Greek, the Koine of their day. This position is in full accord with the facts as we know them." And since Hellenistic Greek is a native growth, we may speak of Marcan Greek as "real" Greek.

But the Marcan enigma is not easily solved, and many are the questions that here press for answer. Was the Koine an entity homogeneous in texture and well-defined in detail? Did it admit of local coloring in the far-flung provinces of the Empire? Was it perhaps like a reservoir (or "Sammelbecken") gathering in its ample basin diverse rills and rivulets of speech? It seems almost impossible to answer exactly. But the enigma deepens when we wish to know whether St. Mark's diction is indebted for some details to her nobler sister, the literary Koine of the day. To judge from what is happening in our own midst, one may suppose that the two great currents of the Koine

---

[1] See the qualified statement in Blass (4), with a reference to Norden.

must have intersected here and there. Moreover, was St. Mark acquainted with the type of composition called Diatribe (or short ethical treatise common in his time)? Was he familiar with any of the jargons so plentiful in official-ridden communities? Is his diction plain man's speech throughout, or have any of the refractions of everyday speech, such as the *sermo familiaris* of polite conversation, the *sermo plebeius* of the man in the street, the *sermo rusticus* of the farmer, or the *sermo castrensis* of the soldier, strayed into his narrative? St. Mark, the boy raised at Jerusalem and Cyprus, the young missionary traversing Asia Minor, the interpreter of St. Peter in the capital, the later Bishop of cosmopolitan Alexandria, must have spoken to men of various strata of society.

And if we had done searching the prose of Hellenistic life to find the elements of Marcan speech, there would yet remain the vast field of poetry, both older and contemporary. Critics have observed that the Koine meets at various points the language of epic, lyric, and especially dramatic poetry (Radermacher). The Greek Papyri show that Homer and Euripides were popular with the common man. It would be curious to know whether St. Mark ever glanced at a line of contemporary verse, or whether he confined his reading to the Septuagint and the Hebrew Bible, or whether he did any reading at all. Of course, when Homer and Thucydides and Xenophon and Plato are cited as witnesses to the sense of certain idioms occurring in the second Gospel, it is assumed that idioms in use at a period prior to St. Mark somehow contrived to live, though probably not always with the same vigor, and that we are not acting absurdly if we expect to detect traces of such life even in St. Mark.[1] In so vast a territory as the Roman Empire, in which the spoken word was the principal medium of communication, who would set bounds to "the winged word" and forbid it to roam about? Good and honest Greek idioms did not come into St. Mark's Gospel by a direct route from the golden treasury of Greek literature, but were carried into it on the wings of living speech.

But suppose we had exhausted the external sources of Marcan Greek, there is yet the writer's individuality staring us in the face. A written composition is not a mere conglomeration of words, phrases, or clauses, like so many *disiecta membra* that have met by chance; but there is a secret Something that binds them together—a spiritual power that fuses them into a living stream of thought. The second Gospel does not reach the level of literary speech, but even there words were

---

[1] For an illustration, see above, Note I on "Marcan Ἤρξατο."

welded together to make sense and express sentiment. The mystery is all the deeper because there we face two personalities, without being able to make separate assignments to voucher and interpreter.

Problems like these may be full of interest to the student of language; but until scholars are able to unravel the mystery, *we have a right to enjoy the second Gospel with the helps already at our disposal.* Of one thing we must be sure: the second Gospel deserves loving study because it is unique; unique *perhaps* in point of time, in the sense that it *may* be the first Christian utterance in *Greek*; unique in rush and forward movement; unique in brevity and compactness; unique in ruggedness of construction; unique in graphic detail and vigorous phrase; unique in its ultimate relation to the prince of the Apostles.

There is no lack of treatises on the Koine. Robertson's *Grammar* shows (pp. 49–75) the numerous aspects of the language problem in the New Testament and weighs the pros and cons in the interesting debate between the Hellenist and the Semitist. Milligan's "General Introduction" to his *Vocabulary* is brimful of details. In recent years the possible presence of Latinisms in the second Gospel has attracted attention. The student may be warned against hasty inferences, and should ponder Robertson's guarded statement (110): "Blass thinks that the syntax [of the NT] shows a greater Latin influence [than the vocabulary], but admits that it is difficult to tell the difference between native development in the Greek and a possible Latin bent. It is indeed difficult to speak with decision on this point. Ultimately Greek and Latin had great influence on each other, but at this stage the matter is at least too doubtful to appeal to with confidence." "Though the bulk of the NT," says Moulton (20), "comes to us from authors with Roman names, no one will care to assert that Latin was the native language of Paul or Luke or Mark." Blass discusses with much detail "Ungriechische Elemente" and "Latinismen" in the New Testament (4 and 5; with interesting notes in "Nachträge"). For the latest literature on Latinisms in NT, see Blass, p. 291. See the notes on Mk., 5, 43, εἶπεν δοθῆναι αὐτῇ φαγεῖν. 11, 32, εἶχον Ἰωάννην ὅτι ἦν. 15, 15, τὸ ἱκανὸν ποιῆσαι. 14, 65, ῥαπίσμασιν αὐτὸν ἔλαβον. Moulton 18; 20; 71; 75; 100 ff.; 142; 208; 212 f.; 247. Joüon discusses Latin influence in his notes on Mt. 18, 10; 21, 46. Mk. 5, 43; 11, 32; 15, 15. Lk. 7, 4; 12, 58; 14, 18. Abel xxxiii–xxxvi. Lagrange cvi, cvii. It has been surmised that the second Gospel was originally written in Latin; see *JThSt.*, 29, 375 ff. Cf. *ib.*, pp. 346 ff.

T. Points of Syntax

1. The Aoristic Present

Note the judicial tone in Mk. 2, 5, ἀφίενται: "Your sins are here and now forgiven." *Memoirs* 150. Swete makes the amazing statement that the forgiveness is regarded as continuous, beginning from that hour, and renders, "thy sins are receiving forgiveness." But absolution from sin is instantaneous in operation and comprehensive in effect: αἱ ἁμαρτίαι denotes the man's sins *as a unit;* nor does present absolution deal with the future. In grammatical parlance ἀφίενται is an aorist-present. Smyth 1853; 1924 a. Dana 174. Burton 9 and 13. Blass 320, w. reff. Robertson 865. Moulton 119; 247. Gildersleeve 188; 189; 192. Mayser 32, 2 with notes.

Since the Greek aorist had power to express concentrated action (Gildersleeve 260–262) and to denote the immediate past (Moulton 135), there was no pressing need for using the present in the same function. If ἤσθην could mean "I *am* delighted here and now" (Gild. 262. Smyth 1937), the present ἤδομαι could be reserved mainly to express *action in progress*. Aorist-presents are therefore comparatively rare in ancient Greek. Blass gives no references to older Greek. Brugmann (546) sees an aorist-present in verbs compounded with perfective prepositions.[1] He explains ἔχω=ἔλαβον, ἔσχον (Mayser takes ἔχω= ἔσχηκα; p. 133). On the aoristic (?) use of φέρειν, see Moulton 129, w. footnote, and cf. Mk. 11, 2.

Gildersleeve (on *Pyth.* 2, 50) denies the existence of an aorist-present in ancient Greek; but his 'Specific Present' (189) will often serve the purpose (Mayser, p. 132 footnote). Xen. *Anab.* 1, 8, 26, τὸν ἄνδρα ὁρῶ, "I see my man." *Cyr.* 7, 2, 27, ἤδη σοι λέγω, "I assure you here and now." Gerth (382, 7, b at end) notes that present tense forms do not invariably have a conative sense. He compares Pl. *Civ.* 390 e, δῶρα θεοὺς πείθει, "Gifts (not only tempt, but) actually beguile gods." Smyth 1853, δίδωμι, "I make a present" (not only "I offer"). So. *Oed. Tyr.* 41, ἱκετεύομέν σε, "We here and now beseech thee." Xen. *Cyr.* 7, 2, 26, ἀπο-δίδωμι ἤδη γυναῖκα, "I here and now restore to you your wife." Gildersleeve (192 and 188) distinguishes between the present as a tense of *continuance* and the present as a tense of *attainment*. Mayser (132) refers to Rodenbusch who endeavors to show that there are

---

[1] "Der Sprache ist somit ein Mittel an die Hand gegeben, die aoristische Aktionsart auch in der Zeitstufe der Gegenwart auszudrücken. Ein Ansatz zu einem punktuellen oder Aorist-Praesens ist beim Verbum ἀπ-έχω gemacht."

sporadic instances in Greek in which a present expression coincides with the occurrence denoted by it, not only in a linear-perfective, but also in the so-called punctiliar sense. Cf. Ignatius *Trall.* 11, 1, οὗ ἐὰν γεύσηται τις, παραυτὰ ἀπο-θνῄσκει (*ipso facto dies*). See Moulton, p. 114. Aeschylus *Choe.* 3, κατ-έρχομαι (note again the perf. prepos.).

Furthermore, the historic present may represent the narrative aorist. Smyth 1883 a. Gerth 382, 2. Blass (321) states that the Aktionsart of the historical present is mostly *punctiliar* in spite of the present form ("wird trotz der praesentischen Form meist punktuell bleiben"). The context makes the reference clear. See Dana's description of the aorist-present (174). Davis 401 (b).

For possible Marcan instances, see 1, 2, κατασκευάσει (with comment by Brugmann 546). 3, 26, τέλος ἔχει (often in the Papyri= τετέλεσται. Witkowski, p. 190). 4, 12, συνιῶσιν. 3, 28, ἀμὴν λέγω. 11, 24, λέγω. 9, 25, ἐπιτάσσω. 12, 20, ἀποθνῄσκων. 14, 22, ἐστίν. John 11, 41, εὐχαριστῶ.

In the parallel passage St. Luke (5, 20) has ἀφέωνται, a true perfect: "are forgiven and stay forgiven"; on a par with βεβάασι in *Iliad* 2, 134; see Brugmann, 547. St. Mark and St. Luke express different aspects of the same thing; the former, the act of forgiving, leaving the result to be inferred; the latter, the result, leaving the act to be implied. Gildersleeve 227.

2. Coincident Action

Action may be coincident in two ways; first, when two verbs denote different aspects of the same act; secondly, when two verbs denote different, but closely related, acts. Thus *Iliad* 4, 73, ὣς εἰπὼν ὄτρυνε, "so saying, he spurred on." His words (εἰπών) were words of encouragement (ὄτρυνε). Thuc. 8, 90, 2, ἀπέστειλαν ἐπιστείλαντες, "they despatched . . . with orders." The act of despatching (ἀπέστειλαν) was accompanied by instructions (ἐπιστείλαντες). Brugmann 555, Anm. ("Sachliche Koinzidenz: ineinanderfallende Handlungen" and "Sachlich einander berührende Handlungen"). Mk. 6, 37, ἀποκριθεὶς εἶπεν and 6, 27, ἀποστείλας ἐπέταξεν.

Coincident action may be expressed by two aorists, by two durative forms, or by a combination of the two. Gildersleeve 330–336; 343; 345. Smyth 1872, c, 2; 2062 a; 2096; 2103; 2141; 2147 b; 3042 h; Moulton 131; Blass 339, 1 (w. reff., p. 310); Mayser, p. 169. Gerth 601, 6; 389 Anm. 8. Jacobsthal 63. Howard, p. 452 ff.

It is important to know that coincidence of action may be expressed by two *finite* forms (joined by καί). Mk. 3, 5, ἐξέτεινεν καὶ ἀπεκατέστη. Compare Mk. 6, 50, ἐλάλησεν καὶ λέγει with Mt. 28, 18, ἐλάλησεν λέγων. Mk. 8, 25, διέβλεψεν καὶ ἀπεκατέστη. *Iliad* 9, 393, "If ever the gods save me, *and* I reach my home," ἤν . . . με σαῶσι θεοὶ καὶ οἴκαδ' ἵκωμαι.

In Acts 25, 13, if the aorist ἀσπασάμενοι is genuine, it expresses coincident action, for the phrase κατήντησαν ἀσπασάμενοι is equivalent to κατήντησαν καὶ ἠσπάσαντο. The two actions overlap in point of time; the καταντῆσαι denotes the meeting with Festus and all that this meeting involved; the καταντῆσαι and the ἀσπάσασθαι happened on the same occasion. Moulton has the correct interpretation; p. 132, with footnote, and note on p. 238.

Phrases like ἀποκριθεὶς εἶπεν and ἐλάλησεν λέγων are commonly treated under the head of "Marcan Redundancy"; but Greek literature is full of examples of a similar coupling of verbs of *saying*, from Homer down. One is at a loss to see why St. Mark is blamed for redundancy when such redundancy is almost part and parcel of the ancient Greek diction. Cf. ἀπαμείβετο φώνησέν τε—ἔπος φάτο φώνησέν τε—καὶ μίν φωνήσας ἔπεα πτερόεντα προσηύδα—Pl. *Apol.* 19, says: τί δὴ λέγοντες διέβαλλον οἱ διαβάλλοντες? Arist. *Wasps* 795, ἦ δ' ὃς λέγων. Howard points out with how little certainty this Greek idiom can be said to have an Aramaic basis: "It is *hard* to say when the participle is really pleonastic, but a Semitic flavor clings to the following examples (ἀποκριθεὶς εἶπεν, etc.)." As for ἐλάλησεν λέγων, Lagrange (S. Matth. lxxxix) finds it "a dozen times in the Elephantine papyri and accepts it as commonly spoken, but *not very pure Aramaic.*" It is a great pity to see how much energy has been wasted by some scholars to demonstrate their pet dogma of St. Mark's "Redundancy,"—a pity, because it is easier to label an expression outright than to find a rational explanation for its use. See *Memoirs*, on 12, 23, p. 168. For the sense of ἀποκριθείς in such "redundant" phrases, see Note L.

U. Glimpses of Marcan Rhetoric

With regard to the use of rhetoric in the New Testament, writers are cautious and, naturally, divided in their opinions. See, for instance, Blass-Debrunner 458 ff. and 485 ff., and Robertson, 1194 ff. (with an important addendum on "the rattle of dry bones"; 1206). As to the second Gospel in particular there is a general reluctance to credit its author with any ability to enhance his composition by means of figures

of style or rhetorical devices. Nevertheless, when all due allowances
have been made, writers are agreed that of all the Gospels St. Mark's
abounds in picturesque descriptions and, moreover, there is the fundamental fact that he was *human* and that, in his day, even ordinary people were able to employ freely the lighter touches of rhetorical speech.
The Sophists of the second century "had audiences who could appreciate every artistic device" (Wright, *Philostratus*, Introd., xvi). Then, if
ever, rhetoric was in the air. If rhetoric stands for the sum of those
qualities of expression by which meaning is specially recommended to
the hearer (Rannie), traces of such qualities should be expected to
appear in the second Gospel, for this, more than any other Gospel, was
from start to finish *spoken* speech (see Note Q). As our Lord in addressing the common people in Palestine, so in turn St. Peter in speaking to
the *pusillus grex* at Rome, would by a natural instinct be careful to
press the lesson on those simple folk and, in order to do so, would naturally employ such (more or less rhetorical) modes of expression as were
then in vogue. There is a "natural esthetic," as has been rightly said
(Robertson, with reference to I Cor. 13 and Hebr. 11). At times
rhetoric "enters expression insidiously and may be difficult of detection
in its elementary stages" (Rannie). When this happens, the effect of
rhetoric is achieved by an absence of rhetorical devices. Of this, too,
there are traces in St. Mark.

The following are among those Marcan passages that owe their
effectiveness to a complete absence of rhetoric: their power is in the
bare thought. See the note on 11, 23.

1, 8 : Βαπτίσει ὑμᾶς ἐν πνεύματι ἁγίῳ.

2, 10: ἐξουσίαν ἔχει ἀφιέναι ἁμαρτίας ἐπὶ τῆς γῆς.

3, 28: πάντα ἀφεθήσεται τοῖς υἱοῖς τῶν ἀνθρώπων.

3, 29: οὐκ ἔχει ἄφεσιν εἰς τὸν αἰῶνα.

9, 19: ἕως πότε πρὸς ὑμᾶς ἔσομαι.

10, 18: οὐδεὶς ἀγαθὸς εἰ μὴ εἷς ὁ θεός.

10, 43: οὐχ οὕτως δέ ἐστιν ἐν ὑμῖν.

11, 23: ὃ λαλεῖ γίνεται.

12, 17: τὰ Καίσαρος ἀπόδοτε Καίσαρι.

12, 27: ὑμεῖς οὖν πολὺ πλανᾶσθε.

14, 22: τοῦτό ἐστιν τὸ σῶμά μου.

15, 25: ἦν δὲ ὥρα τρίτη καὶ ἐσταύρωσαν αὐτόν.

15, 37: ὁ Ἰησοῦς ἀφεὶς φωνὴν μεγάλην ἐξέπνευσεν.

St. Mark has several examples of effective parallelism, as 1, 8; 2, 21–22; 2, 27; 3, 24–26; 2, 17; 4, 4 ff.; 4, 12; 4, 25; 4, 39; 6, 28; 8, 17–18; 8, 34 ff.; 9, 37; 9, 43 ff.; 10, 27; 10, 29 ff.; 10, 33–34; 12, 14; 12, 29 ff.; 13, 24–25; 13, 31; 16, 19–20. For parallelism, see Barry 194; Campbell 82; Demetrius *On Style* 23, 250; Norden *AK* and *ATh, passim;* Schütz, *Der parallele Satzbau;* Aristotle *Rhet.* III ix 7 ff.; Adams *Lysias*, p. 348. *Memoirs,* Ch. V, "Glimpses of Marcan Art," p. 39 ff.

For instances of Marcan flexibility of expression, see Note P. Contrast 10, 12 ἀπολύσασα with 10, 11 ὃς ἂν ἀπολύσῃς; 10, 51 τί σοι θέλῃς ποιήσω with 10, 36 τί θέλετε ποιῆσαί με ὑμῖν; 10, 46 ἐκπορευομένου with ἔρχονται in the same verse; 2, 2 ἐλάλει with 5, 35 ἔτι αὐτοῦ λαλοῦντος; 2, 9 ἆρον with 2, 12 ἄρας; 9, 43 ἀπελθεῖν used in the same passive sense as 9, 45 βληθῆναι. Variety is a charm even in the speech of simple men.

St. Mark knows the force of synonyms, as in 13, 33 and 34: βλέπειν, γρηγορεῖν, ἀγρυπνεῖν. He knows the importance of repetition, both as a means of emphasis (as ἵνα γρηγορῇ, γρηγορεῖτε, γρηγορεῖτε. See also 8, 26–38; 9, 43–45–47), and as a means of reproducing the colloquial (and emphatic) tone of the teacher (2, 20, τότε, ἐν ἐκείνῃ τῇ ἡμέρᾳ; 3, 24–26 μερισθῇ–στῆναι; 14, 30 σύ, σήμερον, ταύτῃ τῇ νυκτί; etc.). For chiasm, see 1, 5 πᾶσα–πάντες; *Memoirs* 168, on 12, 14. Holzmeister, *De forma chiastica in NT. adhibita (Verbum Domini* 14, 337 ff.). For paronomasia, see 7, 37 and 12, 14, w. note in *Memoirs.* For asyndeton, see 14, 6.7. For periodic structure, see 15, 42; 5, 26–28, etc. For hendiadys, see 1, 45. For sentence balancing and the disposal of the common element, see 1, 45; 9, 14; 9, 22; w. general note above, p. 122. For parataxis, see Note A. For hysteron proteron, see on 12, 8. For Marcan rhythm, see above, p. 125. Robertson's final estimate of the Greek diction of the NT (pp. 1207, 1208: "The chief treasure of the Greek tongue is the N.T." "Grammar is nothing unless it reveals the thought and emotion hidden in language") is well worth pondering.

B. BRIEF NOTES ON SPECIAL PASSAGES

I, 1: THE SUPERSCRIPTION

1. Κατὰ Μᾶρκον: *according to, as told by, Mark.* The Gospel is Christ's, the presentation, Mark's. But from Plato down, κατά w. acc. may be a substitute for the subj. genitive. *M. Vocabulary,* 322, II, b.

1. ἀρχή: *a summary;* Zorell 178. Headings need no article; Moulton 82. Moreover, in the sense of "beginning," ἀρχή and ἀρχήν often function as predicates even when the rest of the sentence is not the grammatical, but only the logical, subject. Here: "The beginning of the Gospel (was as follows)." Pl. *Ph.* 58 c, ἀρχὴ δ' ἐστὶ τῆς θεωρίας, ἐπειδάν: "The festival opens when . . ." Isocr. *Anti.* 117, ἀρχὴ αὕτη στρατηγίας ἐστίν: "This is the first requisite of good strategy." Cf. Mk. 13, 8, ἀρχαί. In the use or non-use of the definite art., Greek feeling and the modern point of view are often far apart. Dana 145 ff. Smyth 1118 ff. Gild. 514 ff. Moulton 81 ff. Wackernagel II, 131 ff. For the rendering of the Gr. art. in AV, see Roberts 89 ff. See *Special Note* on 5, 30.

εὐ-αγγέλιον: in cpds., εὐ is often negligible (Gild. *BM.* 207); in εὐ-αγγέλιον the prefix needs to be stressed: *Message of salvation; saving message,* rather than merely "good news; glad tidings" ("Heilsbotschaft," rather than "Freudenbotschaft"). *Gospel* means "good story," rather than "story of God" (Skeat). εὐ-αγγέλιον (originally "reward for good news"; Homer) later came to mean a written embodiment of the good news. Ἰησοῦ: probably obj. gen. Contrast Θεοῦ in v. 14.

There are several correct ways of reading the opening verses 1–4. V. 1 looks like a superscription for the whole Gospel, or like a heading for the section dealing w. the Baptist. Some take vv. 1 and 4 as parts of the same sentence: "The beginning of the Gospel was (ἐγένετο) John." Others join 1 and 2, w. verb understood in 1. The interpretation here preferred considers 2 and 3 as protasis to v. 4. See *Memoirs* 46. ἀρχή may denote a person: "primus praeco boni nuntii" (Zorell 178). Cf. Plut. *Cimon* 5, 3, οὐκ ὀλίγοις (Κίμων) ἀρχὴ τοῦ θαρρεῖν ἐγένετο.

I, 2–8. The Mission of John the Baptist

(Lk. 3, 1–18. Mt. 3, 1–12; 11, 10. Jn. 1, 6; 1, 19–30; 3, 28).

2. γέγραπται: *it is written* once for all; it is on record. Every one of Mark's perfects, if strictly interpreted, makes excellent sense; but since from the 3d century B.C. on, the Gr. pf. began to weaken, we cannot be sure that Mark always used it in the older sense. Blass 340 ff. Dana 182 ff. Moulton 140 ff. Brugmann 556. Wackernagel I, 170. The *result* of an action, ordinarily expressed by the pf. (Smyth 1945), may be implied in an aorist, "the shorthand of the perfect" (Gild. 227). Burton 74 ff.; 82. Contrast Mk. 16, 14, ἐγηγερμένος with 16, 6, ἠγέρθη, "He is risen." Davis 403.

Ἠσαΐᾳ: "Mark quotes from the two prophets (Isaias and Malachi) under the name of Isaias, the *Messianic* prophet *par excellence*" (Lagrange). ἐγώ: in the Koine, the personal pron. is not necessarily emphatic as in older Gr. Cf. 1, 8. Blass 277. Dana 134, 1 Note. Smyth 930; 1190. Moulton 84. μου: here reflexive. Dana 134, 2. Smyth 1222. Blass 283.

ἀποστέλλω: perhaps a vision of the future. Gild. 194 ff. Smyth 1879. Dana 174. But the pres. may be aoristic: "I here and now send forth." Smyth 1853. See on 2, 5, ἀφίενται, and Note T. The exact force of a Gr. tense is frequently doubtful because the writer has not chosen to speak more clearly.[1] κατασκευάσει: Simple or final future? Dana 178; 252. Gild. 267. *Will* or *shall prepare?* For "Shall" in the NT, see Moulton 150. Note κατά: for the intensive or perfectivizing force of certain prepositions in compound verbs (ἀπό, διά, κατά, ἐκ, σύν, ἀνά), see Moulton 111 ff.; Howard 112–130. Wackernagel II, 181.

3. φωνὴ βοῶντος: *a voice is crying* (Isaias 40, 3); so in the Hebrew. But see Note R. The Gr. as such may mean "a (mere) voice," which would be John's humble reference to himself (Jn. 1, 23). Cf. Eur. *HF.*, 111, ἔπεα μόνον, "a voice, no more"; ib., 229, οὐδὲν ὄντα πλὴν γλώσσης ψόφον, "nothing but a voice's sound." One is reminded of δῖα θεάων, etc.; Smyth 1316; 1064; so here perhaps = βοῶν βοώντων. Moreover, as we say of one deeply attentive that he is *all ears*, so φωνὴ βοῶντος was perhaps intended to mean that John was *all voice* = one crying with might and main. Mark's symbol in Christian art is a lion.

---

[1] It is often said that "the Greek is remarkable for combining the utmost precision and lucidity with the greatest simplicity" (Flagg, *Attic Prose*, 102); but the same writer admits that "every language must *of course* work more or less by suggestion and implication, in one direction or another."

ἑτοιμάσατε, ποιεῖτε: the aor. views the preparation of the road as a whole and a finished product (τὴν ὁδόν; sing.!); the pres. looks to the ever-recurring details of repair; *keep in constant repair* (τὰς τρίβους; plur.!). Blass 337. Smyth 1924 ff. Contrast Mk. 9, 22, βοήθησον w. 9, 24, βοήθει; 10, 21, πώλησον w. ἀκολούθει; 2, 9, ἆρον w. περιπάτει.

4. The text here used has ὁ before βαπτίζων and no ὁ before κηρύσσων; hence the phrase ὁ βαπτίζων down to ἁμαρτιῶν may be an apposition to 'Ιωάννης. *Memoirs* 65. Without the art., ἐγένετο βαπτίζων may be ingressive or complexive aorist to ἦν βαπτίζων. ἐγένετο may be joined to ἐν τῇ ἐρήμῳ, "he came into the desert" (for ἐν=εἰς, see Blass 218), and to κηρύσσων, "and became a preacher." Smyth 1857. For μετάνοια in NT, see Dirksen; also *Classical Bulletin*, May 1933, p. 60. Both ἐν τῇ ἐρήμῳ and εἰς ἄφεσιν ἁμαρτιῶν are felt as common elements to βαπτίζων and κηρύσσων; see Colometry, B 7. μετανοίας is a descriptive gen. Dana 90. John's baptism "had something to do with repentance." Brugmann 451. Howard p. 440. Löfstedt, *Syntactica* I 83 ff. Blass 162. Smyth 1290 ff.

5. ἐξεπορεύετο: the imperfects in vv. 5–8, fringed by an aor. at either end (ἐγένετο), describe John's ministry. Gild. 211. Smyth 1898; 1908–1909; 1929. For Mark's picture of the Baptist, see *Memoirs* 45–46. For ἐξ- in cpd. verbs, see Note G. ἐβαπτίζοντο: Smyth 1736.

πᾶσα-καὶ-πάντες: Chiasm. Smyth 3020. See Note U. Watch καί wherever it occurs. Note H. Since the inhabitants of J. are included in the wider term ἡ 'Ιουδαία χώρα, καί before οἱ 'Ι. particularizes (*Memoirs* 65). Cf. Mk. 3, 16, καὶ τῷ Σίμωνι. 16, 7, καὶ τῷ Πέτρῳ. 13, 34, καὶ τῷ θυρωρῷ. Smyth 2868 ff. For the limited scope of πᾶς, see Note D.

ἐν τῷ ποταμῷ: the penitents were *in* the water, but the rite of baptism cannot be inferred from the phrase, any more than from ἀναβαίνων in v. 10. It was customary among the Jews to baptize by immersion. For the effect of John's baptism, see *Memoirs* 147. Note the graphic touch in ἐξομολογούμενοι. Howard 119. *M. Vocabulary* 224. αὐτῶν: peccata sua. Dana 140, 2.

6–7. ἦν ἐνδεδυμένος: a periphrastic use of the participle. Dana 203. Smyth 1857 (important); 1961; 2091. Gild. 191; 291. Botte 73. This use is not the same as that of the progressive tenses in English. Moulton 226 f. Cf. 10, 22, ἦν ἔχων. μέλι ἄγριον: *Memoirs* 147. ἔρχεται: Smyth 1881. Botte 51. Dana 174, 2. Gild. 194. ἔρχεσθαι in NT is hallowed from its association w. the Messias = ὁ ἐρχόμενος. Cf. Mk. 14, 62; 13, 35; 13, 26; 12, 9; 11, 9; 11, 10. αὐτοῦ after οὗ is redundant. Moulton 84 f. ὁ ἰσχυρότερος: *one who* or *he who* is stronger. Generic or particular art. Smyth 1119 ff. Dana 147.

8. ἐγώ, αὐτός: emphatic by contrast. Smyth 1190 ff.; 1204 ff. Dana 134; 137. See on v. 2, ἐγώ. ἐβάπτισα: Smyth 1927. For the rendering of the Gr. aor., see Weymouth (*passim*); Burton 52–55; Moulton 135–140. ἐν (an interesting prep.!): often instrumental, without losing its local color. *In* or *with* the Holy Spirit? See on 1, 23. *Memoirs* 147. Note the colometrization of v. 8; the parallelism is perfect. Colometry, B 3.

Special Note: The precise force of NT αὐτός is disputed. Moulton 86 ("generally unmistakably emphatic in nom."); Dana 138 Note; Wackernagel II 86 ("occasionally emphatic, as in old Gr.; generally unemphatic, as in modern Gr."). In Mk. 1, 8 old Gr. would use ἐκεῖνος; Wackernagel *ib.* For ἐγώ and σύ, see W. I 108. Cf. Hunt, *Sel. Pap.* (2nd or 3d century A.D.) p. 306 (Loeb): εὔχομαί σε ὑγιένεν, καὶ ἐγὼ αὐτὸς ὑγιένω. The weight of αὐτός, evidently, varies with the context.

I, 9–13. BAPTISM AND TEMPTATION OF JESUS
(Mt. 3, 13—4, 11. Lk. 3, 21–22; 4, 1–13. Jn. 1, 32–34; 1, 51)

9. ἐγένετο: resumes the narrative; see on 1, 5, ἐξεπορεύετο. Gild. 211. For the phrase (καὶ) ἐγένετο (καὶ) ἦλθεν, etc., see Burton 357 ff.; Joüon on Lk. 3, 21; 5, 1; 9, 28. Mt. 2, 7; 7, 28. ἐβαπτίσθη: permissive pass. Smyth 1736. Gild. 167. εἰς and ἐν are at times used without distinction. Blass 205. Smyth 1659 b. Mark lingered (imperfects: Gild. 205) in describing John's ministry, but hurries (aorist) over Christ's baptism. The Gr. impf. does not argue *objective* importance, nor does the aor. imply *objective* insignificance. Gildersleeve 206.

10. εὐθύς: w. ἀναβαίνων. See on 1, 18. This adverb occurs over 40 times in Mark. Note K. *Memoirs* 56. The subject of εἶδεν may be *Jesus* or *John.* Some refer εἶδεν to John, but ἀναβαίνων to Jesus. See Dean on 1, 10. Moulton 69, "Nominativus pendens." Dana 83. Smyth 3008 e. For the force of σχίζομαι, see *Memoirs* 148. εἰς αὐτόν: εἰς, of direction toward which; *upon.* See Mt. 3, 16. *Memoirs* 184, 185. Dana 111. Mark does not say that this was the *first* descent of the Holy Spirit on Jesus. *Memoirs* 182.

11. ἐγένετο ἐκ: the voice rang out *in* the sky. Gr. stresses the starting-point. Note G. Smyth 1660. Mk. 11, 8, ἐκ τῶν ἀγρῶν. For the "surveying use" of ἐξ see Jebb on So. *Ant.* 411. ὁ υἱός μου: My Son; ἀγαπητός: My only Son. For ἀγαπητός, cf. Zorrell, *al.* εὐδόκησα: the aor. of what has just happened. Moulton 135. Dana 181. Gild. 262. *I am*

well pleased. The reference is primarily to Christ's self-abasement in His baptism. See on 7, 13, παρεδώκατε.

12. ἐκ-βάλλει: no hint of force or violence; see L&S., s.v. βάλλω. The context decides the tone of βάλλω and its cpds. For the historical pres., see Smyth 1883; Dana 174; Gild. 199, 200. It does not necessarily view a past action with the vividness of a present occurrence. Wackernagel I, 163 ff. For the hist. pres. in English, see Moulton 121.

13. Does τεσσεράκοντα ἡμέρας modify ἦν or πειραζόμενος? As the narrative ἐγένετο in v. 4 was followed by the descriptive ἐξεπορεύετο, so here the narrative ἐκβάλλει (Smyth 1883 a) is followed by the descriptive ἦν πειραζόμενος. Gild. 214. For a glimpse of Marcan art, see *Memoirs* 46. Mark is a great epitomizer. *Memoirs* 56. Is ἦν the complete pred. (Smyth 918), or does it go w. πειραζόμενος? Smyth 1857. Dana 203. See on 1, 6. The words ἦν ἐν τῇ ἐρήμῳ may, but need not, mean: He came into the desert. Gild. 212. Cf. Mk. 1, 23. Nor does the impf. necessarily imply that Jesus was tempted repeatedly or throughout the 40 days. Gild 205. πειραζόμενος: Smyth 1872 (subsequent action?); "tested," rather than "tempted."

I, 14–20. The Beginnings of the Ministry in Galilee
(Mt. 4, 12–22. Lk. 4, 14–15; 5, 1–11)

14. μετὰ τὸ παραδοθῆναι: articular infin. Smyth 2034. Dana 191. Burton 392 ff. ἦλθεν εἰς: 1) He set out for Galilee; see on 1, 10. Smyth 1924. 2) He went to Galilee; Smyth 1927. 3) He went through (deep into) G.; see Mk. 16, 15. The precise sense of κηρύσσων (Smyth 1872) will depend on the force of ἦλθεν εἰς. τοῦ θεοῦ: subj. gen. The message deals with Jesus Christ (v. 1), but is sent by God.

15. For this topic outline of our Lord's inaugural sermon, see *Memoirs* 47. πεπλήρωται: *the period*, which had to elapse before the coming of the Messias, has been filled up=*is ended*. Do not miss the force of Mk.'s perfects; see on 1, 2, γέγραπται. The pres. impv. prescribes a course of action, and is more quiet and less abrupt than the aor. would be. Moulton 189. See on 1, 3. In demanding obedience from man, our Lord allows for slow compliance (but see on 10, 21, δός). For an echo of this μετανοεῖτε, see Mk. 6, 12, μετανοῶσιν (pres. subjv.). In Acts 3, 19 the aor. insists on immediate action. *Memoirs*, two notes on **1, 15**; p. 148. ἐν τῷ εὐαγγελίῳ: for εἰς τὸ εὐ.?

16. παράγων εἶδεν: there are scores of exx. in this Gospel (as in all Gr. literature) of an aor. coupled w. a durative tense. Analyze each

occurrence of this idiom, and bear in mind Gild.'s warning (212; 214).
Smyth 1872. Mark calls the Lake of Gennesaret *the Sea of Galilee*.

17. Is δεῦτε here a hypothetical impv. (Smyth 1839: if you come . . .),
or is it an absolute command (come; I will . . .)? See Note A. ποιήσω:
could be hortatory subjv. Smyth 1797. *Let Me make you*. Cf. Aesch.
Choe. 171, μάθω, "let me learn." Gerth 394, 4. ποιέω w. infin., Smyth
2142. What kind of aor. is γενέσθαι? Smyth 1924–1927.

18. εὐθύς: w. καί (and at once, *sc*. they followed); not w. ἀφέντες (no
sooner had they left than they followed). This use of εὐθύς is rare in
the classics. But see So. *Ant*. 1005, and Thuc. 3, 36, 6, καταστάσης
εὐθὺς ἐκκλησίας, "A meeting was held at once." See on 1, 10. ἠκολούθησαν: ingressive or complexive aor.? Smyth 1924 ff.

19. καὶ αὐτούς: *ipsos quoque;* belongs only to ἐν τῷ πλοίῳ, not to
καταρτίζοντας; *like the others*, they were in their boat. *Memoirs* 67.
Thus πάλιν in 15, 13 modifies ἔκραξαν, not σταύρωσον. Cf. 2 Cor. 2, 1,
πάλιν–ἐν λύπῃ. Great care is needed to ascertain the precise reference of
a word or phrase to other words in the same sentence. In reading aloud,
the ref. is made clear by a change in the tone or by pausing. See Colometry, B 6. For the "ear-mindedness" of the ancients, see Hendrickson, *Classical Journal*, 25, 181 ff.

20. ἀπ-ῆλθον: see Note G.

I, 21–39. PREACHING AND MIRACLES IN GALILEE

(Mt. 4, 13; 4, 23; 7, 28–29; 8, 14–15; 9, 35. Lk. 4, 31–44).

21. For a rendering of this verse, see *Memoirs;* but several words
are doubtful. Does εὐθύς modify τοῖς σάββασιν (on the very first Sabbath. Smyth 1153 e N; as in Latin *plane vir*, an excellent man), or does
it qualify εἰσελθών (see on 1, 10)? Does εἰσελθών go w. εἰς Καφαρναούμ
or w. εἰς τὴν συναγωγήν? The partic. εἰσελθών may be intended merely
to resume εἰσπορεύονται: and no sooner had He entered (*sc*. the city)
than He began to teach. For this kind of resumption, see on 10, 46,
ἔρχονται (ἐκπορευμένου. Mt. 9, 31, ἐξελθόντες, and 32, ἐξερχομένων.
Gerth 486.

22. ἐξεπλήσσοντο: descriptive ipf.; an indefinite plural; Smyth 931 d;
people were lost in wonder. ἐκπλαγῆναι: Note M. For ἦν διδάσκων, see
on 1, 6. Dana 203. For the connotations of ἐξουσία, see Mk. 1, 27;
2, 10; 3, 15; 6, 7; 11, 28; 13, 34. "A free hand to do as one pleases"
(Rickaby).

23. καὶ εὐθὺς ἦν ἐν τῇ συναγωγῇ: *at once there came*, better than *at*

once there was. See Note P at end. Gild. 212. Joüon on Mk. 1, 13. ἐν: *in* or *into.* Blass 218. Common in the Koine. A man may be "in the grip or power of a demon" or a demon may be "in a man."

24. τί ἡμῖν καὶ σοί: what have you to do with us? *Leave us alone.* A formula, used to deprecate undue interference. John 2, 4 (well explained by Vassall-Phillips, 212 ff.). Smyth 1479. ἦλθες: see on 1, 11, εὐδόκησα. The prolepsis in οἶδά σε τίς εἶ is excellent Greek. Kaegi 176, 5. ὁ ἅγιος may be vocative. Joüon on 1, 24. ἀπολέσαι: Sm. 2009.

25. φιμώθητι, ἔξελθε: two pungent aorists (Gild.). Moulton 189; 172. See on 1, 3, ἑτοιμάσατε, and on 1, 15, μετανοεῖτε. Cf. 11, 29 and 30, ἀποκρίθητε.

26–27. σπαράξαν: threw him into convulsions, or, threw him on the ground. *M. Vocabulary* 582; Joüon. Note the people's incoherent way of speaking: διδαχὴ καινὴ κατ' ἐξουσίαν. For Mark's editorial καί before τοῖς πνεύμασιν, see *Memoirs* 47; also 173, note on 14, 58. ἐθαμβήθησαν, συνζητεῖν: punctiliar, durative; see on 1, 16.

28. ἐξῆλθεν: ingressive or complexive aor.? *Memoirs* 68. εἰς: *for* or *into?* εὐθὺς 1) temporal, *at once, without delay;* see on 1, 10; 2) local, *on and on, straight on;* see 1, 29. πανταχοῦ: of Place Whither; like εἰς. Note F. Cf. Xen. *Hell.* 2, 2, 7, ἔπεμψε πρὸς Ἆγιν εἰς Δεκέλειαν, He sent *to* Agis *in* Deceleia.

30–33. λέγουσιν: who? Perhaps an indefinite pl.; see on 1, 22. Greek readily allows the subj. of a clause to be gathered from the context. Gild. 71. ἤγειρεν, κρατήσας: coincident action. Gild. 339 and 345. Smyth 1872 c. See Note T. ἀφῆκεν, διηκόνει: aor. coupled w. impf. See on 1, 16. The Gr. indicative is often modal; *she could now wait on them.* Note E. Result impf., Smyth 1899; 1896. ἦν ἐπισυνηγμένη: Gild. 236; of rapid completion. Smyth 1953. This v. is not a parenthesis, for it does not interrupt the narrative.

34. πολλούς: refers to the same group as πάντας in v. 32; it does not necessarily imply that some of the sick went away without a cure. The πάντες brought to Jesus were πολλοί. ἤφιεν: a detail of the general topic (ἐκβαλεῖν). Gild. 211. For the modal tone of the negative impf., see Gild. 216; Smyth 1896. *He would not let speak.* Note E.

35–36. ἐξῆλθεν, ἀπῆλθεν: He went out of the house and left the city. No tautology. Mark follows our Lord step by step; graphic description; Demetrius 209. προσηύχετο: the background for κατεδίωξεν: our Lord's sweet rest in prayer is rudely interfered with. προσηύχετο is also the result of ἀπῆλθεν: "and there He gave Himself to prayer" (Dean). See on 1, 16, παράγων εἶδεν. Smyth 1899. *Memoirs* 149. κατεδίωξεν:

one of Mark's "strong" words. Moulton: "he hunted Him down."
Perfective κατά; see on 1, 2, κατα-σκευάσει. Howard 121.

38. ἀλλαχοῦ εἰς: Note F. See on 1, 28. ἐξῆλθον: "came out of,"
sc. Capharnaum, or, "was sent" from heaven. Cf. Lk. 4, 43, ἀπέσταλμαι
(v. l. ἀπεστάλην). The Synoptics are familiar w. the idea of our Lord
"being sent from heaven." Mk. 9, 37, τὸν ἀποστείλαντά με. For active
verbs used in a pass. sense, see Smyth 1752. Mk. 9, 29, ἐξελθεῖν, "to
be driven out." 9, 45, ἀπελθεῖν=9, 47, βληθῆναι. Conversely, Mk. 16,
19, ἀνελήφθη, rose to heaven (or, was taken up). Smyth 815. Mk. 9, 4,
ὤφθη, appeared; 2, 20, ἀπαρθῇ, departs.

39. How do you construe ἦλθεν κηρύσσων εἰς–εἰς? Memoirs 69.
κηρύσσων may go w. εἰς τὰς συναγωγάς. The double use of εἰς may be an
example of Parallel Orientation (but here the wider term follows).
Note F.

I, 40–45. CLEANSING OF A LEPER
(Mt. 8, 2–4. Lk. 5, 12–16)

40. ἔρχεται: historical pres. Moulton 120; 139. Smyth 1883 a.
See on 1, 12. The Gr. hist. pres. is not confined to animated discourse.
Wackernagel, I, 163. Contrast ἔρχεται in 1, 7. Smyth 1881. Do all
three participles, παρακαλῶν, γονυπετῶν, and λέγων, express the same
nuance? Smyth 1872.

41. σπλαγχνισθείς: our Lord's heart went out to him. Memoirs 150.
L&S; e.g., ἄ-σπλαγχνος, heartless. Contrast the peremptory καθαρίσθητι
(as in 1, 25) with the milder 1, 15, μετανοεῖτε. For the "tone" of the
impv., see Moulton 172, 189.

42. In the classics εὐθύς generally precedes the partic. See on 1, 10
and 1, 18. The aorists ἀπῆλθεν and ἐκαθερίσθη describe the same fact;
coincident action. See on 1, 31. No tautology; Mark's narrative re-
produces the people's comment: "The leprosy has left him!" and "He
is cleansed!" For Mark's editorial καί, see Memoirs on 14, 58.

43. ἐξέβαλεν: no harshness implied; see on 1, 12; but "verbis gravi-
bus eum iussit abire." ἐμβριμησάμενος: may merely mean that our
Lord spoke forcibly to the man, ordering him not to publish the cure.
If the word meant a rebuke "for entering a house" (of which there is
no hint in the text), it would stand more naturally at the beginning of
v. 41 (before σπλαγχνισθεὶς ἐκτείνας).

44. μηδενὶ μηδέν: excellent Gr. Smyth 2760. For the prohibitive
aor., see Smyth 1841. Moulton 122 ff. ὅρα: does not affect the con-

struction. Smyth 1797 a; 1800. The phrase εἰς μαρτύριον αὐτοῖς may modify προσένεγκε or ἃ προσέταξεν. It occurs again in 6, 11 and 13, 9, but need not there have the same sense as here. The plur. αὐτοῖς may refer to "the priests" or to "priest and people" or to "whom it may concern," like indefinite ἐκεῖνος. Smyth 1258. See 15, 6, αὐτοῖς.

45. ἤρξατο w. pres. inf.; common in NT; never merely "he began." It means, through all Gr. literature, "he proceeded to do," with intention to continue. See Note I. Joüon: "il se mit à proclamer." *Memoirs* on 13, 5. πολλά: may be adverb (Joüon: 'bien haut'), *loudly*, or object to κηρύσσειν. The grateful man had *a great deal* to say about Jesus and his cure. The very wording shows how he struggled to express his gratitude. *Memoirs* 69. πολλά (adverb) and τὸν λόγον may be common elements; see Colometry, B 7. πολλά occurs again in 3, 12; 4, 2; 5, 10; 5, 23; 5, 26; 5, 38; 5, 43; 6, 20; 6, 34; 8, 31; 9, 12; 9, 26; 12, 27 (πολύ); 15, 3. ὁ δέ: the leper; αὐτὸν δύνασθαι: sc. Jesus; Gild. 71. εἰς πόλιν: "into town." Smyth 1128.

Note this peaceful close: καὶ ἤρχοντο πρὸς αὐτὸν πάντοθεν. Our Lord withdrew to desert places, to seek rest or avoid provoking His enemies; but *people came to Him from everywhere*. The quiet impf. invites our eyes to follow the masses streaming out to see Him. Gild. 205. Cf. Mk. 15, 47, ἐθεώρουν ποῦ τέθειται. The rhythm is excellent; note the sonorous "o" sounds: ἤρχοντο, πρός, αὐτόν, πάντοθεν. Colometry, B. 8, w. footnotes 46, and 47.

II, 1–12. HEALING OF A PARALYTIC

(Mt. 9, 1–8. Lk. 5, 17–26; 6, 8. Jn. 16, 19; 5, 8. Mk. 3, 20; 6, 31)

1–3. δι᾽ ἡμερῶν w. ἠκούσθη. *Memoirs* 69. ἐστίν: regular, as in indirect discourse. Smyth 2614. Dana 284. ἐλάλει: a result (Smyth 1899) of συνήχθησαν, and background for ἔρχονται (Smyth 1883 a; aoristic). The relation of tenses is not affected by our punctuation marks. 1, 16. τὸν λόγον: art.; easily understood by Mark's first readers: "the message of salvation." Smyth 1120 a. For the sequence καὶ ἐλάλει, καὶ ἔρχονται, see on 2, 18; Note A. While Jesus was discoursing —suddenly men came in. φέροντες, αἱρόμενον; vivid, not pleonastic; Demetrius *On Style* 209.

4. μὴ δυνάμενοι: in NT, μή "encroaches" on classical οὐ. Some distinctions made by grammarians are hardly to the point. Blass 426 ff. Dana 241. The precise sense of ἐξορύξαντες is disputed. *Memoirs* 70,

and 150; see Joüon. αὐτῶν: Jesus saw *their* faith, which includes that of the paralytic. *Memoirs* 194.

5. ἀφίενται: not at all durative, but an aorist-present. Smyth 1853. Remission of sin is instantaneous and comprehensive. Jesus speaks in the tone of a judge (the Son of Man! *Memoirs* 70 and 150). Cf. ἐστίν in 14, 22. In the classics the pres. as a "tense of attainment" is rare. Gild. 192. Blass 320. Burton 13. Dana 174. Cf. Moulton, 114, on ἀπο-θνήσκειν; Brugmann, 546, on δια-φεύγειν. See Note T.

6–7. καθήμενοι: *in the audience;* not necessarily *seated.* See on 2, 13. Thus Mk. 16, 19, ἐκάθισεν: does not refer to posture, but denotes the quiet and lasting possession of kingly power and glory. For the periphrastic tenses, see Smyth 1857. Dana 203. οὗτος, οὕτως: perhaps used contemptuously, like Latin *iste.* Smyth 1254. Note the Asyndeton: the questioners are excited. See Note A; Blass 462. Another good instance of emotional Asyndeton is 14, 6 and 7.

8–9. τῷ πνεύματι αὐτοῦ: Jesus *read their minds.* The same idea is expressed differently in 10, 51, ἀποκριθείς. τί ἐστι εὐκοπώτερον: *Memoirs* 150. περιπάτει: the pres. is picturesque; *be up and about again.* Smyth 1864 a.

10. ἵνα: probably introducing, as often, an independent sentence. See on 5, 23. Almost=*I want you to understand;* cf. 14, 49. Moulton 41, 205, 211. But cf. Blass 483. There is no need here to assume an Anacoluthon or an Ellipse. See the rendering in *Memoirs.*

12. ἐξῆλθεν (punctiliar) and ἐξίστασθαι (durative). Smyth 1908; 1909. πάντας: *all,* but without including the Scribes. Note D. οὕτως: often in NT felt as a subj. or obj. noun; Zorell; Joüon on Mt. 9, 33. Cf. Mk. 4, 30, πῶς ὁμοιώσωμεν and ἐν τίνι θῶμεν. Joüon: "ne semble guère grec"; but cp. Thuc. 5, 85: εἰ ἀρέσκει ὡς λέγομεν, "whether our proposal suits you" (C. F. Smith); also compare *Hom. Hymn Dem.,* 172 with Mk. 5, 16 πῶς ἐγένετο.

II, 13–22. Call of Levi

(Mt. 9, 9–17. Lk. 5, 27–39. Jn. 1, 43; 3, 29; 16, 20)

13–14. ἐξῆλθεν: continues the narrative. The foll. imperfects point out details. Gild. 211. παράγων εἶδεν: as in 1, 16. καθήμενον: not necessarily in a sitting posture; perhaps "staying." See on 2, 6. The word often means *sit quiet, sit idle, sit doing nothing,* but of all this nothing need be implied here. *M. Vocabulary* 312; L&S. ἀκολούθει: pres. impv.

See on 1, 15. Our Lord allows for slow compliance; or the pres. pictures a course of action: "be one of My constant followers." Gild. 415. ἠκολούθησεν: ingressive; "became a follower." Gild. 239. Dana 180.

15. γίνεται: Burton 357 ff. ἠκολούθουν: descriptive impf.; not necessarily a pluperfect (Joüon). Joined paratactically to ἦσαν πολλοί: "there were at that time many *who* followed Him." Note A. Mk. 9, 4. αὐτοῦ: in whose house?

16–17. ἁμαρτωλῶν καὶ τελωνῶν: one art. for both nouns. Smyth 1143. Is this a case of Parataxis: "the publicans, *that is to say*, that reprobate class of men"? See Note A. Cf. 15, 1, καὶ ὅλον; 9, 35, καὶ διάκονος. Note the strict parallelism in v. 17, which helps to fix the memorable saying in our memory. Colometry, B. 3. Barry 194.

18–19. οἱ δέ: the questioners do not want to know why the Pharisees were fasting, but why, *when* everybody else was fasting, Christ's disciples did not fast. Parataxis: Note A. καὶ ἦσαν: background for καὶ ἔρχονται; as in 2, 2. δύνανται: often used of moral propriety, decency, etc. Almost: "is it fair that they should fast?" At times ability to do is identical with readiness; see on 10, 38; 9, 39; 15, 31; 6, 5.

20 ff. ὅταν ἀπαρθῇ: the first (covert) reference to our Lord's death. The pass. need not mean forcible or violent removal. Pass. verbs often require an active rendering, as πορευθῆναι, to march, travel. Arist. *Wasps* 51, ἀρθεὶς ἀφ' ἡμῶν, "after leaving us." So here: "when He departs from them." Smyth 815. See on 1, 38, ἐξῆλθον. Cf. Joüon on ἐν ἐκείνῃ τῇ ἡμέρᾳ. ἡμέρα is sometimes = Latin *dies*, *time*. Study the colometrization of 21 and 22. Colometry, B 4. For the thought, see *Memoirs* 151. βλητέον: Smyth 2152.

II, 23–III, 6. "MASTER OF THE SABBATH"
(Mt. 12, 1–14; 22,16. Lk. 6, 1–11. Jn. 6, 6–11; 11, 33)

23. παραπορεύεσθαι; παρά sometimes implies stealth. Howard 123 a, at end. Cf. Mk. 9, 30, "avoiding the high-ways"; 3, 2, παρετήρουν. ἤρξαντο: Note I. We expect ὁδὸν ποιοῦντες τίλλειν; but the Gr. partic. may carry the main thought of a sentence. Smyth 2147 a. Eur. *HF.* 1230, βλέποντι σημαίνεις κακά, "I see the ills thou namest." *ib.*, 1235. Donovan, on Tertiary Predicates, 424–429.

25–26. χρείαν ἔσχεν καὶ ἐπείνασεν: no tautology; Note A. The Gr. could say χρείαν ἔσχεν (as we say: "he caught a cold") and χρείαν ἔσχεν αὐτόν, as in Mk. 16, 8. οὐκ ἔξεστιν: an *echo* of the phrase in v. 24; so ἀφιέναι in 2, 7 echoes ἀφίενται in 2, 5. Cf. 5, 39, οὐκ ἀπέθανεν (5, 35); 6, 12, μετανοῶσιν (1, 15).

27–28. Note the sharply pointed saying in v. 27, as in 2, 17. Colometry, B 3 and 4. *Memoirs* 152. For the sense of ὥστε, see the commentators; esp. Knabenbauer. Since we must assume that our Lord's words were intelligible to His hearers, it is natural to think that in the reported speeches a link or two in the chain of reasoning may at times be missing. John 21, 25. *Memoirs* 152. κύριός ἐστιν: he has authority in the matter of the Sabbath. Excellent Greek. Xen. *Hell.* 2, 2, 18, ἐκείνους κυρίους εἶναι εἰρήνης καὶ πολέμου. For "Son of Man," see *Memoirs* 188; Joüon, p. 601. Note καί before τοῦ σαββάτου; *also*, sc. as of many other things; or *even;* a thrust at those Pharisees who kept the Sabbath for its own sake.

III. 1–2. ἦν ἐκεῖ: *there was there;* perhaps better: *there came there.* For ἦν, see on 1, 23; Gild. 212. For ἐκεῖ = ἐκεῖσε, see Bauer; class. and late. χείρ: may be *hand* or *arm.* For ἐξηραμμένην, etc., see Note P. Gild. 628, 629. Everywhere in Mark we encounter excellent *idiom.* τὴν χεῖρα: the art. as possess. pron. Smyth 1121. Dana 139, 3. In παρετήρουν note παρά: "stealthily" or "narrowly"? Howard 123, a. See on 2, 23, παρα-πορεύεσθαι.

3–4. ἔγειρε: rise *(and step)* εἰς τὸ μέσον. Common Ellipsis; Smyth 3017. Cf. Pl. *Phaedo* 116 a: ἀνίστατο εἰς οἴκημά τι. τὸ μέσον: the open space between speaker and audience. Mk. 14, 60. Joüon on Mt. 14, 6 and Lk. 5, 19. Note the alternatives: ἢ κακοποιῆσαι, ἢ ἀποκτεῖναι. An instance of Brachylogy; Smyth 3017 m; Gerth 597 k. See the rendering in *Memoirs* 73. Acquaintance with the wide prevalence of Gr. Brachylogy, and its various forms, is indispensable for correct interpretation. Cf. Thuc. 6, 29, 1, ἕτοιμος ἦν δίκην δοῦναι· εἰ δ' ἀπολυθείη, ἄρχειν [*sc.* ἠξίου].

5–6. συν-λυπούμενος: perfective or intensive prep. See on 1, 2, κατασκευάσει. Howard 127; Moulton 111. Zorrell, 1252, compares συγχαίρω. ἐξέτεινεν and ἀπεκατεστάθη: coincident aorists; Gild. 345; two aspects of the same fact. Note T. To be coincident, aorists need not be in the partic. Where does εὐθύς belong? See on 1, 10; 1, 18. ἐδίδουν (here a result-impf.) occurs again in 4, 8; 6, 7; 6, 41; 8, 6; 15, 23. ἀπολέσωσιν: final clauses prefer the aorist (of attainment). For συμβούλιον διδόναι, see Joüon. The ὅπως-clause expands κατ' αὐτοῦ (κατά here in a hostile sense). Note C. See on 3, 9; 13, 19.

III, 7–19. Concourse. Call of the Twelve Apostles
(Mt. 4, 25; 10, 1–4; 12, 15–16; 15, 30. Lk. 6, 17–19;
4, 41; 6, 12–16; 9, 54)

7 ff. Mark at his worst, or at his best (?). See Note Q. *Memoirs* on on 12, 23; also *Memoirs*, Chapter III. ἀκούοντες: Smyth 1885. Some mss. have (the needless change to) ἀκούσαντες (Mk. 2, 17; 3, 21; 4, 15; 5, 17). εἶπεν ἵνα: common in the Koine; *he told them to* . . . ἵνα μὴ θλίβωσιν: explains and expands the phrase διὰ τὸν ὄχλον. Notes C and Q.

Special Note. The πλοιάριον in 3, 9 is a πλοῖον in 4, 1. Diminutives in NT show the same frequency as in the Koine generally and, as again in the Koine, have largely lost their original significance. This is especially true of diminutives from the intimate language of the nursery and the speech of the streets. Diminutives are nouns formed from other nouns by the addition of certain suffixes, as -ιο-; -ιδ-ιο-; -αρ-ιο-; -ασ-ιο-; -ισκος. They are deteriorative or hypocoristic (expressing relative smallness; disparagement; contempt; familiarity; affection; also admiration and love); many diminutives are terms of endearment: ὑποκοριστικά. Smyth 852 ff.; Howard 138; Robertson 82 and 118; Bauer, *Wörterbuch* XVI; Blass 111, 3. See the List of Words for κυνάριον. Marcan diminutives are: παιδίον, θυγάτριον, κοράσιον, ὠτίον (ὠτάριον), ψιχίον, ἰχθύδιον, βιβλίον, κυνάριον, παιδίσκη, νεανίσκος.

10–11. ἐθεράπευσεν: "had cured." Smyth's rule (1943) should be extended to include independent sentences. Gild. 253, quoting Thuc. 7, 1, 3. It is important to know this. Wackernagel I, 151. Mk. 4, 41, ἐφοβήθησαν (*Memoirs* 81) and ἔλεγον (Smyth 1907); 6, 52, συνῆκαν. ἐπιπίπτειν: graphic, "tumble over." ὅταν: w. impf., denoting repetition. Koine Greek. Smyth 2409. Goodwin *MT.*, 249. Moulton 168. ὅτι: before σύ, has the value of quotation marks. An old Gr. idiom, overdone in NT. Smyth 2590 a.

12–13. ἵνα, of *purport* rather than *purpose;* "warned them not to make Him known." *Memoirs* 187, 188. How is ἵνα used in 14, 38? Moulton 207. φανερόν: see 6, 14. τὸ ὄρος: "the mountainous region." πολλά: see on 1, 45. οὓς ἤθελεν αὐτός: "men of His own choosing"; but it is not certain that αὐτός can bear so much emphasis. See Moulton 85, and Joüon's note; Frisk 44; Blass 283; 288; Dana 137; *M. Vocabulary* 94. For αὐτός in the classics, see Smyth 1204 ff.; Gild. 654, 655. ἀπό in cpds. stresses the starting-point, though the writer's mind is on the goal; not "went away" but "went." Note G. See *Special Note* on I, 8.

14–15. ἵνα ὦσιν μετ' αὐτοῦ, "that they might be His constant companions." Cf. 16, 10. Compare the demoniac's request in 5, 18; John 15, 27; Mt. 12, 3. ἵνα ὦσιν, after ποιεῖν=εἶναι. See on 1, 17; consecutive-final conjunction. Dana 220. ἵνα ἀποστέλλῃ: w. the subject shifted. Gild. 71. For the pres., see Smyth 1876. On this depend two infinitives, joined by καί, although ἔχειν ἐξουσίαν is only a detail in the missionary activity. The disciples' power over the demons was their credentials. So also 6, 7. Parataxis: Note A.

16 ff. τοὺς δώδεκα: Smyth 1120 b. For particularizing καί before ἐπέθηκεν, see *Memoirs* 74. See on 1, 5, καί, and Note H. It is not certain that Simon received his surname on this occasion; the καί- clause may be a parenthesis. John 1, 42. Another parenthesis in Mk. is 10, 21. Blass 458; 465. For the sense of *Boanerges*, see Joüon. ὃς καί: *the same who; who later; who, by the way*. Smyth 2881.

III, 20–35. DRIVING OUT THE DEMONS BY BEELZEBUL
(Mt. 12, 24–32; 46–50. Lk. 11, 15–22; 8, 19–21)

20–21. ἔρχονται) (συνέρχεται: wherever our Lord *went*, the crowds *went along;* but see 14, 53, "assembled." ὥστε: Dana 270, 1 and 5 w. note; Burton 234 ff. οἱ παρ' αὐτοῦ: we expect οἱ παρ' αὐτῷ; but Gr. stresses the starting-point. Note G. Smyth 1660. The same phrase in the neuter occurs in 5, 26. The οἱ παρ' αὐτοῦ need not be the same as those that arrived (ἔρχονται) in v. 31; nor need our Lord's mother have been with them. As for those who ἔλεγον ὅτι ἐξέστη, see Knabenbauer, Lagrange, al. ἔλεγον may be an indefinite pl.: *it was rumored*. See on 1, 22, ἐξεπλήσσοντο. Why would people wish to "arrest" Jesus?

22–23. Note Mk.'s editorial καί before the second ὅτι, and study the effect of the quotation-marks employed in *Memoirs* 75; see *Memoirs* 173, 174, note on 14, 58. Beelzebul: *Memoirs* 153. ἐν, almost "in collusion with." See on 1, 23. Dana 112. πῶς: expressing impossibility, or absurdity, in the lively form of a rhetorical question. Smyth 2640. Note Q.

24–25. ἐάν: of remote eventuality; Blass 371 ff.; εἰ in 26="if," *sc.* "as you say." Study the colometrization of these verses, and see the renderings in *Memoirs* 75 and 153. οὐ δυνήσεται: stronger than οὐ δύναται. See on 8, 3. Note the variation between σταθῆναι and στῆναι; between ἐὰν μερισθῇ and εἰ ἀνέστη. Note P.

26. The opening καί sounds like *therefore; and so too.* Note H.
μεμέρισται: a noteworthy pf., hinting at a fixed condition, the inevitable
result of ἀνέστη. See on 1, 2, γέγραπται. Smyth 1945. τέλος ἔχει: a
bare and rugged phrase, as here applied to Satan.[1] ἔχει is either an
aor.-pres. (see on 2, 5, ἀφίενται: "has *ipso facto* an end"; almost=
ἔσχεν, parallel w. ἀνέστη; cf. *si hoc feceris, stultus fueris*), or a pf. (*has,
that is, has already met w.,* his end; parallel w. μεμέρισται) or a fut.
(=*involves* destruction; *has to face* his end. L&S. A I and III); "is
doomed to extinction." Note B. For ἔχει="has received," cf. Aesch.
Choe. 164.

27. ἀλλά: ill-boding; "now mark," "now let Me warn you." Smyth
2775. Dana 211. Botte 79. Brugmann 606, 4. τοῦ ἰσχυροῦ: the art. of
an imaginary strong man (generic) or a reference to σατανᾶς (particular). Smyth 1122; 1120; Gild. 563. Dana 146 ff. See on 1, 7. Our
Lord here draws a very practical conclusion from what precedes.

καὶ τότε . . . . διαρπάσει: Mark writes as Jesus had spoken (Note Q)
and as Peter had narrated the incident. The last colon merely *enforces*
what has already been said or implied. Critics have found fault w.
such "slovenly" writing! διαρπάσει: modal; Note E. "Then he *may*
or *can* plunder," the antithesis to οὐ δύναται διαρπάσαι. The Gr. fut.
is particularly apt to be modal. Smyth 1910 a. Gild. 267. So ἐρεῖς,
"one may say" (Wackernagel, I 206), *dixerit quispiam. Memoirs* 76.

28. ἀμήν: *Memoirs* 154. ἀφεθήσεται: again the modal ft.; see on 27.
May be forgiven, *sc.* when all conditions for forgiveness (faith; sorrow
for sin; etc.) are present. See Joüon on Mt. 5, 43, and 7, 4; also Mt.
12, 31, *pourra* être remis. Note E. This modal nuance is frequent in
Hebrew (Joüon); but Mark did not have to know Hebrew or Aramaic
to use a simple Greek idiom. Note R.

29–30. οὐκ ἔχει ἄφεσιν: splendid Greek. Turner says: "very un-
Greek"! *Can never obtain forgiveness.* Notes B and E. This sense is
required to match modal διαρπάσει and ἀφεθήσεται in vv. 27 and 28.
The question is of what *can* or *cannot* be done, not of what *will* actually
be done. *Memoirs* 154 and 190. ὅτι ἔλεγον: "they had said, you know
(remember)"; see on 4, 41 ὅτι.

31 ff. καὶ ἔρχονται: *Memoirs* 154 and 191. See note on v. 21. ἐστῶ-
τες: not necessarily a reference to posture. See on 2, 6. ἀποκριθείς:
Note L. *Memoirs* 154. The words ἡ μήτηρ, etc., are *echoes* of what the
people had said to Jesus; see on 2, 26. For the repetition of the key-

---

[1] The phrase τέλος ἔχει occurs elsewhere in a different sense; cf. Archilochus,
104 B (Loeb L., p. 156) and Sophocles, *Epic Poems*, 3 A (Loeb L., p. 424).

words ἡ μήτηρ, etc., see Note Q. Our Lord's way of teaching is popular, emphatic, and, above all, clear. Demetrius 211.

IV, 1–34. PARABLES
(Mt. 13, 1–23; 31–34. Lk. 8, 4–18; 13, 18–19)

IV. 1–2. ἤρξατο: Note I. *Memoirs* 169, on 13, 5. For the idyllic setting of our Lord's discourse, see *Memoirs* 53, 54, and 77. ὥστε: Dana 270. πρός: often w. the acc., denoting rest. Dana 119. ἐπὶ τῆς γῆς: a graphic touch, added for contrast with ἐν τῇ θαλάσσῃ. Demetrius 208–209. For the parallelism in v. 2, see Colometry, B 4. "Parable": *Memoirs* 154.

3–4. ἀκούετε: pres. impv.; invites sustained attention; *lend your ears.* Contrast 7, 14, ἀκούσατε. Smyth 1835 b. See on 1, 2. Eur. *HF.* 1255, ἄκουε δή νυν, at the beginning of a lengthy exposition. *M. Vocabulary* 19. ἐξῆλθεν: render by the lively present. Smyth 1930; 1931. Gild. 255 ff. ὁ σπείρων: Smyth 2052. τοῦ: w. infin. Smyth 2032. Burton 397. Dana 268. For the aor., see Smyth 1927. ἐν τῷ σπείρειν: Smyth 2033. Burton 406. Dana 191 ff. σπείρειν: pres., as background to ἔπεσεν. Smyth 1898 and 1899. For perfective κατά- in κατέφαγεν, see on 1, 2, κατασκευάσει; we say "eat *up.*"

5. εἶχεν: in the recurrence of the verb ἔχω Jouön scents Aramaic influence; but such recurrence is far from being un-Greek. Note Q. οὐκ εἶχεν: *did not have* or *could not have.* Smyth 1890, 1896. Gild. 216. γῆν πολλήν, matched against βάθος γῆς: Note P. The seed had no earth, but plenty of sunshine; hence εὐθὺς ἐξανέτειλεν.

6. διὰ τὸ μὴ ἔχειν ῥίζαν; for διά, see Burton 406 ff. Smyth 2034. Dana 191 ff. It seems harsh to say, *the seed had no root;* better, *it could not take or strike root.* This negative pres. infin. represents a negative impf.: Gild. 216. Smyth 1896. See on v. 17. Besides, ἔχω is often found in potential phrases: Note B. Verse 7 is typical of the simple Marcan narrative: καί, καί, καί, καί. Note H.

8. ἐδίδου: a solitary impf., coming after a string of aorists. The fate of the seed fallen on bad soil is summarily dealt with in aorists (vv. 4–7; Smyth 1927, w. notes); that of the seed in good soil is stated in two imperfects, expressing surprise and lingering vision. Gild. 205. Note a similar contrast between Mk. 1, 5, ἐβαπτίζοντο and 1, 9, ἐβαπτίσθη. *This at last produces fruit.* The impf. ἐδίδουν (very common in Gr. literature) is often perplexing; see 6, 7; 6, 41; 8, 6; 15, 23. See Gild. 205; 212. ἔφερον is sometimes aoristic; Moulton 129.

9-10. The inf. ἀκούειν after ὦτα seems to be consecutive-final: "ears such as to be able to hear" (= δυνάμενα ἀκούειν. Blass 393; 400). Cf. Smyth 2004-2011. Compare our English phrase: "His is a name *to stir* the fancy." Hence: "He that has ears to hear My words." οἱ περὶ αὐτόν: note the presence of others besides the Twelve; this is important for interpreting τοῖς ἔξω in v. 11. ἀκουέτω: see on ἄκουε in v. 3.

11. δέδοται: A splendid pf.! The secret *has already been entrusted* to the disciples, for the acceptance of the Call to discipleship *entitled* them to full enlightenment as to the nature of the Kingdom of God. δέδοται refers to God's decree in eternity which ruled that those who would follow Jesus should in time know the secret. The amount of meaning a single word may sometimes contain may be seen, for instance, from Eur. *Ion* 1291, ἔκτεινα, explained by Smyth 1926 b; Gerth 386, 12 (with many illustrations); or from Keats's line:

> So their two brothers and their *murdered* man
> Rode past fair Florence,

where *murdered* means *murdered in anticipation;* "whom they were about to murder." Genung 149. *Memoirs* 155. δέδοται: Iliad 5, 428.

τὰ πάντα γίνεται: generally rendered *all things* (needed for their instructions) *come to them* in parables. See Joüon; Lagrange; etc. Menander 537 K, 6. However, in view of Eur. *HF.*, 603, πάντα σοι γενήσεται, "If here thou bide, *all shall go well with thee*" (Way), the phrase (τὰ) πάντα γίνεταί τινι was perhaps proverbial for "all is well with one." So here: As to those outside, *all is well with them* if they but receive Christ's teaching *in parables*, whereas the true disciple asks for additional instruction in the hidden meaning of the parables. Hence, if we take the dative to be that of interest or relation (Smyth 1474 ff.; 1496), our Lord means to say: *Those outside are perfectly content with parables.* A capital sense! The same dative occurs in 11, 23, ἔσται αὐτῷ, "it shall be *as he desires*" (almost = αὐτῷ βουλομένῳ. Smyth 1487).

12. ἵνα: *final* or consecutive. "Parables may serve as a judgment on those who have rejected Christ's teaching" (Plummer). *Memoirs* 155. For the scope of ἵνα in Koine Gr., see Dana 220; Moulton 206 ff. Note the fine use of the tenses in this passage. συνιῶσιν (with perfective συν-; Moulton 111) is probably aoristic (*grasp*), to match ἴδωσιν. ἐπιστρέψωσιν, ἀφεθῇ: "So free is the Greek in its omission of the subject

that there is often a sudden change of subject without further warning"
(Gild. 71). Cf. Mk. 9, 18.

13–14. καὶ πῶς: Smyth 2872. πάσας τὰς παραβολάς: *all the other parables*, or, *the parables in general.* Mk. 7, 3, καὶ πάντες. πάσας in this idiom
is not necessarily due to Aramaic influence. ὁ σπείρων: the art. refers
back to v. 3.

15–16. The Greek in 15 ff. is harsh, but intelligible. Most translators retain the harshness in their renderings. οἱ–ὅπου: *the ones in
whom.* Study the effect intended by the change of tense in ἐσπαρμένος
(15), σπειρόμενοι (16), and σπαρέντες (20). Mark does not "confuse"
his tenses! See 5, 15 (δαιμονιζομένῳ) w. foll. variants.

17. οὐκ ἔχουσιν ῥίζαν: the same phrase as in v. 6, but here even
more harshly applied to human beings. ἔχω is often used in Potential
Phraseology (Note B). Fickle hearers do not give the Word of God
a chance to take root in them; *do not let it strike root* in their hearts. Cf.
Eur. *H.F.*, 732, explained in Note B. Plautus *Poen.* 11: *fac populo
audientiam:* "give the people *a chance* to hear us." For the meaning of
σκανδαλίζεσθαι, see Note N. *Memoirs* 155.

18–20. Note the force of the article w. γῆ, ἄκανθαι, etc.; all *familiar*
objects. This nuance should not be overlooked in the translation.
Smyth 1120, a, b, c. *Memoirs* 156; and cp. the rendering in *Memoirs*
77 f. "The path," *sc.* along the Palestinian field; "the rocky ground,"
sc. which every hearer could see with his own eyes.

21–25. ἔρχεται: *is brought in.* Smyth 1752. See on Mk. 1, 38,
ἐξῆλθον. βλέπετε: of intellectual sight; hence coupled with ἀκούετε.
"Pay close heed to what you are being told. Hear with the closest
attention." τοῖς ἀκούουσιν: Smyth 2052. Conditional or causal in
sense. ἔχειν, often = "have wealth or capital"; οἱ ἔχοντες, "the well-to-
do"; classic. Bauer 517.

26–27. The man has sown the seed (βάλῃ); after that *he is asleep*
during the night, νύκτα, and wakes up (ἐγείρηται) [*and is awake*] during
the day, ἡμέραν. Smyth 1582. Dana 90, 4. For the ellipsis (*and is
awake*), see on 3, 3, ἔγειρε; 16, 2, ἔρχονται; ἐγείρηται does not directly
mean *he is up and about* (Joüon: être debout). *Memoirs* 79. καὶ between νύκτα and ἡμέραν: "alternately, by turns." Smyth 2870. See
on Mk. 1, 5, and Note H.

28 ff. αὐτομάτη, etc.: note the splendid explanatory Asyndeton.
Smyth 2167 b. *By an inward force; of itself.* Recognized by Joüon as
"un grécisme"; there is nothing like this "en sémitique"; an important
admission from an Orientalist. See Note R. For παραδοῦναι, "to per-

mit," see Bauer 982. Note the rhetorical questions in 30. Smyth 2640.
The hearer is taken into consultation by the speaker. πῶς does not
here inquire into the *manner* of likening; watch οὕτως and πῶς. Bauer;
Zorell. See on 2, 12, οὕτως.

31. ἐπὶ τῆς γῆς: the repetition of this phrase is not necessarily "une
dittographie anticipante du second" (Joüon), but rather an echo of
actual speech. Note Q. Another reminiscence of Peter's preaching is
ὅταν σπαρῇ in two different senses. *Memoirs* 80. Joüon renders correctly: *quand on le sème* and *une fois semé*, respectively. So again Mk.
12, 23, ἐν τῇ ἀναστάσει and ὅταν ἀναστῶσιν. See on 4, 37, τὸ πλοῖον.

32 ff. τοῦ οὐρανοῦ: the birds that roam *the air*. ὥστε: Dana 270;
occurs in 1, 27; 1, 45; 2, 2; 2, 12; 3, 10; 3, 20; 4, 1; 4, 32; 4, 37; 9, 26;
15, 5. Cf. 2, 28; 10, 8. ἀκούειν: in a very special sense: *hear and heed*.
Zorell 55. ἐλάλει, ἐπέλυεν: customary action. Smyth 1893.

IV, 35-41. THE STORM
(Mt. 8, 18; 8, 23-27. Lk. 8, 22-25)

36. παραλαμβάνουσιν: Jesus is already ἐν τῷ πλοίῳ. "They take Him
along with them, ὡς ἦν (excellent Gr.), *as He was*, without further ado
or preparation." The clause might mean: they took Him *into* their
boat. For εἰς and ἐν, see Blass 218. Also possibly: ὡς ἦν ἐν τῷ πλοίῳ,
"because He was already in the boat." Blass 453, 2.

37-38. ἤδη tallies well w. the tendential present γεμίζεσθαι. Smyth
1878. Dana 174, 4. τὸ πλοῖον: twice in the same verse. See *Memoirs*
on 7, 15. Note Q. καὶ ἦν αὐτός: *meanwhile the Master was asleep*.
Smyth 1204 ff. Dana 137. διεγείρουσιν: here *they wake Him up;* not
so in 39. ἀπολλύμεθα: finely analyzed by Moulton 114: "We recognize in the perfective verb (*sc.* ἀπό-) the sense of an *inevitable* doom,
under the visible conditions, even though the subsequent story tells
us it was averted." Howard 115.

39. διεγερθείς: Jesus awoke when addressed by the disciples; and
at once rebuked *them;* then He *rose to His full height* and rebuked the
elements. Cf. Mt. 8, 25, ἤγειραν, and Mt. 8, 26, τότε ἐγερθείς. The
two imperatives (σιώπα and πεφίμωσο) apply to the two nouns (ἄνεμος
and θάλασσα) respectively. In this entire pericope Mark presents things
in pairs. *Memoirs* 81. σιώπα, πεφίμωσο: Gild. 408. Note the calm
majesty of these imperatives, and contrast the aorists in 1, 25. Wackernagel, I 170; Smyth 1864 c and N.

40. These two questions were not uttered in the same breath; see

Mt. 8, 26. Our Lord first calmed the disciples (gently reproving them for their fear, τί δειλοί); then, rising to His height, He rebuked the elements. When, *after* the γαλήνη had set in, the disciples express astonishment (instead of downright faith), He chid them for their unbelief: πῶς οὐκ ἔχετε; Lk. 8, 25. Mark joins the two questions here, and gives the two separate reasons for them in v. 41. *Memoirs* 156. Note the pluperfect rendering of ἐφοβήθησαν and ἔλεγον. See on 3, 10. Luke's φοβηθέντες implies religious awe rather than mere fright (Lk. 8, 25).

41. Note that, in point of time, the contents of this verse (εἶπεν) precede those of v. 40. The stilling of the storm did *not end* in the disciples' unbelief. τίς ἄρα: Smyth 2787. Dana 212. ὅτι: (we ask this question) *because.* See 3, 30. Dana 222. Arist. *Wasps* 267, τί πέπονθεν, ὡς οὐ φαίνεται: "The fellow's not in sight. What's the matter with him?"

V, 1–20. HEALING OF THE GERASENE

V. 1–2. εἰς, εἰς: Note F. αὐτοῦ, αὐτῷ: Smyth 2073 a; rare in the classics; common in NT. ὑπήντησεν αὐτῷ: *there met Him;* better, *He met.* Joüon on Mt. 8, 28. Ceteris paribus, it makes no difference whether A meets B or B meets A. Kaibel appeals to this principle to explain the so-called Hysteron Proteron, on So. *El.* 1235. See Mk. 12, 8, ἔβαλον. Aeschylus, *Choe.* 3, ἥκω καὶ κατέρχομαι.

3 ff. οὐδέ, οὐκέτι, οὐδείς: excellent Greek. "Accumulation of Negatives." Smyth 2760 ff. διὰ τὸ αὐτὸν δεδέσθαι: note διά; that's how we *know* that the man was untamable. Articular infin.: Smyth 2034. Dana 191, 192. πολλάκις: usually joined to an aorist. Smyth 1893 a; 1930. Gild. 249. δεδέσθαι: see on 1, 2, γέγραπται. A notable case of Parataxis: "*although* he had been fettered, yet . . ." Note A. νυκτός: genitive of time; Smyth 1444; Dana 90, 4, "night-time; day-time." καί, before ἐν τοῖς ὄρεσιν: *and* or *or.* Smyth 2870. Mk. 4, 27. Note H. For the gesture of προσκύνησις, see J. A. Scott, *Class. J.*, 17, 403.

7–8. τί ἐμοὶ καὶ σοί: see on 1, 24. μή με βασανίσῃς: he does not wish to be sent back to hell; Lk. 8, 31 has εἰς τὴν ἄβυσσον. ἔλεγεν: Jesus "was about to say." *Memoirs* 156. The demon probably expected Jesus to say ἔξελθε: Gild. 213. If ἔλεγεν expresses an explicit command, why was it not at once obeyed? *Memoirs* 187. Blass 329.

9 ff. λεγεών: *Memoirs* 156. παρεκάλει: impf.; Mark is already thinking of the aor. in v. 12; where the shift in tense denotes a shift in tactics. *Memoirs* 156; 157. A verb in the impf. generally furnishes the

background for a following aorist. Smyth 1899. ἔξω τῆς χώρας: almost euphemistic for being sent *to hell*. Lk. 8, 31. Mt. 8, 29.

12–13. παρεκάλεσαν: in sharp contrast w. παρεκάλει. Gild. 214. Mark has many aorists and imperfects that illustrate each other. See on 1, 16. *Memoirs* 156. They *ended by* asking. Blass 328. A Gr. aorist always implies "Abschluss," completion, or attainment. Note the two senses of εἰς. Eur. *HF.*, 1276, εἰς νεκροὺς ἀφικόμην. ἐπνίγοντο: a notable result impf. Smyth 1899. It is Mark's rule to close his narratives with an impf. denoting result. 5, 20, ἐθαύμαζον. See on 5, 43. For the aor. παρεκάλεσαν, see Thuc. 3, 36, 2, γνώμας ἐποιοῦντο καὶ ἔδοξεν αὐτοῖς: "they held a debate and *finally* determined" (Smith) = ποιουμένοις αὐτοῖς ἔδοξεν.

14. οἱ βόσκοντες: note the force of the pres. part. Strictly speaking, they *had been* their keepers. Smyth 1872 a; 1887. Cf. 5, 15, δαιμονιζόμενον, so referred to even after his cure. ἦλθον: ingressive, *they set out;* ἔρχονται: complexive aor. (Smyth 1883 a), *they came;* Mark is graphic; cf. 11, 13, ἦλθεν, ἐλθών. Note pf. and aor. in ἰδεῖν τί ἐστιν τὸ γεγονός; just so in *Iliad* 22, 450, ἴδωμ' ἅτιν' ἔργα τέτυκται. Burton 88. Dana 182 ff. See on 1, 2, γέγραπται.

15. θεωροῦσιν: with wide wondering eyes they look at him. The word may be used of a general reviewing his army. Cf. also Isocr. *To Nic.* 48, of witnessing a show: θεωροῦντες τοὺς ἀγῶνας καὶ τὰς ἀμίλλας. L&S: "look at, behold, gaze at, gape, contemplate, observe"; cf. θεωρία. Mk. 15, 47. καί before σωφρονοῦντα may be paratactic; seated and clothed *because* he was now in his senses. Note A. ἐσχηκότα: of "action now over and gone," as *fuimus Troes*, "we are Trojans no more." Brugmann 547. For the addition of τὸν ἐσχηκότα, etc., see Note C.

16–17. πῶς: see on 4, 30; *what* or *how* it had happened. διηγήσαντο: governs both πῶς and περί; excellent Greek. Xen. *Cyr.* 1, 4, 7, where φυλάττοιεν governs both ἀπό and εἴ τι; Isoc. *To Nic.* 30, τὰς γιγνομένας and ὅταν θαυμάζωσιν. ἤρξαντο παρακαλεῖν: Note I. They made a point of asking, asked in good earnest. The aor. in ἀπελθεῖν adds abruptness to the insult offered to Jesus. *Memoirs* 157.

18 ff. αὐτοῦ, αὐτόν: see on 5, 2. The impf. παρεκάλει prepares us (see on 1, 16) for the aor. οὐκ ἀφῆκεν. For ἵνα μετ' αὐτοῦ ᾖ, see Note B. The same μετ' αὐτοῦ as in 3, 14. εἰς, πρός: Note F. πεποίηκεν, ἠλέησεν: Parataxis; Note A. *What He had done in His pity*. An abiding benefit (πεποίηκεν) was bestowed on the man by a transient act of pity (ἠλέησεν). Another ὅσα may be supplied before ἠλέησεν. ὅσα: *what a great* blessing. ἤρξατο: Note I. ἐθαύμαζον: result impf., as 5, 13, ἐπνίγοντο.

V, 21–43. Jairus. The Woman with the Hemorrhage

(Mt. 9, 18–26. Lk. 8, 41–56)

21–22. πάλιν εἰς τὸ πέραν goes w. συνήχθη. See on 2, 1, δι' ἡμερῶν. εἰς τὸ πέραν and ἐπ' αὐτόν: Note F. πίπτει: "throws himself down," better than "falls"; cf. 14, 35, ἔπιπτεν, said of our Lord.

23. πολλὰ λέγων, "pleading warmly"; Iliad I 35, πολλὰ ἠρᾶτο; for πολλά, see on 1, 45. ἵνα: introduces an independent sentence. Dana 220. See on 10, 51. σωθῇ καὶ ζήσῃ: not tautologous; σωθῇ: "to be snatched from death"; ζήσῃ: "to come back to the full enjoyment of life." The phrase expresses the fond father's wishes more adequately than either word alone would do. Mark's prose is throughout an echo of living speech. Note Q. Memoirs 168, on 12, 23; also 192: "Imposition of hands."

24–25. ἀπῆλθεν: followed by two descriptive impfs. Note A. Mark might have said: ἀκολουθοῦντος ὄχλου and συνθλιβόντων αὐτόν. οὖσα: she had been. Smyth 1885. Dana 173, 1, c. Smyth 1872. ἐν ῥύσει; we may compare Eur. HF. 1266, ἔτ' ἐν γάλακτι ὄντι, "when I was yet a suckling"; or Isocr. Anti. 39, τοὺς ἐν κακοῖς ὄντας, "those in trouble." For ἐν in general, see L&S.; Bauer; Zorell; Dana 112; Blass 218 ff.

26–29. Note the periodic structure; and see Colometry, A 3, and B 3. Another Marcan period is in v. 33. μηδέν; for μή, "encroaching on οὐ" in NT, see Blass 426; Moulton 170 f. Both verses 29 and 30 open with καὶ εὐθύς; for the colometry involved, see Memoirs 49 and 50. σώματι: the woman had "a sensation."

30. ἐν ἑαυτῷ: refers to mental perception; as in 2, 8. ἐπι-γνούς: coming after the simple ἔγνω, the prep. seems to imply "coming close after; following immediately upon." Howard 120, "in addition"; see on 6, 33.

ἐξελθοῦσαν: the participial pred. after ἐπιγνούς. Smyth 2106 ff. Jesus perceived (the fact) that His power had gone out. Memoirs 157. Blass, 474, 5, b cites Gild. 622: Jesus "knew the out-going power," which is hardly satisfactory, unless ἐξελθοῦσαν contains the main thought (Smyth 2147 a): knew "the going-out of the power." Note τὴν δύναμιν: the (= His inherent) power; Smyth 1121. ἐξ αὐτοῦ is brachylogical for τὴν ἐν αὐτῷ δύναμιν ἐξελθοῦσαν ἐξ αὐτοῦ. Smyth 1660 a. Cf. Aesch. Choe. 107, λέξω τὸν ἐκ φρενὸς λόγον, "I will voice my inmost thoughts" (Smyth). ἐξέρχεσθαι may have a passive sense; Smyth 1752; as in Mk. 9, 29, ἐξελθεῖν. Jesus "was conscious that the power within Him (His healing power) was roused or stirred to action";

or, since Jesus exerted His power deliberately, "conscious of putting forth the power that was in Him."

Special Note. The Greek article deserves most careful study. In the NT its use is, in the main, in agreement with earlier Greek. In general an articular construction emphasizes *individuality, identity;* anarthrous nouns or phrases, on the other hand, emphasize *nature, character, essence.* Dana 145–150; Smyth 1099–1189; Davis 384–388; Moulton *passim;* Gildersleeve 514 ff.; Blass 249–276; Brugmann 496, 3; Gerth 457 ff.; Wackernagel II 125 ff.

Examine the article in 5, 30 τὴν δύναμιν; 14, 69 ἡ παιδίσκη; 6, 3 ὁ τέκτων; 14, 18 ὁ ἐσθίων; 14, 21 ὁ ἐμβαπτόμενος; 6, 14 αἱ δυνάμεις; 6, 31 οἱ ἐρχόμενοι; 6, 44 οἱ φαγόντες; 6, 46 τὸ ὄρος; 7, 15 τὰ—τά; 6, 43 κλάσματα; 8, 8 κλασμάτων; 8, 32 τὸν λόγον; 10, 23 τὰ χρήματα; 10, 27 Θεῷ—τῷ Θεῷ? 10, 31 ἔσχατοι—οἱ ἔσχατοι; 16, 17 σημεῖα; 11, 9 ὁ ἐρχόμενος; 12, 7 ὁ κληρονόμος; 12, 27 θεός.

31–33. καὶ λέγεις: "*although* you see, you say." Parataxis; Note A. The impf. περι-εβλέπετο prepares us for the aorists that follow; see on 1, 16. Note the periodic structure in v. 33, and the fine *crescendo* (Moore, *Orations,* xxxiii and xxxi):

ἦλθεν
καὶ προσέπεσεν αὐτῷ
καὶ εἶπεν αὐτῷ πᾶσαν τὴν ἀλήθειαν,

each colon exceeding its predecessor in length and importance. Demetrius 18. Cicero *de or.* III 186 (*melius et iucundius,* w. reference to the rhythm).

34. ἡ πίστις σου: "The statement does not, of course, exclude the *complementary* truth that she was healed by power proceeding from the person of Christ" (Swete). See Note D. σου σέσωκέν σε: the *generally* unpleasant effect of repeated sigmas is here neutralized by the graciousness of the message and the friendly tone of the Speaker. *Class. J.,* 23, 298. Kretschmer, *Sprache,* 6, 3, comments on "die Vermeidung hässlicher Laute wie des s." ὕπαγε εἰς εἰρήνην: *Memoirs* 157. For ὑπάγω (pres. or ft.), see Blass 323, 3; cf. Mk. 14, 21.

Special Note. In all languages, it appears, the letter s can be used at will for pleasant as well as unpleasant effects. It can stir up or soothe the hearer's emotion. Tennyson, for example, knew that sibilants in English are a means of hissing, and we are told (E. A. G. Lamborn, *The Rudiments of Criticism;* Clarendon 1931; p. 36) that he tried to rid his verse of this element, "kicking the geese out of the boat," as he called it. But he also appreciated the softness of s's when used in hushing a passage:

> Music that brings sweet sleep down from the blissful skies,
> Music that gentlier on the spirit lies
> Than tir'd eyelids upon tir'd eyes.

Similarly Shakespeare pictures certain dark-souled men who refuse to submit to the sway of music, and E. H. Pritchard (*Studies in Literature;* Harrap 1919; p. 57) calls attention to the hiss of the *s* in "It is treason, stratagems, and spoils" and the hush of the *s* in "How sweet the moonlight sleeps upon this bank."

For Latin we have Quintilian's testimony in 12, 10, 32, that *s* is *littera absona*. Greek grammarians (as Dionysius of Halic., *de comp. verb.*, 80 UR) ridicule the excessive use of sigma; but J. A. Scott (*AJPh.* 29, 69–77) points out that the free use of sigma in both tragic and comic poetry conclusively disproves the theory that sigma was, essentially, fit only to express anger or contempt. There are some exquisite lines in Aeschylus, Sophocles, Euripides, Pindar, and Aristophanes which abound in esses. It may be noted that each of the following lines (quoted by Scott)

Eur. *Med.* 476: ἔσωσά σ᾽, ὡς ἴσασιν Ἑλλήνων ὅσοι.
Eur. *I.T.* 765: τὸ σῶμα σώσας τοὺς λόγους σώσεις ἐμοί.
Aes. *Eum.* 754: ὦ Παλλάς, ὦ σώσασα τοὺς ἐμοὺς δόμους.

contains a form of σώζω, that very word which brought untold happiness to the woman whom Jesus cured (Mk. 5, 34). The emotional effect of sigma depends on its phonetical value, on the nature of the message conveyed, and on its pronunciation. Pronounced softly or harshly, an *s* will whisper music or hiss contempt. Blass thinks that on the whole the Greeks were averse to sigmatism, for why should they have consented to the all but wholesale disappearance of intervocalic *s*? Dionysius's words are: ἄχαρι καὶ ἀηδὲς τὸ σ καὶ πλεονάσαν σφόδρα λυπεῖ. Kühner-Blass, 15, 1; Buck, *Comparative Grammar* 164; J. A. Scott, *Class. J.*, 23, 298 (a note on Mt. 9, 22); Kretschmer, *Sprache* 6, 3.

35–36. ἀπέθανεν: the pf. might have been used; 15, 44. Gild. 227. Moulton 135. τί ἔτι σκύλλεις; Why *should* you trouble? (Joüon). Note E. λαλούμενον: *as it was being delivered;* graphic. *Memoirs* 45 ff. μὴ φοβοῦ: Smyth 1841. Gild. 415. Dana 290. Moulton 122. πίστευε: present; *hold on to your faith;* after the arrival of the messengers, there was need of this exhortation. See on 1, 3, ποιεῖτε; 1, 15, μετανοεῖτε.

38–39. ἔρχονται εἰς: not in the same sense as εἰσελθών in 39. The verb may mean 1) set out; 2) travel; 3) arrive. Θεωρεῖ (see on 5, 15) governs by a natural Zeugma also ἀλαλάζοντας; Smyth 3048. οὐκ ἀπέθανεν: an emphatic denial of ἀπέθανεν in v. 35; Gild. 245. For other echoes in this Gospel, see on 2, 26.

40–41. κατεγέλων: they *were about to* laugh Him down. Gild. 213, 214. Dana 177. Smyth 1895. For κατά, see on 1, 2, κατασκευάσει. Howard 121: the prep. here indicates "action unfavorable to an object." τοῦ παιδίου: a common element, neatly placed after τὸν πατέρα (not necessarily Aramaic; Joüon). Colometry, B 7. For ταλιθὰ κούμ, see Joüon; Errandonea 297, 1.

42–43. The story proper (as all incidents in Mark) ends with the result impf. περιεπάτει; see on 5, 13, ἐπνίγοντο. The foll. isolated matters of detail are not here represented as results of the miracle (though elsewhere we have ἐξίστασθαι, 2, 12; ἐθαύμαζον, 5, 20; ἐξίσταντο, 6, 51), but as simple occurrences. ἐκστάσει: Smyth 1577.

VI, 1–6. JESUS IN NAZARETH
(Mt. 13, 53–58. Lk. 4, 15–30)

VI. 1. ἔρχεται εἰς: as often, *He set out for*. Historical pres.=ingressive aor. Smyth 1883 a. ἀκολουθοῦσιν: equiv. to a descriptive impf. See on 5, 24. Parataxis, Note A, καί, καί, καί.

2. γενομένου: ingressive. Smyth 1924. Gild. 239. Dana 180. ἤρξατο: Note I. ἐκπλήττεσθαι: Note M. πόθεν: asks for source or origin; Note G, at end; so does τίς (Blass), "where is it coming from?" An ominous question: if His wisdom is "given to Him," who else but God could be the Giver? Perhaps τίνες εἰσίν should be understood w. αἱ δυνάμεις. "Is it a rare phenomenon to see men refusing to acknowledge genius in a former classmate?" (Lagrange). Joüon sees Aramaic influence in διὰ τῶν χειρῶν; but many of our Lord's miracles were actually wrought διὰ τῶν χειρῶν; and why should the phrase be un-Greek? So. *El.* 1350, "by whose hands I was spirited away," οὗ ἐξεπέμφθην χεροῖν. Hesiod *Theog.* 701, ὀφθαλμοῖσιν ἰδεῖν ἠδ' οὔασι ὄσσαν ἀκοῦσαι; and in 718, χερσὶν νικήσαντες. Mark is graphic, and sure of his Greek.

3 ff. ἀδελφός: *Memoirs* 191. οὐκ ἐδύνατο (ποιῆσαι): *Memoirs* 193. Both the meaning of the verb and the negative tense emphasize that Christ "could not," even if He would work miracles here. Smyth 1896. Thus the force of a Gr. verb is often strengthened by the tense.

See on 5, 17, ἀπελθεῖν. ἐθαύμαζεν: the result impf. See on 5, 13. For editorial καί, see *Memoirs* on 14, 58; 3, 22.

VI, 7–13. The Mission of the Apostles
(Mt. 10, 1; 9–15. Lk. 9, 1–6; 10, 1)

7–8. ἤρξατο: Note I. δύο δύο: Moulton 97. ἐδίδου: a detail, as usual, in the impf. Gild. 211. See on 5, 24. For a harmonization of the foll. account w. Mt. and Luk., see *Memoirs* 157, 158. For αἴρω, see on 13, 15 and 6, 29; John 20, 15; not only "I take up" what I have, but also "I go and get; fetch." See Appendix II.

9–10. A sudden transition from indirect to direct discourse was not unknown to good Gr. writers. Xen. *Hell.* 2, 1, 25, μεθορμίσαι παρῆνει πρὸς πόλιν· οὗ ὄντες ναυμαχήσετε, ἔφη, ὅταν βούλησθε. *Anab.* 1, 9, 25; 5, 6, 37. See Note Q. χιτῶνας: the use of two tunics was a luxury; 14, 63. μένετε: of lodging permanently. For Mk.'s ἕως ἂν ἐξέλθητε Luke (9, 4) uses Parataxis: καὶ ἐκεῖθεν ἐξέρχεσθε. Note A.

11 ff. εἰς μαρτύριον αὐτοῖς: as a warning to them. See on 1, 44; 13, 9. The sense of the phrase varies with the context. ἐκήρυξαν: the principal event (aor.); the foll. impfs. give details. Gild. 211. The present μετανοῶσιν is an echo of μετανοεῖτε in our Lord's inaugural sermon, 1, 15. See on 2, 26.

VI, 14–29. Herod and John the Baptist
(Mt. 14, 1–12. Lk. 9, 7–9; 3, 19–20)

14–15. ἐγήγερται: see on 1, 2, γέγραπται; the same event is referred to by the aor. in v. 16. Cf. Mk. 16, 6 and 16, 14. Gild. 227. The aorist expresses simple occurrence and implies result; the perfect expresses result while implying occurrence. αἱ δυνάμεις: Smyth 1120 a and b. ὡς εἷς τῶν προφητῶν, "like all the prophets"; Joüon.

16 ff. ἀκούσας ἔλεγεν: resumes ἤκουσεν καὶ ἔλεγεν of v. 14. ἀποστείλας ἐκράτησεν: coincident aorists. Note T. Gild. 345. αὐτός: see Joüon on Mt. 3, 4. "It was the same Herod who . . ." Lk. 3, 23. ἐφοβεῖτο: "held in reverence." The use of repeated καί's in v. 20 is obtrusive: the reader is to relish each individual item. Note A. Blass 460, 3.

22 ff. αἴτησον: Moulton 160. Blass 316. For a glimpse of Marcan Art in this section, see *Memoirs* 49. The modal shades of θέλω and ἤθελον are not always obvious. Is ἤθελεν in v. 19 "she would have

liked" or "she was determined"? For θέλω and βούλομαι, see Bauer, and *M. Vocabulary.* Cf. θέλω in I Cor. 7, 7, and see Note E.

26 ff. διά w. acc.: not the same as διά w. gen. Contrast οὐκ ἠθέλησεν here with οὐκ ἤθελεν above; Gild. 245 and 216; Joüon renders "il n'osa pas." ἀποστείλας: like πέμψας in Isocr. *Anti.* 123. ἀποστείλας, ἐπέταξεν: coincident action. Note T. ἔθηκαν: common for "bury," as in 15, 47. Arist. *Wasps* 386.

VI, 30–56. RETURN OF THE DISCIPLES. FEEDING THE CROWD
(Mt. 14, 13–36. Lk. 9, 10–17. Jn. 6, 1–21)

30 ff. οἱ ἐρχόμενοι: Smyth 2052. ὑμεῖς αὐτοί: "all by yourselves"; αὐτός in the sense of "alone" is common Gr. Smyth 1209 a. Joüon prefers "you too." καὶ ἀναπαύσασθε: Parataxis: Note A. In v. 33, do not overlook ἐπί in ἐπ-έγνωσαν. Howard, 120, "in addition"; Mk. 5, 30. Hence: *many more.* ἐσπλαγχνίσθη: *Memoirs* on 1, 41, p. 150.

37 ff. ἀποκριθείς: Note L. συμπόσια συμπόσια: *Memoirs* 54. Moulton 97; Joüon. ἐδίδου: a special detail. See on 4, 8. The Gr. impf. invites the reader to look at the scene with the eyes of the imagination. Gild. 205. V. 42: a notable case of Parataxis; Note A. οἱ φαγόντες: Smyth 2052. For ἀπό in 6, 43, see *Special Note* on 7, 28.

45 ff. ἐμβῆναι καὶ προάγειν: ἐμβάντας προάγειν. The tenses are correctly used. ἀπολύει: indirect discourse, as part of what Jesus said. Blass 383, 1. Class. Gr. would prefer ἄν w. the subjv. ὀψία: the late afternoon or the early evening. ἐν τῷ ἐλαύνειν: "in trying to make headway." Smyth 2033. Dana 191, 192. The sense of παρελθεῖν ("come to" or "pass by") is disputed. προσεύξασθαι: *Memoirs* 194, 195.

49–50. εἶδον καὶ ἐταράχθησαν: Parataxis; Note A. ἐλάλησεν: "spoke to," rather than "conversed with"; Joüon. ἐγώ εἰμι: *It* is I. Excellent Greek. Xen. *Hell.* 1, 6, 28, ὅτι οἱ Ἀθηναῖοι εἶεν, "that it was the Athenians." Cf. Mk. 13, 6; 14, 62.

51 ff. πρός, εἰς: Parallel Orientation. Note F. ἐξίσταντο: impf. of result, as usual. 5, 42. οὐ συνῆκαν: explains why the disciples were utterly amazed at the stilling of the storm, instead of acknowledging Christ's Divinity outright—the same Divinity that had multiplied the loaves the evening before. *Memoirs* 159. "They *had* not understood." ἦν πεπωρωμένη: "*had been* in a state of callousness or blindness." See on 3, 10, ἐθεράπευσεν; 4, 41, ἐφοβήθησαν.

55–56. The subj. of περιέδραμον need not be the same as that of

208   THE GOSPEL OF ST. MARK

ἤρξαντο. Gild. 71. ἤρξαντο: Note I. ὅτι ἐστίν: indirect discourse. Smyth 2597. Note the Koine use of ἄν w. the impf. and aor. Moulton 166.

VII, 1–23. "THE THINGS THAT DEFILE A PERSON"
(Mt. 15, 1–20)

VII. 1–2. It is not clear whether ἐλθόντες modifies τινὲς only, or also οἱ Φαρισαῖοι. Memoirs 93. See Mt. 15, 1. The art. οἱ is probably generic (Smyth 1122. Gild. 563 ff. Dana 147), though possibly particular (the Pharisees, sc. of that country). Smyth 1120. ἰδόντες τινὰς ὅτι ἐσθίουσιν: Prolepsis of the subject. Kaegi 176, 5. Smyth 2182. See on 1, 24. ἐσθίουσιν: Smyth 2614. Dana 284. κοιναῖς: "profane"; well explained by Joüon. M. Vocabulary 350: "a specifically Jewish usage."

3. γάρ: The Pharisees, "you must know," . . . ; Smyth 2808; a kind of footnote. καὶ πάντες: adding the wider term, οἱ Ἰουδαῖοι, to the narrower, οἱ Φαρισαῖοι. Augmentative καί. Smyth 2869. "Like the Jews generally"; "and, in fact, all the Jews." Note H. πυγμῇ: the word has not yet been satisfactorily explained; the general sense is, of course, "carefully; scrupulously." ἐάν: a general present condition; Smyth 2337.

4. ἀγορά: 1) market-place; 2) public place or street; 3) market-goods. ἀπό: local or temporal. Hence 1) returning from the street; 2) [they do not eat goods] bought in the market. In Greek, prepositional phrases may function as subject or object. Smyth 928. κρατεῖν: Smyth 2008 ff.; "as binding them," "as obligatory"; the present, of a rule of life.

5–6. ἔπειτα: resumes verse 2. Smyth 2080. καλῶς: ironically or seriously? Occurs again in v. 9. πόρρω ἀπέχει ἀπ' ἐμοῦ: compare the expression with Iliad I, 562, ἀπὸ θυμοῦ μᾶλλον ἐμοὶ ἔσεαι, and w. Archilochus 25 (Loeb L., p. 110), ἀπόπροθεν γάρ ἐστιν ὀφθαλμῶν ἐμῶν.

7–12. διδάσκοντες διδασκαλίας, etc.; Smyth 1563 ff. Memoirs 94; 159. ἵνα τηρήσητε: a fine aorist, denoting attainment; "to keep intact." In v. 10, note the editorial καί; see on 14, 58; Memoirs 173. θανάτῳ etc.: Smyth 1577. The construction begun in v. 11 is not continued in v. 12. Smyth 3004, Anacoluthon. But see the rendering in Memoirs 94. κορβᾶν: see Joüon; and Memoirs 160.

13–14. ἀκυροῦντες: see on 7, 19, καθαρίζων. ᾗ (=ἥν) παρεδώκατε: by no means otiose. Note C. The aorist "of what has just happened" (in the lifetime of the persons addressed). Moulton 135 ff. "Which you are handing down." The παραδοῦναι is still going on; hence our Lord's censure. A similar aorist is ἀφήκαμεν in 10, 28. Note the sharp aorists ἀκούσατε and σύνετε, as though expressing urgency or impatience. See on 1, 3, ἑτοιμάσατε. Contrast 4, 3, ἀκούετε. Blass 337.

15 ff. οὐδέν ἐστιν, etc.: one of the most vivid sentences in the whole Gospel. The secret of vividness (sc. exact narration overlooking no detail) is explained by Demetrius 209–220. For the repetition of "a person" (not an idle addition!), see Memoirs 160–161. οὕτως: thus; sc. as your question shows. Smyth 1245. οὕπω νοεῖτε: perhaps modal, "can you not yet see"? Note E. For ὦτα ἀκούειν, see on 4, 9.

19. καθαρίζων may modify ἀφεδρῶνα, or λέγει. Blass 137, 3. Moulton 69; 225. See note on 1, 10, ἀναβαίνων. Mark is familiar with the use of the Gr. partic. as expressing a verdict on an action just mentioned. See 7, 13, ἀκυροῦντες; 7, 3, κρατοῦντες; 8, 11 and 10, 2, πειράζοντες. In Gr. literature εὖ ποιῶν is common in this sense. Smyth 2062. Gerth 486, 6. The part. is in apposition to the subject of the preceding sentence. And thereby He declared all foods clean. For a Greek reader the part. καθαρίζων is not too far away (Lagrange) from λέγει. In Eur. Iph. T., the verb λέγει in line 16 is qualified by ἀναφέρων in line 23! ἔσωθεν; Place from; agrees with ἐκ; Note F.

VII, 24–30. THE SYROPHOENICIAN WOMAN

(Mt. 15, 21–28)

24 ff. οὐδένα ἤθελεν: the imperfect, cut short by a negative aor. Gild. 214, 216. Our Lord's "will" to remain incognito was not absolute. εὐθὺς ἀκούσασα: no sooner than; for εὐθύς, see on 1, 10. αὐτῆς: superfluous after ἧς. ἠρώτα: impf.; the ἐρωτᾶν continues through the entire story. Blass 328. Smyth 1891.

27–28. If our Lord was at the time εἰς οἰκίαν (v. 24), His remark about τὸν ἄρτον would be suggested by His being at table (Joüon). ἀπεκρίθη: a very felicitous instance of this verb; see Memoirs 154, on 3, 33; Note L. Our Lord's words were disheartening: "the dogs under the table cannot have the children's bread"; but the good lady touched them with a sudden radiance, by showing that, while His statement was perfectly true, it would not prevent Him from granting her request: for all that the little dogs under the table claim is the crumbs from the children's bread. καί before τὰ κυνάρια may mean but, or and; either will fit the context. ἀπὸ τῶν ψιχίων: partitive ἀπό; Blass 169. Smyth 1355.

Special Note on the "So-called Partitive Genitive": Davis 343 (i); Blass 164, 169; Dana 90, 7; Robertson 502, 519; Moulton 72, 73, 102, 223. In Mk. this genitive is often strengthened by the addition of ἐκ or ἀπό. Note that such prepositional phrases may act as subject or object of a verb. Cf. 7, 28 ἀπὸ τῶν ψιχίων; 7, 4 ἀπ' ἀγορᾶς (may be object to ἐσθίουσιν); 6, 43 ἀπὸ τῶν ἰχθύων; 6, 33 ἀπὸ πασῶν τῶν πόλεων; 12, 2 λάβῃ ἀπὸ τῶν καρπῶν; 5, 35 ἔρχονται ἀπὸ τοῦ ἀρχισυναγώγου; 7, 11 ὃ ἐὰν ἐξ ἐμοῦ; 9, 17 εἷς ἐκ τοῦ ὄχλου; 11, 8 κόψαντες ἐκ τῶν ἀγρῶν; 11, 14 ἐκ σοῦ καρπόν; 12, 44 ἐκ τοῦ περισσεύοντος (*bis*); 14, 23 ἔπιον ἐξ αὐτοῦ (14, 25); 14, 69 ἐξ αὐτῶν ἐστιν; 16, 12 δυσὶν ἐξ αὐτῶν. Smyth 928; 1306 ff.; 1341 ff.

29–30. διά w. acc.: "thanks to; because of." ἐξελήλυθεν: action "now over and gone." See on 5, 15, τὸν ἐσχηκότα. βεβλημένον: *thrown*, perhaps by the departing demon; or, simply, *lying*. 9, 42, βέβληται. The use of ἐξελθὼν ἐκ in v. 31 need not mean that our Lord had actually been within τὰ ὅρια of heathen territory. Brugmann 508, ἐκ = ἀπό, as in *Iliad* 3, 273.

VII, 31–37. THE DEAF-MUTE
(Mt. 15, 29–31)

31 ff. φέρουσιν: *lead;* not "carry"; even the Latin *portare* may be so used. ἔβαλεν: no hint of force or unseemly haste; see on 1, 12, ἐκβάλλει. πτύσας: seems to qualify ἥψατο: *with His saliva.* ἐφφαθά: see Joüon. ἐλάλει: of the result, as usual; Smyth 1899. "He *could* now speak correctly." For a rendering of 37, see *Memoirs* 97 and 48. On Paronomasia, see *Memoirs* 168, on 12, 14. For the pf. πεποίηκεν, cf. *Iliad* 2, 272, μυρία ἐσθλὰ ἔοργε. See Adams's note on Lysias 12, 22, εἰργασμένοι εἰσιν, "they are responsible for the deed." See Note U.

VIII, 1–10. SECOND FEEDING
(Mt. 15, 32–39)

VIII. 1–2. This account of a miraculous feeding is not a doublet of the first, given in 6, 35 ff. *Memoirs* 161. "It is not to be wondered at that the Savior repeated a miracle which foreshadows the Eucharist" (Lagrange). πολλοῦ ὄντος or ὄντος alone may be the predicate. Smyth 918. For NT μή, see Blass 426 ff. Cf. Dana 241; Moulton 169 ff. σπλαγχνί-

ζομαι: *Memoirs* on 1, 41, p. 150. ἡμέραι τρεῖς: an independent nominative. Moulton 70. Dana 83. προσμένουσιν: Smyth 1885. Gild. 202.
Dana 174, 5.

3. ἐκλυθήσονται: modal future, "they must break down." See Note
E. Cf. 10, 7, καταλείψει. 3, 28, ἀφεθήσεται. The same homely word occurs in Isoc. *Anti.* 59, ἵνα μὴ ἐκλυθῶ: "in order that I may not break
down utterly" (Norlin). Note ἥκουσιν: "they are here, *have* come."
Smyth 1886.

4. ἀπεκρίθησαν: *Memoirs* on 3, 33, p. 154; Note L. πόθεν: quite common in Gr. of a source of information (Mk. 6, 2), a source of being
(12, 37), or of resources, as here. Arist. *Wasps* 305, πόθεν ὠνησόμεθ'
ἄριστον: *where* or *how* can we buy a dinner? See Note G, at end.
δυνήσεται: modality twice expressed, by the meaning of the word and
by the tense. See on 3, 25.

6 ff. ἐδίδου: see on 6, 41. The present παρατιθῶσιν views the act as
repeated, from man to man. The aorist παρέθηκαν sums up. Smyth
1927; Gild. 238; note the sg. τῷ ὄχλῳ; see on 1, 3, ἑτοιμάσατε. For
ἔφαγον, etc., see on 6, 42. περισ., σπυρίδας: two accusatives; "in the
way of fragments, they gathered seven basketfuls." καὶ εὐθύς: 1, 18.

VIII, 11–21. THE LEAVEN OF THE PHARISEES
(Mt. 16, 1–12)

11–12. οἱ Φαρισαῖοι: the Ph. of that locality. Smyth 1119. See
on 7, 1. ἤρξαντο: Note I. ἀπὸ τοῦ οὐρανοῦ: *in* the sky. Note G. Smyth
1660. Cf. 11, 8, and 1, 11. εἰ δοθήσεται: see Joüon; an emphatic *not*.
For the repetition of σημεῖον and γενεά, see on 7, 15. *Memoirs* 160.
Note Q.

13–14. πάλιν goes w. ἐμβάς. The word has the same senses as Latin
rursus (Souter), or the Engl. *again*. ἀπῆλθεν: *set out for* the opp. shore.
The incident here narrated takes place ἐν τῷ πλοίῳ. ἐπελάθοντο: may
be simultaneous with ἀπῆλθεν. Mt.'s ἐλθόντες in 16, 5 agrees w. Mark.
If ἀπῆλθον meant *they arrived*, ἐπελάθοντο would be *they had forgotten*.
Gild. 253. For the sequence of thought in this section, see *Memoirs* 162.

15 ff. Note the parallelism: καὶ διεστέλλετο—καὶ διελογίζοντο: *now
it so happened* that He exhorted, and that they disputed. οὔπω νοεῖτε:
may be modal. See Note E. οὔπω νοεῖτε οὐδὲ συνίετε: Perhaps a
Hendiadys; "is the light not yet dawning on you?" By our Lord's own
question (vv. 19, 20), there were two feedings. Mark did not tamper
with our Lord's words. μνημονεύετε ὅτε: Smyth 2395 A, n.

VIII, 22–26. Cure of a Blind Man

22 ff. φέρουσιν: *bring, lead*. For the indefinite pl., see on 1, 22, ἐξεπλήσσοντο. εἴ τι βλέπει: may be modal. See Note E. So βλέπω: "I can see." For the man's incoherent way of speaking, see *Memoirs* 100 and 162. Note Q. ἐνέβλεπεν: impf. of result, as usual. He *could* now see.

VIII, 27–39. Peter's Confession. Prediction of the Passion
(Mt. 16, 13–28. Lk. 9, 18–27)

27 ff. *Memoirs* 43, and 162. ὁ Χριστός: Smyth 1152. ἐπιτιμάω always means *to speak sternly* (Joüon). ἤρξατο: Joüon's note is misleading. With the inf., the word never means that something is done "la première fois." Note I. δεῖ: of the necessity imposed upon Christ by the Father. For διδάσκειν ("enseigner") and μετὰ τρεῖς ἡμέρας, employed in the usual Jewish way of reckoning, see Joüon.

32–33. ἤρξατο ἐπιτιμᾶν: who Whom? Note I; for ἐπιτιμάω, see on 8, 30. *Memoirs* 162. ὕπαγε: foll. by a pause, go back; *sc.* join the other disciples. ὀπίσω μου is a renewal of the original call in Mk. 1, 17. "Come; follow Me." Peter had forgotten that he must follow Jesus as a docile disciple, not as a master or critic. See, however, Joüon on Mt. 16, 23. In no case did Jesus order Peter to leave Him altogether (Swete!) and go out of His sight! Joüon, too, separates ὕπαγε from what follows; but his explanation of ὀπίσω μου = "Arrière de moi" seems erroneous. In Mk., ὀπίσω μου is the stereotyped expression for *follow me*. It is a mistake to compare Mt. 4, 10. ὕπαγε ὀπίσω μου, taken together, may mean: "go back to your place behind me."

34. *Memoirs* 162. ὀπίσω μου ἐλθεῖν = ἀκολουθῆσαι. The addition of καὶ ἀράτω marks the extent to which, if need be, the ἀπαρνήσασθαι must be carried in the service of Christ. "Every Christian is radically ready for martyrdom; this is implied in the state of grace in which he lives. He must lay down his life rather than renounce Christ or a single truth of the Christian faith" (Vonier, *Christianus*, p. 9). This ἀπαρνήσασθαι having been accomplished in one resolute act of the will (Lk. adds 'daily'), the disciple *may come* (ἀκολουθείτω: Smyth 1839) and follow Jesus. The use of θέλει does not imply that the following of Christ, as here inculcated, is a matter of supererogation. The case in 10, 21 is different.

35. *Memoirs* 163. Jesus illustrates in various ways (vv. 35–37) the futility of refusing to follow Him, in view of the brevity and perishableness of human *life*, which one may wish to prefer to martyrdom. σῶσαι τὴν ψυχήν: the same as Eur. *HF.*, 1146, τί δῆτα φείδομαι ψυχῆς ἐμῆς, "Why should I spare my life?" For the undertone in ἀπολέσει, see *Memoirs* 101; for the fut., see on 8, 3. "Will save it *in the end*"; when will this take place or how? A hint at the resurrection of the body. Knabenbauer refers to 2 Cor. 4, 17. Note ἄν w. ft. indic.; Moulton 43; Blass 380, 3.

36–37. Note the commercial terms ὠφελήσει, κερδῆσαι, ζημιωθῆναι. The world with its material wealth is pitted against the unselfish servant of Christ. Physical life at its best may imply the possession of worldly goods; but the brevity of human life is proof that this possession cannot be compared with eternal life (which includes the resurrection; for it is only through the resurrection that the ψυχή is completely recovered: σώσει αὐτήν).

38. *Memoirs* 163. Such combinations as μὲ καὶ τοὺς ἐμοὺς λόγους (the person and something belonging to the person) are very common in the Gr. Tragedies (esp. Sophocles). Cf. Eur. *HF.*, 1135, σὺ καὶ τὰ σὰ τόξα: *you and your bow*. Gerth 521, 2. Xen. *Cyrop.* 5, 5, 16, ἐπὶ σὲ καὶ τὴν σὴν χώραν: *against you and your country*. The insult, implied in ἐπαισχυνθῇ, is directed both against the Person of Christ (μὲ) and against His Gospel (τοὺς ἐμοὺς λόγους). ἐν τῇ δόξῃ: almost = *wrapt in glory*. For ἐν and the great variety of its subtle uses, see Bauer, Zorell, and *M. Vocabulary.* New Testament ἐν is full of interest. Cf. 1, 23, ἐν τῷ πνεύματι; and St. Paul's ἐν Χριστῷ.

In interpreting verses 34–38, it is essential to recognize 1) the various senses of ψυχή; and 2) the use of γάρ "in coördinate clauses," for which in English *and* or *but* must be substituted (Weymouth, *Rendering into English;* pp. 44 ff.; with many illustrations). Note the use in the *Memoirs* of *for* in 35; *clearly*, in 36; *or*, in 37; *furthermore* (as introducing another line of reasoning, parallel to 34) in 38.

IX, 1–13. TRANSFIGURATION
(Mt. 17, 1–13. Lk. 9, 28–36)

IX. 1–2. *Memoirs* 163. οὐ μή: an emphatic denial. Smyth 2756 b. Dana 242. ἐληλυθυῖαν: passive; "set up; established." Smyth 1752. See Joüon. ἴδωσιν: ingressive. Smyth 1924. Dana 180. Gild. 240; 241.

μετεμορφώθη: reflexive, rather than passive; 9, 4, ὤφθη: "He appeared"; 16, 10, πορευθεῖσα, "she went." Smyth 815.

3 ff. οὕτως: superfluous after οἷα. ὤφθη: see note above. καὶ ὤφθη καὶ ἦσαν: Note A. ἀποκριθείς: Note L. Memoirs 164. So again in 9, 6. καλόν: "opportune"; Lysias 13, 6, κάλλιστος καιρός: "an excellent opportunity." καὶ ποιήσωμεν: Parataxis; Note A.

7 ff. Does ἐγένετο go with ἐπισκιάζουσα? Dana 203. Smyth 1857. Or does it mean "formed"? Smyth 917; 918. ἐκ τῆς νεφέλης: Note G. ἀγαπητός: see on 1, 11. ἀκούετε: present imv., here of a rule of life; see on 4, 3. ἀλλά: = "except," εἰ μή. Not necessarily an Aramaism; Gerth 534, 5. Memoirs 164.

10 ff. καί: and so; and indeed. Note H. ἐκράτησαν τὸν λόγον: see Joüon. Probably, "they kept the matter to themselves," as commanded by Jesus. συνζητοῦντες: "except that they discussed." Smyth 2066; 2069. ἀποκαθιστάνει: Smyth 1879. For Elias, see Memoirs 164. καὶ πῶς: Smyth 2872. ἀλλά: "well," "eh bien" (Joüon). See on 3, 27. ἐποίησαν ὅσα ἤθελον: a euphemism for wanton treatment.

IX, 14–29. THE EPILEPTIC BOY
(Mt. 17, 14–21. Lk. 9, 37–42)

14 ff. The two common elements, περὶ αὐτούς and συνζητοῦντας, belong to both ὄχλον πολύν and γραμματεῖς. See Colometry, B 7. ἐκ τοῦ ὄχλου: Note G. "In the crowd." ἤνεγκα: Moulton 135. ὅπου: often = "when"; Isocr. Anti. 208. For ῥήσσει, see Joüon on 1, 26. Note how frequently the subject is changed without further warning. Gild. 71. ἀποκριθείς: Note L. For the rhythm and parallelism in our Lord's reply, see Colometry, B 3, 4, and 8.

20–21. ἰδών: referring to πνεῦμα. Smyth 1013 ff. ἰδὼν αὐτόν might be nominativus pendens. See on 1, 10, ἀναβαίνων. πεσών: he was thrown down. Smyth 1752. So. Ant. 474, πίπτειν μάλιστα: "are soonest broken." πόσος χρόνος ἐστίν: "how long is the time," = "how much time has elapsed," ὡς = "since . . ." γέγονεν: refers to possession as a condition now existing. Smyth 1885 b; 1945. Gild. 203. Burton 88. Moulton 145 ff. ἐκ παιδιόθεν. "from (the beginning of) his childhood"; Joüon.

22 ff. βοήθησον: contrast the more subdued βοήθει in v. 24. See on 1, 3, ἑτοιμάσατε. σπλαγχνισθείς: coincident w. βοήθησον. See Note T. Memoirs 164. τὸ εἰ δύνῃ: Smyth 1153 g. δυνατά: all things can be done "for a believer" or "by a believer"? Smyth 1488. How did the

boy's father understand the statement? βοηθεῖν w. dat.: "help a thing" or, as here, "bring help against (=to ward off) a thing"; *remedy, cure;* see L&S. ἀπιστία: see *Memoirs* on v. 23. "Lack of faith," not "weak faith"; 16, 14.

25 ff. Note the majesty of tone in: ἐγὼ ἐπιτάσσω σοι. Aorist-present; Burton 13; see note on 2, 5, and Note T. ἀπέθανεν: *he is dead.* We emphasize the result; Greek merely registers the occurrence. Moulton 135 ff. For ἀποθνήσκω in Mk., cf. 5, 35; 5, 39; 12, 19; 12, 20; 12, 21; 12, 22; 15, 44. Gild. 227. τῆς χειρός: *Memoirs* 192. ἐξελθεῖν: "cannot *be driven out.*" Smyth 1752. Cf. 9, 43, ἀπελθεῖν and 45, βληθῆναι.

IX, 30–32. SECOND PREDICTION OF THE PASSION
(Mt. 17, 22. 23. Lk. 9, 43–45. Jn. 7, 1)

30 ff. παρα-πορεύεσθαι: *travel* by a side-way, hence *avoiding the highway.* See on 2, 23. οὐκ ἤθελεν: as in 7, 24. παραδίδοται: Smyth 1879. Note the use of ἀποκτανθείς after ἀποκτενοῦσιν: *although put to death.* Cf. 4, 32, ὅταν σπαρῇ. ἠγνόουν: *Memoirs* 106 and 164.

IX, 33–50. INSTRUCTION OF THE APOSTLES
(Mt. 18, 1–35. Lk. 9, 46–50)

35 ff. θέλει: *would like to be* or *is determined to be.* Note E. The precise force of θέλω is not always clear. ἔσται: modal fut; Note E: *He must be; he will have to be.* Smyth 1910 a. καὶ πάντων διάκονος, explains ἔσχατος. Note A. Why δέχηται after δέξηται? The pres. of this verb is either aoristic (Smyth 1853) or denotes result (Smyth 1887). V. 37 is continued in 41, after the interruption caused by John's remark, vv. 38–40. *Memoirs* 165.

38 ff. John's remark was perhaps suggested by the phrase ἐπὶ τῷ ὀνόματι, in v. 37. Possibly John wanted to change the unpleasant subject; or Mark inserted the incident here because he was reminded of it by that phrase. ἐκωλύομεν: a tendential impf.; Dana 177; *we were for hindering him.* Hence μὴ κωλύετε in v. 39. Gild. 415. Joüon on 9, 38. καὶ δυνήσεται goes closely w. ὅς ποιήσει: no one can do these two things taken together and at the same time. Note A. The same paratactic καί in Lk. 24, 18. δυνήσομαι occurs in 3, 25; 8, 4; and 9, 39. Brugmann 559, 5 Anm.

41–42. For the opening γάρ, see *Memoirs* 164, 165. This verse continues 37. ποτίσῃ ποτήριον: Smyth 1563 ff. σκανδαλίσῃ, foll. by the pres. σκανδαλίζῃ. *Memoirs* 107. Note N. καλόν ἐστιν: *it is* or *would be more tolerable*. *Memoirs* 165. Note E. Splendid parataxis: περίκειται καὶ βέβληται: Note A.

43 ff. Study the perfect symmetry of vv. 43, 45, 47. See Colometry B, 4. Verses 44 and 46, identical with 48, are omitted in the better mss. Note the positive καλόν followed by ἤ: Blass 245, 3. Moulton 236. ἀπελθεῖν: see on 9, 29, ἐξελθεῖν=βληθῆναι in v. 45. Note the parallel orientation in εἰς τὴν γέενναν and εἰς τὸ πῦρ. Note F.

48 ff. οὐ τελευτᾷ, οὐ σβέννυται: an appalling thought, made more appalling still by its stark expression; for the full force of the negative universal present (Gild. 189), see Note E; cf. also 10, 43 οὐκ ἐστίν, and 11, 23, ὃ λαλεῖ γίνεται. Colometry B, 3. καὶ πᾶσα θυσία: Parataxis; Note A. *Just as* every sacrifice. . . . The connection of thought in vv. 49 and 50 is not entirely clear. Joüon comments on καί before εἰρηνεύετε: it may mean *et* "sans connexion logique"; *et néanmoins;* or *et ainsi vous aurez la paix entre vous*. ἐν ἑαυτοῖς: the refl. pron. of the third person is sometimes used for that of the first or the second. Smyth 1230. Note also that "Reciprocal and reflexive may occur in the same sentence without difference of meaning": Smyth 1232. Dana 140; 141.

X, 1–16. MARRIAGE. CHILDREN
(Mt. 19, 1–15. Lk. 18, 15–17)

X. 1 f. ἀναστάς: *departing*, rather than "rising"; as in 7, 24. ἔρχεται εἰς: *He set out for*, as often, rather than "He arrived." For the histor. pres., see Smyth 1883 a. καὶ πέραν: "and that, too, by keeping to the other side of the Jordan"; Note A. Note the symmetry of the two cola, καὶ συμπορεύονται, καὶ ἐδίδασκεν. Colometry B, 4. Our Lord was as unwearied in teaching as the crowds were in flocking to Him. πειράζοντες: expressing the writer's verdict. See on 7, 19.

4 ff. Note the apodictic aorists γράψαι and ἀπολῦσαι; divorce was a simple process under Moses. ἀπὸ ἀρχῆς κτίσεως: *in* the beginning; Note G. Dates need no article. ἐποίησεν, etc.: generally rendered, He made *them male and female;* but the Greek reads: made them "a male and a female," which here seems to mean "one male and one female." ἕνεκεν τούτου: because of this (institution of matrimony). καταλείψει: modal fut., expressing a law of nature: "*must* leave"; Note E. So προσκολληθήσεται and ἔσονται. Note εἰς w. acc. for the pred. noun. Dana 111.

9 ff. μὴ χωριζέτω: pres. impv.; of a rule of conduct. Gild. 415. πάλιν: as the Pharisees had questioned Jesus, so *now* the disciples *for their part* or *in turn* ask Him. Mark has over twenty-five instances of πάλιν. For the colometrization of 11 and 12, see Colometry, B 4. Note ἀπολύσασα as against ἂν ἀπολύσῃ: Note P. Marcan πάλιν is interesting; cf. 2, 1; 5, 21; 8, 13; 10, 10; 10, 24; 11, 3; 14, 61; 14, 69; 14, 70; 15, 4; 15, 12; 15, 13.

14 ff. μὴ κωλύετε: Gild. 415. Smyth 1841. Moulton 122. οὐ μή: Dana 242. Smyth 2756. παιδίον: nominative. In v. 16 almost every word or phrase reveals our Lord's affection for little children. For κατ-ευλόγει, see 1, 2, κατασκευάσει. τιθείς: pres. partic., "one by one." Smyth 1876. Dana 173, 3.

X, 17–31. THE RICH MAN. RICHES
(Mt. 19, 16–30. Lk. 18, 18–30)

18 ff. ἀγαθόν: *Memoirs* 165. The commandments are expressed in the prohibitive aorist. Gild. 415. Smyth 1841. Moulton 122 ff.; = "have nothing at all to do with . . ." ἀποκριθείς: no question had been asked; Note L. ἐφυλαξάμην: in its usual sense, *I have guarded against.* Matthew and Luke do *not* "correct" Mark (Moulton 159!), but use the active in an entirely different sense, *I have kept.* ταῦτα πάντα: may mean "these sins" or "these commandments." *Memoirs* 165.

21. ἐμβλέψας, ἠγάπησεν: ingressive. Gild. 239. πώλησον and δός: aorists, where we might expect the present (see on 1, 15, μετανοεῖτε); but these aorists denote a condition (Smyth 2061 and 2067) to be fulfilled before the ἀκολουθεῖν can be entered upon. *Memoirs* 166. What is the object of δός? The man's κτήματα or the proceeds realized from the sale? καί sometimes means *or;* Smyth 2870. καὶ ἕξεις: a parenthesis. The phrase ἄρας τὸν σταυρόν resumes and reiterates πώλησον, etc. See on 8, 34. "Having *thus* taken up your cross."

22 ff. ἦν ἔχων: he was "the owner" of large estates; Dana 203; Smyth 1857; Gild. 191; 192. τὰ χρήματα: art., Smyth 1120; the goods *of this world.* ἀποκριθείς: Note L. καὶ τίς: Smyth 2872. For the rendering of 27 see *Memoirs* 111. δυνατόν: cf. Callimachus fr. 27 (137): ῥέξαι δαίμονι πᾶν δυνατόν.

28 ff. ἤρξατο: Note I. ἀφήκαμεν: sc. on that memorable occasion when Jesus called them; 1, 17. ἀφήκαμεν, complexive; ἠκολουθήσαμεν, ingressive aorist. ἀποκριθείς: Note L. Study the colometry of vv. 29

and 30. νῦν ἐν τῷ καιρῷ τούτῳ; by no means pleonastic. Joüon takes νῦν as *déjà*. ἐρχομένῳ: as often, in a fut. sense. Smyth 1881. Note ἐμοῦ as distinguished from τοῦ εὐαγγελίου: see on 8, 38. Why is anarthrous ἔσχατοι followed by οἱ ἔσχατοι?

X, 32–45. Third Prediction of the Passion.
The Sons of Zebedee
(Mt. 20, 17–28. Lk. 18, 31–34; 22, 25–27)

32 ff. There is a pause after ὁδῷ. Not a case of periphrastic part. Smyth 2062. For ἦν προάγων, see Dana 203. οἱ δέ: here, as occasionally in old Gr., introducing "a fresh act of the subj. of the preceding clause" (Leaf, on *Iliad* 8, 321). Latin would use *idem*. Xen. *Anab.* 4, 2, 6. *Odyssey* 22, 86. Herod. 1, 66. Eur. *Or.* 35. See Gerth 469, 2. Here ἀκολουθοῦντες carries the main thought, while ἐφοβοῦντο expresses a subordinate thought. For this common Gr. idiom, see Smyth 2147 a. *Iliad* 1, 191, ὁ δ' (the same person as ὅ γε in 190) Ἀτρεΐδην ἐναρίζοι. Donovan on Tertiary Predicates, 424 ff. It is an error to assume that Mark here refers to three different groups. Schaefer's explanation is correct: "folgten aber, (wenn auch) schweren Herzens." καί, καί, καί: in the typical Marcan manner. Note H.

37 ff. δὸς ἡμῖν ἵνα καθίσωμεν: give us *the right* to sit. Note B. αἰτῶ and αἰτοῦμαι: Moulton 160. Dana 156, note ii. Blass 316, 2. δύνασθε: "are you *ready*"; their ability consists in their readiness. *Memoirs* 166. For δύνασθαι almost = ἐπίστασθαι, see Isocr. *Demon.* 28. πίνω: modal; "have to drink." Smyth 1879. For the metaphor in *cup* and *baptism*, see *Memoirs* 166.

40. After ἀλλ' οἷς ἡτοίμασται supply τὸ ἐμὲ δοῦναι. Most exegetes supply "a place" as subject to ἡτοίμασται, which is less satisfactory. Not, "for whom a place has been reserved," but "in whose favor (οἷς) it has been decreed by the Father that I should assign a special place." Our Lord assigns special places to none for carnal considerations, but always in due conformity with the will of the Father; *He* does the actual assigning, hence τὸ ἐμὲ δοῦναι ἡτοίμασται. Note the splendid pf. See on 1, 2, γέγραπται, and on 4, 11, δέδοται.

41 ff. ἤρξαντο: see Note I. οἱ δοκοῦντες ἄρχειν: "the distinguished rulers." Eur. *Tro.* 613. δοκῶ, as often, "to have a good reputation; to be distinguished": τὰ μηδὲν ὄντα opp. to τὰ δὲ δοκοῦντα (Eur.). οὐχ οὕτως δέ ἐστιν ἐν ὑμῖν a rebuke, finely worded, but emphatic: "it *is* not

so" for "it must not be so." Note E. But see Lagrange and Knabenbauer.

ἔσται: modal; Smyth 1910 a; *must be.* See on 10, 7. ἀντὶ πολλῶν:
for *all*, who in reality are *many*. Christ died for all; one Savior, but the
saved are countless. *Memoirs* 166. εἶναι πρῶτος: simple, but class.
Greek. Thuc. 6, 28, 2: πρῶτοι εἶναι, "to have first place."

X, 46–52. BARTIMAEUS
(Mt. 20, 29–34. Lk. 18, 35–43)

46. ἔρχονται: *they arrive* at Jericho, or, more probably, *they set out*
for Jericho. ἐκ-πορευομένου may denote our Lord's leaving Jericho
(so all commentators), or, better, His leaving Peraea *for* Jericho.
Hence ἐκπορευομένου describes the journey denoted by ἔρχονται. It
was on this outward-bound (ἐκ) journey from Peraea to Jericho that
Bartimaeus was cured. Where? ἀπὸ Ἰεριχώ, *at a distance from Jericho;*
not far from J. *Iliad* X, 151: the messengers found Diomedes ἐκτὸς
ἀπὸ κλισίης, "outside close-by his hut." See *Verbum Domini* 10 (1930),
231 ff.; 297 ff. For other solutions of this crux, see Soubigou 457.
For ἐκπορευομένου referring back to ἔρχονται, cf. Mt. 9, 32, where
ἐξερχομένων refers back to ἐξελθόντες in v. 31. Gerth 486, 1. For ἀπό,
cf. Eur. *Tro.* 523, ἀπὸ πέτρας σταθείς. Gerth 430. For the colometrization of this verse, see Colometry, B 6 (on Pauses). "And as He was
on the high road—some distance from (=near) Jericho— ..."

47 ff. ἤρξατο: Note I. ἐλέησον: the same *sharp* cry for pity as in
Arist. *Wasps* 393, ἐλέησον καὶ σῶσον. ἵνα ἀναβλέψω: an independent
sentence: *O Master, I wish to see.* See on 5, 23; 14, 49. For ῥαββουνί,
see Joüon. On the whole scene, see *Memoirs* 167. ἠκολούθει: the impf.
of result, as usual in Mark.

XI, 1–26. ENTRY INTO JERUSALEM. THE FIG-TREE. PRAYER
(Mt. 21, 1–22. Lk. 19, 29–48)

XI. 1–2. Parallel Orientation; see the colometrization, Note F, and
the rendering, *Memoirs* 114. It is immaterial to the Greek which of
the two villages is named first; no defence of the order in Mk. is needed.
See Lagrange. εὐθὺς εἰσπορευόμενοι: see on 1, 10; *Just as you enter.*
ἐφ᾽ ὃν οὐδεὶς οὔπω ἐκάθισεν: Jesus conforms to custom, "nam ad usus
sacros adhiberi solebant iumenta nondum usibus humanis mancipata."

For Him to insist on this respect shown to His Person, was as natural as to maintain that He was King. Note the aorist of total negation: Gild. 245. φέρετε, beside λύσατε, may be aoristic: Moulton 129, w. footnote. Smyth 1853.

3 ff. τί ποιεῖτε τοῦτο: another bit of splendid Greek. Smyth 2647. The pres. is conative. Smyth 1878. ἀποστέλλει: Smyth 1879; the fut. sense (not so in 11, 1) is helped by εὐθύς, *without delay;* see on 1, 10. ἔξω ἐπὶ τοῦ ἀμφόδου: *in the street outside;* but see Joüon. καθώς in v. 6 is felt as object to εἶπεν; see on 2, 12, οὕτως. For ἐκ τῶν ἀγρῶν, see Note G.

9 ff. οἱ προάγοντες, as it were, the vanguard; οἱ ἀκολουθοῦντες: the rear. It was an impromptu procession, but conducted with order and solemnity. Cf. the parallel accounts. ὁ ἐρχόμενος: *qui mittendus est;* Smyth 1752; one of our Lord's proper names; see on 1, 7. The Kingdom of God "is to come," ἐρχομένη, "to be established or *restored.*" See on 9, 1, ἐληλυθυῖαν, and 4, 21, ἔρχεται, in a passive sense.

11 ff. εἰς—εἰς: Parallel Orientation. Note F. ἀπό and ἐκ are sometimes used interchangeably. 7, 31, ἐκ τῶν ὁρίων(?). Blass 209. Brugmann 508; 506. ὁ γὰρ καιρός: For the difficulty in the use of γάρ, see *Memoirs* 167. For εἰ ἄρα, see Smyth 2796. ἀποκριθείς: Note L. ἤκουον: modal; they could hear it. Contrast ἤκουσαν in v. 18.

15–16. ἤρξατο: Note I. τῷ ἱερῷ: τὸ ἱερόν is wider than ναός and includes the Temple grounds. οὐκ ἤφιεν: "He would not permit." Gild. 216. Smyth 1896. σκεῦος: "pratiquement tout objet, et spécialement tout récipient"; Joüon.

17–18. ἐδίδασκεν: impf., of detail accompanying the main action (= διδάσκων). κληθήσεται: not merely *shall be called,* but *shall be considered; shall be* what its name implies. Joüon on Mt. 5, 9; Lk. 1, 32; etc. See Bauer's pertinent comment (p. 622). Claimed as an Aramaism, but *Hom. Hymn Demeter* 79 says: Zeus gave Demeter to Hades κεκλῆσθαι ἄκοιτιν, to be (called) *his legitimate wife.* πεποιήκατε: true pf.; 1, 2, γέγραπται. ἤκουσαν: they actually heard about it; different from ἤκουον, they were within hearing distance. ἐξεπλήσσετο: Note M.

19 ff. ὅταν: w. indic., as often in the Koine. Moulton 168, 239. It is incorrect to say that ἐξεπορεύετο is *equivalent* to an aorist (Joüon). Smyth 1889; descriptive impf.; the conclusion of the action is to be inferred from the context. παρα-πορευόμενοι; essentially the same as in 9, 30; the context must supply the terminus relationis implied in παρά. ἀποκριθείς: Note L. Our Lord's statement was an "answer" to Peter's thoughts. ἔχετε: the pres., of continued faith.

Special Note on the Vocative. Mk. 9, 19 is the only instance in this

Gospel of ὦ with the nominative. The expression is an emphatic exclamation, rather than a mere address. The articular nominative in the vocative function occurs 1, 24 (where ὁ ἅγιος may, however, be predicate or in apposition to an implied σύ); 5, 8 τὸ πνεῦμα τὸ ἀκάθαρτον; 5, 41 τὸ κοράσιον; 14, 36 ἀββᾶ ὁ πατήρ; 9, 25 τὸ ἄλαλον πνεῦμα; 15, 29 οὐὰ ὁ καταλύων; 15, 34 ὁ θεός μου; 3, 4 ἴδε ἡ μήτηρ μου does not belong here. The article, as usual, gives definiteness. Elsewhere the simple vocative is used. Cp. 1, 24; 2, 5; 4, 38; 5, 7; 5, 34; 7, 28; 8, 33; 9, 5; 9, 17; 9, 38; 10, 17; 10, 20; 10, 24; 10, 35; 10, 47; 10, 51; 11, 21; 12, 14; 12, 19; 12, 32; 13, 1; 14, 37, 14, 45; 15, 18. In classical Greek the use of ὦ before the vocative is "familiar," while its omission has a touch of dignity, reserve, impressiveness. "In English we obtain the same effect by exactly the opposite means" (Adam, quoted by Moulton 71). In Mk., every instance of the vocative without the interjection shows that the noun is uttered under stress of emotion. 2, 5 τέκνον: an affectionate address; so in 5, 34; 10, 24; etc.; 4, 38 διδάσκαλε: said in breathless excitement (with a touch of indignation) by frightened disciples; 15, 19 βασιλεῦ: the soldiers are mocking Christ; 10, 51 ῥαββουνί: reminds one of Mary's tender address in John 20, 16. Each case should be examined on its own merits and in its own context. Dana 84; Davis 341; Smyth 1283–1288; Moulton 71; Blass 146–147; J. A. Scott, "Additional Notes on the Vocative," *Am. J. Ph.*, xxvi, 32–43.

23. καὶ μὴ διακριθῇ: Parataxis; Note A; *without hesitating*. πιστεύῃ: the present as in ἔχετε πίστιν. ὃ λαλεῖ γίνεται: *what he says comes true*, a phrase that can hardly be surpassed as an expression of implicit confidence. Other passages where the pres. indic. is used to good advantage are (see note U):

2, 10: ἐξουσίαν ἔχει ἀφιέναι ἁμαρτίας ἐπὶ τῆς γῆς.

3, 29: οὐκ ἔχει ἄφεσιν εἰς τὸν αἰῶνα.

10, 43: οὐχ οὕτως δέ ἐστιν ἐν ὑμῖν.

12, 27: ὑμεῖς οὖν πολὺ πλανᾶσθε.

9, 48: οὐ τελευτᾷ, οὐ σβέννυται.

14, 22: τοῦτό ἐστιν τὸ σῶμά μου.

For the subjective tone of ἔσται αὐτῷ, see on 4, 11, τὰ πάντα γίνεται. All his *wishes* will come true: Smyth 1486; 1481; 1487.

24 ff. *Memoirs* 197, 168. The aor. ἐλάβετε represents an ἐλάβομεν (Moulton 135) spoken by petitioners who are suddenly made aware that their prayers have been answered. See Knabenbauer, Lagrange, al. For this happy result, the pres. πιστεύετε is a necessary preliminary.

See 22, ἔχετε πίστιν. πιστεύετε, καὶ ἔσται: Note A; "*If* you believe, you will receive"; Smyth 1839. στήκετε: "la position ordinaire dans la prière." Joüon on Mk. 11, 25 and Mt. 6, 5. οὐκ ἀφίετε: Smyth 2691 ff. Blass 428. Gerth 511, 4 b.

XI, 27–33, "By What Authority?"
(Mt. 21, 23–27. Lk. 20, 1–8)

27–28. οἱ, οἱ, οἱ: Smyth 1144; 1143. Note the precision of the questioners in 28: *Memoirs* 168. To label such writing as pleonastic is to miss the point. Note Q. ποίᾳ: practically = τίνι. Blass 298, 2. The origin of Christ's ἐξουσία is in question; hence the more precise question: ἢ τίς, etc. The demonstrative ταύτην is expanded and made clear by the ἵνα-clause. Note C. Just so ὑμῶν in 7, 13 is made clear by ᾗ παρεδώκατε.

29 ff. Our Lord is willing to answer (ἐρῶ) on two conditions; hence καί between ἐπερωτήσω and ἀποκρίθητε. These two verbs are joined paratactically to ἐρῶ. Smyth 1839. Note the sharp Asyndeton: τὸ βάπτισμα τὸ Ἰωάννου; the fatal question comes like a bolt from the blue. Cf. the rendering in the *Memoirs*. Equally peremptory is the aor. impv.; see on 1, 25; "answer outright." ἐξ οὐρανοῦ: a reverential reference to God; see on 13, 14, ὅπου οὐ δεῖ.

32. ἐφοβοῦντο: different in tone from the aor. in 12, 12. εἶχον: perhaps a Latinism. See Note S, and Pref. Note to Vocabulary. Blass 5, 3; 397, 2. Moulton, "Latinisms," *passim.* ὄντως: belongs probably in the ὅτι-clause.

XII, 1–12. The Wicked Tenants
(Mt. 21, 33–46. Lk. 20, 9–19)

XII. 1 ff. ἤρξατο: Note I. Note the colometrization of vv. 1 and 2. Parataxis and the parable style go well hand in hand. ἀπὸ τῶν καρπῶν: the quasi-object of λάβῃ: "his share of the vintage." Prepositional phrases may function as object or subject. Smyth 928 a. Mk. 6, 43, ἀπό. For κεφαλαιόω, see Joüon. Note the anacoluthon in v. 5; the sense is clear. Smyth 3004.

6 ff. For ἀγαπητόν, see on 1, 11; perhaps = μονογενῆ. For the art. w. the predicate, ὁ κληρονόμος, see Smyth 1152. Lk., 20, 15, reverses the order, ἐκβαλόντες ἀπέκτειναν. To a Greek reader the order was immaterial. See on 11, 1. Smyth 3030. For Hysteron Proteron in Homer,

see Classen; Kaibel on So. *El.* 1235. The mere fact that ἐξέβαλον is placed after ἀπέκτειναν is not a proof that the ἐκβαλεῖν took place after the ἀποκτεῖναι. Cf. 1, 31. ἤγειρεν κρατήσας. Cf. Xen. *Cyr.* 1, 4, 11, ὁ Κῦρος ἐδίδου ἄρας τοῖς παισίν, "took it away and gave it."

9 ff. The words ἐλεύσεται, etc., were probably spoken by the hearers; see Mt. 21, 41. Verse 10 continues the parable. οὐδέ: "Yes; and . . . . not also." Smyth 2932. λίθον: assimilated in case to ὅν; it may also be object to ἀπεδοκίμασαν; *quem lapidem . . . , eum.* Inverse Attraction: Smyth 2533. εἰς w. acc. after ἐγενήθη: supplies the pred. noun. 10, 8. Dana 111.

12. ἐζήτουν: from now on they sought; impf. The aor. ἐφοβήθησαν differs in tone from ἐφοβοῦντο in Mk. 11, 18. They would have liked to arrest Jesus, but (= καί; see on 1, 5) they suddenly took alarm. Smyth 2871; 1924. ἔγνωσαν may be simultaneous w. ἐφοβήθησαν or prior to it. First they understood the drift of the parable; then they took alarm; this alarm paralyzed their efforts to arrest J.

XII, 13–17. "Render to Caesar"
(Mt. 22, 15–22. Lk. 20, 20–26)

14–15. For the symmetry in v. 14, see *Memoirs* 168. For Chiasm and Paronomasia, see Smyth 3020 and 3040. Note the precision in formulating the captious question. *Memoirs*, p. 168, on 12, 23. For the meaning of ὑπόκρισις, see Zorell, Bauer; also *Classical Bulletin*, Jan. 1934. πειράζετε: not "tempt to sin," but "put to the test." ἵνα ἴδω: may be an independent clause; 5, 23; 10, 51.

17. ἀποκριθείς: now Jesus "answered" the question put to Him in v. 14. Note ἀπό-δοτε, as more precise than δῶμεν in v. 14: the poll tax is thereby qualified as *due* to Caesar (ἀπό: *back*, to whom it belongs). The unexpected addition of καὶ τὰ τοῦ θεοῦ . . . . is perhaps (so Deissmann) meant as a much-needed warning to the questioners: "but be sure you also render to God what is God's"; a case of Parataxis. Note A.

XII, 18–27. The Resurrection of the Dead
(Mt. 22, 23–33. Lk. 20, 27–38)

18–20. οἵτινες: for the class. nuance of this pron., see Smyth 2496. Blass 293. μή: "encroaching" on οὐ. Blass: 426. Dana 241. ἀποθάνῃ καὶ καταλίπῃ: coincident action: Note T. Since ἀποθνῄσκων in v. 20

cannot have its usual meaning ("a-dying; about to die"), the perfectivizing prepos. ἀπό gives to the durative pres. an aoristic nuance; Brugmann 546; Smyth 1853; Moulton 114.

21–27. ἀπέθανεν μὴ καταλιπών: coincident; Note T; Moulton 132 ff. Gild. 345. ὅταν ἀναστῶσιν after ἐν τῇ ἀναστήσει is not otiose. *Memoirs* 168. See on 4, 31, ὅταν σπαρῇ, and Notes C and Q. "At the rising" is a date; ὅταν ἀναστῶσιν adds a personal touch: "when these people rise again." οὐκ ἔστιν Θεός: is Θεός subject or predicate?

XII, 28–40. THE FIRST COMMANDMENT. "SON OF DAVID"
(Mt. 22, 34–46. Lk. 20, 39–47; 10, 25–28)

28 ff. Note the clever use of three participial clauses before the main verb: προσελθών, ἀκούσας, εἰδώς, ἐπηρώτησεν. Compare the Latin rendering of the Vulgate. ποία: perhaps = τίς. Blass 298, 2. πάντων: neuter; not "of all commandments," but adverbially "of all." ἀγαπήσεις: imperative future. Smyth 1917. Note the idiomatic use of ἐξ; Note G. The heart is conceived as the *source* of love.

31 ff. δευτέρα αὕτη (not ἡ δευτέρα): "*the* following is *second* in importance." μείζων: lit.: "a greater commandment than these there is none." ἀπεκρίθη: Note L.; "had expressed himself." οὐκέτι: a relative term; see Note D. πῶς: is felt both with λέγουσιν and with ἐστίν. For πόθεν, see on 8, 4, and Note G, at end.

38 ff. βλέπετε has two objects; one, a prepositional phrase (ἀπό); the other, a number of accusatives. This is not slovenly writing. See Note Q; and cf. Isocrates *To Nic.* 30: εἶναι μὴ τὰς . . . γιγνομένας and ἀλλ' ὅταν. See note on 5, 16. κατ-εσθίοντες: this reminds classical readers of the suitors of Penelope, who ate and ate (ἐσθίοντες; present) until they had eaten *up* (κατά) the house of Odysseus. Moulton 114. For μακρὰ προσευχόμενοι, see *Memoirs* 169. See Joüon on 38 and 40 (θέλειν = *aimer*, a Semitism; as οἰκία = *les biens*).

XII, 41–44. THE WIDOW'S MITE
(Lk. 21, 1–4)

41 ff. ἐθεώρει: significant word and tense; Gild. 205; θεωρέω occurs in 16, 4; 15, 47; 15, 40; 12, 41; 5, 38; 5, 15; 3, 11. See note on 5, 15. Note the various tenses in which βάλλω is used in this section; there is no confusion here. ἐκ τῆς ὑστερήσεως ἔβαλεν: almost an Oxymoron. Smyth 3035. ἐκ: used for symmetry with ἐκ τοῦ περισσεύοντος; "in

spite of." ὅλον τὸν βίον: See Note C. The principle here implied was known to the ancient philosophers (Arist. *Nicom.* 4, 1, 19), but was not effective as a principle of life (Lagrange).

XIII, 1–37. THE GREAT ESCHATOLOGICAL DISCOURSE
(Mt. 24. Lk. 21, 5–36)

XIII. 1 ff. For evidences of "Markan Art" in this chapter, see *Memoirs* 57 ff. For βλέπεις in a question expressing wonder, cf. Eur. *Tro.* 611, τάδ᾽ εἰσορᾷς; For οὐ μή, see Smyth 1804. εἰς τὸ ὄρος: in the Koine εἰς and ἐν interchange somewhat. Blass 205; 218. Smyth 1659. ταῦτα seems to refer to the destruction of Jerusalem or of the Temple: Smyth 1240 ff. ταῦτα πάντα: a reference to the end of the world: Mt. 24, 3, συντελείας τοῦ αἰῶνος. Note πάντα: *this world* or *universe;* Latin: *omnia.* μέλλῃ: Gild. 272. *Memoirs* 169.

5 ff. ἤρξατο: *Memoirs* 169. Note I. ἐγώ εἰμι: excellent Greek; I am *he;* I am *it; it* is I. See on 6, 50. Cf. Xen. *Hell.* 1, 6, 28, ὅτι οἱ Ἀθηναῖοι εἶεν, "that *it* was the Athenians." Mk. 14, 62. ἀρχαί: predicate. εἰς μαρτύριον αὐτοῖς: see on 1, 44. V. 10 is probably a parenthesis (*Memoirs* 169), occasioned by the mention of βασιλέων. δεῖ, as often: *it is decreed.*

11 ff. ἄγωσιν: carry off into captivity; drag away forcibly. Common Gr.; Eur. *Tro.* 577, δεσπόται μ᾽ ἄγουσιν. οἱ λαλοῦντες: *the speakers;* Smyth 1152; 2052. ἔσεσθε μισούμενοι: Dana 203. μισούμενοι: an eyesore, an object of disgust. ὁ ὑπομείνας: Smyth 2052. ὁ ὑπομείνας w. εἰς τέλος: a clear case of complexive or resultative aorist. Smyth 1927; 1926. For the connotations of σώζω, see 3, 4; 5, 23; 5, 28; 5, 34; 6, 56; 8, 35; 10, 26; 10, 52; 13, 13; 13, 20; 15, 30; 15, 31; 16, 16.

14 ff. *Memoirs* 170. ἐστηκότα: either masc. sg., referring to some person, or nt. pl., referring to βδέλυγμα and ἐρήμωσις. The phrase ὅπου οὐ δεῖ avoids a direct reference to the Temple or to the Holy Land; so in 11, 30, ἐξ οὐρανοῦ, "from God." Note ἆραι in the sense of "to go and get"; cf. 6, 8 and 6, 29. ὁ εἰς τὸν ἀγρόν. Smyth 1659. Blass 205. τοιαύτη: superfluous after οἵα. ἣν ἔκτισεν: see Note C; so οὓς ἐξελέξατο, in v. 20. For the colometry of v. 19, see *Memoirs* 58.

20 ff. The aor. ἐσώθη ("would be saved") considers the "saving" as thing to be attained: would attain to salvation; σωθῆναι = τυχεῖν σωτηρίας. See Blass 360, 3. οὓς ἐξελέξατο: see on v. 19. μὴ πιστεύετε: pres. impv.; of resistance to temptation. Smyth 1841. Gild. 415. ἔσονται ἐκπίπτοντες: a majestic phrase, suited to the collapse of the universe. Smyth 1857. Dana 203. ἐρχόμενον: see on Mk. 1, 7, ἔρχεται.

27 ff. A difficult passage. Do not join ἀπ' ἄκρου γῆς directly with ἕως ἄκρου οὐρανοῦ. Colometry B, 6 on Pauses in reading. *Memoirs* 127. The two designations that go together are ἐκ τῶν τεσσάρων ἀνέμων and ἀπ' ἄκρου γῆς. Parallel Orientation: Note F. The prepositional phrase ἕως etc. complements ἐπισυνάξει. οὐρανοῦ: *atmosphere: air.* I Thess. 4, 17, ἐν νεφέλαις εἰς ἀέρα.

28 ff. τὴν παραβολήν: note the art.; Dana 146 ff. Smyth 1118. Either *"this* illustration" or "learn *the* illustration (lesson) *which* it conveys." γένηται: ingressive aor.; ἐκφύῃ: pres.; denoting the process of putting forth leaves. οὕτως καὶ ὑμεῖς γινώσκετε: "in a similar way you also may know." Note the vague ταῦτα, as in v. 4; see *Memoirs* on 13, 4, p. 169. The precise sense of γενεά is often doubtful; the word occurs in 8, 12; 8, 38; 9, 19; and 13, 30.

31–32. παρελεύσονται: *will* or *may* pass away? Will sky and earth actually pass away? Or is the sense: even if sky and earth (which seem indestructible) should pass away, yet my words will never fail to be true? See the commentators. For the modal future, see on 3, 28, ἀφεθήσεται. For the meaning of v. 32, see *Memoirs* 200. ὁ πατήρ: here, as contrasted with the Son of Man (that is, the Son of God), stands for the Blessed Trinity. *Memoirs* 188.

34. ὡς ἄνθρωπος: brachylogical; "it is as when. . ." By all means separate ἀφεὶς τὴν οἰκίαν αὐτοῦ by a pause from ἀπόδημος. See the rendering in *Memoirs* 128; and *Memoirs* 170. Not a case of tautology. For the need of pauseful reading, see Colometry B, 6. ἀπόδημος is, strictly, "a man away from home"; not "one going away." This man, regarded as away from home, *gave* orders to his slaves, *sc.* when he left home, ἀφεὶς = ὅτε ἀφῆκε. τὴν ἐξουσίαν: art.; Smyth 1120; each slave had *his* ἔργον and *his* corresponding ἐξουσία. καὶ before τῷ θυρωρῷ (who is already included in the general term τοῖς δούλοις) is probably adverbial, and particularizing; see on 1, 5, καί, and on 3, 16, καὶ ἐπέθηκεν. Note H.

35–37. ἔρχεται: Smyth 1881. For the cases in designations of time, Smyth 1444 ff.; 1539 ff.; 1582 ff. Blass 161 and 186; Dana 90, 4. μὴ εὕρῃ: Smyth 2223. λέγω, λέγω: I say; I mean.

XIV, 1–11. ANOINTING AT BETHANY
(Mt. 26, 1–16. Lk. 22, 1–6. Jn. 12, 1–8)

XIV. 1 ff. τὰ ἄζυμα: an explanation of τὸ πάσχα. Notes H and A. ἦν: *was to be.* Gild. 213. μή: *let it not be done;* if necessary, a verb governing μή is easily supplied. μὴ ἔσται: Smyth 2220; 2229. πιστικῆς: see

Joüon. ἦσαν ἀγανακτοῦντες: Is this a periphrastic use of the partic.? Dana 203. Smyth 1857. Gild. 191, 291. *Memoirs* 170, 171.

5 ff. ἠδύνατο: Gild. 363. The subj. of δοθῆναι is easily gathered from the context. Mk. 10, 21; 4, 25. *Memoirs* 54, 55; 171. ἔργον: often used in NT for a "work" as outward evidence of an interior state of mind. Hence qualified here by καλόν; not of physical, but of moral, beauty. Note the Asyndeton in our Lord's discourse. For the psychology of asyndeton, see Note A at the very end. After ὁ ἔσχεν ("she was able"; Smyth 2000 a) supply ποιῆσαι. Smyth 3017. Gerth 597.

8 ff. Mary's anointing was, in the providence of God, to take the place of (="to be as good as": εἰς. Dana 111) the regular (art.; Smyth 1120 e) embalmment; ἐνταφιασμός does not mean "burial"; see Zorell 445. προέλαβεν: used, quite naturally, w. infinitive. *She has anticipated the anointing of My Body*. (τὸ) μυρίσαι: object noun. Cf. Eur. *HF*. 535, πρόσθεν ἥρπασ' ἃ σὲ λέγειν ἐχρῆν. For προ-, *just in time*, see Pernot 205. *Memoirs* 171.

XIV, 12–25. LAST SUPPER
(Mt. 26, 17–29. Lk. 22, 7–22. Jn. 13, 21–26)

12 ff. ἔθυον: Smyth 1893 ff. θέλεις: Smyth 1806. ἐξῆλθον καὶ ἦλθον: note the circumstantial way of narrating, proper to eye-witnesses. Note Q. ὁ ἐσθίων μετ' ἐμοῦ: "*One* who eats with Me." Smyth 2052. Our Lord revealed the traitor neither here nor in v. 20. εἷς καὶ εἷς: followed by ἄλλος; see the rendering in *Memoirs* 130.

21 ff. ὑπάγει, like ἔρχεται, future; Smyth 1881; Blass 323, 3. ὁ ἄνθρωπος ἐκεῖνος, refers back, somewhat awkwardly, to τῷ ἀνθρώπῳ ἐκείνῳ. Havers compares Pl. *Apol*. 27, τὴν γραφὴν ταύτην, after ταῦτα. See Note Q. ἐσθιόντων: "supper" was still going on, or, before supper was over. τοῦτό ἐστιν: probably aoristic; "is here and now changed into"; "devient." Smyth 1853; and Note T. *Memoirs* 172 and 201.

24 ff. τῆς διαθήκης: descriptive genitive (common in NT; rare in classical Greek). Cf. Thuc. 3, 82, 7: ὅρκοι ξυναλλαγῆς, "oaths of reconcilement." So 1, 4, βάπτισμα μετανοίας. Dana 90. Brugmann 451. τὸ ἐκχυννόμενον: Smyth 1872 and 1879. ὑπὲρ πολλῶν: see 10, 45. The Eucharist is a Sacrifice. οὐκέτι οὐ μὴ πίω: Smyth 2754.

XIV, 26–52. GETHSEMANI
(Mt. 26, 30–58. Lk. 22, 31–55. Jn. 18, 1–18)

27 ff. σκανδαλισθήσεσθε: Note N. προάξω ὑμᾶς εἰς: for a rendering, see *Memoirs* 131; so again in 16, 7. For the poignancy of our Lord's

reply to Peter in v. 30, see *Memoirs* 54. Colometry B, 6. ἕως=ἕως ἄν; Blass 383. ἤρξατο: Note I. Jesus yielded deliberately to the feelings expressed by the two infinitives. περίλυπος: "My soul is sunk (περί) in sadness."

35 ff. ἔπιπτεν: *threw Himself down.* Descriptive impf.; Gild. 205. παρέλθη: passive; Smyth 1752; for the active, see παρένεγκε in v. 36: *spare* and *might be spared.* τί: for the relative; Koine Greek. Blass 298. ἔρχεται: *returns;* common Greek. ἵνα: of the purport or of the purpose of the prayer? See on 3, 12. Dana 220. Moulton 206 ff. εἰσέλθητε: Smyth 1752. τί ἀποκριθῶσιν: they had nothing to say *by way of excuse* or *in explanation* of their conduct. Note L. See 9, 5.

41 ff. For a rendering of 41, see *Memoirs* 133. τὸ λοιπόν: implies the notion of *continuing.* παραδίδοται: pres.; of the immediate future. Not so in 9, 31. κατεφίλησεν: perfectivizing prepos.; kissed Him *effusively.* Cf. 10, 16, κατευλόγει. ἀποκριθείς: Jesus "remonstrated with them." Note L. ἐξήλθατε: aor.; of what has just happened; Moulton 135. ἵνα: introducing an independent clause; as often. 5, 23; 12, 15. κρατοῦσιν: tendential pres. Dana 174. See Joüon's comment on εἷς τις νεανίσκος. Mark's reference to himself?

XIV, 53–72. PETER'S DENIAL OF CHRIST
(Mt. 26, 59–75. Lk. 22, 56–71. Jn. 18, 17–27)

53 ff. συνέρχονται: the sense is doubtful; some mss. omit αὐτῷ; see on 3, 20. πρὸς τὸ φῶς: just so in Arist. *Wasps* 772, ἡλιάσει πρὸς ἥλιον: "he will bask in the sun." οὐχ εὕρισκον: Gild. 216; Smyth 1896; they were of course "disappointed." Note Mark's editorial καί in joining the two statements of the witnesses. *Memoirs* 135 and 173 on 14, 58. οὐδέ: "and . . . again . . . not"; sc. as in verse 55. Mark notes the perplexity of Caiaphas: "And thus again their testimony did not agree." καταλύσω: modal, for δύναμαι καταλῦσαι (Mt. 26, 61). Note E. Smyth 1910 a.

60–61. εἰς μέσον: Joüon: "équivaut à 'devant' toute l'assemblée." The word μέσος does not always answer to our "midst"; cf. 3, 3; 6, 47; 7, 31; 9, 36. οὐκ ἀποκρίνῃ: perhaps modal in tone: *"can you not, will* you not, answer? Have you nothing to say?" Note E. See *AJPh.* 54 (1933), p. 52; Arist. *Plut.* 17, ἀποκρινόμενος οὐδὲ γρῦ, "He *will* not (refuses to) answer at all" (Peppler). "When the present indicative represents a durative act of the present that is continued into the future, then in association with the negative it may express resistance to pressure or refusal."

62–64. ὄψεσθε: uttered in a threatening tone; not so ὄψονται in 13, 26. See Moulton 150 ff. Smyth 1910 a; 1912. μετὰ τῶν νεφελῶν: elsewhere (13, 26) ἐν νεφέλαις. Smyth 1687 and 1691. ἠκούσατε: Moulton 135: "you have *just* heard; *you hear.*" τί ὑμῖν φαίνεται; like "quid vobis videtur?" A Latinism? See *JThSt.* 1920, p. 198 (Turner). κατέκριναν: "they decided" (ἔκριναν) "against Him" (κατά), saying "that He had incurred the penalty of" or "should be liable to" (ἔνοχον εἶναι) "death." Cf. Xen. *Cyrop.* 3, 1, 9, αὐτὸν καταδικάζειν σεαυτοῦ πάντα τὰ ἔσχατα παθεῖν.

65 ff. ἤρξαντο: See Note I. For Peter's denial of Christ, see *Memoirs* 174. Does Peter's reply in v. 68 reflect mental agitation? ἡ παιδίσκη: *The* servant-girl *there;* Smyth 1120; hence, *the* door-keeper; not the same woman as μία in v. 66. πάλιν: *in turn;* see on Mk. 15, 13. ἤρξατο πάλιν λέγειν: "she in turn busied herself, saying," Note I.

70–71. πάλν: in two different senses (always like Latin *rursus*. Souter). ἤρξατο ἀναθεματίζειν: Note I. Peter "burst out cursing"; almost, "launched forth" into a series of protestations. οὐκ οἶδα: may mean "I have nothing to do with" (Bauer). τὸν ἄνθρωπον τοῦτον: said of his Master and Lord!

72. τὸ ῥῆμα ὡς εἶπεν: colloquial; see Note Q. Cf. 1 Cor. 4, 17, τὰς ὁδούς—καθὼς διδάσκω. ἐπιβαλὼν ἔκλαιεν: "he *set to* and cried"; Moulton 131. The phrase ἐ.ἐ. means what Mark would generally express by saying ἤρξατο κλαίειν. Note I. See *M. Vocabulary*, p. 235. Joüon: "Le français 'il *éclata* en pleurs' exprime bien que le commencement de l'action est subit et *violent.*" No doubt, Peter "broke into sobs and tears."

XV, 1–20. JESUS BEFORE PILATE

(Mt. 27, 1–2; 11–31. Lk. 22, 66; 23, 1–25. Jn. 18, 28—19, 16)

XV. 1 ff. καί before ὅλον: *that is to say,* the whole Sanhedrin. 1, 5; 9, 35; Note H. συμβούλιον: see Joüon. ὁ βασιλεύς: Smyth 1152. σὺ λέγεις: Mt. has εἶπας; both tenses are correct. Smyth 1939: πῶς ἔλεξας, ὅπως λέγεις. Smyth 1887. Blass 441, 3: σύ seems to be emphatic (You said it; I should not have said it, had I not been asked). οὐκ ἀποκρίνῃ: modal? See on 14, 60. Note E. ἴδε: *listen* to all the charges; ἴδε, not ἰδέ. Blass 364, 2.

6 ff. αὐτοῖς: to the people; cf. 1, 44, εἰς μαρτύριον αὐτοῖς; note the dative: "as a favor to them"; see *Memoirs* 174, on 15, 9. ἠτοῦντο: see on 6, 22. ἀναβοήσας: some mss. read ἀναβάς. For ἤρξατο, see Note I. ἀπεκρίθη: Pilate *argued* or *expostulated* with them; Note L. πάλιν in v. 13: a reference to ἀναβοήσας in v. 8; they shouted *again;* they raised *another* shout; or: they shouted *back*. The adverb qualifies ἔκραξαν, but not what follows.

14 ff. γάρ: well, what . . . ? Smyth 2805. τὸ ἱκανὸν ποιῆσαι: claimed as a Latinism, *satis facere*. Blass 5. Moulton 20. παρέδωκεν: does not here denote that final "surrender" of Jesus into the hands of the Jews (as in John), but the "handing Him over" to the soldiery for custody; Zorell. ἵνα σταυρωθῇ may go closely w. φραγελλώσας; a kind of scourging inflicted w. a view to crucifixion. αὐλή: see Joüon.

XV, 21–41. THE CRUCIFIXION
(Mt. 27, 32–56. Lk. 23, 26–49. Jn. 19, 17–30)

23 ff. ἐδίδουν: sharply intersected by οὐκ ἔλαβεν; see on 1, 16. Note Mt.'s more precise statement: γευσάμενος οὐκ ἠθέλησεν πιεῖν; 27, 34. τίς τί: Smyth 2646. ὥρα τρίτη καί: Parataxis, Note A. The fact of the Crucifixion was already mentioned in 24; hence, the tone here rests on the hour of the Crucifixion; *when*. The precise force of ὥρα τρίτη is disputed; see Lagrange.

29 ff. ὁ καταλύων: vocative. Dana 84. Blass 147. Moulton 70. Smyth 1288. σῶσον, καταβάς: coincident aorists. Note T. Gild. 345. ἐγένετο: fell over the whole land *and lasted;* Smyth 3017; Gerth 597; Brachylogy is widely used in Gr. literature. ἐπί w. acc., of motion toward. ἐγκατέλιπες: Moulton 135; may be rendered by the present. *Memoirs* 174. For ἄφετε, and on Mark's workmanship, see *Memoirs* 175. αἵ in v. 41 refers only to the three women named in 40. *Memoirs* on 3, 31, p. 191.

XV, 42–47. THE BURIAL OF JESUS
(Mt. 27, 57–61. Lk. 23, 50–55. Jn. 19, 38–42)

42 ff. καὶ αὐτός: *ipse quoque*, sc. like the other pious persons mentioned just before. ἦν προσδεχόμενος: true periphrastic use of the partic. Dana 203. Smyth 1857. τολμήσας: ingressive aor., "boldly, courageously." Smyth 1924. ᾐτήσατο: Moulton 160. Smyth 1719. τέθνηκεν, ἀπέθανεν: Gild. 227. For ἐθεώρουν, see on 12, 41 and 5, 15. "They

noted carefully." See Colometry, B 8. Note the magnificent rhythm in the closing verse:

$$\underset{\smile\smile}{\dot{\epsilon}\theta\dot{\epsilon}\acute{\omega}\rho\text{ovv}} \underset{-}{\pi\text{o}\hat{v}} \underset{\smile}{\tau\dot{\epsilon}\theta}\underset{-}{\epsilon\iota\tau\alpha\iota}.$$

XVI, 1–8. THE RESURRECTION

(Mt. 28, 1–8. Lk. 24, 1–12. Jn. 20, 1–10)

XVI. 1–2. λίαν πρωΐ: very vague; technically "it was still night," Jn. 20, 1. The ὄρθρος began about the cockcrow, 2:30 A.M., and lasted until the ἕως appeared; half an hour later or so, the ἥλιος "rose." ἔρχονται they set out *and arrived;* see on 5, 3, ἔγειρε, and 15, 33, ἐγένετο. Cf. Xen. *Hell.* 2, 3, 13, ἐλθεῖν ἕως καταστήσαιντο: "to come [*and stay*] until they had established." Vergil *Aeneid* 6, 13, *subeunt* lucos atque tecta: they *enter* the grove and [*approach*] the house; see Norden. The women left the house ὄρθρου βαθέως (Lk. 24, 1), when the ὄρθρος was in its *last* stages, hence, just before the ἕως began; this ἕως lasts in Palestine about half an hour; so when the sun peeped over the hills, the women arrived at the tomb. Cf. Pl. *Crito* 43 a, ὄρθρος βαθύς: correctly rendered by Fowler, "just before dawn." See Appendix III.

3 ff. ἔλεγον: on their journey "they had been saying." Cf. 4, 41, ἔλεγον. Smyth 1906. Gild. 224. ἀνα-βλέψασαι: ἀνά, "w. eyes raised"; wonderingly. ἀποκεκύλισται: significant pf.; significant for those pious women; one can hear their sigh of relief, when one appreciates the ft.: ἀποκυλίσει! A sentence introduced by γάρ does not necessarily account for a statement immediately preceding; here the reference is to ἔλεγον πρὸς ἑαυτάς.

6 ff. See Colometry, B 6. καὶ τῷ Πέτρῳ, already included in τοῖς μαθηταῖς; hence, "and in particular to Peter." See on 3, 16; 1, 5. Particularizing καί: Note H. Lk. 23, 27, πλῆθος καί "and, especially," γυναῖκες. προάγει: fut.; Smyth 1879. 14, 21 ὑπάγει. Note the implication: He goes before you= "Go to G. to meet Him." Verse 8 is not "a ragged edge" (Plummer). Isocr. *To Dem.* closes section 31 with: παροξυντικὸν γάρ. See *Memoirs* 8 and 9. Note that προάγει ὑμᾶς, in this context, implies a command: Go to Galilee; He expects to see you there.

XVI, 9–13. APPARITIONS OF JESUS

(Lk. 24, 13–15)

9–20. Much has been written on the authorship of the closing verses of this Gospel. The stylistic differences between this ending and the

rest of the Gospel are evident, but hardly weighty enough to disprove
Marcan authorship. *Memoirs* pp. 8, 9. See the commentators, esp.
Knabenbauer and Lagrange. Whoever may be the author of vv. 9–20,
their canonicity is certain.

9–13. Note ζῇ and ἐθεάθη: Mark does not confuse his tenses. "He
was seen; He *is* alive." ἐγηγερμένον: pf.; contrast ἠγέρθη in v. 6. Gild.
227. See *Memoirs* on 16, 9 (πρῶτον) and 16, 13; pp. 175, 176.

XVI, 14–20. THE SENDING OF THE APOSTLES. THE ASCENSION
(Mt. 28, 18–20. Lk. 24, 36–49. Jn. 20, 19–23)

15 ff. εἰς may be joined to πορευθέντες or to κηρύξατε. For πάσῃ τῇ
κτίσει, see Joüon. σημεῖα: predicate; "in the way of signs." τοῖς
πιστεύσασιν: the plural does not *necessarily* mean that each individual
Christian would work those signs; nor does the future *necessarily* imply
that signs would be wrought at all times. *Memoirs* 176. Note D. As a
matter of fact, signs are being wrought down to this day.

19–20. *Memoirs* 176. The Ascension took place 40 days after the
Resurrection. ἀνελήφθη: need not mean *He was taken up;* perhaps,
merely, *He rose.* Smyth 815. Christ rose by His own power, as well
as by the power of the Father. ἐκάθισεν: ingressive aor.; *took His seat.*
See on 2, 6, καθήμενοι. The signs which the Apostles work accompany
them: παρ-ακολουθήσει; they are also witnesses to the truth of their
preaching: hence, ἐπ-ακολουθούντων, in its technical sense. See *M. Vocabulary;* "ratify"; Bauer. For the force of ἐπί, cf. Pl. *Erastae* 134,
ἐπ-εγέλασαν, "they laughed *their approval.*" For the sonorous ending
of the Gospel, see Colometry, B. 8. For τῶν before σημείων, see Smyth
1120 b; cf. v. 17.

Χρῶ τοῖς εἰρημένοις, ἢ ζήτει βελτίω τούτων.

— Isocrates, *To Nicocles,* 38

Καὶ μὴ θαύμαζε, εἰ πολλὰ τῶν λεγομένων ἐστὶν ἃ καὶ σὺ γιγνώσκεις.

— Isocrates, *To Nicocles,* 40

LIST OF WORDS

(See *Prefatory Note*, pp. 131 ff; and, *Note S*, pp. 173 ff.)

A

ἀββᾶ (Aramaic), voc., *father.*

'Αβιάθαρ (indecl.) *Abiathar.*

'Αβραάμ (indecl.) *Abraham.*

ἀγαθοποιέω *do what is good.*

ἀγαθός, ή, όν *good,* in the broadest sense.

ἀγανακτέω *am indignant.*

ἀγαπάω *love;* perhaps *caress;* Bauer 7.

ἀγαπητός, ή, όν *beloved;* also *only=* μονογενής; 1¹¹; 9⁷; 12⁶.

ἀγγαρεύω *press into service, force.*

ἄγγελος, ου, ὁ *angel; messenger.*

ἀγέλη, ης, ἡ *herd.*

ἅγιος, α, ον *sacred, holy.*

ἄγναφος, ον (cloth) *not yet dressed; un-shrunken.*

ἀγνοέω *do not grasp.*

ἀγορά, ᾶς, ἡ *market-place; public place, street; market-goods, provisions.*

ἀγοράζω *buy.*

ἀγρεύω *catch, trap, ensnare.*

ἄγριος, α, ον *wild.*

ἀγρός, οῦ, ὁ *field; farm;* pl. *countryside.*

ἀγρυπνέω *am awake, am careful.*

ἄγω, tr., *bring; carry off;* intr., *go, de-part.*

ἀδελφή, ῆς, ἡ *sister; Memoirs* 191.

ἀδελφός, οῦ, ὁ *brother; Memoirs* 191; Moulton-M., 9.

ἀδημονέω *am distressed, bewildered.*

ἀδύνατος, ον *impossible.*

ἀεί *always.*

ἄζυμος, ον *unleavened;* τὰ ἄ., *Feast of the Unleavened Bread.*

ἀθετέω *slight, disappoint; nullify.*

αἷμα, ατος, τό *blood.*

αἴρω *lift, take up* (and *bear*); *go and get; lift and remove. Memoirs* 158, on 6⁸.

αἰτέω *ask, beg, demand;* Moulton 160.

αἰτία, ας, ἡ *cause; guilt.*

αἰών, ῶνος, ὁ *life; age, long space of time; eternity; world* = Latin *saeculum.*

αἰώνιος, ον *everlasting, eternal.*

ἀκάθαρτος, ον *unclean.*

ἄκανθα, ης, ἡ *thorn.*

ἀκάνθινος, η, ον *made of thorns.*

ἄκαρπος, ον *fruitless.*

ἀκοή, ῆς, ἡ *fame; rumor; ear.*

ἀκολουθέω *follow.*

ἀκούω *hear, listen; heed; understand.*

ἀκρίς, ίδος, ἡ *locust.*

ἄκρον, ου, τό *edge, end, extremity; highest* or *farthest point.*

ἀκυρόω *render worthless.*

ἀλάβαστρος, ου, ὁ and ἡ; τὸ ἀλάβαστρον; *alabaster flask; Memoirs* 171.

ἀλαλάζω *wail.*

ἄλαλος, ον *speechless.*

ἅλας, ατος, τό *salt.*

ἁλεεύς, έως, ὁ *fisherman.*

ἀλείφω *anoint.*

ἀλεκτοροφωνία, ας, ἡ *cockcrow.*

ἀλέκτωρ, ορος, ὁ *cock.*

'Αλέξανδρος, ου, ὁ *Alexander.*

ἀλήθεια, ας, ἡ *truth;* ἐπ' ἀληθείας *truth-fully.*

ἀληθής, ές *truthful.*

ἀληθῶς *truly, really; of course; certainly.*

ἀλίζω *salt, season.*

ἀλλά *but; mark!* Dana 211; Smyth 2775. Joüon on 9, 13.

ἀλλαχοῦ *elsewhere* =ἀλλαχόσε.

ἀλλήλων *one another, each other; among themselves.* Smyth 1277.

ἄλλος, η, ον *other; different; besides.* Smyth 1272.

ἅλς, ἁλός, ὁ *salt.*

ἅλυσις, εως, ἡ *chain; manacle.*

'Αλφαῖος, ου, ὁ *Alpheus.*

ἁμάρτημα, ατος, τό *sin, fault.*

ἁμαρτία, ας, ἡ *sin.*

ἁμαρτωλός, οῦ, ὁ *sinner; sinful.*

ἀμήν (Hebrew) *verily, truly;* ἀμὴν λέγω ὑμῖν: *Memoirs* 154. Dana 227.

ἄμπελος, ου, ἡ *vine.*

ἀμπελών, ῶνος, ὁ *vineyard.*

ἀμφιβάλλω *cast the net; fish.*

ἄμφοδον, ου, τό *street.*

ἄν; Smyth 1761; Dana 228; ὃς ἄν *whoever.*

ἀνά *up; through;* ἀνὰ ἑκατόν *in groups of one hundred each.* Dana 105. Smyth 1682.

ἀναβαίνω *come up, ascend, go up; sprout.*

ἀναβλέπω *look up; receive (recover) sight.*

ἀναβοάω *cry out; raise a shout.*

ἀνάγαιον, ου, τό *upper room.*

ἀναγινώσκω *read.*

ἀναγκάζω *force, compel.*

ἀναθεματίζω *declare anathema; curse.*

ἀνάκειμαι *recline.*

ἀνακλίνω *make recline.*

ἀνακράζω *cry out, scream.*

ἀναλαμβάνω *take up;* pass. *go up.*

ἄναλος, ον *saltless.*

ἀναμιμνήσκω *remind;* pass. *remember.*

ἀναπαύω *cause to rest;* pass. *take a rest*

ἀναπηδάω *leap up.*

ἀναπίπτω *lie down, recline.*

ἀνασείω *stir up.*

ἀνάστασις, εως, ἡ *resurrection.*

ἀναστενάζω *groan; sigh.*

ἀναστῆναι, aor. to ἀνίσταμαι.

ἀνατέλλω *go up, rise..*

ἀναφέρω *take* or *lead up.*

ἀναχωρέω *withdraw.*

Ἀνδρέας, ου, ὁ *Andrew.*

ἀνέβην, aor. to ἀναβαίνω.

ἀνέβλεψα, aor. to ἀναβλέπω.

ἀνεβόησα, aor. to ἀναβοάω.

ἀνέγνων, aor. to ἀναγινώσκω.

ἀνέκραξα, aor. to ἀνακράζω.

ἀνελήφθην, aor. pass. to ἀναλαμβάνω.

ἀνεμνήσθην, aor. to ἀναμιμνήσκομαι.

ἄνεμος, ου, ὁ *wind*

ἀνέξομαι, ft. to ἀνέχομαι.

ἀνέπεσα, ἀνέπεσον, aor. to ἀναπίπτω.

ἀνέσεισα, aor. to ἀνασείω.

ἀνεστέναξα, aor. to ἀναστενάζω.

ἀνέστην, aor. to ἀνίσταμαι.

ἀνέτειλα, aor. to ἀνατέλλω.

ἀνέχομαι *bear with.*

ἀνήρ, ἀνδρός, ὁ *man; husband.*

ἄνθρωπος, ου, ὁ *human being; man.*

ἄνιπτος, ον *unwashed.*

ἀνίσταμαι *rise.*

ἄνομος, ον *lawless.*

ἀντάλλαγμα, ατος, τό "what is given either in order to keep or to acquire anything" (Thayer); *exchange.*

ἀντί *for; in behalf of.* Dana 106. Smyth 1683.

ἄνωθεν *from above.*

ἀπαγγέλλω *bring news, report.*

ἀπάγω *lead* or *take away.*

ἀπα΄ρω *take away;* pass. *depart.*

ἁπαλός, ή, όν *tender.*

ἀπαντάω *meet.*

ἀπαρνέομια *deny, disown; renounce.*

ἅπας, ασα, αν *all, whole, entire.*

ἀπάτη, ης, ἡ *deceitfulness, glamour.*

ἀπεκατεστάθην, aor. pass. to ἀποκαθιστάνω.

ἀπεκτάνθην, aor. pass. to ἀποκτείνω.

ἀπέρχομαι *go away, come away.*

ἀπέχω *am far away;* ἀπέχει intr. *it is enough; the time is up.* Joüon on 14, 41.

ἀπήγγειλα, aor. to ἀπαγγέλλω.

ἀπήνεγκα, aor. to ἀποφέρω.

ἀπήρθην, aor. pass. to ἀπαίρω.

ἀπηρνησάμην, aor. to ἀπαρνέομαι.

ἀπιστέω *disbelieve.*

ἀπιστία, ας, ἡ *unbelief.*

ἄπιστος, ον *unbelieving.*

ἀπό *from, off;* Dana 108; Smyth 1684; *at a distance from;* Gerth 430, 1.

ἀποβάλλω *throw off.*

ἀποδημέω *am abroad.*

ἀπόδημος, ον *away from home; travelling.*

ἀποδίδωμι *give back; pay.*

ἀποδοκιμάζω *reject.*

ἀποθνήσκω *die.*

ἀποκαθιστάνω *restore.*

ἀποκεφαλίζω *behead.*

ἀποκόπτω *cut off.*

ἀποκρίνομαι *answer, reply;* see Note L.

ἀπόκρυφος, ον *hidden, secret.*

ἀποκτείνω *kill.*
ἀποκτέννω; see ἀποκτείνω.
ἀποκτενῶ, ft. to ἀποκτείνω.
ἀποκυλίω *roll away.*
ἀπολαμβάνω *take aside.*
ἀπόλλυμι *destroy, kill; lose; mid. perish; die; am lost.*
ἀπολοῦμαι, ft. to ἀπόλλυμαι.
ἀπολύω *set free; dismiss; divorce.*
ἀποπλανάω *lead astray.*
ἀπορέω *have qualms of conscience.*
ἀποστάσιον, ου, τό *divorce.*
ἀποστεγάζω *unroof.*
ἀποστέλλω *send away* or *forth; apply.*
ἀποστερέω *defraud.*
ἀπόστολος, ου, ὁ *apostle.*
ἀποτάσσομαι *bid farewell.*
ἀποφέρω *take* or *lead away.*
ἅπτομαι *touch, lay hold of.*
ἀπώλεια, ας, ἡ *loss, waste.*
ἄρα, inferential; *then, therefore; under the circumstances; really.* Dana 212. Smyth 2787.
ἀργύριον, ου, τό *silver; money.*
ἀρέσκω *please.*
ἀρθήσομαι, ft. pass. to αἴρω.
Ἀριμαθαία, ας, ἡ *Arimathia.*
ἀριστερός, ά, όν *left.*
ἀρνέομαι *deny.*
ἄρρωστος, ον *weak; ailing.*
ἄρσην, εν *male.*
ἄρτος, ου, ὁ *loaf of bread; food; meal.*
ἀρτύω *season, make savory.*
ἀρχή, ῆς, ἡ *beginning; summary.*
ἀρχιερεύς, έως, ὁ *high priest.*
ἀρχισυνάγωγος, ου, ὁ *ruler* or *official of the synagogue.*
ἄρχω *rule;* mid. *set myself to do, set about doing;* see Note I.
ἄρχων, οντος, ὁ *prince; ruler.*
ἀρῶ, ft. to αἴρω.
ἄρωμα, ατος, τό *spice.*
ἄσβεστος, ον *unquenchable.*
ἀσέλγεια, ας, ἡ *lewdness.*
ἀσθενέω *am sick.*
ἀσθενής, ές *weak.*
ἀσκός, οῦ, ὁ *wine skin; bottle.*
ἀσπάζομαι *greet; salute.*

ἀσπασμός, οῦ, ὁ *greeting.*
ἀστήρ, έρος, ὁ *star.*
ἀσύνετος *without discernment.*
ἀσφαλῶς *safely; carefully.*
ἀτιμάζω *dishonor.*
ἄτιμος, ον *unhonored.*
αὐλή, ῆς, ἡ *court yard* = *praetorium.* Joüon on Mt. 26³.
αὐξάνω *cause to grow.*
αὐτόματος, ον *by an inward force.*
αὐτός, ή, όν *self.* Smyth 1204; Dana 137.
αὐτοῦ, etc., = ἑαυτοῦ.
ἀφαιρέω *cut off.*
ἀφεδρών, ῶνος, ὁ *privy; sink; drain.*
ἀφεθήσομαι, ft. pass. to ἀφίημι.
ἀφεῖλον, aor. to ἀφαιρέω.
ἄφεσις, εως, ἡ *remission.*
ἀφίημι *send away; leave, quit; allow, let; remit.*
ἀφίω = ἀφίημι.
ἀφρίζω *foam.*
ἀφροσύνη, ης, ἡ *folly.* Joüon on 7, 22.
ἀχειροποίητος, ον *not made with hands.*

B

βάθος, ους, τό *depth.*
βάλλω *put, place; throw.*
βαπτίζω *dip; drench; wash; baptize.*
βάπτισμα, ατος, τό *baptism; flood.* Memoirs 166, on 10³⁸.
βαπτισμός, οῦ, ὁ *washing.*
βαπτιστής, οῦ, ὁ *baptist.*
Βαραββᾶς acc. ᾶν, ὁ *Barabbas.*
Βαρθολομαῖος, ου, ὁ *Bartholomew.*
Βαρτιμαῖος, ου, ὁ *Bartimaeus.*
βασανίζω *torment.*
βασιλεία, ας, ἡ *dominion, rule, sway; royalty; kingdom;* Memoirs 148, on 1¹⁵.
βασιλεύς, έως, ὁ *king.*
βαστάζω *carry, bear.*
βάτος, ου, ἡ *thorn-bush.*
βδέλυγμα, ατος, τό *abomination; horror.* Memoirs 170, on 13¹⁴.
βεβαιόω *confirm; seal.*
Βεελζεβούλ, indecl.; *Beelzebul.* Memoirs 153, on 3²².
Βηθανία, ας, ἡ *Bethany.*
Βηθσαϊδά *Bethsaida.*

Βηθφαγή *Bethphage.*

βιβλίον, ου, τό *bill (of divorce).*

βίβλος, ου, ἡ *book.*

βίος, ου, ὁ *livelihood; life.*

βλάπτω *hurt.*

βλαστάω *sprout.*

βλασφημέω *blaspheme; use abusive language.*

βλασφημία, ας, ἡ *blasphemy; abusive language.*

βλέπω, *look, see; take heed; beware of, guard against.*

Βοανηργές *Boanerges, sons of thunder.* Joüon on 3, 17.

βοάω *call; cry.*

βοηθέω *bring help (for* or *against); cure, remedy.*

βόσκω *feed; tend.*

βουλευτής, οῦ, ὁ *councillor.*

βούλομαι *wish, want.* Bauer 553. Blass 101.

βροντή, ῆς, ἡ *thunder.*

βρῶμα, ατος, τό *food.*

Γ

Γαδαρηνός, οῦ, ὁ *a Gadarene;* inhabitant of Gadara in the Decapolis.

γαζοφυλάκιον, ου, τό *treasury (chest).*

γαλήνη, ης, ἡ *calm.*

Γαλιλαία, ας, ἡ *Galilee.* Γαλιλαῖος, ου, ὁ *Galilean.*

γαμέω *marry;* γαμίζω *give* a daughter *in marriage.*

γάρ. Smyth 2803. Dana 213.

γαστήρ, τρός, ἡ *belly.*

γέεννα, νης, ἡ (Aramaic); *gehenna; hell.*

Γεθσημανεί garden of *Gethsemani.*

γεμίζω *fill; swamp.*

γενεά, ᾶς, ἡ, *race; set of people; generation.*

γενέσια, ων, τά *birthday celebration.*

γένημα, ατος, τό *fruit.*

γεννάω *beget; bear.*

Γεννησαρέτ Lake of *Gennesaret.*

γένος, ους, τό *birth; kind; race, nationality.*

γεύομαι *taste.*

γεωργός, οῦ, ὁ *husbandman; tenant; farmer.*

γῆ, γῆς, ἡ *earth; soil; land; region.*

γίνομαι *become; am born; appear; come to pass, happen.*

γινώσκω *learn to know; understand; feel, become aware.*

γλῶσσα, ης, ἡ *tongue.*

γναφεύς, έως, ὁ *fuller.*

Γολγοθᾶ *Golgotha.*

γονεύς, έως, ὁ *parent.*

γόνυ, ατος, τό *knee.*

γονυπετέω *kneel.*

γραμματεύς, έως, ὁ *Scribe.* Memoirs 149, on 1²².

γραφή, ῆς, ἡ *Scripture (text).*

γράφω *write; draw up.*

γρηγορέω *am awake.*

γυμνός, ή, όν *lightly clad; bare.*

γυνή, αικός, ἡ *woman; wife.*

γωνία, ας, ἡ *corner.*

Δ

δαιμονίζομαι *am possessed by a demon.*

δαιμόνιον, ου, τό *demon; evil spirit.*

δάκρυον, ου, τό *tear.*

δάκτυλος, ου, ὁ *finger.*

Δαλμανουθά *Dalmanutha.*

δαμάζω *tame.*

δαπανάω *spend.*

δαρήσομαι, ft. pass. to δέρω.

Δαυίδ *David.*

δέ. Smyth 2834. Dana 214.

δεῖ *it is necessary* or *decreed; must; ought.*

δείκνυμι *show.*

δειλός, ή, όν *timid, cowardly.*

δεῖπνον, ου, τό *meal; banquet.*

δέκα *ten.*

Δεκάπολις, εως, ἡ *the Decapolis,* a group of ten cities east of the Sea of Galilee.

δένδρον, ου, τό *tree.*

δεξιός, ά, όν *right;* τὰ δεξιά *the right side.*

δέρω *flay; beat.*

δερμάτινος, η, ον *leathern.*

δέσμιος, ου, ὁ *prisoner; bound in chains.*

δεσμός, οῦ, ὁ *bond; impediment.*

δεῦρο *hither;* impv. *come here.*

δεῦτε pl. of δεῦρο.

δεύτερος, α, ον *second;* ἐκ δευτέρου *for the second time.*

δέχομαι receive, welcome.

δέω bind, chain.

δηνάριον, ου, τό denarius, a Roman coin worth about 20 cents, but with a purchasing power much greater than that.

διά, w. gen., through; after the lapse of; by way of; across; w. acc., on account of; for the sake of. Dana 109. Smyth 1685.

διαβλέπω see through the mist on my eyes; see clearly.

διαγίνομαι pass; elapse.

διαθήκη, ης, ἡ covenant; last will and testament.

διακονέω wait on.

διάκονος, ου, ὁ servant.

διακόσιοι, αι, a two hundred.

διακρίνομαι doubt, waver.

διαλέγομαι converse.

διαλογίζομαι debate, reason, discuss; am puzzled.

διαλογισμός, οῦ, ὁ reasoning, thought, purpose.

διαμερίζομαι divide (among themselves).

διάνοια, ας, ἡ mind.

διανοίγω open.

διανοίχθητι, impv. aor. pass. of διανοίγω.

διαπαντός continually.

διαπεράω cross over.

διαρπάζω plunder.

διαρρήσσω tear.

διασκορπίζω scatter.

διασπάω tear asunder.

διαστέλλομαι charge, admonish, order.

διατί why?

διαφέρω carry across.

διαφημίζω circulate, spread.

διδασκαλία, ας, ἡ teaching.

διδάσκαλος, ου, ὁ teacher.

διδάσκω teach, instruct.

διδαχή, ῆς, ἡ teaching, instruction.

δίδωμι offer; give.

διεγείρω wake up; pass. raise myself to full height.

διέρχομαι go or cross over; pass through.

διηγέομαι tell in detail.

διήνεγκον, aor. to διαφέρω.

διηνοίχθην, aor. pass. to διανοίγω.

δίκαιος, α, ον just; good.

δίκτυον, ου, τό net.

δίς twice.

δισχίλιοι two thousand.

διωγμός, οῦ, ὁ persecution.

δοκέω fancy; οἱ δοκοῦντες the distinguished (rulers).

δόλος, ου, ὁ guile.

δόξα, ης, ἡ glory.

δοξάζω praise, extol.

δοῦλος, ου, ὁ slave; servant.

δρέπανον, ου, τό sickle; reapers (?).

δύναμαι have power, can, am able; 10^{38} am ready.

δύναμις, εως, ἡ power; might; miraculous deed.

δυνατός, ή, όν possible

δύνω go down.

δύο two.

δύσκολος, ον difficult; δυσκόλως w. difficulty.

δώδεκα twelve.

δῶμα, ατος, τό house.

δωρέομαι donate, grant.

δῶρον, ου, τό gift.

E

ἔα ah, ha!

ἐάν if; when; = generalizing ἄν, ever. Smyth 2323. Dana 228; 216.

ἑαυτῶν, οἷς, οὕς refl. pron. of the three persons. Smyth 329; 1218. Dana 140.

ἐγγίζω come near.

ἐγγύς near; at hand.

ἐγείρω raise up; arouse; pass. rise; wake up; ἔγειρε, rise!

ἐγήγερμαι, pf. pass. to ἐγείρω.

ἐγκαταλείπω abandon.

ἐγώ I.

ἔθνος, ους, τό nation, race; pl. the Gentiles.

εἰ if. 8^{12} = assuredly not (Hebraism?); εἰ δὲ μή otherwise. Smyth 2346. Dana 217.

εἶδον, aor. to ὁράω.

εἰκών, όνος, ἡ image; head on a coin.

εἰμί am.

εἶπα, εἶπον, aor. to λέγω, etc.

εἰρηνεύω *am at peace.*

εἰρήνη, ης, ἡ *peace.*

εἰς *into, in; toward, for; as good as;* often
= ἐν. Dana 111. Smyth 1686.

εἷς, μία, ἕν *one;* εἷς κατὰ εἷς: see *Memoirs*
130, on 14, 19.

εἰσέρχομαι *go* or *come into; call upon.*

εἰσπορεύομαι *enter; creep in.*

εἶτα *then, thereafter.*

ἐκ, ἐξ *out of; from;* Smyth 1688. Dana
110.

ἕκαστος, η, ον *each; every.*

ἑκατόν *one hundred.*

ἑκατονταπλασίων, ονος, *hundredfold.*

ἐκβάλλω *put out; throw out; drive out;
prompt* one *to do.*

ἐκδίδομαι *let out.*

ἐκδύω *strip.*

ἐκεῖ *there; thither.* Bauer 371.

ἐκεῖθεν *from there.*

ἐκεῖνος, η, ο *that; ille.* Smyth 1257.

ἐκθαμβέομαι *am frightened* or *astounded.*

ἐκθαυμάζω *wonder greatly.*

ἐκλέγομαι *select, choose.*

ἐκλεκτός, ή, όν *elect.*

ἐκλύομαι *faint, break down.*

ἐκπερισσῶς, *beyond all bounds.*

ἐκπεσοῦμαι, ft. to ἐκπίπτω.

ἐκπίπτω, *fall down from.*

ἐκπλήσσομαι, *am struck* (w. fear or joy).
Note M.

ἐκπνέω *breathe my last.*

ἐκπορεύομαι *go out; journey forth* or *along*
(10⁴⁶).

ἔκστασις, εως, ἡ *bewilderment: panic.*

ἐκτείνω *stretch out.*

ἐκτινάσσω *shake off.*

ἕκτος, η, ον *sixth.*

ἐκφέρω *lead out.*

ἔκφοβος *terrified.*

ἐκφύω *put forth* (leaves).

ἐκχύννομαι *am poured out.*

ἐλαία, ας, ἡ *olive.*

ἔλαιον, ου, τό *olive oil.*

ἐλαύνω *row.*

ἐλεέω *pity.*

Ἑλληνίς, ίδος, ἡ *a Greek (heathen) woman.*

ἐλωΐ (Aramaic), *my God!*

ἐμβαίνω *go into; embark.*

ἐμβάπτομαι *dip (my hand).*

ἐμβλέπω *look steadily at.*

ἐμβριμάομαι *express indignation.*

ἐμός, ή, όν *mine.*

ἐμπαίζω *mock; speak jestingly.*

ἔμπροσθεν *before.*

ἐμπτύω *spit at.*

ἐν *in.* Smyth 1687. Dana 112.

ἐναγκαλίζομαι *embrace.*

ἐναντίον *before.*

ἐναντίος, α, ον *contrary;* ἐξ ἐναντίας *facing.*

ἔνατος, η, ον *ninth.*

ἕνδεκα *eleven.*

ἐνδιδύσκω *put on.*

ἐνδύω *put on.*

ἐνειλέω *wrap up.*

ἕνεκα, ἕνεκεν *on account of.*

ἐνεργέω *am operative.*

ἐνέχω *have a grudge.*

ἔννυχα *in the night.*

ἔνοχος, ον *guilty; deserving of.*

ἔνταλμα, ατος, τό *commandment.*

ἐνταφιασμός, οῦ, ὁ *embalmment; Memoirs*
171, on 14⁸.

ἐντέλλομαι *enjoin.*

ἐντολή, ῆς, ἡ *commandment.*

ἐντρέπομαι *have regard for.*

ἕξ *six.*

ἐξάγω *lead forth.*

ἐξαίφνης *suddenly.*

ἐξανατέλλω *rise up.*

ἐξανίστημι *raise up.*

ἐξάπινα *suddenly.*

ἐξαυτῆς *at once, here and now.*

ἐξέρχομαι *go out* or *forth; am driven out;
am sent forth.* Smyth 1752.

ἔξεστι *it is allowed.*

ἑξήκοντα *sixty.*

ἐξίσταμαι *am astonished; out of my mind.*

ἐξομολογέομαι *confess.*

ἐξορύττω *dig out* or *up.* Joüon on 2⁴.

ἐξουδενεῖσθαι *be set at naught.*

ἐξουσία, ας, ἡ *power, right, authority.*

ἔξω *outside.*

ἔξωθεν *from outside.*

ἑορτή, ῆς, ἡ *feast.*

ἐπαγγέλλομαι *promise.*

ἐπαισχύνομαι *am ashamed.*

ἐπακολουθέω *follow* in token of approval; *am witness to;* Bauer 438: "begleiten und beglaubigen." Moulton-Milligan 228. *Memoirs* 176.

ἐπανίσταμαι *rise up against.*

ἐπάνω *over; more than.*

ἐπαύριον *on the morrow.*

ἐπεί *seeing that;since,because.* Dana 218.

ἔπειτα *thereupon.*

ἐπερωτάω *question, ask.*

ἐπί *at; on.* Smyth 1689. Dana 113.

ἐπιβάλλω, tr. or intr., *dash into;lay upon;* 14⁷² = ἄρχομαι *set to.*

ἐπίβλημα, ατος, τό *patch.*

ἐπιγινώσκω *know (well).*

ἐπιγραφή, ῆς, ἡ *inscription.*

ἐπιγράφω *write upon; inscribe.*

ἐπιθυμία, ας, ἡ *desire.*

ἐπιλαμβάνομαι *lay hold of.*

ἐπιλανθάνομαι *forget.*

ἐπιλύω *interpret.*

ἐπιπίπτω *make a rush upon.*

ἐπιρράπτω *sew upon.*

ἐπισκιάζω *overshadow.*

ἐπίσταμαι *know, understand.*

ἐπιστρέφω *turn myself about;* pass. *turn round.*

ἐπισυνάγω *bring together to.*

ἐπισυντρέχω *run together.*

ἐπιτάσσω *enjoin, command.*

ἐπιτίθημι, *put* or *lay upon; surname* (w. ὄνομα).

ἐπιτιμάω *reprove; speak sternly to.*

ἐπιτρέπω *allow, permit.*

ἑπτά *seven.*

ἐργάζομαι, *work; do.*

ἔργον, ου, τό *work; task;* (visible) *proof* or *evidence* of inner state of mind; 14⁶.

ἐρέω, ἐρῶ, ft. to λέγω.

ἐρημία, ας, ἡ *desert.*

ἔρημος, ον *secluded;* ἡ ἔρημος (γῆ), *desert.*

ἐρήμωσις, εως, ἡ *desolation; Memoirs* 170, on 13¹⁴.

ἔρχομαι *come, go; set out; arrive; am brought; am sent.* Smyth 1752.

ἐρωτάω *ask; request.*

ἐσθίω, ἔσθω *eat.*

ἔσχατος, η, ον *last.*

ἐσχάτως, w. ἔχω *am dying.*

ἔσω *into.*

ἔσωθεν *from within.*

ἕτερος, α, ον *different; other.*

ἔτι *still, as yet.*

ἑτοιμάζω *prepare.*

ἕτοιμος, η, ον *ready.*

ἔτος, ους, τό *year.*

εὖ *well; finely.*

εὐαγγέλιον, ου, τό *good news; message of salvation; Gospel.* See on 1, 1.

εὐδοκέω *am well pleased.*

εὐθέως, εὐθύς *at once; straight.*

εὐθύς, εῖα, ύ *straight.*

εὐκαιρέω *have leisure for.*

εὔκαιρος, ον *opportune.*

εὐκαίρως *opportunely.*

εὔκοπος, ον *easy.*

εὐλογέω *bless.*

εὐλογητός, οῦ, ὁ *the Ever-Blessed.*

εὑρίσκω *find.*

εὐσχήμων *respectable.*

ιεὐχαριστέω *say grace.*

εὐώνυμος, ον *left;* ἐξ εὐωνύμων *at the left side.*

ἐφφαθά; see on 7, 34.

ἐχθρός, οῦ, ὁ *foe, enemy.*

ἔχω, *have, possess; hold, keep;* esp. *have wealth;* intr. w. adverbs, *am in a certain state*

ἕως *until; while.*

ἕως, prep., adv., *as far as; up to.*

Z

ζάω *live.*

Ζεβεδαῖος, ου, ὁ *Zebedee.*

ζημιόομαι *forfeit, lose, am punished.*

ζητέω *seek, wish to see; ask for; cast about.*

ζύμη, ης, ἡ *leaven.*

ζωή, ῆς, ἡ *life.*

ζώνη, ης, ἡ *girdle.*

H

ἤ *or; in other words.*

ἠγανάκτησα, aor. to ἀγανακτέω.

ἠγάπησα, aor. to ἀγαπάω.

ἡγεμών, όνος, ὁ magistrate.
ἡγνόουν, ipft. to ἀγνοέω.
ἡγόρασα, aor. to ἀγοράζω.
ἤγρευσα, aor. to ἀγρεύω.
ἡδέως gladly.
ἤδη already; by now.
ἠθέτησα, aor. to ἀθετέω.
ἠκολούθησα, aor. to ἀκολουθέω; ipft.
 ἠκολούθουν.
ἤκουον, ἤκουσα, ἠκούσθην: to ἀκούω.
ἥκω am come. Smyth 1886.
ἤλειψα, aor. to ἀλείφω.
Ἠλίας, ου, ὁ Elias.
ἤλιος, ου, ὁ sun.
ἡμεῖς, ἡμῶν, ἡμῖν, ἡμᾶς, we. Smyth 325;
 1190.
ἡμέρα, as, ἡ day; time.
ἥμισυ, ους, τό one half. Smyth 297.
ἠνοίγησαν, aor. pass. to ἀνοίγω.
ἦρα, aor. to αἴρω.
ἤρεσα, aor. to ἀρέσκω.
ἤρθην, aor. pass. to αἴρω.
Ἡρῴδης, ου, ὁ Herod.
Ἡρῳδιανοί, οἱ the Herodians =Herod's
 partisans.
Ἡρῳδιάς, άδος, ἡ Herodias.
Ἠσαΐας, ου, ὁ Isaias.
ᾔτησα, aor. to αἰτέω; ipft. mid. ᾐτούμην.
ἤφιον, ipft. to ἀφίημι (ἀφίω).
ἡψάμην, aor. to ἅπτομαι.

Θ

Θαδδαῖος, ου, ὁ Thaddeus.
θάλασσα, ης, ἡ the Sea (=Lake of Ti-
 berias).
θαμβέω terrify.
θανάσιμος, ον deadly.
θάνατος, ου, ὁ death.
θανατόω cause one's condemnation to
 death.
θαρσέω have courage.
θαυμάζω wonder, admire; express admiration.
θαυμαστός, ή, όν wonderful.
θεάομαι see, view.
θέλημα, ατος, τό will.
θέλω wish, will, desire, like. Bauer 229;
 553.

θεός, οῦ, ὁ God.
θεραπεύω attend to; cure.
θερισμός, οῦ, ὁ harvest (-time).
θερμαίνομαι warm myself.
θέρος, ους, τό summer.
θεωρέω behold, note carefully.
θηλάζω nurse; give suck.
θῆλυς, εια, υ female.
θηρίον, ου, τό wild beast.
θησαυρός, οῦ, ὁ treasure.
θλίβω press against.
θλῖψις, εως, ἡ pressure, tribulation, distress.
θνήσκω die.
θορυβέομαι make a noise.
θόρυβος, ου, ὁ noise, tumult.
θρίξ, τριχός, ἡ hair.
θροέομαι am agitated.
θυγάτηρ, τρός, ἡ daughter.
θυγάτριον, ου, τό little daughter.
θύρα, as, ἡ door; entrance.
θυρωρός, οῦ, ὁ door-keeper.
θυσία, as, ἡ sacrifice.
θύω sacrifice.
Θωμᾶς, ᾶ Thomas.

I

Ἰάειρος, ου, ὁ Jaïrus.
Ἰακώβ, Ἰάκωβος, ὁ Jacob; James.
ἰάομαι, pass. am cured.
ἰατρός, οῦ, ὁ physician.
ἴδε look! behold!
ἰδεῖν, aor. to ὁράω.
ἴδιος, a, ον one's own; κατ᾽ ἰδίαν privately.
ἰδού see here! see there!
Ἰδουμαία, ἡ Idumea.
ἱερεύς, έως, ὁ priest.
Ἰεριχώ, οῦς, ἡ Jericho.
ἱερὸν, οῦ, τό, temple; including the temple
 halls, temple grounds, etc.
Ἱεροσόλυμα, ατος, τά Jerusalem.
Ἱεροσολυμίτης, ου, ὁ inhabitant of Jerusalem.
Ἰησοῦς, οῦ, ὁ Jesus.
ἱκανός, ή, όν fit; considerable; τὸ ἱ. ποιεῖν =
 satisfacere, gratify.
ἱμάς, άντος, ὁ strap.
ἱματίζω clothe.

ἱμάτιον, ου, τό cloak, outer garment.

ἵνα, final and consecutive: in order that; so that; also descriptive of content, that. Dana 220. Moulton, passim.

Ἰορδάνης, ου, ὁ Jordan.

Ἰουδαῖος, a, ον Jewish; ὁ Ἰ. Jew; ἡ Ἰ. χώρα Judea.

Ἰούδας, a Judas.

Ἰσαάκ, indecl., Isaak.

Ἰσκαριώθ the man from Kerioth; Iscariot.

ἴσος, η, ον tallying, concordant.

Ἰσραήλ, indecl., Israel.

ἵστημι place, set; ἵσταμαι am set up; stand, stop.

ἰσχυρός, ά, όν strong, mighty.

ἰσχύς, ύος, ἡ strength.

ἰσχύω am able or strong.

ἰχθύδιον, ου, τό little fish.

ἰχθύς, ύος, ὁ fish.

Ἰωάννης, ου, ὁ John.

Ἰωσῆς, ῆ or ῆτος, ὁ Joses.

Ἰωσήφ, indecl., Joseph.

K

καθαιρέω take down.

καθαρίζω cleanse, purify.

καθαρισμός, οῦ, ὁ cleansing.

καθέδρα, ας, ἡ seat.

καθεύδω am asleep.

κάθημαι sit.

καθίζω sit down.

καθώς just as; inasmuch as.

καί and. Note H. Smyth 2868. Dana 221.

καινός, ή, όν new.

καιρός, οῦ, ὁ (fixed) time.

Καῖσαρ, αρος, ὁ Caesar.

Καισαρία, ας, ἡ Caesarea.

κακολογέω curse.

κακοποιέω do what is bad.

κακός, ή, όν bad; evil.

κακῶς badly; κ. ἔχω am ill.

κάλαμος, ου, ὁ reed.

καλέω call.

καλός, ή, όν good; fertile; excellent, fair; fortunate.

καλῶς finely, cleverly, well, to the point; κ. ἔχω, am well.

κάμηλος, ου, camel, dromedary.

κἄν even if = καὶ ἐάν; and if.

Καναναῖος, ου, ὁ Cananean. Zorell 655.

Καπερναούμ indecl., Capharnaum.

καρδία, ας, ἡ heart; mind.

καρπός, οῦ, ὁ fruit.

καρποφορέω bear fruit.

κατά down from; against. Smyth 1690. Dana 114.

καταβαίνω come or go down; κατάβα: Smyth 684.

καταβαρίνω weigh down

καταγελάω laugh to scorn.

καταδιώκω hunt down or out.

κατάκειμαι lie down; recline.

κατακλάω break in pieces.

κατακόπτω cut.

κατακρίνω condemn.

κατακυριεύω lord it over.

καταλαμβάνω lay hold of.

καταλείπω leave behind.

καταλύω pull down.

κατάλυμα, ατος, τό lodging.

καταμαρτυρέω witness against.

καταπέτασμα, ατος, τό veil, curtain.

καταράομαι curse.

καταρτίζω mend.

κατασκευάζω prepare.

κατασκηνόω pitch my tent; dwell, have shelter.

καταστρέφω upset.

κατατίθημι lay down, deposit.

κατέφαγον, aor. to κατεσθίω.

καταφιλέω kiss effusively.

καταχέω pour down.

κατέναντι over against; facing.

κατεξουσιάζω grind down.

κατεσθίω eat up.

κατευλογέω bless fervently.

κατηγορέω accuse.

κατοίκησις, εως, ἡ home.

κάτω, below; ἕως κ., to the bottom.

καυματίζω burn up.

Καφαρναούμ Capharnaum.

κενός, ή, όν empty-handed.

κεντυρίων, ωνος, ὁ centurion.

κεράμιον, ου, τό pitcher.

κερδαίνω gain.

κεφαλαιοῦν *smite on the head* (?); *ill-treat.* Moulton-Milligan 342. Bauer 674. Joüon on 12⁴.

κεφαλή, ῆς, ἡ *head.*

κῆνσος, ου, ὁ *census; poll-tax.*

κηρύσσω *preach, proclaim.*

κινέω *shake.*

κλάδος, ου, ὁ *branch.*

κλάω *break.*

κλαίω *weep.*

κλάσμα, ατος, τό *fragment.*

κλέπτω *steal.*

κληρονομέω *inherit.*

κληρονομία, ας, ἡ *inheritance.*

κληρονόμος, ου, ὁ *heir.*

κλῆρος, ου, ὁ *lot.*

κλίνη, ης, ἡ *bed; couch.*

κλοπή, ῆς, ἡ *theft.*

κοδράντης, ου, ὁ *quadrans,* a quarter of a Roman *as.*

κοιλία, ας, ἡ *belly.*

κοινός, ή, όν *common; unwashed;* levitically *unclean.*

κοινόω *defile.*

κόκκος, ου, ὁ *grain.*

κολαφίζω *beat with the fist.*

κολλυβιστής, οῦ, ὁ *money-changer.*

κολοβόω *shorten.*

κοπάζω *cease (raging).*

κόπος, ου, ὁ *trouble.*

κόπτω *cut.*

κοράσιον, ου, τό *little girl.*

κορβᾶν (Aramaic) *votive offering.* Joüon on 7, 11.

κόσμος, ου, ὁ *world.*

κούμ (Aramaic) *rise!*

κόφινος, ου, ὁ *basket.*

κράβαττος, ου, ὁ *mat.*

κράζω *cry, shout.*

κρανίον, ου, τό *skull.*

κράσπεδον, ου, τό *tassel.*

κρατέω *hold fast* or *cling to; arrest.*

κρημνός, οῦ, ὁ *precipice.*

κρίμα, ατος, τό *judgment.*

κρυπτός, ή, όν *hidden.*

κτῆμα, ατος, τό *possession; estate.*

κτίζω *found; create.*

κτίσις, εως, ἡ *creation.*

κύκλῳ, adv., *round about.*

κυλίομαι *am rolling.*

κυλλός, ή, όν *maimed.*

κῦμα, ατος, τό *wave.*

κυνάριον, ου, τό *dog* in the house (opp. to ferocious street dog); also *pet dog.*

κύπτω *stoop.*

Κυρηναῖος, ου, ὁ *a native of Cyrene,* a flourishing city in North Africa.

κύριος, ου, ὁ *master, lord, owner.*

κωλύω *hinder, stop.*

κώμη, ης, ἡ *village.* κωμόπολις, εως, ἡ *country town.*

κωφός, ή, όν *deaf; dumb.*

Λ

λαῖλαψ, απος, ἡ *tempestuous wind, squall;* "a storm breaking forth from black thunder clouds in furious gusts" (Thayer). Joüon on 4, 37.

λαλέω *speak, talk, explain.*

λαμβάνω *take, lay hold of, receive, accept; get, obtain;* 14⁶⁵: *treat one to.*

λανθάνω *escape the notice of; am hidden.*

λαός, οῦ, ὁ *people, populace.*

λατομέω *cut, hew.*

λάχανον, ου, τό *vegetable, garden-herb.*

λέγω, *speak, say; think* (=speak to myself), 5²⁸; *mean,* 13³⁷.

λεγεών, ῶνος, ἡ *a Roman legion;* a body of soldiers whose number differed at different times (6000 ?).

λέπρα, ας, ἡ *leprosy.*

λεπρός, οῦ, ὁ *leper.*

λεπτόν, οῦ, τό *small coin;* "a very small brass coin, equivalent to the eighth part of an *as*" (Thayer).

Λευίς *Levy.*

λευκαίνω *whiten.*

λευκός, ή, όν *white.*

λῃστής, οῦ, ὁ *robber; bandit.*

λίαν *very much.*

λίθος, ου, ὁ *stone.*

λιμά (Aramaic) *why?*

λιμός, οῦ *famine.*

λογίζομαι *reckon; class.*

λόγος, ου, ὁ *speech, talk; saying, message; argument; account; thing related.*

λοιπός, ή, όν *remaining; οἱ λοιποί the rest.*
λυπέομαι *am grieved.*
λύτρον, ου, τό *ransom.*
λυχνία, ας, ἡ *lamp-stand.*
λύχνος, ου, ὁ *lamp.*
λύω *loose, unhitch.*

M

Μαγδαληνός, ή *a native of Magdala, a* place on the western shore of the Lake of Galilee.
μαθητής, οῦ, ὁ *disciple.*
μακράν *far.*
μακρόθεν *from afar; at a distance.*
μακρός, ά, όν *long.*
μᾶλλον *more; on the contrary, rather.*
μανθάνω *learn.*
Μαρία, ας, ἡ *Mary.*
μαρτυρία, ας, ἡ *testimony, evidence.*
μαρτύριον, ου, τό *testimony.* See on 1, 44.
μάρτυς, υρος, ὁ *witness.*
μαστιγόω *scourge.*
μάστιξ, ιγος, ἡ *"scourge" = malady, ail-* ment.
μάτην *in vain, to no purpose.*
Ματθαῖος, ου, ὁ *Matthew.*
μάχαιρα, ας, ἡ *sword.*
μέγας, μεγάλη, μέγα *great, large; loud;* *intense, severe, utter.*
μεγιστάν, ᾶνος, ὁ *courtier, high dignitary.*
μεθερμηνεύω *interpret.*
μεθόρια, ων, τά *border, frontier; vicinity.*
μείζων, ον *greater.*
μέλει μοί τινος *am concerned about.*
μέλι, ιτος, τό *honey.*
μέλλω *am about to.*
μέν. Smyth 2895. Dana 232.
μένω *stay, abide; lodge.*
μερίζω *portion out; divide.*
μέριμνα, ης, ἡ *care.*
μέρος, ους, τό *district.*
μεσονύκτιον, ου, τό *midnight.*
μέσος, η, ον *middle; τὸ μέσον, the midst;* *mid-; ἀνὰ μέσον into the heart of.*
μετά *with.* Smyth 1691. Dana 115.
μεταμορφόομαι *change my appearance.*
μετανοέω *repent, am converted, do penance.*
μετάνοια, ας, ἡ *repentance; conversion.*

μετρέω *measure.*
μέτρον, ου, τό *measure.*
μέχρις οὗ *till.*
μή, negative particle; Smyth 2702. Dana 241. Blass 426.
μηδέ *not even; and—not.*
μηδείς, εμία, ἐν *no one.*
μηκέτι *no longer.*
μηκύνομαι *shoot up straight.*
μήποτε *never.*
μήτηρ, τρός, ἡ *mother.*
μήτι *can it be that? = numquid.*
μικρός, ά, όν *little; small; μικρόν a little* (distance or while).
μισέω *hate.*
μισθός, οῦ, ὁ *reward.*
μισθωτός, οῦ, ὁ *hired man.*
μνῆμα, ατος, τό *tomb.*
μνημεῖον, ου, τό *tomb.*
μνημονεύω *remember.*
μνημόσυνον, ου, τό *remembrance.*
μογιλάλος, ον *speaking w. difficulty.*
μόδιος, ου, ὁ *bushel, a dry measure hold-* ing about a peck.
μοιχαλίς, ίδος, *adulterous; unfaithful to* God.
μοιχάομαι *commit adultery.*
μοιχεία, ας, ἡ, *adultery*
μοιχεύω *commit adultery.*
μόνος, η, ον *alone; only; μόνον, adv., only;* κατὰ μόνας, *apart, alone.*
μονόφθαλμος, ον *deprived of one eye.*
μορφή, ῆς, ἡ *form.*
μύλος, ου, ὁ *millstone.*
μυρίζω *anoint.*
μύρον, ου, τό *myrrh.*
μυστήριον, ου, τό *mystery; secret.*
Μωϋσῆς *Moses.*

N

Ναζαρέτ, indecl. *Nazareth.*
Ναζαρηνός, οῦ *of Nazareth.*
ναί *yes indeed; true.* Dana 233.
ναός, οῦ, ὁ *sanctuary.*
νάρδος, ου, ἡ *nard.*
νεανίσκος, ου, ὁ *youth.*
νεκρός, οῦ, ὁ *dead man.*
νέος, α, ον *young; new.*

νεότης, ητος, ἡ *youth.*
νεφέλη, ης, ἡ *cloud.*
νηστεία, ας, ἡ *fasting.*
νηστεύω *fast.*
νῆστις, ὁ, ἡ; acc. pl. νήστεις; *fasting.*
νίπτω *wash.*
νοέω *think, understand.*
νόσος, ου, ἡ *sickness.*
νουνεχῶς *sensibly.*
νυμφίος, ου, ὁ *bridegroom.*
νυμφών, ῶνος, ὁ *wedding chamber;* οἱ υἱοὶ
   τοῦ ν., *wedding guests*
νῦν *now.*
νύξ, νυκτός, ἡ *night.*

Ξ

ξέστης, ου, ὁ *household utensil; dish.*
ξηραίνω *make dry, wither.*
ξηρός, ά, όν *dry; withered.*
ξύλον, ου, τό *wood; club.*

Ο

ὁ, ἡ, τό *the.* Dana 145. Smyth 1118.
ὁδός, οῦ, ἡ *way, path.*
ὀδούς, όντος, ὁ *tooth.*
οἰκία, ας, ἡ *house.*
οἰκοδεσπότης, ου, ὁ *owner of a house.*
οἰκοδομέω *build.*
οἰκοδομή, ῆς, ἡ *building.*
οἶκος, ου, ὁ *household.*
οἶνος, ου, ὁ *wine.*
οἷος, α, ον (such) *as; qualis.*
ὀλίγος, η, ον *little.*
ὁλοκαύτωμα, ατος, τό *burnt offering.*
ὅλος, η, ον *whole; all.*
ὄμμα, ατος, τό *eye.*
ὀμνύω, ὄμνυμι *swear, make oath.*
ὁμοιόω *liken.*
ὁμοίως *similarly.*
ὀνειδίζω *reproach, revile.*
ὀνικός, w. μύλος, the upper *millstone*, requiring an ass (ὄνος) to turn it.
ὄνομα, ατος, τό *name.*
ὄντως *really.*
ὄξος, ους, τό *vinegar.*
ὄπισθεν (from) *behind.*
ὀπίσω *behind;* see note on 8³³.

ὅπου *where;* also *when.*
ὅπως *in order that.*
ὁράω *see, look;* ὤφθην *was seen* or *ap-*
   peared.
ὀργή, ῆς, ἡ *anger.*
ὀρθῶς *correctly.*
ὅρια, ων, τά *borders, territory.*
ὁρκίζω *adjure.*
ὅρκος, ου, ὁ *oath.*
ὁρμάω *rush.*
ὄρος, ους, τό *hill, mountain.*
ὀρύττω *dig*
ὀρχέομαι *dance.*
ὅς, ἥ, ὅ rel. pronoun; *who, which;* ὁ μέν
   some; ὅ ἐστιν, *that is;* ὃς ἐάν = ὅς ἄν;
   ὃς καί *the same who.*
ὅσος, η, ον *as, quantus;* pl. *as many as;*
   sometimes *as great as.*
ὅσπερ *the very one who.* Smyth 2495.
   Dana 235.
ὅστις, ἥτις, ὅτι indef. rel. pronoun; *who,*
   which, whoever.
ὀσφύς, ύος, ἡ *waist; loins.*
ὅταν *when, whenever.*
ὅτε *when; because.*
ὅτι *that; because.* Dana 222.
οὐ, οὐκ, οὐχ *not.* Smyth 2688. Dana 240.
   οὐ μή: Smyth 1800 c; 1804; 1919;
   2754; 2755. Dana 242.
οὐά *bah.*
οὐαί *woe; alas!*
οὐδέ *not even; nor, and not, not—either.*
   See on 14⁵⁹. Smyth 2930.
οὐδείς, εμία, ἐν *no one.*
οὐδέποτε *never.*
οὐκέτι *no longer.*
οὖν *then, therefore.* Smyth 2955. Dana
   223.
οὔπω *not yet.*
οὐρανός, οῦ, ὁ *sky, heaven, atmosphere.*
οὖς, ὠτός, τό *ear.*
οὔτε *neither—nor.*
οὗτος, αὕτη, τοῦτο *this, that.*
οὕτω(s) *thus, so.*
ὀφθαλμός, οῦ, ὁ *eye.* Joüon on 7, 22.
ὄφις, εως, ὁ *serpent.*
ὄχλος, ου, ὁ *crowd.*
ὀψέ *late.*

ὄψιος, α, ον, late; ἡ ὀψία late evening; early night.

Π

παιδιόθεν from a child.

παιδίον, ου, τό little child.

παιδίσκη, ης, ἡ slave-girl; door-maid.

παίω strike.

πάλαι (long ago), for some time past.

παλαιός, ά, όν old.

πάλιν again, in turn; back; =Latin rursus.

πάμπολυς, υ very large.

πανταχοῦ everywhere.

πάντοθεν from everywhere

πάντοτε always.

παρά from; to; along; with. Dana 116. Smyth 1692.

παραβολή, ῆς, ἡ parable = illustration, simile, similitude, figure, allegory, dark saying. proverb, etc.

παραγγέλλω order, command.

παράγω, intr., pass by or along.

παραγίνομαι come (to).

παραδέχομαι receive warmly.

παραδίδωμι hand down or over, surrender, imprison (Zorell).

παράδοσις, εως, ἡ a handing down; tradition.

παρακαλέω beg, entreat.

παρακολουθέω follow, attend, accompany.

παρακούω overhear, disregard.

παραλαμβάνω take along.

παραλυτικός, οῦ, ὁ paralytic.

παραπορεύομαι pass along; go out of my way; avoid the highway.

παράπτωμα, ατος, τό fault.

παρασκευή, ῆς, ἡ preparation.

παρατηρέω observe closely.

παρατίθημι set before; serve.

παραφέρω take away, remove.

παρέρχομαι pass by.

παρέχω cause.

παρίσταμαι be at hand; be present.

παρόμοιος, α, ον similar

παρρησία, ας, ἡ freedom of speech; dat., boldly.

πᾶς, πᾶσα, πᾶν all; whole.

πάσχα, τό indecl., paschal lamb; passover. See Zorell, and Bauer.

πάσχω experience; suffer.

πατάσσω strike.

πατήρ, τρός, ὁ father.

πατρίς, ίδος, ἡ country.

πέδη, ης, ἡ fetter.

πεζῇ on foot, by the land route.

πείθω persuade; πέποιθα trust.

πεινάω hunger.

πειράζω test, try, sound, tempt.

πειρασμός, οῦ, ὁ test, trial, temptation.

πέμπω let go, send.

πενθερά, ᾶς, ἡ mother-in-law.

πενθέω mourn.

πεντακισχίλιοι, αι, a five thousand.

πέντε five.

πεντήκοντα fifty.

πέραν (on, from, to) the other side.

περί round, about; concerning. Smyth 1693. Dana 117.

περιάγω go round, travel about.

περιβάλλομαι put on.

περιβλέπομαι look round.

περικαλύπτω cover.

περίκειμαι lie round.

περίλυπος, ον very sad.

περιπατέω walk about; live.

περισσεύω abound; τὸ περισσεῦον surplus.

περίσσευμα, ατος, τό what is left over.

περισσόν, οῦ, τό; ἐκ περισσοῦ exceedingly.

περισσότερος, α, ον, more severe; more than ordinary.

περισσῶς abundantly, extravagantly, furiously.

περιστερά, ᾶς, ἡ dove.

περιτίθημι place round.

περιτρέχω run about.

περιφέρω carry about.

περίχωρος, ου, ἡ (sc. γῆ) surrounding country.

πετεινόν, οῦ, τό fowl, bird.

πέτρα, ας, ἡ rock.

Πέτρος, ου, ὁ Peter.

πετρώδης, ες rocky, stony.

πηγή, ῆς, ἡ source.

πήρα, ας, ἡ wallet, bag.

Πιλᾶτος, ου, ὁ Pilate.

πίναξ, ακος, ἡ *platter.*
πίνω *drink.*
πιπράσκω *sell.*
πίπτω *fall; throw myself.*
πιστεύω *believe, trust.*
πιστικός, ἡ *pure, genuine.*
πίστις, εως, ἡ *faith, confidence.*
πλανάω *lead astray;* mid. *am wide of the mark.*
πλείων, ονος, *more;* πλεῖστος, η, ον *most; very large.*
πλέκω *plait.*
πλεονεξία, ας, ἡ *covetousness.*
πλῆθος, ους, τό *multitude.*
πλήν *beside; but.*
πλήρης, ες (sometimes indecl.) *full; ripe.*
πληρόω *fill up, fulfill, end.*
πλήρωμα, ατος, τό *filling; patch; complement.*
πλησίον (adv. to πλησίος), ὁ *neighbor.*
πλοιάριον, ου, τό (little) *boat.*
πλοῖον, ου, τό *boat.*
πλούσιος, α, ον *rich.*
πλοῦτος, ου, ὁ *riches.*
πνεῦμα, ατος, τό *spirit; (Holy) Ghost.*
πνίγω *drown.*
πόθεν *whence?*
ποιέω *do, make.*
ποικίλος, η, ον *diverse.*
ποιμήν, ένος, ὁ *shepherd.*
ποῖος, α, ον *what kind of ; qualis.*
πόλεμος, ου, ὁ *war.*
πόλις, εως, ἡ *city.*
πολλάκις *often.*
πολύς, πολλή, ὑ *much, great, abundant;* πολλά, adv., *much, earnestly.*
πολυτελής, ές *costly.*
πονηρία, ας, ἡ *malice.*
πονηρός, ά, όν *evil, bad, wicked.*
πορεύομαι *go, travel.*
πορνεία, ας, ἡ *fornication.*
πόρρω *far.*
πορφύρα, ας, ἡ *purple cloak.*
πόσος, η, ον ; pl. *how many?*
ποταμός, οῦ, ὁ *river.*
ποταπός, ή, όν *how wonderful.*
πότε *when?* ἕως πότε *how long?*

ποτήριον, ου, τό, *cup. Memoirs* 166, on 10³⁸.
ποτίζω *give one to drink.*
ποῦ *where?*
πούς, ποδός, ὁ *foot.*
πραιτώριον, ου, τό = *praetorium,* the palace of the Roman procurator.
πρασιά, ᾶς, ἡ *flower bed.*
πρεσβύτερος, α, ον *older;* οἱ πρ. *the Elders; Memoirs* 159, on 7⁵.
πρίν *before.*
πρό *before, in front of.* Dana 118. Smyth 1694.
προάγω *go before; walk, march, row ahead.*
προαύλιον, ου, τό *vestibule.*
προβαίνω *forward.*
πρόβατον, ου, τό *sheep.*
προείρηκα, pf. to προ-αγορεύω *have foretold.*
προέρχομαι *arrive before.*
πρόθεσις, εως, ἡ *presentation, display; Memoirs* 152, on 2²⁶.
πρόθυμος, ον *willing.*
προλαμβάνω *anticipate.*
προμεριμνάω *be anxious beforehand.*
πρός *near; facing.* Smyth 1695. Dana 119.
προσάββατον, ου, τό *eve of the Sabbath.*
προσαίτης, ου, ὁ *beggar.*
προσδέχομαι *await.*
προσέρχομαι *approach.*
προσευχή, ῆς, ἡ *prayer.*
προσεύχομαι *pray.*
πρόσκαιρος, ον *lasting but for a time, fickle.*
προσκαλέομαι *call into my presence.*
προσκαρτερέω *be ready for constant service.*
προσκεφάλαιον, ου, τό *cushion, pillow.*
προσκολλάομαι *cling to.*
προσκυλίω *roll up to.*
προσκυνέω *pay homage.*
προσλαμβάνομαι *take to myself.*
προσμένω *cling to.*
προσορμίζομαι *moor.*
προσπίπτω *fall down before.*
προσπορεύομαι *come to.*

προστάττω enjoin.
προστίθημι add.
προστρέχω run toward.
προσφέρω bring to.
πρόσωπον, ου, τό face; βλέπειν εἰς
   πρόσωπόν τινος: Zorell 229; Bauer
   225.
πρόφασις, εως, ἡ pretext.
προφητεύω prophesy.
προφήτης, ου, ὁ prophet.
πρύμνα, ης, ἡ stern.
πρωΐ early in the morning.
πρωτοκαθεδρία, ας, ἡ front seat.
πρωτοκλισία, ας, ἡ first seat.
πρῶτος, η, ον first.
πτύω spit.
πτῶμα, ατος, τό corpse.
πτωχός, οῦ, ὁ beggar.
πυγμῇ, "with the fist"? carefully. Joüon
   on 7, 3
πῦρ, πυρός, τό fire.
πύργος, ου, ὁ tower.
πυρέσσω have a fever.
πυρετός, οῦ ὁ fever.
πωλέω sell.
πῶλος, ου, ὁ colt.
πωρόω harden; blind; make callous.
πώρωσις, εως, ἡ blindness; hardness.
πῶς how? what?

Ρ

ῥαββί Rabbi; master!
ῥαββουνί my master! Joüon on 10, 51.
ῥάβδος, ου, ὁ staff.
ῥάκος, ους, τό cloth.
ῥαντίζω sprinkle.
ῥάπισμα, ατος, τό blow on the face.
ῥαφίς, ίδος, ἡ needle.
ῥῆμα, ατος, τό word; saying.
ῥήσσω, burst; throw to the ground.
ῥίζα, ης, ἡ root.
Ῥοῦφος, ου, ὁ Rufus.
ῥύσις, εως, ἡ flow.

Σ

σαβαχθανεί (Aramaic) thou hast forsaken.
σάββατον, ου, τό Sabbath; pl. τὰ σάββατα;

ἡ μία τῶν σ., the first day of the week =
   our Sunday.
Σαδδουκαῖος, ου, ὁ, Sadducee.
σαλεύω shake, cause to wander.
Σαλώμη, ης, ἡ, Salome.
σανδάλιον, ου, τό sandal.
σάρξ, ρκός, ἡ flesh; human nature or
   being.
σατανᾶς, ᾶ, ὁ Satan; adversary.
σβέννυμι quench.
ἑαυτοῦ, ῷ, όν thyself.
σέβομαι worship.
σεισμός, οῦ, ὁ earthquake.
σελήνη, ης, ἡ moon.
σημεῖον, ου, τό sign; miracle.
σήμερον to-day.
Σιδών, ῶνος, ἡ Sidon.
Σίμων, ωνος, ὁ Simon.
σίναπι, εως, τό mustard.
σινδών, όνος, ἡ sheet.
σῖτος, ου, ὁ grain; corn.
σιωπάω am silent.
σκανδαλίζω, give offense to; surprise and
   shock; am a temptation (or an occasion
   of sin) to. Note N.
σκεῦος, ους, τό utensil, furniture, vessel.
   Joüon on 11, 16.
σκηνή, ῆς, ἡ tent, booth, tabernacle.
σκιά, ᾶς, ἡ shadow.
σκληροκαρδία, ας, ἡ hardness of heart.
σκοτίζω darken.
σκότος, ους, τό darkness.
σκύλλω trouble.
σκώληξ, ηκος, ὁ worm.
σμυρνίζω drug.
σός, σή, σόν your; thy.
σοφία, ας, ἡ, wisdom; learning.
σπάομαι draw.
σπαράσσω tear; throw into convulsions.
   Joüon on 1, 26.
σπεῖρα, ας, ἡ company of soldiers.
σπείρω sow.
σπεκουλάτωρ, ορος, ὁ executioner.
σπέρμα, ατος, τό seed.
σπήλαιον, ου, τό den.
σπλαγχνίζομαι am touched at heart; my
   heart goes out to.
σπόγγος, ου, ὁ sponge.

σπόριμα, ων, τά *crops.*
σπόρος, ου, ὁ *seed.*
σπουδή, ῆς, ἡ *eagerness, haste.*
σπυρίς, ίδος, ἡ *basket.*
στάσις, εως, ἡ *riot.*
σταυρός, οῦ, ὁ *cross.*
σταυρόω *crucify.*
στάχυς, υος, ὁ *ear of corn.*
στέγη, ης, ἡ *roof.*
στενάζω *sigh.*
στέφανος, ου, ὁ *crown.*
στήκω *stand.*
στιβάς, άδος, ἡ *twig, branch.*
στίλβω *glisten, am white.*
στολή, ῆς, ἡ *long robe.*
στρατιώτης, ου, ὁ *soldier.*
στρώννυμι *spread.*
στυγνάζω *look gloomy.*
σύ, σοῦ, σοί, σέ *thou; you.*
συγγενής, οῦς, ὁ *relative.*
συγκάθημαι *am seated among.*
συγκαλέω *call together.*
συζεύγνυμι *yoke together.*
συκῆ, ῆς, ἡ *fig-tree.*
σῦκον, ου, τό *fig.*
συλλαμβάνω *capture.*
συμβαίνω *happen.*
συμβούλιον, ου, τό *consilium* and *concilium; deliberation, decision.* Joüon on 3, 6.
συμπνίγω *choke.*
συμπορεύομαι *travel with; assemble.*
συμπόσιον, ου, τό *table company.*
σύν *with.* Smyth 1696. Dana 120.
συνάγω *bring together.*
συναγωγή, ῆς, ἡ *synagogue.*
συνακολουθέω *accompany.*
συναναβαίνω *go up together with.*
συνανάκειμαι *recline together with.*
συναποθνήσκω *die together with.*
συνέδριον, ου, τό *Sanhedrin;* the great council at Jerusalem, consisting of seventy-one members, Scribes, Elders, and high priests.
συνεργέω *coöperate.*
συνέρχομαι *come together.*
σύνεσις, εως, ἡ *understanding.*
συνζεύγνυμι *join together.*

συνζητέω *discuss together with.*
συνθλίβω *crush* or *press against.*
συνίημι *understand.*
συνκάθημαι *sit together with.*
συνκαλέω *call together.*
συνλαλέω *converse with.*
συνλυπέομαι *am grieved;* perhaps "am utterly distressed."
συνπνίγω, *choke.*
συνσπαράσσω *convulse.*
συνσταυρόω; see συστ.
συντελέω *accomplish.*
συντηρέω *shelter.*
συντρέχω *run together.*
συντρίβω *crush, break in pieces.*
Συροφοινίκισσα, ης, ἡ *a Syrophoenician woman.*
σύσσημον, ου, τό *signal.*
συστασιαστής, οῦ, ὁ *fellow rioter.*
συσταυρόω *crucify together with.*
σφόδρα *very (much).*
σχίζω *split;* pass. *burst open.*
σχίσμα, ατος, τό *rip, rent.*
σώζω *save, cure.*
σῶμα, ατος, τό *body; corpse.*
σωφρονέω *am in my right senses.*

T

ταλιθά (Aram.) *maiden.*
ταράσσω *disturb.*
ταχύ *quickly, readily.*
τὲ *and.*
τέκνον, ου, τό *child; son.*
τέκτων, ονος, ὁ *carpenter; worker in wood?*
τελευτάω *die.*
τέλος, ους, τό *end;* in cl. Greek and in the Papyri, τέλος ἔχει is often = τετέλεσται; Witkowski, p. 139.
τελώνης, ου, ὁ *tax* or *toll gatherer; publican.*
τελώνιον, ου, τό *toll booth; custom house.*
τέρας, ατος, τό *wonder; sign.*
τέσσαρες, *a four.*
τεσσεράκοντα *forty.*
τέταρτος, η, ον *fourth.*
τετρακισχίλιοι, αι, *a four thousand.*
τηλαυγῶς *clearly (even at a distance); distinctly.*

τηρέω *observe, keep.*
τίθημι *place, put.*
τίλλω *pluck.*
Τιμαῖος, ου, ὁ *Timaeus.*
τιμάω *honor.*
τίς, τί *who? what?* τί ἡμῖν καὶ σοί; = *leave us alone.*
τὶς, τὶ *some one, anyone.*
τοιοῦτος, αὕτη, οὖτον *such.*
τολμάω *have courage.*
τόπος, ου, ὁ *place.*
τότε *then.*
τράπεζα, ης, ἡ *table, counter.*
τράχηλος, ου, ὁ *neck.*
τρεῖς, τρία *three.*
τρέμω *tremble.*
τρέχω *run.*
τριάκοντα *thirty.*
τριακόσιοι, αι, *a three hundred.*
τρίβος, ου, ἡ *path.*
τρίζω *grind.*
τρὶς *thrice.*
τρίτος, η, ον *third;* τὸ τρ. *for the third time.*
τρόμος, ου, ὁ *trembling.*
τρύβλιον, ου, τό *dish.*
τρυμαλιά, ᾶς, ἡ *eye of a needle.*
τύπτω *beat.*
Τύρος, ου, ἡ *Tyre.*
τυφλός, ή, όν *blind.*

Υ

ὑγιής, ἐς *sound, hale.*
ὕδωρ, ατος, τό *water.*
υἱός, οῦ, ὁ *son.*
ὑμεῖς, ὧν, ἶν, ἆς *you.*
ὑμνέω *chant a hymn.*
ὑπάγω *go; see on* 8³³.
ὑπακούω *obey.*
ὑπαντάω *meet.*
ὑπέρ *for.* Dana 121. Smyth 1697.
ὑπερηφανία, ας, ἡ *pride.*
ὑπερπερισσῶς *beyond bounds.*
ὑπηρέτης, ου, ὁ *servant.*
ὑπό *under; by.* Smyth 1698. Dana 122.
ὑποδέομαι *bind under (my feet).*
ὑπόδημα, ατος, τό *sandal; shoe.* Joüon on 1, 7.
ὑποκάτω *from underneath.*

ὑπόκρισις, εως, ἡ *hypocrisy; acting a part.*
ὑποκριτής, οῦ, ὁ *hypocrite.* See *Class. Bulletin,* Jan. 1934.
ὑπολήνιον, ου, τό *wine vat.*
ὑπομένω *hold out.*
ὑποπόδιον, ου, τό *foot-stool.*
ὑποστρέφω *turn back.*
ὑστερέω *be lacking.*
ὑστέρησις, εως, ἡ *deficiency, want.*
ὕστερον *later.*
ὑψηλός, ή, όν *high.*
ὕψιστος, η, ον *highest.*

Φ

φαγεῖν, aor. to ἐσθίω; *eat, take a meal.*
φαίνομαι *appear;* τί φαίνεται; *what is your verdict?*
φανερός, ά, όν *well known.*
φανερόω *make known.*
φανερῶς *openly.*
φάντασμα, ατος, τό *phantom; spectre.*
Φαρισαῖος, ου, ὁ *Pharisee.*
φέγγος, ους, τό *ray; light.*
φέρω *bring, take, carry.*
φεύγω *flee, run off, hurry away.*
φημί *say, remark.*
φθόνος, ου, ὁ *envy.*
φιλέω *love.*
Φίλιππος, ου, ὁ *Philip.*
φιμόω *muzzle, silence.*
φοβέομαι *fear.*
φόβος, ου, ὁ *fear.*
φονεύω *murder.*
φόνος, ου, ὁ *murder.*
φραγελλόω *scourge;* Lat. *flagellare.*
φραγμός, οῦ, ὁ *fence.*
φρονέω *think.*
φυλακή, ῆς, ἡ *watch; prison.*
φυλάττομαι *guard against.*
φύλλον, ου, τό *leaf.*
φυτεύω *plant.*
φωνέω *call.*
φωνή, ῆς, ἡ *voice.*
φῶς, ωτός, τό *light, glow.*

Χ

χαίρω *rejoice.*
χαλάω *let down.*

χαλκίον, ου, τό bronze vessel.
χαλκός, οῦ, ὁ copper; money.
χαρά, ᾶς, ἡ joy.
χεῖλος, ους, τό lip.
χειμών, ῶνος, ὁ winter.
χείρ, ρός, ἡ hand; arm.
χειροποίητος, ον made by the hand of man.
χείρων, ον worse.
χήρα, ας, ἡ widow.
χιλίαρχος, ου, ὁ chiliarch = military trib-
une.
χιτών, ῶνος, ὁ tunic, under-garment.
χλωρός, ά, όν green.
χοῖρος, ου, ὁ swine.
χορτάζω feed; give one plenty to eat.
χόρτος, ου, ὁ grass.
χοῦς, χοός, ὁ dust.
χρεία, ας, ἡ need; distress.
χρῆμα, ατος, τό thing.
Χριστός, οῦ, ὁ Christ, = the Anointed.
χρόνος, ου, ὁ time.
χωλός, ή, όν lame.
χώρα, ας, ἡ land; country.
χωρέω am able to hold.
χωρίζω separate.

χωρίον, ου, τό place.
χωρίς without; apart from.

Ψ

ψευδομαρτυρέω bring false witness against.
ψευδοπροφήτης, ου, ὁ pseudoprophet, false
prophet.
ψευδόχριστος, ου, ὁ pseudochrist, false
messias.
ψιχίον, ου, τό crumb.
ψυχή, ῆς, ἡ soul; life.

Ω

ὦ oh.
ὧδε here.
ὠδίν, ῖνος, ἡ birth-pang.
ὥρα, ας, ἡ hour; time; ordeal.
ὡς as; about; like; since.
ὡσαννά (Hebrew) Hosanna; a cry of joy
= Save!
ὡσαύτως in like manner.
ὡσεί as, as it were.
ὥστε so that.
ὠτίον, ου, τό ear.
ὠφελέω benefit.

APPENDIX I

Marcan Departures from Classical Greek

The subjoined list records words, phrases, and constructions in the
second Gospel that deviate from the more rigid classical standards
familiar to the student. In the case of idioms used more than once,
generally only their first occurrence in the Gospel has been noted.
Occasionally the purpose of a note is not to point out a Marcan departure from older Greek, but to warn the student against hastily assuming such a departure, as in 1, 5, where one might be tempted to suppose
that the use of the singular verb followed by two subjects is contrary to
classical Greek. The abbreviations used are as follows: Bl. = Blass;
Sm. = Smyth. For fuller information regarding discrepancies between
older and Koine Greek, recourse should be had to such larger works,
as Robertson's, Deissmann's, Moulton's *Prolegomena* and *Vocabulary*,
Blass-Debrunner's *Neut. Grammatik;* etc.

The following list is not exhaustive.

I

2. καθώς: since Aristotle for ὡς. ἐγώ: would cl. Gr. omit this pronoun here? Sm. 1190. Dana 134, 1. μου: for cl. τὸν ἐμὸν ἄγγελον
or τὸν ἐμαυτοῦ ἄγγελον or τὸν ἄγγελον. Sm. 1222; 1199; Kaegi 64, 3.

4. ἐν: "in" or "into." Sm. 1659. Bl. 218.

5. ἐξεπορεύετο: sing.; Sm. 966a.

7. αὐτοῦ: cl. Gr. would omit. Bl. 297.

8. ἐγώ, αὐτός: Sm. 1190; 1204 ff. Dana 137. βαπτίσει: Sm. 539e.

9. ἐγένετο ἦλθεν: Bl. 442, 5; for cl. ἐγένετο ἐλθεῖν 'Ιησοῦν. Sm. 1985.

13. τεσσεράκοντα: cl. τετταράκοντα. Sm. 33; 33D. σατανᾶ: for cl. decl.,
see Sm. 227.

15. ὅτι: rare in cl. Gr. Sm. 2590a.

16. ἁλεεῖς: nom. for ἁλιεῖς; Sm. 33 D; acc. for ἁλιέας or ἁλιᾶς; Sm.
276; 277.

21. σάββασιν: dative of 3d decl. Sm. 282.

23. ἐν πνεύματι: = ἔχων πνεῦμα. Dana 112 ii. ἀνέκραξεν: ἀνέκραγεν.
Sm., p. 703.

27. πρὸς ἑαυτούς: Sm. 1231; 1218. ὑπακούουσιν: pl.; Sm. 958; 959.

28. πανταχοῦ: =πανταχόσε; cl. Sm. 342. Bl. 103.

31. διηκόνει: Att. ἐδιακόνει.

32. ἔδυσεν: =ἔδυ. Sm. 819. Bl. 75.

34. ἤφιεν: for ἀφίει or ἠφίει. Sm. 782; 450; 746. ᾔδεισαν: post-cl. for ἦσαν or ᾔδεσαν. Sm. 798.

35. πρωΐ: since Homer, for attic πρῴ.

38. ἀλλαχοῦ=ἀλλαχόσε; cl. Sm. 342. Bl. 103. ἵνα: in Koine Gr.often= "so that"; also frequent in N.T. in a non-final sense in object clauses, as ἐρωτᾶν ἵνα; also introducing independent sentences, as in 2, 10; 5, 23; 12, 15. Dana 220.

42. ἐκαθερίσθη: for ἐκαθαρίσθη. Sm. 33; 33D. Bl. 29, 1.

44. ὅρα w. subj.: Sm. 2211 and 2214. σου: cf. 1, 2, μου.

45. ἠρχόμην: cl. ᾖα.

II

1. εἰς οἶκον: Sm. 1659 b.

4. μή: for cl. οὐ. In N.T. οὐ is confined to the indicative, μή may be used w. any other mood. The cl. rules regarding οὐ and μή do not seem to hold for the N.T. Bl. 426. See, however, Dana 241. Sm. 2737. For particulars, see Davis 464–470. Bl. 427–433. προσενέγκαι =προσενεγκεῖν.

14. ἐπὶ τό: cl. ἐπὶ τοῦ.

15. γίνεται: for cl. γίγνεται. Sm. 89. Bl. 34, 4. For the construction, see on 1, 9.

16. τί ὅτι: Sm. 2644. Bl. 299, 4. Davis 381.

20. ἐλεύσονται: cl. Gr. prefers εἶμι, ἀφίξομαι, ἥξω. Sm., p. 698.

21. ἐπιράπτει: for ἐπιρράπτει. Sm. 80.

23. ὁδὸν ποιεῖν: for ὁδὸν ποιεῖσθαι, "pass through." Sm. 1722. στάχυας: Sm. 272.

24. ἴδε: for ἰδέ: Sm. 424 b.

25. ἐπείνασεν: for cl. ἐπείνησεν. Sm. 394. Bl. 70, 2; 88.

III

4. ψυχή=τὶς, ἄνθρωπος.

5. ἀπεκατεστάθη: see Sm. 451. Bl. 69, 3.

6. ἐδίδουν: =cl. ἐδίδοσαν. Sm. 746 b and 416.

9. εἶπεν ἵνα: Koine Gr., for cl. εἶπεν or ἐκέλευεν w. inf.

11. ὅταν w. impf.: for cl. εἰ w. opt. Sm. 2340.

14. ἵνα: for cl. ἐποίησεν εἶναι; see 1, 17 and on 1, 38.

17. υἱοὶ βροντῆς: the nominative is cl.; Bl. 143. Sm. 940. Dana 83, 3.
24. σταθῆναι: =cl. στῆναι. Bl. 97, 1. Sm., p. 701.
28. ὅσας ἐάν=ὅσας ἄν.
33. ἀποκριθείς; cl. aor. ἀπεκρινάμην. Sm. 811 ff.

IV

1. παρά w. acc.=w. dative.
4. ὁ μέν–: cl. τὸ μέν–τὸ δέ. Sm. 1107.
9. ὦτα ἀκούειν: "strange Gr." (Bl. 393, 6; 400, 2) for ὥστε ἀ., or δυνάμενα ἀκ.
13. οἴδατε: late for ἴστε. Sm. 796.
25. ὃς οὐκ ἔχει: cl.; Sm. 2691 ff.; ἔχω, cl. for "I have means," "am rich."
29. παραδῶ : παραδῷ.
31. The construction is somewhat confused.
32. ὑπὸ τὴν σκιάν: Sm. 1659 b. See 4, 38 ἐπί.
34. ἰδίοις: Koine for cl. τοῖς ἑαυτοῦ μαθηταῖς.. Bl. 286.
41. ὑπακούει: sing. Sm. 966 c.

V

2. αὐτοῦ–αὐτῷ: not uncl. Sm. 2073.
6. αὐτῷ: for cl. αὐτόν. Bl. 151.
7. κράξας: for cl. κραγών. Sm., p. 703.
13. εἰσῆλθον: pl.; Sm. 958; 959.
22. εἷς=τὶς. Bl. 247, 2.
23. ἵνα: see on 1, 38. ἔζησα=ἐβίων. Sm., p. 698.
26. μηδέν: Dana 241; for cl. οὐδέν. Sm. 2240. Bl. 426.
29. ἴαται: passive; Sm. 813. Bl. 311. ἀπό: hardly cl. See Bl. 211 and 180; so again 34: ὑγιὴς ἀπό (like Lat. *liber ab*). Sm. 1684.
42. ἐκστάσει: dat.; cl. Sm. 1577.
43. γνῶ:=γνῷ.

VI

7. δύο δύο: Koine for ἀνὰ δύο. Bl. 248, 1.
8. παραγγέλλω ἵνα: see on 1, 38.
10. ὅπου ἐάν: for cl. ὅπου ἄν.
17. ἐγάμησεν: for ἔγημεν. Bl. 101. Sm., p. 691.
22. ὃ ἐάν=ὃ ἄν.
25. θέλω ἵνα δῷς: see 10, 35 and 36.
27. σπεκουλάτορα=speculatorem. Bl. 5, 1, b.

29. ἔθηκαν = ἔθεσαν.

34. μὴ ἔχοντα: see on 2, 4; here = "*if* or *when* they have not."

38. ἰχθύας: late for ἰχθῦς. Sm. 272.

39. συμπόσια συμπόσια: see on 6, 7, δύο δύο; so πρασιαὶ πρασιαί in v. 40.

49. ἀνέκραξαν = ἀνέκραγον. Sm., p. 703.

56. ὅπου ἄν w. indic.: Sm. 2340; past general condition.

VII

13. παρεδώκατε = παρέδοτε. Sm. 755.

25. αὐτῆς: redundant after ἧς.

26. τῷ γένει: more commonly τὸ γένος; but see Bl. 197. Sm. 1516 with a; 1600; 1577.

28. ἐσθίουσιν; pl. Sm. 958. ἀπό: for partitive genitive. Sm. 1684 N.

35. ἠνοίγησαν = ἀνεῴχθησαν. Sm., p. 687.

36. μᾶλλον περισσότερον: w. redundant μᾶλλον; but see Sm. 1084.

VIII

2. ἡμέραι τρεῖς παραμένουσιν: *nominativus pendens;* Sm. 3008; 940. Dana 83, 4.

3. ἀπό: redundant w. μακρόθεν. Bl. 104.

12. εἰ δοθήσεται: Semitic; Bl. 454, 5.

15. βλέπετε w. ἀπό: Semitism. Bl. 149. Sm. 1684.

19. εἰς: = "destined for"; cl. Bl. 206, 3. Sm. 1686.

28. εἰς = τὶς.

31. ἀποκτανθῆναι = ἀποθανεῖν.

36. κερδῆσαι = κερδᾶναι. Sm. 518; also p. 702.

IX

3. οὕτως: redundant after οἷα. λευκᾶναι = λευκῆναι. Sm. 518.

8. ἐξάπινα, late for ἐξαπίνης.

11. ὅτι = τί; why?

17. τὸν υἱόν μου: for τὸν ἐμὸν υἱόν. Kaegi 64. Sm. 1222.

18. ὅπου ἐάν: see on 6, 10. εἶπα: rare in Attic. Sm., p. 695.

19. πρός με: see Sm. 187, N. 2.

20. ἰδών: w. τὸ πνεῦμα; Sm. 1013; grammatically ἰδών may refer to ὁ παῖς: see Sm. 3008 e; 940. Dana 83, 4.

21. ἐκ παιδιόθεν: Sm. 342 w. notes; ἐκ is redundant, as in 8, 3.

24. κράξας: = κραγών. Sm., p. 703.

31. ἀποκτανθείς: for cl. ἀποθανών. Sm., p. 704.

43. καλόν ἐστιν . . . . ἤ: ἤ after positive; an extension of cl. usage. Bl. 245, 3. Gerth 540, Anm. 2.

50. τὸ ἅλας: for cl. ὁ ἅλς.

X

8. εἰς σάρκα: for σάρξ. Bl. 145.

11. γαμήσῃ: for cl. γήμῃ. Sm., p. 691.

17. εἷς = τὶς.

20. ἐφυλαξάμην: cl.; "I guarded against." Sm. 1597. ταῦτα: Sm. 1253.

21. σε ὑστερεῖ: σοί? Bl. 180, 5 and 189, 3.

23. εἰσελεύσονται: for cl. ft. εἶμι. Sm., p. 698.

28. ἀφήκαμεν: cl. ἀφεῖμεν more common. Sm. 755.

34. ἐμπαίξουσιν: for cl. ἐμπαίσονται. Sm., p. 710.

37. δὸς ἵνα: see on 1, 38.

45. τὴν ψυχὴν αὐτοῦ: = ἑαυτόν.

XI

6. ἀφῆκαν: ἀφεῖσαν. Sm. 755 and 777.

12. ἐπείνασεν: for cl. ἐπείνησεν. Sm. 394.

16. ἤφιεν: = ἠφίει; Sm. 450; 746; 782.

19. ὅταν ἐγένετο: for ὅτε ἐγένετο or γένοιτο; see on 6, 56.

21. ἴδε = ἰδέ. Sm., p. 700.

25. στήκετε for ἐστήκητε (pf. ἔστηκα). Sm., p. 700.

26. εἰ οὐκ ἀφίετε: either μή or οὐ: Sm. 2691.

32. εἶχον: like Latin habebant. Bl. 397, 2; 157, 3.

33. οἴδαμεν: rare for ἴσμεν. Sm. 796.

XII

5. οὕς: for τοὺς μέν, τοὺς δέ. Sm. 1107.

6. ἐλεύσομαι: for εἶμι, ἥξω, ἀφίξομαι. Sm., p. 698. ἀπολέσει: for ἀπολεῖ. Sm. 539 b; 488.

10. ἐγενήθη εἰς κεφαλήν: = ἐγένετο κεφαλή. Sm., p. 691. For εἰς, see 10, 8.

22. ἀφῆκαν = ἀφεῖσαν.

42. μία = τὶς.

XIII

3. εἰς τὸ ὄρος: Sm. 1659 b.

4. εἰπόν = εἰπέ.

19. τοιαύτη: redundant after οἵα.

28. γινώσκετε: for γιγνώσκετε. Sm. 89.

33. οἴδατε: ἴστε. Sm. 796.

XIV

3. κατέχεεν: aor.? or impf. for κατέχει? Sm. 543 a; 397; 134. Blass 89.
7. εὖ ποιεῖν: cl. w. accus.
10. ἀρχιερεῖς: acc. pl. Sm. 275–277.
11. παραδῶ: παραδῷ.
14. ὅπου ἐάν: ὅπου ἄν. *Passim.*
19. εἷς κατὰ εἷς: Bl. 305.
21. εἰ οὐκ: μή? Sm. 2691?
32. ἕως: ἕως w. ἄν.
40. ᾔδεισαν: ᾔδεσαν. Sm. 798.
44. δεδώκει: ἐδεδώκει. Augment. Sm. 438.
48. ἐξήλθατε = ἐξήλθετε.
49. ἤμην = ἦν. Kühner-Blass 298, 4.

XV

1. συμβούλιον ποιήσαντες: Latinism? Bl. 5. παρέδωκαν: παρέδοσαν. Sm. 755.
7. πεποιήκεισαν: ἐπεποιήκεσαν; so παραδεδώκεισαν in v. 10. Sm. 438.
15. τὸ ἱκανὸν ποιῆσαι: Latinism? Bl. 5. So also φραγελλώσας.
23. ἐδίδουν: ἐδίδοσαν.
47. τέθειται: κεῖται. Sm. 767.

XVI

2. τῇ μιᾷ = τῇ πρώτῃ.
3. ἀποκυλίσει: ἀποκυλιεῖ. Sm. 539 e. πρὸς ἑαυτάς: either Sm. 1218 or 1231.
6. ἔθηκαν: ἔθεσαν. Sm. 755. ἴδε ὁ τόπος:= ἰδοὺ ὁ τ.; sg. ἴδε in addressing more than one; Sm. 1010.
9. ἐκβεβλήκει: Sm. 438.
11. ἐθεάθη: passive; Sm. 813 c.

APPENDIX II

"A Staff was all they were allowed to have"
Mk. 6, 8

As usual, the universal statement (μηδὲν αἴρωσιν) is given first, then follow the exceptions (εἰ μή); just so in 6, 5: first, οὐδεμίαν δύναμιν, then, εἰ μὴ ἐθεράπευσεν.

According to St. Mark, Jesus allows the carrying of ῥάβδον μόνον; according to St. Luke, He forbids even this. Many attempts have been made to solve this "difficulté célèbre." Some authors treat the discrepancies between Mk. and Lk. as of no account, because there is agreement as to the gist of our Lord's injunctions: the disciples were to exercise the utmost poverty and to trust to divine Providence (Maldonatus).

Mt.'s (10, 9) μὴ κτήσησθε is clear: "do not acquire." The negative aorist is sweeping, the prohibition total. Smyth 1841. Gildersleeve 245; 415. Moulton 122–126. "To acquire" is to get what one does not have or to get something in addition to what one has. The disciples, then, are forbidden to make any special preparations for their missionary tour, as, for instance, by providing themselves with an extra staff (ordinarily every disciple had one) or with another pair of sandals, etc. (so Zahn; Dausch; Knabenbauer). Lagrange makes light of such "subtilté," but no subtlety is needed to read μὴ κτήσησθε aright.

We obtain the same sense if we interpret Mk.'s αἴρω in keeping with the context. Its general meaning is "to take, take up, take along"; but in *a given context* a person who is to *take* a thing with him may first have to secure possession of it; hence αἴρω often means "to fetch; to go and bring." In John 20, 15, Mary is willing to *go and secure possession* of the Body of Jesus: κἀγὼ αὐτὸν ἀρῶ. In Mk. 6, 29, the disciples of the Baptist "fetched his body" (preceded by the unnecessary ἦλθον καί). In 13, 15, the disciples are forbidden to go down into the house "in order to take something," ἆραί τι. There are contexts, therefore, in which ἆραι clearly overlaps with κτήσασθαι.

Accordingly, our Lord tells His disciples not to waste time in running about, with not a little anxiety, to provide themselves with traveling conveniences for their missionary trip. St. Matthew is right in saying they were *not to acquire* a staff in addition to the one they already possessed; St. Mark is right in saying they were *allowed to carry* the staff they already possessed. And note the fine idiom in εἰ μὴ ῥάβδον μόνον. A common feature of Greek is Brachylogy in its various forms. (Smyth 3017 and 3018; Blass 480, 483; Gerth 597, with twelve pages of illustrative material). Thus, from a preceding word its opposite must often be supplied, esp. an affirmative from a negative. In So. *OT*. 241, αὐδῶ is understood from the negative ἀπ-αυδῶ (Jebb). In So. *El*. 71, a word like δέξασθε must be supplied from the negative μὴ ἀποστεί-λητε (Kaibel). Often, when οὐκ ἔξεστιν precedes, a following ἀλλά suggests that χρή is to be supplied, and *vice versa*. This observation of Kaibel's is important for Mk. 6, 8, for from the preceding μηδὲν αἴρωσιν (which in tone is equivalent to μηδὲν χρὴ αἴρειν) we should supply ἔξεστιν αἴρειν or ἔξεστιν ἔχειν. "Do not go and procure anything for your journey—but, of course, *you are allowed* (ἔξεστιν) *to have* and carry a staff." This may be taken as a parenthesis, thrown in by our Lord, perhaps in reply to a question, or a remonstrance, from some disciple. St. Mark is noted for his many parentheses. In this acceptation μόνον is peculiarly appropriate: *the only thing* you are allowed to have—is a staff. Of course, ῥάβδον may be direct object to αἴρωσιν: they should not take anything with them except a staff (*sc*. the one they always had with them).

The present αἴρωσιν (or Lk.'s αἴρετε) is no obstacle to this interpretation; for, first, some texts read ἄρωσιν; besides, if the present is genuine, it forbids a course of action, rather than a single act; and most of all, even when there is reference to a single act, the negative present implies resistance to pressure (as much as the negative imperfect does: Gildersleeve 216; 415; 416. Smyth 1840; 1841). The sense then would here be: "Take nothing—in spite of temptations to the contrary." For εἰ μή (= ἀλλά) in ellipsis, see Blass 480, 6; Smyth 2346, with notes; Gerth 577, 6.

The nuances of Marcan αἴρω may be seen in the foll. passages: 2, 3; 2, 9; 2, 11; 2, 12; 2, 21; 4, 15; 4, 25; 6, 8; 6, 29; 6, 43; 8, 8; 8, 19; 8, 20; 8, 34; 10, 21; 11, 23; 13, 15; 13, 16; 15, 21; 15, 24; 16, 18. The sense of *acquiring* is conspicuous in 6, 29; 13, 15; 13, 16; 15, 24. Cf. Lk. 6, 29 (an interesting way of acquiring!).

For a rendering of Mk. 6, 8 and 9 (with the parallel accounts in Mt. 10, 9 and 10, and Lk. 9, 3), see *Memoirs*, pp. 87 and 158. Knabenbauer: "Virgam *ne comparent;* proinde, si virgam ad manum habent, tollant eam; sin minus, pergant sine ulla mora." Dausch: "Die Aposteln sollen sich *nicht besonders* rüsten, etwas einen *besonderen* Wanderstab oder, falls ihre Sandalen bereits schadhaft sind, ein paar *neue* anschaffen." Similarly Zahn, *al*.

APPENDIX III

The Greek designations of time for the early morning hours

Mk. 16, 2

The following definition of ὄρθρος is given by Phryn. Epit. Anecd. Bekker 54, 8 (see *Philologus* 43, 594): ὄρθρος, ἡ ὥρα τῆς νυκτός, καθ' ἣν ἀλεκτρυόνες ᾄδουσιν, ἄρχεται δὲ ἐνάτης ὥρας καὶ τελευτᾷ εἰς διαγελῶσαν ἡμέραν.

Νύξ—Σκοτία—Night		'Ημέρα—Day	
ab. 2:30 A.M. gallicinium	Rising—Time	"Εως	"Ηλιος ἀνατέλλων
ἅμα ὄρθρῳ	ὄ ρ θ ρ ο s		
	ὄρθρος βαθύς	"Dawn"	
	ἡ ἐπιφώσκουσα		Sunrise
πάνυ πρῴ = λίαν πρωΐ		30 or 40 minutes	
νυκτὸς ἔτι οὔσης			
σκοτίας ἔτι οὔσης			

Explanation.—Just as ἕως or "dawn" is the first division of ἡμέρα or "day," so ὄρθρος (from ὀρ-, as in ὄρνυμι; hence "rising-time") is the last division of νύξ or "night." It begins about 2:30 A.M. when the cock crows. Its *last* section is called ὄρθρος βαθύς, because then it is "deepest" or "farthest advanced," *sc.* from midnight. The phrase is classical (see Plato, *Crito*, 43 a, where Fowler correctly renders "just before dawn"). In *Crito* πάνυ πρῴ is narrowed down to ὄρθρος βαθύς; so Mk.'s λίαν πρωΐ (a vague and somewhat hyperbolic expression, but in the Marcan manner) is narrowed down by Lk.'s ὄρθρου βαθέως. The pious women left home (ἔρχονται. Mk. 16, 2) λίαν πρωΐ or ὄρθρου βαθέως (Lk. 24, 1) or πρωΐ σκοτίας ἔτι οὔσης (John 20, 1) or τῇ ἐπιφωσκούσῃ (*sc.* ὥρᾳ. Mt. 28, 1), "at an early hour on the first day of the week." Leaving their house ὄρθρου βαθέως, the women must have arrived at the Sepulchre about 30 or 40 minutes later, ἡλίου ἀνατείλαντος. In the Orient the period called ἕως is of the briefest duration. The sense attributed above to Lk.'s ὄρθρου βαθέως is confirmed by P. *Lips.* I, 40, ii, 10: ὀψὲ πάνυ βαθείας ἑσπέρας (see M.-M. *Vocabulary* 101).

A NOTE INSTEAD OF A BIBLIOGRAPHY

Considering the elementary nature of this volume, I do not think it necessary to add a special bibliography to the notes on literature scattered throughout the book. I may assure the reader that I have tried to keep in touch with the latest scholarship. A word must, however, be said about certain abbreviations used in the text:

"Gildersleeve B. M." stands for Professor Miller's *Selections from the Brief Mention.*

"Dana" refers to the *Manual Grammar* by Professors Dana and Mantey. Macmillan.

"Blass" means A. Debrunner's "Bearbeitung" of Blass's *Neut. Grammatik;* 6. A.

"Hofmann *Synt.*" = H.'s *Lateinische Grammatik: Syntax und Stilistik.*

"Howard" refers to H.'s revision of Moulton's grammar.

"Moulton," without any qualification, stands for M.'s *Prolegomena.*

"M.-M. Vocabulary" stands for *Vocabulary of the Greek Testament,* by Professors Moulton and Milligan.

"Havers" stands for the *Handbuch der erklärenden Syntax.*

"Joüon" = *L'Evangile de Notre-Seigneur Jésus-Christ.* Paris: Beauchesne, 1930.

In connection with the *Plates* at the end of this volume, I wish to call attention to a 32-page booklet containing specimens of NT texts, gathered from a variety of well-known manuscripts, by Professor Dr. Heinrich Joseph Vogels (who very kindly permitted me to use his text in the present work): "Übungsbuch zur Einführung in die Textgeschichte des Neuen Testamentes" (Bonn: Hanstein; 1928); with it may be used the same author's "Handbuch der Neutestamentlichen Textkritik"; Münster; Aschendorff; 1923.

Ἐρευνᾶτε τὰς Γραφάς

The facsimiles on Plates I and II illustrate what is meant by a "sense-line" arrangement. On Plate I, colon 1 contains a verb and the indirect question it governs:

significans—qua morte honorificabit Deum.

Colon 2 contains a whole sentence made up of three very short phrases:

et hoc cum dixisset—dicit illi—sequere me.

Colon 3 contains a subject with its modifier and a verb with its object:

conversus autem Petrus—videt discipulum.

Colon 4 contains two phrases describing the object of the preceding colon:

quem diligebat Jesus—sequentem.

Colon 5 adds another descriptive relative clause:

qui et recubuit in cena.

Colon 6 rounds out the preceding sentence and starts a new one:

super pectus eius—et dixit illi.

Colon 7 contains the words of the direct question asked by the disciples:

Domine—quis est qui tradidit te?

Colon 8 contains a clause introducing another direct question:

hunc ergo videns Petrus dicit ad Jesum.

Colon 9 gives the direct question and starts a new sentence:

Domine—hic autem quid? Dicit illi Jesus:

Colon 10 contains part of a conditional clause:

si eum volo sic manere.

Colon 11 completes the conditional clause, gives the apodosis, and adds a sharp command:

usque dum venio, quid ad te? tu me sequere.

Colon 12 introduces a new sentence:

exivit ero hic verbus aput fratres.

From the description just given it appears that every colon, with the exception of 6 and 9, "makes sense" inasmuch as the words in each are intimately connected with one another and express a word-group. One may wonder why cola 6 and 9 contain parts taken from different sentences or different syntactical groups and thus destroy the word-group proper to each line. In the Latin version, it may be observed, there is space enough in colon 5 for the phrase *super pectus eius*, while in the Greek original the corresponding phrase, ἐπὶ τὸ στῆθος αὐτοῦ, could not have been crowded into the preceding line. In colon 9 the copyist may have desired to save space by running into the line such disparate things as a direct question and a clause introducing a new sentence. That he was aware of the heterogeneous character of the line seems evident from his use of a punctuation mark at the end of the question. The only other punctuation mark used in the entire selection is at the end of colon 8.

Compared with the passage from St. John, the selection from St. Paul has several noteworthy colometric features of its own. First, the twelve cola are much shorter throughout. Secondly, in arranging his cola the copyist was wisely guided by a due regard for the double Epanaphora in the original, that is, the fivefold repetition of οὐ, and the fourfold repetition of πάντα. Lastly, the key-word of the whole passage, ἡ ἀγάπη, received as much prominence in colon 11 as colometry is capable of giving, by assigning to a single word an entire line. Here, as in the selection from St. John, each colon "makes sense," but it is easy to see that each of the two copyists had his own conception of what precisely constitutes "sense." That there is a more or less in the sense-making power of words is the most obvious lesson of these two facsimiles.

ⲤΗΜΕΝⲰΝΠΟΙⲰΘΑΝΑΤⲰΔΟΞΑⲤΕΙΤΟΝΘΝ
ΚΑΙΤΟΥΤΟΕΙΠⲰΝΛΕΓΕΙΑΥΤⲰΑΚΟΛΟΥΘΕΙΜΟΙ
ΕΠΙⲤΤΡΑΦΕΙⲤΔΕΟΠΕΤΡΟⲤΒΛΕΠΕΙΤΟΝΜΑΘΗΤΗΝ
ΟΝΗΓΑΠΑΙΗⲤ ΑΚΟΛΟΥΘΟΥΝΤΑ
ΟⲤΚΑΙΑΝΕΠΕⲤΕΝΕΝΤⲰΔΕΙΠΝⲰ
ΕΠΙΤΟⲤΤΗΘΟⲤΑΥΤΟΥ ΚΑΙΕΠΕΝΑΥΤⲰ
ΚΕ ΤΙⲤΕⲤΤΙΝΟΠΑΡΑΔΙΔⲰΝⲤΕ
ΤΟΥΤΟΝΟΥΝΕΙΔⲰΝΟΠΕΤΡΟⲤΛΕΓΕΙΑΥΤⲰΙΗΥ
ΚΕ ΟΥΤΟⲤΔΕΤΙ ΛΕΓΕΙΑΥΤⲰΟΙΗⲤ
ΕΑΝΑΥΤΟΝΘΕΛⲰΜΕΝΕΙΝΟΥΤⲰⲤ
ΕⲰⲤΕΡΧΟΜΑΙΤΙΠΡΟⲤⲤΕ ⲤΥΜΟΙΑΚΟΛΟΥΘΕΙ
ΕΞΗΛΘΕΝΟΥΝΟΥΤΟⲤΟΛΟΓΟⲤΕΙⲤΤΟΥⲤ

Codex Bezae Cantabrigiensis (*D*ᵉᵃ): John 21, 19—23

ΟΥΚΑⲤΧΗΜΟΝΕΙ
ΟΥΖΗΤΕΙΤΑΕΑΥΤΗⲤ
ΟΥΠΑΡΟΞΥΝΕΤΑΙ
ΟΥΛΟΓΙΖΕΤΑΙΤΟΚΑΚΟΝ
ΟΥΧΑΙΡΕΙΕΠΙΤΗΑΔΙΚΙΑ
ⲤΥΝΧΑΙΡΕΙΔΕΤΗΑΛΗΘΕΙΑ
ΠΑΝΤΑⲤΤΕΓΕΙ
ΠΑΝΤΑΠΙⲤΤΕΥΕΙ
ΠΑΝΤΑΕΛΠΙΖΕΙ
ΠΑΝΤΑ ΥΠΟΜΕΝΕΙ
Η ΑΓΑΠΗ
ΟΥΔΕΠΟΤΕΕΚΠΙΠΤΕΙ ✝

Codex Claromontanus (*D*ᵖ): 1. Kor. 13, 5—8

Plate I

(Reproduced from "Eberhard Nestle's Einführung in das Griechische Neue Testament"; 4a. von Ernst von Dobschütz; Göttingen: Vandenhoeck und Ruprecht; 1923.)

SIGNIFICANSQUAMORTEHONORIFICABITDM
ETHOCCUMDIXISSETDICITILLISEQUEREME
CONUERSUSAUTEMPETRUSUIDETDISCIPULUM
QUEMDILIGEBATIHSSEQUENTEM
QUIETRECUBUITINCENA
SUPERPECTUSEIUS ETDIXITILLI
DMEQUISESTQUITRADIDITTE
HUNCERGOUIDENSPETRUSDICITADIHM
DMEHICAUTEMQUID· DICITILLIIHS
SIEUMUOLOSICMANERE
USQUEDUMUENIOQUIDADTETUMESEQUERE
EXIUITERGOHICUERBUS APUTFRATRES

Codex Bezae Cantabrigiensis (*d*)

NONAMBITIOSAEST
NONQUAERITQUAESUASUNT
NONINRITATUR
NONCOGITATMALUM
NONGAUDETSUPERINIQUITATEM
CONGAUDETAUTEMUERITATI
OMNIASUFFERIT
OMNIACREDIT
OMNIASPERAT
OMNIASUSTENET
CARITAS
NUMQUAMEXCIDET

Codex Claromontanus (*d*)

Plate II

EXPLANATION OF PLATE III

The selection presented on Plate III contains twelve cola, each colon beginning at the margin on the left. Note that indention is there used, not (as in the Marcan text in the present volume) to mark the beginning of a fresh colon, but to introduce words carried over from the preceding line. The twelve cola from *The Four Gospels* run, therefore, as follows:

1. invenietis infantem
    pannis involutum

2. et positum in praesepi

3. et subito facta est cum
    angelo multitudo
    militiae caelestis

4. laudantium Deum et
    dicentium

5. gloria in altissimo Deo

6. et in terra pax homi
    nibus bonae vo
    luntatis

7. et factum est ut dis
    cesserunt ab eis
    angeli in caelum

8. pastores vero loque
    bantur ad invicem

9. transeamus usque
    in Bethlehem

10. et videamus hoc ver
    bum quod fac
    tum est

11. quod Dominus ostendit
    nobis

12. et venerunt festinantes

INQENIETISINFANTEM
PANNISINUOLUTU
ETPOSITUMINPRAESEPI
EISUBITOFACTAESTCU
ANCELOMULTITUDO
MILITIAECAELESTIS
LAUDANTIUMDET
DICENTIUM
GLORIAINALTISSIMISDO
ETINTERRAPAXINBOM
NIBUSBONAEUO
LUNTATIS
ETFACTUMESTUTDIS
SCESSERUNTABEIS
ANGELIINCAELUM
PASTORESUEROLOQUE
BANTURADINUICE
TRANSEAMUSUSQUE
INBETHLCEM
ETUIDEAMUSHOCUER
BUMQUODFACTUM
EST
QUODDNSOSTENDIT
NOBIS
ETUENORUNTFESTINANTES

Luke 2, 12–16

Plate III

From THE FOUR GOSPELS, in the *Latin* version, made by St. Jerome at the end of the fourth century. Written in uncials, perhaps in North Italy, in the 6th or 7th century. See *Guide to the Manuscripts*, etc., exhibited in the Department of Manuscripts and in the Grenville Library; British Museum, 1906; p. 111.

ITINERARY OF OUR LORD ACCORDING
TO ST. MARK

I. 9: (from Nazareth in Galilee) to the Jordan.
12: into the desert (of Judea, between the Dead Sea and Jerusalem).
14: into Galilee (Nazareth).
16: along the Sea of Galilee.
21: to Capharnaum (north-west end of the Sea: the great highway from Damascus to Judea).
35: into the desert (near Caph.).
38: to the neighboring towns.
39: throughout Galilee.
45: in desert places (in Galilee).

II. 1: again in Caph.
13: by the sea-shore.
23: through the corn-fields.

III. 1: the synagogue of Caph.?
7: along the shore.
13: into "the mountain."
20: Simon's house at Caph.?

IV. 1: by the seaside.

V. 1: the east shore of the Sea of Galilee (Gerasenes).
21: back to the western shore.

VI. 1: at Nazareth.
6: through the villages round about.
32: to a desert place. Topography uncertain.
45: toward Bethsaida.
46: a mountain near by.
53: in the plain of Gennesar: north-west end of the Lake.
56: near-by villages.

VII. 17: "indoors." Where?
24: Tyre and Sidon, west of Galilee, along the Mediterranean.
31: back to the Sea of Galilee: into the Decapolis.

VIII. 1: in the Decapolis?
10: Dalmanutha (a small town on the west shore of the Lake).
13: to the east shore of the Lake.
22: to Bethsaida.
27: north to Caesarea Philippi.

IX. 2: Mount Thabor? Southern end of the Lake.
33: to Capharnaum.

X. 1: from Galilee to Judea, through Peraea, beyond the Jordan.
17: from Peraea westward.
32: on the way to Jerusalem, via Jericho.
46: setting out for Jericho. The blind man is cured before entering Jericho.

XI: 1: near Jerusalem. Bethphage and Bethany, on the Mount of Olives. Back and forth between Bethany and Jerusalem.
12: leaving Bethany.
15: entering Jerusalem.
19, 20: back in Bethany; return to Jerusalem.

XIII. 3: Mount of Olives.

XIV. 3: in Bethany.
17: in Jerusalem, for the Last Supper, etc.

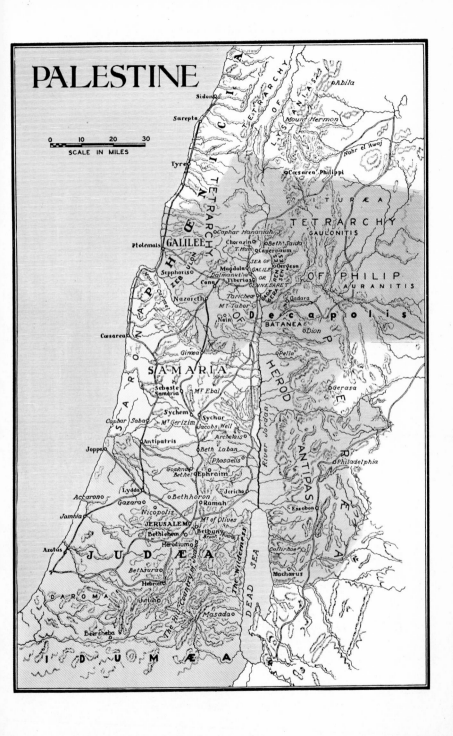

2022. 02. 17